CAFÉ THEOLOGY

EXPLORING LOVE,
THE UNIVERSE
AND EVERYTHING

CAFÉ THEOLOGY

EXPLORING LOVE,
THE UNIVERSE
AND EVERYTHING

MICHAEL LLOYD

StPaul's
theological centre

For:

Julian and Jean
Nigel and Karen
Tim and Carina

'Michael Lloyd is an expert writer who covers many demanding issues in a popular and engaging way. His context is clearly 21st-century thinking, as he seeks to address theology from the viewpoint of the "thinking outside the box" Christian ... The themes that have been covered so frequently by other authors come alive with a fresh and contemporary feel.'

Dianne Tidball, *The Baptist Times*

'This is a marvellous book, because Michael really tackles and finds answers to all the really knotty theological problems.'

Antony Grant, CR

'Mike tackles the vital areas of the Christian faith with boldness and integrity, never flinching from difficult issues or hesitating to give bold answers ... This book could play the part in our generation that C. S. Lewis' *Mere Christianity* did when it first came out.'

Rupert Charkham, Holy Trinity Church Cambridge

'Here is theology you'd be happy discussing with a friend or colleague over a coffee. Free from cringe and jargon, you're frequently made breathless by the awe and wonder of biblical truth.'

Peter Heslam, *EG Magazine*

'*Café Theology* is the best book since a cup of coffee. In fact, it's probably better.'

Christianity Magazine

CONTENTS

CONTENTS

FOREWORD TO THE FIRST EDITION

For many years, Michael Lloyd has been a regular guest speaker at our annual church teaching holiday, Focus. Following a particularly popular series of theology seminars, which Mike put together for Focus in 1998, we asked him to consider putting those talks into written form. This book is the result, and we are delighted to have the opportunity to publish it.

An enthusiastic and inspiring teacher with an infectious wit and great sense of humour, Mike has an amazing ability to make the mysteries of Christian 'theology' accessible and relevant, always thought-provoking, but with a minimum of jargon and a healthy dose of fun!

As a course in theology, it is equally good for personal reading or for study within a pastorate or small group. So whatever your background knowledge or understanding of things theological, if you'd like to know more about theology ... then this book is for you! It is great!

Sandy Millar

Honorary Assistant Bishop in the Diocese of London, and Former Vicar of HTB (1985–2005)

FOREWORD TO THE THIRD EDITION

This is *Café Theology*'s third incarnation, thus beating God, who's only had one. (On every other score, sadly but predictably, it fails to compete.) The first one was orange, the second had a helpful index so you could see where I had stolen my material from, and to this third edition I have added a study guide.

In his generous Foreword, Sandy Millar writes that 'As a course in theology, it is equally good for personal reading and for study within a pastorate or small group.' And I know that a number of groups have used it as the basis for a short series or Lent course (or Lenten penance, more like). I hope that the questions for each chapter will help open up good and illuminating discussion.

This third edition is being published as a St Paul's Theological Centre (SPTC) imprint, as part of a set of theological resources that I and my lovely colleagues there are building up, which gives me the chance to say how much I love working with them and our poor long-suffering students. In the unlikely event of your enjoying this book, you might enjoy one of our courses. Do look us up on sptc.htb.org.uk.

There is always more to be explored about everything, but especially about the Love by whom and for whom we were made. It is my prayer that this book will open up a tiny bit of that 'more' for you.

Talking of love, I have got married since I wrote this book, and would like to thank Abigail for her love, and the extraordinary stimulation and joy – not to mention the flapjacks – she has brought me.

Michael Lloyd

INTRODUCTION

A lot of fun was had choosing the title of this book. Because it goes from Creation to New Creation, I wanted to call it From Primeval Soup to Apocalyptic Nuts, but the publishers told me that it would get put in the cookery section of bookshops. One of my students suggested Everything You Ever Wanted To Know About God But Were Too Stupid To Work Out For Yourself, which has a certain charm, but for some reason did not recommend itself to the publishers. (Sorry, James.)

We thought of calling it The Big Picture, because it tries to show how we can fit into the vast sweep of God's purposes – and thus find meaning. (Then I could have referred to it as My Big Picture Book!)

We toyed with the idea of Mere Theology, because, like C. S. Lewis' Mere Christianity, it tries to present an understanding of the faith that is common to Christians of all types and stripes. This ecumenical approach is in my blood anyway, having Roman Catholic family members, and having worshipped for a while in a United Church in Canada, having been brought up in an Anglo-Catholic church, and then encountered evangelicalism at university, and having worked in a charismatic church and a theological college in the Anglo-Catholic tradition. I believe passionately that different styles of worship reflect different aspects of the nature of God, and that we can therefore enrich our experience of Him by listening to and worshipping with one another.

That is why I have quoted a lot in this book – partly so that readers find their own tradition represented here and feel at home, partly so that they get to read some of the theological greats in their own words, and partly to demonstrate the complementary richness of the various Christian traditions. To try and safeguard against saying things that grate on the ears of Christians from other parts of the Church, I have asked many friends and colleagues to read through the first draft and comment upon it. I am deeply grateful to Nigel Lloyd, Carina Lloyd, Margaret Atkins, Tom Wright, Lynnae Williams, Martyn Percy, John Bardwell, Bill Scott, James Heard, Ana Pollard, Ayla Lepine, Annie Rey, Ed Carlisle, Dave Bookless, Barbara Mearns and in particular my wonderful editors, Jo Glen and Julia Evans, for the time and trouble they took over the script, and John Jarick for kindly sending me a list of errata. I would also like to thank Jeremy Crossley for encouraging me to give the talks that ended up as this book, and Julia and Peter Harvey for all the (not exclusively edible) support they gave me during the writing of it (not that it was inedible, you understand). I am also most grateful to Spurgeon's College for food and fellowship during the writing of this book.

In the end, we went for Café Theology. People sometimes fear – I certainly did – that if you take being a Christian too seriously, you will have to give up much of what makes life enjoyable in order to concentrate on 'spiritual' things. I used to fear that if I were a consistent Christian, I could no longer justify spending time doing the things I most enjoyed, such as listening to music, going to the theatre, walking in the fells, going to cafés with my friends. I have come to believe that this is profoundly wrong. God made us as multi-dimensional beings, and so life lived in company with Him is going to involve living in more dimensions, not fewer. The ordinary pleasures of life are not left behind – they are taken up and properly directed and properly enjoyed. So what I have tried to offer here is a theology that embraces and revels in the variety and physicality and relationality and creativity of God's creation – and enjoys it all in conscious and grateful dependence upon and in dialogue with Him.

I hope it will take you deeper into your faith if you have a faith. I hope it will give you some idea of what Christian faith looks like from the inside, if you don't. And I hope it will help you to a richer and more vibrant enjoyment both of Life and of the Life-Giver. And because so much of that richness in my own life has come from, and been enjoyed with, my family, I dedicate this book with gratitude and love to my brothers and sisters-in-law: Julian and Jean, Nigel and Karen, Tim and Carina.

Michael Lloyd

1 CREATION

Consider these two statements of where we come from and what we are for. First, the atheist philosopher, Quentin Smith, writes:

> The fact of the matter is that the most reasonable belief is that we came from nothing, by nothing and for nothing. ... We should ... acknowledge our foundation in nothingness and feel awe at the marvellous fact that we have a chance to participate briefly in this incredible sunburst that interrupts without reason the reign of non-being.[1]

Secondly, theologian and food critic, Robert Farrar Capon, begins his book, *The Third Peacock*, like this:

> Let me tell you why God made the world. One afternoon, before anything was made, God the Father, God the Son and God the Holy Spirit sat around in the unity of their Godhead discussing one of the Father's fixations. From all eternity, it seems, he had

this *thing* about being. He would keep thinking up all kinds of unnecessary things – new ways of being and new kinds of things to be. And as they talked, God the Son suddenly said, "Really, this is absolutely great stuff. Why don't I go out and mix us up a batch?" And God the Holy Spirit said, "Terrific! I'll help you." So they all pitched in, and after supper that night, the Son and the Holy Spirit put on this tremendous show of being for the Father. It was full of water and light and frogs; pine cones kept dropping all over the place and crazy fish swam around in the wineglasses. There were mushrooms and grapes, horseradishes and tigers – and men and women everywhere to taste them, to juggle them, to join them and to love them. And God the Father looked at the whole wild party and said, "Wonderful! Just what I had in mind!"[2]

In the end, there are basically only two possible sets of views about the universe in which we live. It must, at heart, be either personal or impersonal. It must either be the product of a Person, or the unplanned, unintended by-product of the impersonal + time + chance.[a] Quentin Smith thinks that the universe is ultimately impersonal. He sees life as arbitrary ('for nothing … without reason') and temporary ('briefly'). Robert Farrar Capon, on the other hand, believes that the universe is ultimately personal. It emerges from relationship, creativity, delight, love. It is purposeful ('for the Father', 'to love them') and rooted in permanence ('From all eternity').

There is no more important decision you can make about the universe than this. Is there a Person behind it or not? How you regard the universe, how you treat it, what you hope to get from it and give to it, how you view your own life and work and relationships and goals – all will be shaped decisively by how you answer that question. The Bible doesn't keep us long in suspense about what its answer is: 'In the beginning, God …' (Genesis 1:1).

[a] I owe this phrase to Francis Schaeffer. See for instance his *How Should We Then Live?* (Fleming H. Revell Company, 1976) p.165.

In the Jewish and Christian Scriptures, which begin with these words, we have, I suggest, the overall story which makes sense of our world, and our lives, and our longings, and our values, and our feeble and frustrated fumblings after an understanding of who we are and what we are for.

1. THERE IS A PERSON BEHIND CREATION

The Bible is utterly clear from its opening words that there is a Person behind Creation. It sides unambiguously with the personal view of life, the universe and everything. Before the universe is even mentioned, the Bible has already introduced us to a Person. It seems to me that as human beings, we warm to that, for we are personal beings. The most valuable things we know in our own experience are people, so it doesn't surprise us to know that it is a Person who is behind reality and responsible for it. There are many things about our experience that aren't as we expect, and not as we would want, which do surprise us and to which we do not warm, and we shall be looking at why that might be in Chapter 2. But we relate to the suggestion that there is a Person behind it, because there is a sense of deep calling to deep, of recognition, of kinship, and of belonging.

That there is a Person behind existence has always been foundational to an enriching understanding of who we are, but it has never perhaps been so important as it is today. For we live in (what has every appearance of being) an impersonal world. To the health authority, we're an NHS number; to the Post Office, we're a postcode; to the Inland Revenue, we're a National Insurance number. And while employees of these vital institutions make every effort to remember that behind each statistic is a person, the sheer quantity of applications and forms and letters and houses and phone calls with which they have to deal means that the amount of genuine relationship possible in these interactions is necessarily small. Gone (largely) are the days when your GP would come to your home and have time to talk, and know your family.

Or your bank manager would know your financial situation and its ramifications for your family and other commitments. We live at greater relational distance from all but a small (and sometimes fragile) collection of friends and family members. We cry out for community, but are generally too busy to create it or contribute much to it. And loneliness is, as Mother Teresa observed, one of the most prevalent and depressing features of the Western world. We need to know that our world is not ultimately a cold, empty, impersonal product of time and chance.

And into this situation, the Bible speaks its ancient message with new freshness, force and relevance. There is a Person behind it. Creation is therefore pregnant with the possibility of relationship with the Person who made it, and that transforms our experience of our lives. A painting by your small daughter is much more valuable to you than it would be if it were simply a painting done by someone you didn't know. A simple meal cooked by your husband as a token of love, and eaten together, is much more enjoyable than a gourmet meal eaten alone. Places that you visited with your wife when you were still courting retain a lifelong significance. Life that is lived in relationship with the Person who made you – however tentative and ambiguous that relationship may be – is infinitely richer than one lived in the belief that the universe is ultimately impersonal, and life ultimately unrenewable. Believe that there is a Person behind the whole shebang, and all Creation becomes a trysting-place where we may meet with our Lover.

I had three friends on board the PanAm flight that was blown up over Lockerbie in 1988, and in the papers of one of them, Sarah Aicher, we found this: 'Sometimes I feel that every cell is pregnant, every atom is swollen with the strong, sure love of God for me and for all creation.' What Sarah sometimes felt is, in fact, always the case, because there is a Person behind and within the world in which we live. And that is basically what spirituality is – opening oneself to perceive that occasionally and fleetingly, training oneself to believe that constantly and consistently, and learning to live on that basis significantly and joyfully. This is not a glamorous or ethereal business, but a matter of living ordinary, everyday, mundane life in the company of the Life-Giver. As George Herbert put it in his great poem, *The Elixir*:

> Teach me, my God and King,
> In all things Thee to see,
> And what I do in any thing,
> To do it as for Thee:

'Teach me', it begins, because we need to be taught. Seeing God in everything does not come naturally. It's a skill to be acquired, an art to be learnt. It is one of the tasks required in living a Christian life, and, indeed, a human life. Herbert enjoins us to see God 'in all things' – not just in 'spiritual' things, not just in prayer or in worship, but in *all things*, for all things have been created by God, and we may meet with Him in them all. He may be met with in all things, and all our actions may be done for Him. All dimensions of who we are and what we do may be lived in the warmth and creative quirkiness of relationship.

> A man that looks on glass,
> On it may stay his eye;
> Or if he pleaseth, through it pass,
> And then the heaven espy.

You can look *at* your window, if you like, and notice the smudges and the smears and the raindrops and the bird-droppings, or, in my case, the glazier's squiggles, put there to stop me from walking into the glass and not yet wiped off in the two years or so since the glass was put in. Or you can look *through* it, which, after all, is what a window is for. Similarly, with creation – you can look *at* it, and that's a good thing to do. It's a place of curiosity and wonder and beauty, and, as we shall see, it should be observed and explored and enjoyed and revelled in. But it can also act as a window through which to espy the Beauty and the Love from

which it (and we) sprang. And that can transform everything we do, making drudgery divine:

All may of Thee partake:
Nothing can be so mean,
Which with this tincture 'for Thy sake'
Will not grow bright and clean.

A servant with this clause
Makes drudgery divine:
Who sweeps a room, as for Thy laws,
Makes that and the action fine.

This is the famous stone
That turneth all to gold:
For that which God doth touch and own
Cannot for less be told.

The letters of a seventeenth-century monk called Brother Lawrence have been collected together into a book, under the title, *The Practice of the Presence of God*. In it, he tells of how even the lowliest and most mundane of tasks in the monastery kitchen became for him an opportunity to bask in God's presence and love. The practice of the presence of God is the appropriation and celebration of the fact that there is a Person behind and within our world, and it is the art of enjoying creation as it is intended to be enjoyed.

There are many ways of aiding this practice. Saying Grace over a meal is one such: it is a way of acknowledging that food doesn't just happen. It is not just a mechanical process. Food is not just fuel. Saying Grace is a recognition that we are dependent for our nourishment on a whole chain of suppliers and producers and farmers – a chain of dependence that culminates in the Creator. And a meal is more than the absorption of energy – it is an opportunity for relationship. Saying Grace is an exercise in the practice of the presence of God, for it reminds us that we have not just a meal to be enjoyed and one another to enjoy it with, but also an unseen Guest to eat with and meet with. There is a Person behind it.

2. THERE IS A PURPOSE FOR CREATION

There is a purpose for Creation. It is not just haphazard. It is not just there for us to impose our own purposes on it. We may not simply do what we like with it. Nor are we left to make up our own limited purposes for our own lives. Everyone wants their life to have purpose, but only a person can have purposes. A force cannot have purposes. Electricity cannot have a purpose. Gravity cannot have a purpose. Scientists sometimes speak as if the 'purpose' of DNA, for instance, is to replicate itself; and the sperm with the outboard motor in Larson's cartoon waving to the unmotorised sperm and saying, 'See you guys later!' certainly seems to have a purpose in mind! But that is funny precisely because it personalises the sperm, it attributes to it the sort of intention (and deviousness!) of which only a person is capable. Thus Richard Dawkins concludes, 'The universe that we observe has precisely the properties we should expect if there is, at bottom, no design, no purpose, no evil and no good, nothing but blind, pitiless indifference.'[3] That is consistent with the impersonal view. If there is no Person behind it, there can be no purpose for it, except for the (frequently exploitative) purposes we impose upon it.

But if there is a Person behind it, then creation can have intrinsic purposes, which we are called upon to respect. And we ourselves can have a purposeful place and rôle within it, a rationale, a *raison d'être*, a reason for being here. So what are the purposes of God for creation? Far more, I suspect, than we can ever know, and it would be presumptuous in the extreme to pretend that we have anything more than a provisional and hazy idea of what He intends for His handiwork. But that goes for just about anything one might want to say theologically and the time comes when it is better to risk saying something than to say nothing, especially if you then expect people to splash out £9.99 on a 416-page theological tome! So I want to suggest seven aspects of His purpose about which we may be reasonably (though humbly) confident.

a) Creation is there for the Son

It is appropriate that what creation is for is not a thing but a Person. Its purpose is not ultimately functional but relational. St Paul tells us that 'We look at this Son and see God's original purpose in everything created. For everything, absolutely everything, above and below, visible and invisible, rank after rank after rank of angels—*everything* got started in him and finds its purpose in him' (Colossians 1:16 THE MESSAGE). Or, as a more literal translation puts it: 'in him [ie God's beloved Son] all things in heaven and on earth were created, things visible and invisible, whether thrones or dominions or rulers or powers—all things have been created through him and for him' (NRSV). The word translated 'for' might actually be translated 'to'. All things have been made 'to Him'. In other words, the whole of creation is orientated towards the Son of God who became human in Jesus of Nazareth. Just as a flower is made for sunshine and cannot flourish or indeed survive without it and therefore reaches out towards the light, so creation is made *for* the Son and only flourishes in so far as it is reaching out towards and opening itself up to Him. It depends upon Him for its original existence, for its present flourishing and for its future fulfilment. It is *for* Him in the sense that it needs Him in order to be fully itself. It is *for* Him in the sense that it is the Father's gift to the Son. And it is *for* Him in the sense that it exists for relationship with Him and to bring Him glory.

John of the Cross captures this well in the conversation he imagines between the Father and the Son:

> My heart dreams of your having,
> son, an affectionate bride,
> who for the worthiness in you
> merits a place at our side:
>
> to break bread at this table,
> the same loaf as we two,
> and ripen in acquaintance
> with traits I always knew …
>
> O father, a world of thanks,
> the son to the father replied.
> The depth of my luminous gaze
> I give as a gift to the bride;
>
> I'd have her use it to see
> the kind of father you are:
> how all that I have to my name
> I have from the person you are.
>
> To think she will lie in my arms!
> Be warmed in the noons of your love!
> and in ecstasy never to end
> lift radiant carols above![4]

b) Creation is there to praise its Maker and to reflect His glory

By being itself, creation glorifies God. 'The heavens declare the glory of God' says Psalm 19:1 – not in the same way we do, not verbally nor consciously, but by being themselves, by their beauty, and by being in harmony with the purposes of God. (Of course, the natural order is not always in harmony with the purposes of God, and, again, we shall be looking in Chapter 2 at why that might be.)

Creation's praise of its Maker is difficult to discern, being largely inanimate and inarticulate. It takes humanity to articulate it. We are to be the priests of creation, the point through which creation's praise is offered up to God. Humanity is, to quote Herbert again:

> ... secretary of Thy praise.

> Beasts fain would sing; birds ditty to their notes;
> Trees would be tuning on their native lute
> To Thy renown: but all their hands and throats
> Are brought to man, while they are lame and mute.

> Man is the world's high priest: he doth present
> The sacrifice for all; ...[5]

Just as when ministers lead the prayers in a church service, they are praying not just on their own behalf but on behalf of the congregation, so as human beings we are to praise God, not just on our own behalf, but also on behalf of the rest of creation. We are to be its vocal point – the larynx of creation as it sings the praise of God.

In Psalm 148, the psalmist calls upon creation to magnify its Maker. Sun and moon and stars and sea creatures and snow and clouds and mountains and trees and animals and birds are summoned to praise the Lord. And last of all, human beings, and in particular the chosen people, are called upon to exalt Him. As the summit of creation, human beings sum up creation's praise on their own. There is more happening when we meet together Sunday by Sunday than we usually realise. In the Chapel at Worcester College, Oxford, where I studied for my doctorate, there are all sorts of strange and exotic animals carved into the pews. This is not some sort of pagan idolatry, but a reminder that in our praise we give voice to creation's unconscious testimony and tribute to the Creator God.

Christopher Smart was an eighteenth-century poet who suffered from what was diagnosed as religious mania. His poem, *Rejoice in the Lamb*, written while an inmate in an asylum in Bethnal Green and set to music so memorably by Benjamin Britten, contains a fanciful yet delightful depiction of his pet cat:

> For I will consider my cat Jeoffry.
> For he is the servant of the Living God, duly and
>   daily serving Him.
> For at the first glance of the glory of God in the East
>   he worships in his way.
> For this is done by wreathing his body seven times
>   round with elegant quickness.
> For he knows that God is his Saviour.
> For there is nothing sweeter than his peace when at rest.[6]

Nor is it his cat alone that he sees glorifying God: 'For flowers are great blessings. … For the flower glorifies God … For there is a language of flowers. For flowers are peculiarly the poetry of Christ.' Locked up in his asylum, he had time to observe the things around him, lovingly and lingeringly and perceptively enough to notice that a cat (by being a cat) and a flower (by being a flower) bless their Maker and reflect (in some ways) His glory. He may have been mentally ill, but he was in relationship with God, he was arrestingly creative and he mediated something of creation's praise – and that is more humanity than many of us practise.

c) Creation is there to be beautiful

We tend to think that things need to have their own use and function, that they have to earn their keep, as it were, by being of benefit to us. But to be beautiful is justification enough. When

Solomon built the temple in Jerusalem, we are told that he adorned it with precious stones 'for beauty' (2 Chronicles 3:6 KJV). The precious stones fulfilled no architectural or liturgical function – they were just there to be beautiful. Just by being there and by being beautiful, they reflected something of the beauty of their Creator. In many medieval cathedrals, there are exquisite carvings in places where they will never be seen. In Chinese rod puppetry, the puppeteers not only operate the puppets but also carry out an intricate dance as they do so, even though the audience cannot see them. Similarly, our world is full of places of sheer, staggering beauty, which no one has ever seen. Creation, in the reckless profusion of its beauty, reflects something of the gratuitous glory of God.

d) Creation is there for its own sake and for its own pleasure

When we make things, we tend to make them to serve our purposes and to be useful to us. But God doesn't make things to be *useful* to Him. He doesn't *need* anything. He makes them for their own sake, to be themselves, to have their own integrity, to take their unique place in the harmonious order of creation, and to make a unique contribution to the whole. That is not to say that creation isn't in some sense *for us* – for us to eat, to clothe ourselves with, to explore and to enjoy. But that is not its only purpose. Though God created the physical world with an eye to creating human beings to rule it and appreciate it, He also created it for its own sake. All created things have their own particular place and purpose within the intention and plan of God. Just by the fact that they are, by the fact that they obey their own laws and exist in their own ways, they proclaim something of the nature and glory and beauty of the One who made them and sustains them.

In particular, created things proclaim and please God through the sheer enjoyment of *pleasure*. As the psalmist put it:

> How many are your works, O Lord!
> In wisdom you made them all;

the earth is full of your creatures.
There is the sea, vast and spacious,

teeming with creatures beyond number –
living things both large and small.

There the ships go to and fro,
and the leviathan, which you formed to frolic there.

Psalm 104:24–26

What was this huge sea creature created for? 'To frolic' in its natural habitat. To take pleasure in its physical environment and its physical ability. Despite the kill-joy reputation of the church, the Bible has a high view of pleasure. It revels in the ordinary pleasures of life: 'So my conclusion is this: true happiness lies in eating and drinking and enjoying whatever has been achieved under the sun' (Ecclesiastes 5:18 NJB). Psalm 19:5 exults in our physical strength and prowess and in meeting and mastering the physical challenges of life: the joy of sexual delight and of physical exertion are gloried in. Pleasure is God-given, as even C. S. Lewis' fictional senior devil, Screwtape, acknowledges dismissively to his nephew, Wormwood:

[God]'s a hedonist at heart. All those fasts and vigils and stakes and crosses are only a façade. Or only like foam on the sea shore. Out at sea, out in His sea, there is pleasure, and more pleasure. He makes no secret of it; at His right hand are 'pleasures for evermore'. Ugh! I don't think He has the least inkling of that high and austere mystery to which we rise in the Miserific Vision. He's vulgar, Wormwood. He has a bourgeois mind. He has filled His world full of pleasures. There are things for humans to do all day long without His minding in the least – sleeping, washing, eating, drinking, making love, playing, praying, working. Everything has to be twisted before it's any use to us. We fight under cruel disadvantages. Nothing is naturally on our side.[7]

Pleasure is God-given. It is part of what creation is *for*, and God takes pleasure in the pleasure of His creatures. (Have you frolicked enough recently?!)

e) Creation is to be flooded with the knowledge and presence and glory of God

'For the earth will be filled with the knowledge of the glory of the LORD, as the waters cover the sea' (Habakkuk 2:14). The prophet argues that injustice and violence and imperial expansion are ultimately self-destructive ends, because creation is going to be put right. Negatively, evil will be thwarted: positively, creation will be drenched and saturated with the glory of God. The amount of water there is weighing down on the sea-bed gives us a little glimpse of the amount of glory with which creation will be crammed. That is what God made it for, and that is what He will achieve for it at the renewal of all things. 'The world is charged with the grandeur of God,' said Gerard Manley Hopkins – but not as much as it is going to be when it is re-made.

f) Creation is to be united under the headship of Christ so that everything finds its rightful and delightful place

St Paul tells us that God has 'made known to us the mystery of his will ... to be put into effect when the times will have reached their fulfilment – to bring all things in heaven and on earth together under one head, even Christ' (Ephesians 1:9–10). God's purpose for creation is not just to flood it with Himself, but also to unite it with itself, so that every person and every particle will be at peace, every atom and every angel, every ant and every anteater in harmony, so that all things find their unthreatened and unthreatening place under the cohering and unifying headship of Jesus the Messiah.

At the moment, not everything is united. Some things survive by killing and eating others. (Why? See Chapter 2.) The interests of some things are contrary to the interests of others, and the best we can hope for usually is compromise, where everyone benefits in some areas but has to make sacrifices in others. But when Christ is finally head over all things, what is good for one person will be good for everyone else, and the interests of one thing will be completely compatible with the interests of every other. That degree of harmony, and nothing short of it, is the ultimate destiny of creation.

g) Creation is to join in the relationship and dance of God

Perhaps the best way to speak of this planned harmony is to speak of all things joining in the relationship that is God. Within the being of God, there is an eternal relationship of love. In fact, God is relationship. Within the Godhead, the Father, the Son and the Spirit relate to one another, communicate with one another and love one another. And creation is ultimately made to join in that eternal relationship, which has always gone on and always will go on. We are to be taken up into it, and so is the inanimate order. It's a process that has already begun with the Incarnation, the Resurrection and the Ascension – part of the physical world has already been taken up into God by being part of Jesus' body, and one day the whole of creation will become (not parts of God but) participants in the life and love and dance of God.

In the last chapter of his science fiction novel, *Voyage to Venus*, C. S. Lewis presents us with a vision of the final end of creation, in which, as all things are now united to God, they are therefore in harmony with one another, and join in the great cosmic dance. Particles and animals and human beings, but also themes and truths and ideas all whirl around together in such a way as to complement and enrich one another. And wherever you look, *that* seems to be the centre of the dance, because it is so important to God. And when you look elsewhere, that seems to be the centre too. There is no competition between them for the love of the Father, just as there is (or should be) no competition between children for the love and attention of their parents. It is a long passage and full of flowery language – it is, after all, spoken by an 'eldil' or angel – but I hope that this will give you an idea of Lewis' vision of the purpose and ultimate harmony of creation:

The Great Dance does not wait to be perfect until the peoples of the Low Worlds [ie earth rather than heaven] are gathered into it. We speak not of when it will begin. It has begun from before always. There was no time when we did not rejoice before His face as now. The dance which we dance is at the centre and for the dance all things were made. Blessed be He! ... Each thing was made for Him. He is the centre. Because we are with Him, each of us is at the centre. It is not as in a city of the Darkened World [ie our fallen world] where they say that each must live for all. In His city all things are made for each. When He died in the Wounded World He died not for me, but for each man. If each man had been the only man made, He would have done no less. Each thing, from the single grain of Dust to the strongest eldil, is the end and the final cause of all creation and the mirror in which the beam of His brightness comes to rest and so returns to Him. Blessed be He![8]

Because there is a Person behind creation, there can be a purpose for creation.

3. THERE IS A VALUE TO CREATION

a) We are valued

Everyone wants to be valued. I can't imagine anyone not wanting to be valued. But value, like purpose, is a personal quality. You cannot be valued by a force. You cannot be valued by electricity or gravity. You can only be valued by a person. Here again the personal and impersonal views of life diverge dramatically. On the impersonal view, there is no Person at the heart of reality to value you, and therefore the only value you could have is such finite, fragile and temporary value as you can muster from your fellow human beings. On the personal view, by contrast, there is a Person – an infinite and eternal Person – who planned you, made you, loves you and values you, infinitely and unconditionally. So you have value – intrinsically. It is a fact about who you are. It is given – and not earned. You do not have to achieve your value by being good, or by being popular, by hard work, or by impressive achievement. The sense that our value has to be earned leads either to workaholism (in order to achieve it) or to despair (out of fear that it has been lost or will never be achieved).

If it depended upon other human beings, then we would always be afraid that they might cease to esteem us highly. Our value would always be vulnerable because those who value us might fall out with us or indeed die. On the impersonal view, a slice of our value would necessarily die with them. But if there is an eternal Person behind creation who values us infinitely, then our value is not dependent upon the vicissitudes of our achievements or the fluctuating state of our relationship with family and friends. It doesn't have to be earned and it cannot be forfeited. It is given and grounded in the gracious and gratuitous love of God the Creator. Our value is secure. That does not mean that our *sense* of that value is unchanging. When we lose our job, or a relationship breaks down, our *sense* of self-worth may well take a knock. But not the worth itself. That remains as rock beneath our feet – only more secure.

b) All creation is valued

It is not just human beings that are valued, though we do have a special value as those creatures who have been made in the image of God. We are worth more than many sparrows, says Jesus (Matthew 10:31, Luke 12:7), but that only provides the reassurance Jesus intends if sparrows are themselves of intrinsic worth. And though they are two-a-penny in the market – and probably the only meat that poor people could afford – Jesus insists that every one of them is the object of God's providential concern. Creation is not declared to be very good until human beings are part of it (Genesis 1:31), but every stage and every part of creation is assessed as being good in the eyes of its Maker. Creation has an intrinsic value of its own.

Our planet has paid a high price for the way in which we have forgotten this truth, and failed to treat creation as valuable. In practice, we have acted on the impersonal view that creation has no intrinsic purpose and we may therefore impose our own purposes on it; and that creation has no intrinsic worth beyond what it is worth to us. In the Eighties, the British Secretary of State for the Environment (of all people!) proposed the privatisation of nature reserves – as if the only value they possess is their financial potential. But on the personal view, they have value in their own right, because there is a Person behind the universe who made it and values it.

c) There is a basis for ethics

Stephen Hawking begins his book, *A Brief History of Time*, with the story of a famous scientist giving a lecture on astronomy.

> He described how the earth orbits around the sun and how the sun, in turn, orbits around the centre of a vast collection of stars called our galaxy. At the end of the lecture, a little old lady at the back of the room got up and said: "What you have told us is rubbish. The world is really a flat plate supported on the back of a giant tortoise." The scientist gave a superior smile before replying, "What is the tortoise standing on?" "You're very clever, young man, very clever," said the old lady. "But it's turtles all the way down!"[9]

The thing about all cosmologies, all accounts of how the universe came to be, be they sophisticated and scientific (like the Big Bang Theory) or unsophisticated and mythological (like the turtles), is that, by themselves, they provide no basis for morality. The Big Bang Theory may be true – I believe it is – but, by itself, it doesn't tell you how to live. It may tell you the origin of all things, but not their purpose or their value. For that, you need (not just a cosmology, but) a theology. Mere cosmologies are ethics-free: theological cosmologies are not. For if there is a Person at the heart of things, then personal qualities like value come into play. If there is Someone there who values us and values creation, then all created things have value, and we have the building blocks of a liveable morality.

This seems to me to explain our sense that some things are just wrong. We look at Auschwitz and we want to say that it's just wrong – not that it falls outside the terms of some social contract, nor that it's detrimental to the survival of the species, nor that it's undesirable, nor that it is to be condemned for fear that I might be treated the same way. But that it's wrong. Full stop.

One of the heartening things about the personal view of life is that it enables you to say just that. Belief that there is a God behind the universe and that He values His Creation puts ground under our ethical feet when we feel outrage at some appalling act. Conversely, one of the disquieting things about the personal view of life is that it puts ground under our consciences when they feel moral demand being made upon them. Having a Person at the heart of reality makes morality a matter of right and wrong, not of taste and preference. Human beings have value – intrinsically, absolutely and unconditionally – because God values them. And therefore we have to treat one another accordingly.

As we have already seen, however, it is not only human beings who have value. All created beings have some degree of value in the eyes of their Maker, or they would not have been made. Thus a doctrine of Creation not only provides us with the basis for ethics in general: it also propels us towards an environmental ethic in particular. If things have value, it is possible to treat them in a way that respects that value or in a way that violates that value. If things have a purpose, it is possible to treat them in accordance with that purpose or in opposition to that purpose. There are appropriate and inappropriate ways of treating the physical world. Of course, a doctrine of Creation does not resolve every conflict or answer every question we may want to ask of it in the area of environmental ethics. In a fallen world, the rights and needs of different creatures will clash and we shall be forced to choose between them. But it does give us a basis for valuing all creatures, and a call to respect, so far as we can, the value with which God values them.

4. CREATION IS DISTINCT FROM GOD

Creation is not divine. It is not God. It is not part of God. It is not an emanation from God – it's not a bit of Him that has been let loose on its own. It is different from Him. It is other than Him. It is separate from Him. At various points in the Creation story, we are told that 'God saw that it was good.' And at the end of the whole process, 'God saw all that he had made, and it was very good' (Genesis 1:31). In other words, God is separate enough from what He has made to be able to stand back from it, have a good look at it, assess it and declare it to be good. Just as when we make something, it is separate from us, and we can see what we think of it; so when God creates, creation is separate from Him and can be evaluated (very positively) by Him. When a human artist creates a sculpture, for instance, it is different from her, external to her, distinct from her. It may have something of her character and experience and view of life in it, but it isn't her. If the man she sells it to doesn't like it and destroys it, he may be a cultural philistine, but he will not be had up for murder. Similarly, when God creates, His creation may have something of His glory running through it, but it is not *Him*. It may be a window onto God but it is not God. It may be a place to meet with the Creator, but it is itself creat*ed*, not Creat*or*. It is not divine and it is not to be worshipped.

I have laboured this rather obvious point because, despite being obvious, it is in fact of crucial importance, for this reason. If all things are part of God, then there is evil in God as well as good. Not that creation is evil – it isn't. It is good, as we shall see shortly. But it is a good creation that has gone wrong. We are good creatures that have gone wrong and done wrong. We have polluted our planet and besmirched our own beings. If we were part of God, we would have put evil within His being as well. He would no longer be unambiguously good. Nothing less is at stake here than the goodness of God, which is central to the Christian message. 'This is the message we have heard from him and declare to you: God is light; in him there is no darkness at all' (1 John 1:5).

34

In the Greek and Roman world to which John was speaking, there was a whole pantheon of gods, but they were of highly dubious goodness. They got envious of each other and of particularly beautiful mortals. They bickered and backstabbed and battled for power. You never knew whether they were on your side or against you. You never knew whom to placate if things were going wrong. You might appease one and alienate another. You never knew where you stood. Into that world, the message that there is only one God (so that there is no divine division and no squabbling and no power struggle and no need to play one off against another) and that He is completely and unambiguously good (and therefore consistent and reliable and dependable and not capricious) came as very good news indeed. The goodness of God is part of the gospel.

And that is why it is so crucial to maintain the distinction between God and the world. In the world, there is cruelty: in God, there is not. In Him there is no darkness at all. Hitler once said that he could not see why human beings may not be as cruel as nature. And if nature is divine, then he must be right. But nature is not divine. Nature and God are two different entities. This distinction is essential if we are to maintain the goodness of God – and the goodness of God is essential if we are to maintain sanity and hope in a warped world. For if all is polluted, to whom may we go to be made clean? But if the Source of all things remains pure and true and clean and good, then there is hope that we – ourselves and our world – may be unwarped, cleaned, healed and remade.

5. CREATION IS DEPENDENT UPON GOD

The first four words of the Bible (in English) are 'In the beginning, God ...', not 'In the beginning, the universe ...'. The universe is not the ultimate truth. It is real, it matters, it is (or was made to be) beautiful, it is (as we have seen) valuable, and it is (as we shall see) good, but it is not ultimate. It is not self-existent. It does not depend on itself for its own being. It does not, in Jesus' phrase, have life in itself (John 5:26). It had to be given the life that it has. It depends upon God for its existence, its meaning and its future.

The sun and the moon are not mentioned as such in the story of creation. They are simply called the greater light and the lesser light (Genesis 1:16). This is probably because they were seen as gods by many in the ancient world. There was sun worship and moon worship. And the author or compiler of Genesis wanted to deflate this idea, and to insist that they are not gods – they are just lamps, just God's bedside-lights, as it were! They have been created, just as we have. They are fellow-creatures, not deities. They depend upon the real God for their existence, just as we do.

Mother Julian was a solitary nun who lived in a small cell attached to a church in Norwich in the fourteenth and early fifteenth century. Her writings have been published under the title, *Revelations of Divine Love*. In the first of these revelations, she writes:

> And he [our Lord] showed me more, a little thing, the size of a hazelnut, on the palm of my hand, round like a ball. I looked at it thoughtfully and wondered, 'What is this?' And the answer came, 'It is all that is made.' I marvelled that it continued to exist and did not suddenly disintegrate; it was so small. And again my mind supplied the answer, 'It exists, both now and for ever, because God loves it.' In short, everything owes its existence to the love of God.[10]

Creation is utterly, existentially, moment-by-moment dependent upon the persistent and faithful love of God for it. In order to stress this point, most Christian theologians have insisted that, when God created, He did so *from nothing*. He is a God who 'calls into existence the things that do not exist' (Romans 4:17 NRSV). It wasn't that He had some material around that had been there forever and just decided to do something with it. No, He created whatever material there was. If there were bits of matter or energy or spirit or anything (other than Himself) that He did not create, then there would be things that do not depend upon Him, that are self-existent. And if that were the case, then there would be more than one source for our universe, and reality would be essentially fragmented and fractured. In fact, we wouldn't have a universe at all, but a *multi*verse. All the cohesion and coherence and comprehensibility and consistency and (potential) harmony that come with belief in one God would be lost. That is why theologians have insisted that God created everything *from nothing*, and everything is therefore dependent upon Him.[b]

And because we are dependent upon God for our existence, we are dependent upon Him for our meaning. So we will not ultimately find our meaning 'within' ourselves. That is where many people do look. One Video Club magazine had this blurb about a Meditation video: 'Lasting happiness is found by turning within and exploring the depths of the heart and mind.' No, it isn't! That's the way to get trapped in what Malcolm Muggeridge called 'the deep, dark dungeon of my own ego'. There is a place for self-examination, for sure, but even that we don't do alone – we ask the Spirit of God to illumine our inner beings for us and show us the things that need to be put right (Psalm 139:23–4). We are dependent upon God and therefore we certainly won't expect to find meaning within. We don't have the meaning of our own existence within ourselves. It is only to be found in the God who made us for Himself.

For what is meaning if not belonging to and being part of and being able to contribute to a story that is bigger than our own story, and a community that is wider than our own immediate community? Meaning is belonging to something bigger than oneself. Therefore, by definition, we cannot find that within ourselves. To look for our meaning within is to get more and more cramped, to gain nothing more than we have anyway and already. You cannot find a 'beyond' within. To find meaning, you have to belong to something wider and more overarching and more all-embracing, and that ultimately is to be found only in God, the Source of all things.

[b] For an in-depth exposition of this concept, see Paul Copan and William Lane Craig, *Creation out of Nothing: a Biblical, Philosophical and Scientific Exploration* (Apollos, 2004).

6. CREATION IS ENDOWED WITH ITS OWN ORDER, RATIONALITY AND BEAUTY

If there are many gods, then reality is fractured and fragmented. That is very clear from the Greek and Roman gods who each had their own sphere of expertise, as it were, so that if you were in love with someone, it was to Venus, the goddess of love, that you had to pray. If you wanted to attack your neighbour, it was to Mars, the god of war, that you turned. Unfortunately, however, they were in constant conflict with one another, and would use human beings as pawns in their own battles, as means of getting back at one another. The result was that poor Aeneas, for example, never knew where he was. One goddess was for him, another was against him, and he was torn apart by their antagonism. A polytheistic world-view [ie one which believes in many gods] is necessarily going to be an anxiety-ridden world-view, because you never know who is for you and who is against. A divided concept of reality can give no assurance that fundamental order will not simply collapse into chaos and incoherence. That is why Vitalstatistix, Chief of Asterix's Gallic tribe, is always afraid that the sky is going to fall on his head – because polytheism offers no basis for ongoing order.

If there is one Creator God, however, then there is one created reality. If everything was made by the same Person, then everything is capable of cohering and we expect it to have order. If everything was made by an intelligent Being, then we have a basis for presuming that reality will be rational, that gravity will work in Australia as well as in Austria. Believing that Being to be Beauty itself, we are not surprised to find that creation is beautiful. Now of course, sometimes we do find disorder and ugliness in God's world and we shall be looking at that in Chapter 2. But the point here is that we feel the need to explain the *dis*order, not the order; the pain, not the pleasure; the ugliness, not the beauty. We instinctively and rightly feel that order is the norm, pleasure is the norm, beauty is the norm – these are the basic things, the fundamental things, the deep-down things, the true things, the way things should be.

Ugliness and disorder and pain are the exceptions, the abnormal, the perverted, the things that shouldn't be. We talk of 'the problem of evil' – not the problem of good. And that is a rather significant clue to the goodness, rationality and beauty of the Reality behind our reality. If there is so much evil (and disorder and ugliness) in our world, why do we rebel against it and feel that it has no place, that it *should not be*? Do we perhaps have some half-remembered sense that we were made for something better? That we were made *by* Someone Better?

One of the benefits of believing in one God is that we have a harmonised (and harmonising) view of reality. We know why creation is fundamentally ordered and essentially rational and basically beautiful. We know that reality is broken but not divided. We know that we are inhabitants of one reality that has fault-lines within it, and will one day be healed of those fault-lines – not a whole lot of different realities warring with one another. We know that all the different dimensions of creation, seen and unseen, were created by the one God and were made to be in harmony and peace with one another. We do not suffer from the anxiety that comes from a divided concept of reality. We are not torn apart by conflicting loyalties, or by not knowing who is for us and who is against. We believe in one God, who made one multifaceted, gloriously diverse and potentially harmonious creation – and if that God is for us, who can be against us?

Notice in passing how the last two points, 5 and 6, are necessary for science to function. Because creation is *dependent* upon God for its very existence and its basic form, we cannot know in advance what it is like. God is free – and there is presumably an infinite number of ways He could have chosen to set up His world. So we cannot simply deduce what it must be like – we have to take a look. We have to explore it. We have to do experiments to find out what it is like. If creation were something that existed necessarily, there would be no need for experiments – we could just read off how the world must be from mathematical or philosophical principles. But because it depends upon the free decision of God, we cannot know its deepest nature except by exploration and experiment. There is no substitute for science.

And because creation is *rational and ordered*, experiments are worth doing. If creation were not fundamentally ordered, then you might get different results every time you did the same experiment in the same conditions. So if creation were not dependent, there would be no need for experiment. And if creation were not ordered there would be no possibility of doing experiments. The very fact that science works thus implies that there is an order there to be uncovered. It may be a surprising kind of order. It may be much more complex than we were expecting. But the whole pursuit of science, the whole scientific endeavour implies that we expect our world to be ordered – and belief in God gives us grounds for that expectation. The doctrine of Creation thus provided the soil in which modern science could grow.

Alvin Plantinga puts it well:

> There are stories about early opponents of modern science refusing to count the number of a horse's teeth or look through a telescope to see how many moons Jupiter has. These stories may or may not be true; nevertheless they illustrate a point. If you think you can figure out the number of teeth in a horse's mouth *a priori*, you won't feel obliged to open that horse's mouth and count them. If you think you know just by reasoning that Jupiter has no moons, you won't feel compelled to actually take a look through a telescope to see how many there are. ... On the other hand, if you think the world and its structures are contingent – contingent upon God's freely choosing to make them one way as opposed to other possibilities – you'll think looking to see is the appropriate way to find out. In this way the empirical nature of science, as well as its basic charter, arise out of a theistic way of looking at the world and fit in well with it.[11]

7. CREATION IS OPEN TO GOD

He made it, and He can act within it. He created it, and it is not closed off from Him. 'But now, this is what the Lord says – he who created you, O Jacob, he who formed you, O Israel: "Fear not … When you pass through the waters, I will be with you"' (Isaiah 43:1–2). Because He is the one God and the Creator of all that is, and *everything* is dependent upon Him, then there is nowhere He cannot go with us, no experience that puts us outside His 'patch'. Even a place like Auschwitz is not shut off from Him, as Corrie ten Boom discovered. In her book, *The Hiding Place*, she tells of her experiences in the concentration camp where her sister died, and concludes: 'There is no pit so deep that God is not deeper.'[12]

In the ancient world, they used to think that the gods had their own individual patch. Naaman, the Aramaean general, came to believe that 'there is no God in all the world except in Israel' (2 Kings 5:15) and asked the prophet, Elisha, for a lorry-load – well, two mule-loads, to be historically accurate – of Israelite soil to take back to Aram with him, so that he could pray on a (transported) bit of Yahweh's territory. It was a nice touch, and Elisha doesn't even correct Naaman – but it was totally unnecessary. Yahweh created the whole universe. Aram is just as much His territory as Israel is. The whole cosmos is His patch: wherever we go, He can be with us.

It's easy to mock Naaman for his primitive thinking about God, but it's harder to root out the same attitude from within ourselves. We don't, of course, explicitly believe that you can only worship God on Israelite soil, or in a church, or anything like that. But we do tend to assume that there are areas of our life that God isn't interested in – that He's only interested in the 'spiritual'

or 'religious' bits, and not in our work, or our finances, or our sport or our political views. There tend to be areas of our lives that we don't want to let God into, maybe areas we don't even dare face ourselves. But He is the Creator of everything, everything is open to Him, and there is nothing He is not interested in, nothing He does not want to share with us, go through with us, and transform for us – if we will but invite Him to. There are no no-go areas for God. There are no barriers, save for the ones we erect ourselves.

> Where can I go from your Spirit?
> Where can I flee from your presence?
>
> If I go up to the heavens, you are there;
> if I make my bed in the depths, you are there.
>
> If I rise on the wings of the dawn,
> if I settle on the far side of the sea,
>
> even there your hand will guide me,
> your right hand will hold me fast.

Psalm 139:7–10[13]

In the warmth and love of that omnipresence, we are profoundly and ultimately secure.

8. CREATION IS MULTI-DIMENSIONAL

To return to the opening words of the Bible, 'In the beginning, God created the heavens and the earth.' The phrase 'the heavens and the earth' is, at one level, just a Hebrew idiom meaning the whole of created reality, all that is, the whole shebang. But it is a phrase that also reminds us that 'the earth', the physical universe of which we are a part, is not all there is. It is our natural habitat, and it is all we are usually aware of, but it is not the whole story. There are also 'the heavens'. There are other dimensions to reality than those of which we are normally aware. As the creed reminds us, there are things invisible as well as visible.

The Scriptures constantly pull back the veil on these other dimensions of reality. They insist (not just on the fact that these other dimensions are real, but also) on the fact that they intersect and interact with our own. As Jacob discovered in his dream, there is a ladder set up between heaven and earth, and there is two-way traffic on that ladder (Genesis 28:10–15). When Elisha and his servant were surrounded by the Aramaean army intent upon capturing him, he told his panicking servant that 'Those who are with us are more than those who are with them' (2 Kings 6:16). Then he prayed that God would open his servant's eyes 'so that he may see', whereupon his servant saw the horizon full of the fiery hosts of God.

Like Elisha's servant, we normally do not see these other realities. The most we can do is catch the odd glimpse or hear the odd rumour. (As Francis Thompson put it in his poem, *The Kingdom of God*, 'Tis ye, 'tis your estrangèd faces, That miss the many-splendoured thing.') Elisha, a great man of God, was more aware of these other dimensions than most. But whether we are aware of them or not, they are nonetheless real, and they are part of the nexus of influences upon our own world and our own stories. There are more things in heaven and earth, indeed, than are dreamt of in most of our philosophies.

Flannery O'Connor, the American novelist and short story writer, once commented that the Christian novelist lives in a bigger universe. Other Christian writers, such as C. S. Lewis, have explored and exploited that 'biggerness' imaginatively in their books. Just as Jacob stumbled across a place where heaven and earth intersected, so in Lewis' classic children's book, *The Lion, the Witch and the Wardrobe*, the Pevensie children stumble across a wardrobe which is (occasionally) the point at which the world of Narnia meets our own. Of course, it is not just the Christian novelist who lives in this multi-dimensional universe. We all do. It's just that the creative writer can help the rest of us to believe it, to imagine it and relate to it.

When Charlie Chaplin was told that no life had been discovered on Mars, he is reported as having said, 'I feel lonely.' Not that life on Mars would probably help much. It would be exciting, but it would be more of the same – all in the same dimension. What a Christian world-view offers is other dimensions – and life in (admittedly usually unconscious) interaction with those other dimensions. Such a world-view will not cramp us. It provides us with another axis on which to plot the coordinates of our lives as human beings. It promises us what Dostoevsky called 'the touching of other worlds'.

9. CREATION IS GOOD

Creation is not God, but it is good. It was not a mistake. It was not 'Plan B'. It is good. And in particular, it is a good thing that the world is physical, and that we have bodies. It is not as if God looked at His handiwork and said, 'Whoops, I seem to have given them bodies. That's a bit of a blunder. Better make sure they never use them in any positive or pleasurable way!' No, He looked at all that He had made, 'and it was very good' (Genesis 1:31).

This distinguishes the Judeo-Christian world-view from many other philosophies. The Greek philosopher Plato, for example, saw our physicality as a temporary necessary evil from which we would finally escape into the purely spiritual nature that is our true identity. For Plato, the soul was the important thing, and bodies were an ephemeral encumbrance which we would shed at death. Sadly, that is what many people think that Christianity teaches. NO! For Jews and Christians, creation is good. Physicality is good. We, in all our physicality and materiality, are good. As enfleshed, blood-and-bone beings, we are what God intended. It is a good and God-given thing that the world is physical. Creation is not to be rejected, or regretted, or forsaken, or escaped from, or left behind. Nor are our bodies. And if the Church has ever given the impression that our bodies are bad, or shameful, or somehow squalid, then it has departed from a properly Christian doctrine of creation.

Of course, in a broken world, our bodies can be the occasion of much pain and distress and constriction. Why that is, we shall be considering in Chapter 2 (again!), when we look at the Fall. But God's answer to it is not to downplay or denigrate our physicality: it is to promise its ultimate healing. Salvation is not going to be from this world, but of this world. God's going to save this world, not to save us from it. He will save us and our world together because we belong to it, and it needs us to care for it and give voice to its praises.

More particularly, when we are remade, we shall not be bodiless, but will be given new bodies – new (not-less-than) physical expressions of who we are, to live in a renewed and (not-less-than) physical world. We are not going to be unclothed, says Paul in 2 Corinthians 5:4, but reclothed. God made us as physical beings, and He is not going to go back on that creational intention. He made us as multi-dimensional beings, and salvation is not going to reduce the number of those dimensions. The 'many-splendoured thing' that is creation, is going to be more-splendoured, not less. Creation in all its physicality is going to be restored, not reduced – because creation is not a bad thing, but a good thing that has gone wrong.

Similarly, and this is vital psychologically, we are not bad people – we are good people who have gone wrong. God's fundamental word over us is, 'Behold, you are very good'. He may have to say other words over some of the things that we do. But it is good to be you. You are not a mistake. You are not something that should not be. You are someone whom God made, whom God wants to be, whom He loves and cherishes and values and affirms. And that, of course, goes also for the people you live with and work with and come across – even the ones you find difficult. Once again, a proper doctrine of Creation drives us towards ethics. And that, annoyingly, has implications for how you treat them!

Many of the problems we have – psychologically, ecologically, theologically and evangelistically – stem from forgetting that creation is good. To give one example, someone came to see me pastorally to talk over his depression. I have had depression myself, and know some of the triggers, but we spoke for a long time, and I could not quite work out what lay behind it. Eventually, I asked him about his hopes for the future, and he replied, 'Well, what I would like to do is an art course, but I couldn't justify that.' When I asked why not, he replied, 'Well, it doesn't help extend the Kingdom, does it?' 'Ah', I said, 'I think we've just got to the root of your depression.'

So I tried to reassure him that when God saves someone, He doesn't ask them to become less human. He doesn't ask them to lop off bits of who they are. When He *re*creates someone, He doesn't make them less rich than He did when He created them. (He turns water into wine – not the other way round.) He restores all that He made them to be, and more. Creation is good, and we were created in the image of the Creator. So we are creative, and by being creative, we reflect something of God. Try and lop off your creativity, and you are trying to truncate your humanity. You are saying 'No thank you' to a wonderful part of who God made you to be. And your humanity is going to rebel. That was what was happening inside the young man who came to see me. He needed to know that creation is good, that creativity is good, and that God is glorified when we use the gifts He has given us, joyfully and freely. Salvation does not render creation superfluous – it restores it. And all our God-given gifts with it. Because creation is good.

10. CREATION BELONGS TO GOD

> The earth is the Lord's, and everything in it,
>   the world, and all who live in it,
> for he founded it upon the seas
>   and established it upon the waters.

Psalm 24:1

We want to belong. But to belong to some*thing* is to belong to that which is less than ourselves. And to belong to one another, when the others (and we) are imperfect, is dangerous (as the victims of communism discovered). To belong to the One who made us, and who loves us, is the only safe way to belong.[c]

And it is the deepest way to belong. After all, we and all things ultimately come from God. He is our Origin. Our meaning is to be found in Him and our value comes from Him. All things are properly orientated insofar as they are orientated around Him. All things are properly related to each other insofar as they are properly related to Him. If all things belong to Him, then they can cohere; if different things belong to different people, then creation will fragment and be fought over.

This is a truth that the Scriptures hammer home:

> In his hand are the depths of the earth:
>> and the peaks of the mountains are his also.
> The sea is his and he made it:
>> his hands moulded dry land.

Psalm 95:4–5 ASB

And in Jewish law, land could not be bought or sold permanently, 'because the land is mine and you are but aliens and my tenants' (Leviticus 25:23). Indeed, what was actually being sold was not the land but the number of harvests before the next Jubilee Year, when the land would revert to the family that originally occupied it (Leviticus 25:16).

When the American Government offered to buy land from the American Indians, Chief Seattle made a speech in which he is reported as having replied to this offer: 'How can you buy or sell

---

[c] I am not, of course, suggesting that we should only belong to God and not to anyone or anything else. Such a policy would be impossible and completely undesirable – we are made for and flourish in a whole network of structured and committed relationships. All I am saying is that a) realistically, such other belongings are bound to be a source of some pain as well as joy and fulfillment, in a fallen world; and b) our ultimate *belonging* needs to be to the One who made us and who alone loves us perfectly and infinitely. For a powerful critique of pursuing safety by avoiding human belonging and love see chapter 6 of C. S. Lewis' *The Four Loves*, on 'Charity'.

the sky, the warmth of the land? The idea is strange to us. If we do not own the freshness of the air or the sparkle of the water, how can you buy them?'[14] His puzzlement would have been shared by the ancient Israelites, for the earth belongs to the Lord, and all that is in it. It is not ours to do what we want with. We are but tenant farmers who are accountable for how we use it.

11. CREATION DESERVES A RESPONSE

a) Creation should inspire wonder

At the end of the book of Job, when all the participants have had their say, God finally speaks, answers Job out of the storm, and takes him on a sort of visionary tour of creation. At one level, Job 38–41 is a barrage of questions designed to bring home to Job how minuscule is his own perspective, and how total is God's. But at another, God is applying the beauty of His creation to Job's pain. He introduces him (imaginatively) to the secret places of our world, and to some of its strange inhabitants – the stars, the constellations, the ocean depths, the mountain goats, the wild donkeys, the ostrich and horse, the eagle and hawk, and mysterious creatures such as Behemoth and Leviathan, which may be actual creatures such as the hippopotamus and crocodile, or may be symbolic representations of chaos or political powers. David Atkinson, in his commentary, *The Message of Job*, quotes aptly from the great seventeenth-century writer, Thomas Traherne:

> By an act of understanding, therefore, be present now with all the creatures among which you live; and hear them in their beings and operations praising God in an heavenly manner. Some of them vocally, others in their ministry, all of them naturally and continually. … You are never what you ought till you go out of yourself and walk among them.[15]

Atkinson comments:

> That is perhaps why God takes Job on this tour – to show his
> majesty in his works: to take Job out of himself, to distract him
> from his misery, to broaden his horizons to the creative and
> life-giving majesty of God, and especially to enable him to see
> himself in a new setting. Job, this is where your heart will find
> rest: in finding your own place within the panorama of God's
> purposes for his world. Can you lift your eyes from the ash heap,
> and see the glory of God in his creation? Then you may glimpse
> again how, as Traherne puts it elsewhere, to 'enjoy the world'. …
> Sometimes we will most help distressed people – help them draw
> nearer to God, from the depths of depression – not by teaching
> them doctrine, or by preaching our best sermon, or by showing
> them the error of their ways, but by walking with them round the
> garden, by taking them to see a waterfall or a sunset, by helping
> them recover an enjoyment in the world.[16]

Beauty and wonder are therapeutic.

b) Creation is to be enjoyed

'For everything God created is good, and nothing is to be rejected
if it is received with thanksgiving …' (1 Timothy 4:4). Our job is to
receive it with thanksgiving. And to remind and enable us to do
that, God gave us the Sabbath – a day off in which to worship the
Creator and enjoy the creation. To have a bit of time and space. To
put breaks and breaths into our breathless lives. We are not here just
to do 'religious' things. We are here to enjoy all that creation has to
offer (though, as we shall see, in such a way as to respect creation's
integrity and sustainability). We are here to live fully human lives.

A friend of mine, who is an Anglican vicar, was once attending
a clergy conference. Wanting to get away from his fellow clergy,
as well he might – as Revd Sydney Smith put it, 'Clergy are like
manure: thinly spread, they do a lot of good, but all in a heap, they
are very unpleasant!' – he sought out a television on which to watch

the football. He crept surreptitiously into the television room, only to find the bishop there, watching the football too. In the interval, they discussed why it was that they were the only two watching, and came to the conclusion that they must be the only two with a sufficiently high doctrine of creation! Creation is to be enjoyed. Physicality is to be revelled in. Christians are called upon to live life 'with nowt taken out' – and with thanksgiving.

c) Creation is to be meditated upon

'Consider the lilies of the field', says Jesus in Matthew 6:28 (KJV), and do we? No, we're too busy doing other things – very worthy and important things, often. They just don't leave us time to do the things Jesus told us to do. We are to linger over the things of creation, to ponder them, and to meditate upon them. That is how good science is done (remember Newton's apple). It is how good poetry is written. And, suggests Jesus, it is how good lives are lived. Sister Margaret Magdalen expounds Jesus' saying beautifully in her superb book, *Jesus – Man of Prayer*:

> The disciples are invited to consider, to notice, to learn from the lilies, not by a peremptory glance but by a long, feasting look. 'Consider' has about it the feeling of restful reflection, leisurely appreciation, a freedom of heart to gaze and wonder, and, in doing so, to discover truth. This kind of looking has to be for its own sake, not for any end-product; not with our greedy consumer-society tendency to do something with half an eye on what we can get out of it.
>
> In considering the lilies, which obviously Jesus must have done himself, the disciples would discover a truth not only about trust but, even more, about living provisionally – that is, as those for whom provision has been made.
>
> Jesus singled out for special attention these ordinary, rather despised, parts of creation on which no one placed any value – field flowers, grass, sparrows – which could nevertheless become gateways to contemplation. These were to be the icons

through which the disciples would penetrate the mystery of God's providence and protection, and discover hidden wisdom and truth about God's relationship with his creation. And they would do so by using the eyes of the body and the eyes of understanding.[17]

d) Creation is to be explored

Now the Lord God had formed out of the ground all the beasts of the field and all the birds of the air. He brought them to the man to see what he would name them; and whatever the man called each living creature, that was its name. So the man gave names to all the livestock, the birds of the air, and all the beasts of the field.

Genesis 2:19–20a

As well as inspiring a song by Bob Dylan, this little passage is also important for the scientific mandate that it gives to human beings. For naming the animals involves observing them closely, seeing how different parts of the animal kingdom fit together and relate to one another – in other words, the scientific task of classification, or 'taxonomy', to give it its technical term. As we have seen, Creation is endowed with order and rationality, and will reveal that order and rationality to the careful observer and explorer and experimenter. Not only *can* we (in the words of the seventeenth-century astronomer, Johann Kepler) 'think God's thoughts after Him', but that is our calling. That is part of our human task. Humanity is to be the 'mediator of order', as the great Scottish theologian, Tom Torrance, dubbed us: 'the secret of the universe or its meaning becomes disclosed through man's interaction with it, both as man of science and as man of God.'[18]

Notice how God not only gives this scientific task to human beings, but He also respects its results: 'whatever the man called each living creature, that was its name.' Given the sort of names some parents come up with, He was taking a bit of a risk.

Catherine and I had agreed on the name Millie for a girl weeks before the birth. But now that a baby girl had actually come along I felt an urge to name her after my late mother. I shared the idea with Catherine, who said it was a beautiful thought.

'Your mother sounds like a wonderful person, and I wish I had met you earlier so that I could have known her. It would be a lovely thing to name this baby after the grandmother she will never meet; it's a touching and poetic idea. The only trouble, my darling husband, is that your mother's name was Prunella.'

'I know.'

'Don't you think the world is a cruel enough place into which to bring a new human being without lumbering it with the name Prunella?'

We agreed to sleep on the idea and we took Millie home two days later.[19]

God was, indeed, taking a bit of a risk. But then, He is the sort of God who, having given us freedom, does not keep taking it away again the moment we do something of which he disapproves. And in the scientific enterprise, He encourages us to see new links, to make new connections, to think thoughts that are prompted by but not limited to the order He has Himself given in creation. We can be, indeed we *are to* be, creative – scientifically as in every other way. Our creativity, of course, needs to be responsible and accountable. It must be accountable experimentally – does it fit with reality? And it must be accountable morally – does it fit with the purpose and value of reality? But He has given us keen eyes and curious minds and a desire to explore and question – and He wants us to use them in order to understand and interact with the rich and complex universe in which He has set us. The scientific task is part of the human calling.

e) Creation is to be ruled

'Let us make human beings in our image, in our likeness, and let them rule over the fish of the sea and the birds of the air, over the livestock, over all the earth, and over all the creatures that move along the ground.'

Genesis 1:26

Often, in the ancient world, a king or emperor would set up a statue in a town or city as a sign of his rule. In the capital city, he would rule in person, but in other cities his 'image' would represent his rule on his behalf. The Bible sees human beings as God's image – representing and exercising God's rule on His behalf. In heaven, He rules in person: on earth, we are to rule in His Name, that His rule may come on earth as it is in heaven. We are to be His vice-regents, under Him and over the world, being ruled by Him and ruling creation in His stead.

But – and this is crucial – the sort of rule we are to exercise over creation is to be the sort of rule that God exercises over us, and that is servant leadership. How did Jesus exercise leadership over His disciples? By calling them not servants but friends, by being *their* servant and washing their feet, by dying for them. How did He exercise dominion over nature? By bringing it back into order, by caring for it, by healing the sick, raising the dead, undoing all that mars creation and prevents it from being itself. There is no exploitation in God's rule of us, and therefore there should be no exploitation in our rule over creation. Our rule over creation is to be the same sort of protecting, liberating, healing and enabling rule that God exercises over us.

In the nature miracles of Jesus, we see that dominion over nature which we were created for, but which we abandoned and lost, turning our rule into something damaging and selfishly exploitative. But when we look at Jesus in the pages of the Gospels, we see that proper rule being exercised once again. Here at last is a human being ruling creation as it was meant to be ruled. Here at last is a human being who is utterly obedient to His heavenly Father, and who therefore finds that the winds and the waves obey Him. Here at last is a human being exercising dominion, which, as Colin Gunton defined it in The Triune Creator, is 'a calling to be and to act in such a way as to enable the created order to be itself as a response of praise to its maker.'[20] And that is to be the model for our own interaction with the natural world. By both prayer and cosmic estate management, we are to mimic and mirror the gentle, faithful and self-sacrificial rule of God in Jesus – which enables us and all things to be nothing other than fully themselves.

f) Creation is to be cared for

'The Lord God took the man and put him in the Garden of Eden to work it and take care of it' (Genesis 2:15). We are to care for that part of creation into which God places us. That is God's command, and that is our calling. He made and loves and values creation: we must love and value it too – and show that we do by how we treat it. As John Stott put it, 'Christian people should surely have been in the vanguard of the movement for environmental responsibility, because of our doctrines of creation and stewardship. Did God make the world? Does he sustain it? Has he committed its resources to our care? His personal concern for his own creation should be sufficient to inspire us to be equally concerned.'[21] Furthermore, 'we cannot truly love and serve our neighbours if at the same time we are destroying their environment, or acquiescing in its destruction, or even ignoring the environmentally depleted circumstances in which so many people are condemned to live.'

Forgive me for being starkly practical here, but it seems to me that if we are not practical at this point, we are not being faithful. We need to build basic environmental good practice into our everyday lives. We need to make sure that the detergents we use in our dishwashers and washing machines break down easily into non-toxic components – Ecover and Down to Earth are the biodegradable brands most easily available in British supermarkets. We need to keep asking ourselves whether our planned car journeys are really necessary – travelling by bicycle is cleaner, cheaper, healthier and frequently quicker. We could join a Christian environmental organisation such as A Rocha (the inspiring story of which is told in *Under the Bright Wings*). We could have an energy assessment of our home. We could campaign for our work places and churches to be environmentally responsible. (This book is printed on paper from sustainable sources, I am relieved to say!)

These are just a few of the things that we can do without spending a great deal more time – we have to use detergents anyway, it's just a matter of getting into the habit of choosing environmentally-friendly ones when we go shopping. The point is that we need to live out what we profess to believe. We need to live out our doctrine of Creation. We need to reflect the Creator's love for His world. We need to ask ourselves whether, if anyone looked at our homes, our lifestyles and our direct debits, they would be able to tell that we believed in the intrinsic value and purposefulness of creation. Or do we in practice live as if there were no Person behind it and no value to it and no purpose for it? As if it were there not for Him and for itself – but just for us?

RESOURCES FOR FURTHER READING, PRAYER AND ACTION

Denis Alexander, *Rebuilding the Matrix* (Lion Publishing, 2001). A useful place to start to explore further the relationship between a Christian world-view and modern science.

Tom Torrance, *The Christian Frame of Mind: Reason, Order and Openness in Theology and Natural Science* (Helmers & Howard, 1989). More difficult, but very influential, are the writings of Tom Torrance. This book is probably the easiest to read.

Edith Schaeffer, *Hidden Art* (Norfolk Press, 1971). On how to introduce beauty into our (and others') lives, and how our giving full rein to our creativity can proclaim both the Creator God and the fact that human beings are made in His image.

James Sire, *The Universe Next Door: A Guide to World Views* (IVP, 1976). To look more deeply into some of the different conceptions of how God and world are related.

Sister Margaret Magdalen, *Jesus – Man of Prayer* (part of The Jesus

Library by Hodder & Stoughton, 1987). See the appendix for a practical discussion of how to meditate on creation.

Francis Schaeffer, *Pollution and the Death of Man* (Hodder & Stoughton, 1970). On Christian environmental concern.

Andrew Linzey and Tom Regan, *Compassion for Animals* (SPCK, 1988). For an excellent collection of prayers and readings about the animal realm.

A Rocha

'An international conservation organisation working to show God's love for all creation.' See *Under the Bright Wings*, by Peter Harris (reprinted 2000 by Regent College Publishing, www.regentpublishing.com, ISBN I-57383-1888-3). To enquire further about A Rocha, or to join, write to: A Rocha UK, 13, Avenue Road, Southall, Middlesex, UB1 3BL, tel: 020 8574 5935 or email: uk@arocha.org. Or visit their website at www.arocha.org.

Royal Society for the Protection of Birds

To think about how to make your garden more wildlife-friendly, write to the Royal Society for the Protection of Birds for their leaflet, *Gardening with Wildlife*: RSPB, The Lodge, Potton Road, Sandy, Bedfordshire, SG19 2DL. They can also supply a reading list of other helpful works on environmental gardening.

Eco-Congregation

Eco-Congregation is an ecumenical programme helping churches make the link between environmental issues and Christian faith, and respond in practical action in the church, in the lives of individuals and in the local and global community. See their website: www.ecocongregation.org.

ECOVER

For more information about biodegradable detergents and other products, write to Ecover (UK) Ltd., 165, Main Street, New Greenham Park, Berkshire, RG19 6HN.

Energy Efficiency and Renewable Energy

i. Grant Funding

There is currently government funding available for those interested in installing renewable energy technologies in their homes, churches or community buildings. For more information on how to apply, either contact the Clear Skies programme through their website www.clearskies.org.uk or follow the links to the PV Demonstration programme at the EST's website, www.est.org.uk.

Those who are members of the 'priority group' (ie 10 % or more of their income is spent on energy bills) are eligible for grants from local authorities and energy suppliers to improve the energy efficiency of their homes and so reduce their bills. For more information, contact the local Energy Efficiency Advice Centre (EEAC) on 0845 727 7200, or visit the website, www.saveenergy.co.uk or www.est.org.uk.

ii. Advice

EEACs also help anyone to carry out a Home Energy Check and identify ways of saving energy and money. Even those not in the priority group may be eligible for grant funding or for interest-free loans from energy suppliers.

For churches, the Action Energy programme may provide energy audits and interest-free loans to install energy efficiency measures. More information is available at their website, www.thecarbontrust. co.uk/energy, and helpline, 0800 585794. I am grateful to Hannah Reynolds for this information.

2 FALL

The great November gale killed a plumber in Slough, a lady on her way to demonstrate the boning of a shoulder of lamb to the Bromyard Women's Institute, an aromatherapist from Wakefield, and Reginald Iolanthe Perrin.

Reggie's funeral service bore eerie echoes of his memorial service a quarter of a century earlier. On that occasion he had been present, in disguise. It was difficult for the mourners to realise that this time, at the age of seventy-one, he had gone for good.

'The manner of his death may seem to those who knew him well to be a curiously appropriate full stop at the end of the bizarre sentence that was his life,' intoned the Vicar of Goffley, who hadn't known him at all. 'He was struck by a falling billboard advertising the Royal and General Accident Insurance Company. Ironically, this was the very company with which he was insured. God moves in a mysterious way.'

'Absolutely right,' whispered Reggie's old boss, C. J., who was drawn to clichés like lambs to the slaughter. 'I didn't get where I am today without knowing that God moves in a mysterious way.'[1]

Thus the series of Reggie Perrin novels is perpetuated, and so is the long and noble tradition of making all fictional clergy complete prats. (That's why it's called 'fiction', of course!) But notice the *assumption* that this clerical prat makes in his sermon. He assumes that the billboard falling on Reggie Perrin is an instance of God working, albeit in a mysterious way. Natural disaster – and it is certainly a disaster to have carried off the great Reggie Perrin, inventor of the square hoopla and the insoluble suppository – is the work of God. And all we can do is to shrug our shoulders and comment on the mysteriousness of it all, which basically means that we don't have any good answers to the question of why God might choose to work in that sort of way.

The same assumption is made in Ben Elton's savage satire on reality television, *Dead Famous*, in which one of the contestants is murdered on screen. Chief Inspector Coleridge, the intelligent but somewhat supercilious and fuddy-duddy detective investigating the murder, saw the state of the victim and …

> … knew how much he wanted to catch this killer. He could not abide savagery. He had never got used to it; it scared him and made him question his faith. After all, why would God possibly want to engineer such a thing? Because He moved in mysterious ways, of course; that was the whole point. Because He surpasseth understanding. You weren't meant to understand. Still, in his job it was hard sometimes to find reasons to believe. Sergeant Hooper hadn't enjoyed the scene much either, but it was not in his nature to ponder what purpose such horror might have in God's almighty plan.[2]

It's the same assumption – namely, that when horror happens, it is God who has engineered it. It was intended. It has a place in His plan. That is what Christians are assumed to believe. And it is the same phrase about moving in mysterious ways (taken from a hymn by William Cowper) that is used to obscure the fact that no one can think of any good reason why God might want to engineer such an event.

You find the same thing in one of Gary Larson's *Far Side* cartoons, in which God is looking at His video screen and watching a man walking down the street, blissfully unaware that a ten-ton weight is suspended perilously above him. And God's finger is poised just above a button on His computer, marked 'Smite!' Again, the assumption is that if something nasty happens to someone, then it is God who does it. The assumption is that the way things *are* reflects the way God wants them to be. The assumption is that whatever happens is the will of God. If God is omnipotent, says this way of thinking, then He must get His own way. And the only things that can happen are the things that He wants to happen. The doctrine of the Fall says a decisive **No** to that assumption.

What do we mean by 'the Fall'? '"Fallenness" refers to the perceived gap between the universe as it is now and the universe as it was intended to be in the creation purposes of God. "The Fall" refers to that event or process by which such a gap was brought about.'[3] Metropolitan Anthony Bloom, who was leader of the Russian Orthodox Church in Britain, told the story of one of his first sermons in London, when his English was still somewhat hit and miss. He could not understand why the congregation burst out laughing when he spoke passionately about the 'great yawning abbess between us and God'! Well, the distance between us and God is one result of the Fall. But there is also a yawning abyss between the world as it was intended to be, and the world as it now is – between blueprint and (distorted) reality. In other words, we all know instinctively that the world is not what it could be. We all know that it could and should be a place of beauty and of joy. We all know too that that beauty has been marred and defaced, and that that joy has been mitigated and sometimes overwhelmed by delight-haemorrhaging regret and gut-wrenching tragedy. There is a huge gulf between how we see the world to be, and how we sense it could and should be. There is a hiatus between what it is capable of being and what it is. There is a chasm between how the God we meet in Jesus would want it to be and how we actually experience it. The Fall is the story of how that gap opened up.

Traditionally, the story of the Fall has been associated with the story of Adam and Eve disobeying God, in Genesis 3. Why are things so different from the way God created them to be? Why do they lack that harmony which was always God's intention for them? Because human beings misused the freedom God gave them, and chose to go their own way. By their disobedience, they shut themselves off from God, cut themselves off from each other, came to be at threat from and a threat to the natural world, and set up division within their own beings. Theologically, sociologically, ecologically and psychologically, they became disordered and discordant. They fell from that peace in which and for which they were created. That is what is usually meant by the Fall. What credence we can give to this ancient story in the light of Darwinian science, we shall touch upon later in the chapter. Here we shall examine its explanatory power and significance. What does it mean for our understanding of ourselves and of our world – and of God – today?

1. THE DOCTRINE OF THE FALL MEANS THAT GOD IS NOT THE ONLY ONE WHO ACTS IN HIS WORLD

This is a simple but crucial point. God told Adam and Eve not to eat fruit from one particular tree (Genesis 2:17), and they did eat from it (Genesis 3:6). The first thing to be learnt therefore is that God does not always get His way. He wanted them not to do it, but they did it. He has not pre-programmed His creatures, and He does not compel them. God is not the only actor in the drama of creation. There are others, and He lets them work and operate and act and decide and choose in real ways within the real world He made, even if their choices and actions are not what He would want them to be. They are not just distinct from Him, as we saw in the last chapter – they are also free.

a) The Doctrine of the Fall is thus an affirmation of our free will

The very fact that God told Adam and Eve not to do something and they did it shows that they were created with the gift of their own innate and inherent freedom. The fact that they were able to go against the express command of God demonstrates that He is their Creator and not their Controller. The story of Adam and Eve in the garden thus alerts us to the terrifying but dignifying fact of our freedom. We can make our own choices, go our own ways, shape our own characters, forge our own destinies. We are neither puppets nor robots. We are neither manipulated by God, nor pre-programmed. Our responses and choices are significantly our own. And because our responses are significantly our own, we have responsibility. This can be seen in the way that God holds Adam and Eve accountable after their disobedience (Genesis 3:8f).

b) The Doctrine of the Fall is thus a protest against all forms of determinism

Determinism is the belief that human beings, far from being free and responsible, are in fact determined by particular forces and influences. There are different kinds of determinism. There is genetic determinism, in which we are said to be shaped decisively by the genes we inherit. Our genetic make-up forces us to be the sort of people we are, to make the sort of decisions we make, to have the sort of characters we have and to live the sort of lives we live – and there is nothing we can do about it. It is given, and it is determinative.

Cosmological determinism places our defining moment even earlier. Here, it is the Big Bang that has set in motion a mechanistic process, a causal chain that leads inexorably to the way things are, and the way we are. Life, the universe and everything are the distant but direct products of that event. Everything follows from the set of circumstances with which the universe began. Again, we have no say in it. It's simply the way the atoms fall out.

Environmental determinism suggests that it is the more immediate influences upon us that mould us and shape us – our upbringing, parenting, schooling, and the experiences that happen to us. Again, we are passive. Everything happens to us. We have no impact upon our own beings and our own destinies. We are simply working out for the rest of our lives the influences upon us in our early and formative years.

Theological determinists believe that we are completely determined by God. He has written the script and we just act it out. He decides what will be done to us, and what we will do. It's all fixed in advance by the Almighty Fixer, and there is no contribution we can make to our natures or our futures.

Determinism says we have no freedom. We are simply victims. We are but the flotsam and jetsam of the universe, tossed this way and that by its pressures and its processes. And the doctrine of the Fall says no, God gives us freedom. In none of these ways, and at none of these levels are we determined. Of course we are *conditioned* by all these factors – by our genes, by the way the universe is, the early influences upon us, and our interaction with God. Our freedom is not absolute. But nevertheless we remain responsible beings. There is a *shortfall* between all these different forces upon us and within us, and who we become. Not only are we shaped – we also shape. Not only are we influenced – we also influence. We decide how we respond to those influences, and what sort of effect they have upon us. We have a say. We make a contribution. We are active as well as passive. We have (not complete but) significant freedom.

c) The Doctrine of the Fall is a protest against all tyrannical views of God

The Scriptures present us with a God who is Almighty. In the Old Testament, one of His titles is 'the Lord of hosts'. In the New Testament, Jesus calls God 'The Power' (Matthew 26:64) and He tells us that His Father has more angels at His disposal than Rome has soldiers (Matthew 26:53). All power comes from Him and belongs to Him. He is the Source and the Owner of all power.

He is thus omnipotent. But, as we see from Genesis 3 (and on through the whole Bible), He is not the only one who acts in His world. All power belongs to Him, but He loans it to others. All power comes from Him, but He uses it to empower others. He has more than twelve legions of angels at His disposal, but He does not use them to get His own way at every turn. He allows others to act in ways of their own choosing. He allows His laws to be broken, His appeal to be snubbed, His love to be spurned. He is not a tyrannical sort of god who dictates all that happens.

I take it that God could have prevented all evil from ever happening in His world, by restricting all real choice and action to Himself. If He were the only One who acted in His world, then He could guarantee that His will would be done. He could have ensured that creation went the way He wanted it to go, by keeping a tight and exclusive hold on the reins of power, so that no other creature ever did anything. He could have made us robots. *But He is not that sort of God*. He is not a control freak. And He made us for relationship – as relational beings, not remote-controlled automata. So He made us as real people, making real decisions and acting in real ways, which really affect other things and other people. He is the sort of God who lets us make mistakes, who lets us rebel, who lets us go our own way, and does not insist upon His own. He limits Himself, so that we may be free. He is no despot.

2. THE DOCTRINE OF THE FALL MEANS THAT EVIL, SUFFERING AND DEATH DO NOT BELONG IN GOD'S CREATION

Evil, suffering and death (at least as we now experience it) have no rightful place in God's good world. They are not part of His original purposes. They are not things that He wants to happen. He did not build them into His world. They occur, not because things have gone the way He wanted, but precisely because they haven't. Suffering is part of the story, not part of the set-up. It is part of the process, not part of the purpose.[a] It was not intended. It is not intrinsic. It is neither natural nor normal. It is an alien condition which God did not create, but which we have invited into existence.

And it now stalks our relationships, our work, our reproductive processes, our social, personal and ecological stability, and it threatens our safety, our happiness, our meaningfulness and our *shalom*, our peace (Genesis 3:8*ff*). The insecurity, misery and futility which sour our existence are there, not because God put them there, but, on the contrary, because we have turned away from God and turned in on ourselves – and have also turned, therefore, from the purposes and peace of God. Evil is secondary, not primary. Sin has become second nature to us – but it was never our first nature. As N. T. Wright put it, commenting on Romans 5:12, 'Sin was an intruder, not a native inhabitant, of God's good world.'[4] And the same would go for death. They do not belong.

3. THE DOCTRINE OF THE FALL GIVES US A MANDATE TO FIGHT SUFFERING, EVIL AND DEATH

If evil, suffering and death do not belong in God's world, if they are not His intention, nor part of His will, then we should try to

[a] I am not here denying that God can act in judgment during the course of history in a way that prefigures the final judgment at the end of history. Nor am I denying that some instances of physical and moral evil can rightly be interpreted as God acting in judgment. However, i) this is never to be seen as the normative way of interpreting such events. We should not turn first to such an explanation. We should turn first (and secondly and thirdly and fourthly) to the fact that the world is fallen and distorted and not as God wants it, because He does not always get what He wants. The occurrence of sin proves that. God doesn't want sin and He doesn't want suffering. But in a fallen world, both happen. ii) We could only ever come to the conclusion that a particular instance of suffering was God's act of judgment, on the basis of direct revelation. How else could we know? iii) Even where a particular instance of suffering is rightly interpreted as God's judgment, it is still not what God *wants*, because He did not want the sin that provoked the judgment in the first place. iv) It may therefore be helpful to distinguish between God's *purpose* and God's *plan*. Suffering is never God's purpose. It is never what He wants for any of His creatures. But it can be taken up in some extraordinary way into His plan and worked for good.

remove them from His world. We are mandated to fight against them wherever we realistically and usefully can. In the film *Babe*, the duck has worked out that animals on the farm that perform no useful function are eventually killed. Horses survive because they carry things around and pull ploughs and useful things like that; pigs serve no such practical purpose and so end up as pork pies. Ending up as paté is not a pleasing prospect for an ambitious duck, so he sets about finding a rôle for himself. He hits on the idea of pretending to be a rooster and waking everyone up in the morning. That way, he calculates, he will be too serviceable to be slaughtered. The horse disapproves of such posturing and pretence, and says, rather pompously, 'The secret of happiness is to accept that the way things are is the way things are.' To which the duck replies, 'Hmmph! Well, the way things are stinks!' In other words, the duck has a good doctrine of the Fall, and the horse does not! The horse thinks that the way things are is okay, and that we should knuckle under and accept it. The duck says *no*, the way things are stinks, and we are going to fight against it, one way or another. It is the duck who has the better theology! We are not to accept the way things are, because they are no longer the way God intended them to be.

If you prefer a more literary example, then Camus' *The Plague* illustrates the point perfectly. It's about a priest who has a crisis of conscience over whether he should help the victims of plague in his parish. He wants to, as he has a good heart. He wants to visit them and comfort them and be there for them and with them. But he fears that the plague is the will of God and that therefore, if he fights against the plague, he will be fighting against God. So he desists, and it is the atheist doctor who simply gets on with the job of helping his plague-ridden patients. A proper doctrine of the Fall would have resolved the priest's dilemma. Suffering does not belong in God's world: we are not to accept it or acquiesce in it, let alone ascribe it to God. We are to fight it. And when we fight it, we will find that we have been fighting, not *against* God, but *with* Him and alongside Him. And He alongside and through us.

We are to fight the effects of the Fall at every level. When Adam and Eve disobeyed God, they found themselves alienated from Him. He came looking for them in the garden in the cool of the day – a picture of the fellowship for which they were created. And they hid from Him (Genesis 3:8).

But it was not just their relationship with God that was ruptured. Their relationship with each other was never the same, either. Adam sought to shift the responsibility for what he had done onto Eve (Genesis 3:12). Their previously equal and reciprocal relationship degenerated into domineering power games and unhealthy dependency (Genesis 3:16b). And within one generation, the fissure between them had opened up into a vicious and violent division between one of their sons and another (Genesis 4:1–8).

Not only was their relationship with one another distorted, but also their relationship with the natural world. The ground resisted cultivation and no longer worked in harmony with their needs and aims. The fulfilment of strenuous work gave way to the weariness of burdensome toil. And the ecstatic joy of childbirth was tempered by the excruciating pains of labour (Genesis 3:16–19).

Nor was their relationship with themselves unaffected. From the uninhibited and comfortable nakedness of Genesis 2:25, we read of their shrinking and shame-ridden cover-up in 3:7. The body had become an issue. And what is shame except to be divided against oneself? Who they were was affected at every level by the Fall: we are therefore called to fight the effects of the Fall at every level.

At the level of people being cut off from people, the church is called to be a healing community. As Paul argues in Ephesians 2:14–22, the Cross not only reunites us to God, it also thereby reunites us with one another. And the church exists to live out that reconciliation, and to offer it to others. We are to live in peace with one another (1 Thessalonians 5:13), and we are to be peacemakers (Matthew 5:9). In our families, in our relationships, in our churches, in our workplaces, we are to fight the alienating and estranging effects of the Fall. We may not leave hurts to fester. We may not allow the sun to set on our anger. We need to apologise to those we have wronged. We need, where we can, and where it is appropriate, to make up with those we have fallen out with, and gently and humbly encourage others to do the same.

Nor is this ministry of reconciliation to be attempted at the individual level alone. The Christian Church has always seen itself as having a duty to pray for peace, and to offer itself as a potential peacemaker to wider and more deeply-entrenched divides. As the community in which the hostilities between Jew and Gentile, male and female, slave and free have (in principle) been broken down, it has always looked for ways of breaking down the barriers of race, religion, gender and class wherever it has come across them, and whenever it has been true to its calling.

At the level of people being cut off from nature, again the cure is the Cross. For there, all things were reconciled, says Paul in Colossians 1:20, and by '*all* things', I take it he means 'all things'. It is thus the Cross that underwrites the prophetic vision of a healed creation in which 'the wolf will live with the lamb' (Isaiah 11:6). We cannot bring that about now: only when creation is finally and fully renewed and restored will such a radical transformation take place. However, we can and we should anticipate that prophetic vision by living as harmoniously with our environment as possible.

At the level of people against themselves, we are, again, to be a therapeutic community, which heals by its acceptance, its welcome, its support, its mutual forgiveness, by not writing people off, by not being shocked when people say something we disagree with or consider heretical, by paying people the respect of being listened to and taken seriously. The church that, through word and sacrament and through its very life together, tries to make its members feel loved will have a healing effect on the internal divisions that threaten to tear us apart as a consequence of the Fall.

The divisions at all these levels are all portrayed in Genesis 3 as consequences of the fundamental division between us and God. If, therefore, we are to treat the root cause of the problem, we need to address the broken relationship between people and God. We need to relish the reality of that relationship with God for which we were made, which was ruptured at the Fall, restored (in principle) at the Cross and in which we shall one day revel when we see Him face to face. Until then, we must practise this relationship ourselves and proffer it to others. At the fundamental theological level, we refuse to acquiesce in (though we remain affected by) what happened at the Fall.

Like the duck, we do not accept the *status quo*. Unlike the horse, we do not accept that the way things are is the way things are. The doctrine of the Fall tells us that the way things are is not the whole story. It is not the way things were intended to be. God is not content about the way things are, and neither may we be. The doctrine of the Fall is thus a subversive doctrine. It gives us a different vision to live by. The way things were intended to be and the way things will be – *that's* what is normal. That's our vision. That's our blueprint. That's what we long for and look for and pray for and work for. And we will not rest, our sword shall not sleep in our hand, till God has built Jerusalem, not just in England's green and pleasant land but in every desolate corner of the cosmos.

4. THE DOCTRINE OF THE FALL GIVES US HOPE OF A WORLD WITHOUT EVIL

If the way things are is the way God likes them, then there is no hope that things will ever be different. If this is how He set them up, why would He want to change them? If this was the sort of world He had in mind when He set about the task of creation, then He must be happy with the *status quo*. If murders are 'engineered' by God, then why would He ever want to rid His world of such events? But if the way things are is an affront to God, if He is outraged by the suffering and death of His beloved creatures, then we know that He will not rest until ultimately His world is healed of all its divisions and distortions.

When Jesus comes to the tomb of His friend, Lazarus, we are

told that He 'was outraged in spirit, and troubled' (John 11:33, in Don Carson's translation[5]) and that He wept (John 11:35). He is outraged at the occurrence of sickness and death in what should have been a healthy and harmonious world. His grief is not primarily occasioned by the loss of Lazarus – He knows that He is about to raise him to life. He is aggrieved at the distortion that is death. He is angry with what it has done to God's creatures and God's world. And He is angry and aggrieved at these things without being angry or aggrieved at God.

On the contrary, He is grateful to God (John 11:41–42) and concerned to display His glory (John 11:40). Angry at evil, and grateful to God – it is the doctrine of the Fall that enables us to disentangle those two reactions and direct them appropriately. Like Dylan Thomas, Jesus 'rages against the dying of the light', for the dying of the light was no part of the purpose of Him who is Light.[6]

Jesus raises Lazarus without any apparent fear that in so doing He might be opposing God's will. No, unlike the priest in *The Plague*, He knows that suffering has no valid place in God's world. He is angry at the (secondary, invalid and therefore temporary) place it has. He is angry with fallenness. He delights in fighting it and reversing it and giving life and wiping away tears – *and sees the whole episode as just a taster of that final giving of life and wiping away of tears which will be the culmination of cosmic history*. This resuscitation is a glimpse and a guarantee of the great Resurrection of which He is the focal point (John 11:24–25).

Because evil is secondary, it can be rooted out from creation without taking away anything essential from creation. As Derek Kidner put it, 'Since futility was not the first word about our world, it no longer has to be the last.'[7] Paradoxically, therefore, the doctrine of the Fall turns out to be hopeful and optimistic.

5. THE DOCTRINE OF THE FALL ENABLES US TO HOLD ON TO THE GOODNESS OF GOD

If God gets what He wants, then He wants Auschwitz. If creation is as He made it, He wanted it to be red in tooth and claw. If He 'engineers' murder, then it is difficult to see how He is not responsible for it. It is difficult to see how He can be called 'good'. And that is indeed the conclusion that many thoughtful and sensitive people either come to, or are tempted to come to. In Ingmar Bergman's 1943 film, *Jack among the Actors*, the director gives voice to just this view: 'If there is or ever has been a God, He was a criminal. You people pitifully cry out "God is kind" like a call for help because you know there is no God. I think God committed suicide when He saw this universe He created.' Notice again the same assumption: the world as it now is, is the universe as God created it to be. For God to have made, knowingly and intentionally, the sort of universe we currently experience would seem to be incompatible with His goodness (unless goodness is so redefined as to be meaningless) and sensitive people such as Bergman would, I suggest, be right to reject Him.

Even such a Christian thinker as C. S. Lewis could be tempted down the same path. When his wife died from cancer, he wrote down his brilliantly self-observed reactions and his brutally self-critical reflections in some blank school exercise books, which were later published pseudonymously under the title, *A Grief Observed*. In the early stages of his bereavement, he wrote that he wasn't in much danger of ceasing to believe in God: 'The real danger is of coming to believe such dreadful things about Him. The conclusion I dread is not "So there's no God after all," but "So this is what God's really like. Deceive yourself no longer."'[8] And the reason he was tempted to jettison belief in God's goodness was that He tended instinctively to attribute all the twists and turns of his wife's final illness to the hand of God, to see all their false and shattered hopes along the way as His instruments of torture.

71

But if there has been a Fall, then the universe is *not* now the way God created it to be. He did *not* set it up to be red in tooth and claw. He does not engineer murders. He did not ordain Auschwitz. He did not raise and shatter hopes as a means of trial or of torture. He is not the Cosmic Sadist. We are not to Him 'as flies to wanton boys'[9]. Suffering was not His will or His doing in the first place, He is fighting against it now, and He will uproot it once and for all in the future. A proper doctrine of the Fall therefore enables us to maintain belief in the goodness of God.

I once read a theological book that denied that there had been any Fall. It then went on to say that we need to qualify the statement that 'God is light and in him is no darkness at all' (1 John 1:5 rsv). Now it seems to me that if a Christian theologian gets to the point of having to qualify the goodness of God, then they should ask themselves where they have gone wrong. Because the goodness of God is bedrock. It is part of the gospel. The proclamation of the Kingdom of God would be the worst possible news, if it were not for His goodness. And it is the doctrine of the Fall that makes belief in His goodness tenable.

IS THE WHOLE OF CREATION FALLEN, OR JUST HUMANITY?

Not all Christians agree at this point, and, as far as I know, no denomination has an official position on the subject, but it seems to me to be essential that we regard the whole of creation as fallen. Otherwise, we could exonerate God from engineering man-made events such as murders, but we would still have to see natural disasters and diseases and the cruelty of the animal order as a direct consequence of the way He chose to make the world. And then it is hard to see how creation or Creator could be thought of as good. Without a doctrine of the Fall which encompasses the whole created order, we should presumably have to join in lustily with the Monty Python hymn:

All things dull and ugly
All creatures short and squat
All things rude and nasty
The Lord God made the lot

Each little snake that poisons
Each little wasp that stings
He made their brutish venom
He made their horrid wings

"...all things bright and beautiful"

All things sick and cancerous
All evil great and small
All things foul and dangerous
The Lord God made them all

Each nasty little hornet
Each beastly little squid
Who made the spikey urchin?
Who made the sharks? He did.

All things scabbed and ulcerous
All pox both great and small
Putrid, foul and gangrenous
The Lord God made them all.[10]

But allow a doctrine of the Fall that includes the whole of creation within its scope, and we can deny the premise of that satirical song. All creatures owe their ultimate existence to God, but not necessarily all the characteristics of their natures. Yes, He can be said to have created the snake and the wasp, but He intended that they should live in harmony with the rest of creation – not that they should poison, sting, kill and exploit. Their predatory equipment, their defence mechanisms and the diseases they suffer, inflict or carry are evidence of how far creation has come from the original purposes of God.

73

Without such a doctrine of the Fall, I do not know how we could answer the implied attack of this Pythonesque parody, nor, indeed, how we could watch virtually any nature programme without querying the character of the Creator. Unless we posit the fallenness of the natural order, any argument for the existence of God from the evidence of design in creation simply turns in on itself and proves (if anything) the existence of a god of highly dubious morality. The Monty Python mock-hymn does us the favour of reminding us how selective we often are in our theological consideration of the natural world. It has the benefit of forcing us to face the brutality as well as the beauty of God's world as it currently is. And it serves the purpose of directing us to the biblical doctrine of the Fall if we are to be able to present a morally credible God to our sensitive and intelligent contemporaries.

However, a theological position is not true just because we need it to be. We should not believe in the fallenness of creation just because it gets us out of an apologetic hole. But it is not a doctrine that has recently been cobbled together to shore up some otherwise rather shaky pillars of the Christian position. It has, I want to argue, been a part of a biblical world-view from the start. Eight features of the biblical revelation suggest to me that the fallenness of nature is the presupposition of the Scriptures.

a) The effects of Adam and Eve's disobedience

As we saw earlier, Adam and Eve's rebellion against God did not just affect their relationship with God, with each other and with themselves: it also affected their relationship with the natural order. The world is no longer in harmony with the aims and aspirations of humanity. In some way, the very structures of the natural world seem to have been dislocated and disordered, and no longer work with us or for us. The important point here is that this disharmony was not the way creation was set up – it was the way creation became, as a result of the misuse of our freedom.

b) The uncleanness laws

In the book of Leviticus in the Old Testament, there is a complex network of laws declaring that some animals, birds, insects and fish are unclean and may not be eaten. Some diseases render a person unclean. Some activities and events make someone unclean. Some forms of mildew or mould contaminate clothing or housing. The principles underlying these laws and the rationale for them are not clear and have been hotly debated, but they seem to coalesce around the idea of *normality*. Something is unclean if in some way it is inappropriate or abnormal for the kind of thing it is.

The uncleanness laws are thus a way of saying, 'There is something wrong here. There is something here that is out of joint with God's purposes, which are for health and wholeness.' Any contact with death renders you unclean because death has no direct place in the purposes of God. Disease renders one ritually unclean because God wants our well-being. Menstrual discharges make you unclean, not because there is anything sinful or sleazy about sex in its proper context, but because debilitating pain has no planned or rightful place in the reproductive processes.

More particularly for our present purposes, all carnivorous animals and birds are unclean because they eat meat that still contains the blood, and Jews were forbidden to eat meat that had not been drained of its blood as a testimony to the essential abnormality of carnivorousness. Gentile Christians of most denominations have considered that the uncleanness laws do not apply to them. That does not mean, however, that the instincts and insights that gave rise to the uncleanness laws were ill-conceived or invalid. They were, amongst other things[b], ways of flagging up the fallenness of many features of our world that we might otherwise take to be inbuilt. They were ways of saying, 'No. Death and disease and deformity and decay and predation may be prevalent in our world

---

[b] They were also ways of delineating Israel from the pagan nations, which is one reason why Gentile Christians haven't generally felt bound by them, since the Cross broke down the barriers between Jews and Gentiles. See Acts 11:1–18.

and profoundly deep-rooted. But they are not the norm. They are not God-given. They are not of the essence. They fall short of God's purity and purpose.'

c) The Covenant of Peace

In one of Ezekiel's prophecies, God says 'I will make a covenant of peace with them [ie the people of Israel] and rid the land of wild beasts so that they may live in the desert and sleep in the forests in safety' (Ezekiel 34:25[c]). The covenant is relevant not just to their relationship with God but also to their relationship with nature. The peace it offers is not just peace with their Creator but peace with the creation. There is no suggestion here that God deliberately places us in a hostile environment because it will be good for us to face adversity, learn courage, club together, and all that 'character-building' stuff! On the contrary, what God wants for His people is 'safety'. He wants to remove the threat from us. So He would not have made the world a threatening environment in the first place. It must have been made for peace and *become* hostile. It is hostile because it is fallen, and not the way God intended it to be.

Of course, all that is envisaged here is the *removal* of dangerous animals, not their *reconciliation* – a sort of speciesist apartheid rather than a multi-speciel society! Other parts of the Old Testament saw even further into God's ultimate purposes.

d) Visions of a healed and harmonious future

One of Hosea's prophecies envisages the abolition of the conflict between humanity and its fellow creatures:

> In that day I will make a covenant for them [ie the people of Israel
>   with the beasts of the field and the birds of the air
>   and the creatures that move along the ground.

---

[c] Wild beasts are sometimes used in the Bible as a metaphor for the pagan nations (eg Daniel 7:17), and there may be a hint of that here – ie 'I shall drive out your enemies and allow you to return to the land.' Nevertheless, the reference to the desert and the forests suggests that the primary meaning here is literal.

Bow and sword and battle I will abolish from the land,
> so that all may lie down in safety.

Hosea 2:18

And Isaiah gives us a positive vision of what this will be like:

The wolf will live with the lamb,
> the leopard will lie down with the goat,
the calf and the lion and the yearling together;
> and a little child will lead them.
The cow will feed with the bear,
> their young will lie down together,
> and the lion will eat straw like the ox.
Infants will play near the hole of the cobra,
> and young children put their hands into the viper's nest.
They will neither harm nor destroy on all my holy mountain,
for the earth will be full of the knowledge of the Lord
> as the waters cover the sea.

Isaiah 11:6–9

That's how God wants the world to be. That's the sort of world He's after. That's the sort of world He's promised. That's the sort of world He is working towards. So why would He have set it up to be unharmonious and competitive and violent and predatory in the first place? It wouldn't make sense. It wouldn't be consistent. He would have set creation up one way and then committed Himself to making it utterly different. That would be a major U-turn. Indeed, some heretical groupings on the fringes of the early church called the Gnostics were so impressed by the difference between creation as we see it and creation as God has promised to make it that they suggested that two different gods were involved. One (rather bad) god set it up and another (good) God has come to put it right.

But Christians have always been monotheists. We have always believed in one God. It was the same God who both created the world and redeemed it. It's just that the world is not now the way

He wanted it to be. It has gone wrong. It has got warped. The Creator set it up to be harmonious: it is creatures that have turned it violent. How that may have happened, we shall look at shortly. The important point to notice here is that the doctrine of the Fall doesn't just enable us to hold on to the goodness of God – it also enables us to maintain belief in His oneness and His consistency. There are not two gods involved – just one. And He hasn't changed direction half way through the project – He is the same yesterday, today and forever. He wanted creation to be at peace and He will one day bring it back to that peace which He always intended for it. The conflict, cruelty and carnivorousness of the currently fallen creation will be overcome. (But I promise that nut roasts will taste better in the New Creation!)

e) The nature and healing miracles of Jesus

The nature miracles (ie the stilling of the storm, the feeding of the 5,000 etc) and the healing miracles of Jesus were a declaration of war on the fallenness of God's world. When confronted by illness or disability or hunger or danger or even, on occasions, death, Jesus' instinct and His practice were to heal the illness, to deal with the disability, to relieve the hunger, to dissipate the danger and to restore life. He seems to have given no thought to the benefits of which He was thereby depriving people! He seems not to have shared for a moment the fear of Camus's priest that these disorders might be God's doing. He seems not to have entertained the inadequate notion that suffering is good for you. And He is our window on the will of God.

The nature and healing miracles therefore show us that God does not like disease or danger or death deforming His creatures and defiling His world. He is against these things. He could hardly, then, have built them into the blueprint of creation. To quote the poet, Jack Clemo:

> Christ himself was obviously not at peace with nature, any more than he was at peace with human nature. He often acted in open

defiance of the 'majesty' of creation. When the storm arose on Gennesaret he did not bid the disciples to humble themselves devoutly before the 'great Being' who was trying to drown them. He lashed back at the elements from his bridgehead in the divine kingdom: 'Be still …' All natural catastrophes are symptoms of nature's sickness – fevers, vomits, shiverings: they are not growing pains through which God is slowly evolving a perfect world, but mere reminders that we live in an enemy-occupied zone and that in so far as we are subject to its laws we share its tragedy.[11]

f) The Cross of Christ

A world in which one species has to devour another in order to survive is not the sort of world that one would have expected a good God to create. It is *certainly* not the sort of world that one would have expected the God we meet in Christ to have created. The Cross reveals God as One who lays down His own life that others might live. The natural world is one in which animals kill others that they themselves might live. The movement of the one in reckless self-giving is in a totally opposite direction from the movement of the other in ruthless self-preservation.[12]

Thus, as Tom Torrance, the former Moderator of the General Assembly of the Church of Scotland, put it:

> The Cross of Christ tells us unmistakeably that all physical evil, not only pain, suffering, disease, corruption, death, and of course cruelty and venom in animal as well as human behaviour, but also 'natural' calamities, devastations, and monstrosities, are an outrage against the love of God and a contradiction of good order in his creation. This does not allow us to regard evil and disorder in the universe as in any way intended or as given a direct function by God in the development of his creation, although it does mean that even these enormities can be made by God's incredible power to serve his final end for the created order, much as he has made the dastardly violence of men in crucifying Jesus to serve his healing purpose for mankind,

without in any way justifying our human evil and guilt that brought Jesus to the Cross.[13]

In other words, the whole of creation is fallen. To quote Paul Fiddes, the Baptist theologian, 'The sorrow of the cross, no less than the glory of the resurrection, is God's contradiction of the suffering and death of the present world.' [14]

g) The Resurrection of Christ

The New Testament treats the resurrection of Jesus as a physical event.[d] Indeed, it insists upon the point (Luke 24:36–43). It was not just a 'spiritual' event, whatever that might be, but one that occurred within, and was transformative of, space and time. It was a re-ordering of the very structures of the natural order. It was an undoing of death, a reversal of decay, a removal of the shroud that enfolds all peoples, the sheet that covers all nations (Isaiah 25:7). And one of the implications of Jesus' Resurrection was therefore that death and decay were displeasing to God and needed to be undone. The structures of the natural order were *dis*ordered and needed to be *re*-ordered. He would not abandon His Holy One to the grave or to decay (Psalm 16:10, Acts 2:27), precisely because He would not forever abandon us, His *un*holy ones, to such enemies either. He did not want our lives to be end-stopped, our relationships to be guillotined and our meaning to be mocked by death. Decay is an undoing of creation and therefore a denial of the Creator. Death is a snuffing out of life, and therefore a denial of the Life-giver. The resurrection of Jesus is an undoing of these undoings and a denial of these denials and an implicit declaration of the fallenness of our world.

h) The promised redemption of the whole of creation

The New Testament renews the Old Testament's promise of a healed and restored creation. (In fact, Hans Küng suggests that

[d] For a defence of this point, see *The Resurrection of the Son of God* by N. T. Wright (SPCK, 2003).

'creation healed' is a pretty good definition of the Kingdom of God.) When Jesus refers to the culmination of history, He speaks of the 'renewal of all things' (Matthew 19:28), and His apostles follow suit. St Peter holds out the hope of 'universal restoration' (Acts 3:21 NRSV). St Paul's letter to the Romans tells us that 'creation itself will be liberated … and brought into the glorious freedom of the children of God' (8:21). In his letter to the Colossians, he considers how 'all things' have in principle been reconciled by the Cross of Christ (1:20). And in the penultimate chapter of the Bible, we are given a glimpse of creation healed, with God 'making everything new' (Revelation 21:5).

Two points follow from this. First, these promises are an affirmation of creation. If God is going to remake His creation, then He must regard it as worth remaking. We saw in the first chapter that creation has value. Nowhere do we see the reality of that value more clearly than in God's determination to remake it now that it has been marred. In that determination, we see His love for it and His commitment to it. And if we look at the Cross of Christ, we may see the extent of that determination, the depth of that love and the cost of that commitment. He will stick with it in its suffering, and He will see it through to glory. What greater affirmation could there be?

Secondly, these promises are an affirmation of the fallenness of creation. If creation is in need of being renewed, it must lack in some degree that life that God intended for it. If it is in need of restoration, it must have got broken. If it is in need of liberation, it must have become enslaved. If it is in need of reconciliation, it must have become alienated. If it is in need of healing, it must be sick. And Paul does not hesitate to come to that conclusion. Creation, he says, 'was subjected to futility' (Romans 8:20 NRSV). It is in 'bondage to decay' (Romans 8:21), and 'groans in a sort of universal travail' (Romans 8:22 THE MESSAGE).

The Scriptural assumption of the fallenness of creation seems to me to mesh with our own sense of outrage and protest at the apparent pains of predation and the damage and desolation brought about by disaster, disease and death. It seems to me to be vital that we do not add to people's proper problems with such enormities as the suggestion that they are the consequence of God's creative purpose. If we try and live without the doctrine of the fallenness of all things, if we see the world as it currently is as having flowed without hiatus from the hand of its Creator, then it will be difficult to believe in the goodness of such a God without doing violence to our own hearts and minds.

And we shall, I suggest, make it very difficult for sensitive and intelligent men and women to come to faith. For example, the great naturalist, David Attenborough, was interviewed by Michael Palin (one of the Python team, of course) to mark his fifty years as a broadcaster. And in response to a question about the needless violence of the natural world (epitomised by distressing footage of a whale tossing a seal about in triumph, toying with it before devouring it), he said this:

> I often get letters ... from people who say they like the programmes a lot, but I never give credit to the Almighty Power that created nature. To which I reply and say it's funny that people, when they say this is evidence of [the] Almighty, always quote beautiful things – orchids and humming birds and butterflies and roses. But I always have to think too of a little boy sitting on the banks of a river in West Africa who has a worm boring through his eyeball turning him blind before he's five years old. And I reply and say, 'Well, presumably the God you speak about created the worm as well, and I find [it] baffling to credit that action to a merciful God ...'

Quite! As the late Anglo-Catholic theologian, N. P. Williams, put it in his book on the doctrine of the Fall:

> If savagery and cruelty are the expressions of a fundamental law, how evil must be that law, and how deep its discordance with the will of the all-loving Creator revealed by Christ, who clothes the lilies of the

field, and without whom not one sparrow falls to the ground. If we face the facts candidly, we must admit that no one of us, if he had been in the position of Demiurge [ie creator], would have created a universe which was compelled by the inner necessity of its being to evolve the cobra, the tarantula, and the bacillus of diphtheria. How, then, shall that God, the infinite ardours and pulsations of whose love bear the same relation to our weak emotions of sympathy and fellow-feeling as the infinity of His wisdom does to our dim and limited knowledge, have done so? *The answer can only be that He did not do so*; that He did not create such a universe; that, in the words of the most ancient scriptures of our monotheistic faith, in the beginning 'God saw every thing that He had made, and, behold, it was very good.' To explain evil in Nature, no less than in man, we are compelled to assume a Fall – a revolt against the will of the Creator, a declension from the beauty and glory which God stamped upon His work at the beginning.[15]

So the reason for natural evil is not that God wants it. Not because He set up creation that way. Not because it plays a necessary rôle in the operation of a physical world. But because things have gone profoundly wrong.

The question then arises, Why? Why have they gone wrong? How did creation come to deviate from God's good and harmonious purpose for it? If it isn't God's fault, whose fault is it? And to that question we now turn.

HOW DID CREATION COME TO BE FALLEN?

This question has, of course, received a variety of different answers. Not all Christian thinkers agree that creation is fallen, and not all those who do would agree with the answer I am about to give. No Christian denomination has pronounced on the issue, it is part of no creed, and what follows therefore has no official standing. It is not taught in the Bible as such. It is not official church teaching. It is not the approved 'Alpha' position. I have tried in this book to concentrate on that which is common to most Christians and to eschew that which divides them. I make an exception here simply because this is an issue with which Christians often struggle, and here is an approach to it which I have found helpful, both intellectually and pastorally, and which others too have found makes sense. I offer it to you to weigh and consider. In the resources section at the end of this chapter, you will find other books which will introduce you to some of the other options. But here is one way through the woods.

As I said at the beginning of this chapter, the doctrine of the Fall has traditionally been associated with the story of Adam and Eve. When we ask the question, 'Whose fault is it?', many Christians respond that it is *our* fault, humanity's fault, because everything was alright before Adam and Eve rebelled. There is much truth in this position, and we must certainly not answer the question in a way that denies human responsibility or we shall end up denying our humanity.

However, a closer look at the first three chapters of the Bible suggests that things had gone wrong with creation *even before* Adam and Eve's disobedience. First, there is the serpent. However one interprets the serpent, here is one piece of the creation that is working in direct opposition to the commands of God, even before the human Fall. Secondly, God commands humanity to 'fill the earth and subdue it' (Genesis 1:28), which suggests that there was already that which needed to be subdued. There was already that which was opposed to the rule of God, and which, as His vice-regents, human beings were to subdue. Thirdly, it is worth remembering that Eden was only a garden, and not the whole of creation. Thus, even if Adam and Eve are thought of as living in complete harmony with their environment, this does not mean that the whole of creation was similarly at peace. God here acts rather like a Blue Peter presenter and says, 'Here's a bit I did earlier. Now you go out and spread that order and that harmony to the rest of creation'!

If, however, things were fallen even before our first parents fell, then the question becomes even more acute: who was responsible for that fallenness? Through what agency were things already warped? One of the points we noted about the creation was that it is multi-dimensional. There are other dimensions to it than the ones of which we are usually aware. I want now to suggest that there is some reality to which the biblical language of angels and demons refers. Part of the multi-dimensionality of our world is that God has created other free, imaginative and intelligent beings than human beings. Though human beings have a special place, value and rôle in God's creation, we are not the only beings to have free will, nor necessarily even the highest. There are also what the Orthodox Church calls the 'holy, bodiless powers'. They too have freedom and, in Jewish, Christian and (with differences) Islamic tradition, some have used that freedom to rebel against God. There was a rebellion within the spiritual realm long before human beings even emerged.

There was, in other words, a prior Fall of the angels. And together with other writers (such as C. S. Lewis, E. L. Mascall, Hans Urs von Balthasar, and the American philosophers Alvin Plantinga and Stephen Davis), I want further to suggest that the different dimensions of creation are so interrelated that rebellion within the spiritual realm caused a hugely destructive disruption within all the other dimensions as well. The angelic rebellion actually distorted the whole way in which the material creation developed, luring it away from God's original harmonious purposes, and introducing division, disorder, pain, predation, cruelty and killing, disease and death.

As we saw earlier, however, God is committed to His creation. He doesn't give up on it despite its divisions. He works in and through that messy, nasty, competitive, violent process to ensure the emergence of human beings from the bloody matrix of a fallen world. He didn't want that violent, competitive mess, but He works from where creation is, not from where He would like it to be. That is His way. And once human beings have emerged, it is then God's intention that they should undo the evil that's already happened. He calls them to *subdue* the earth, to rid it of the pain and suffering that have crept into creation as a result of the angelic Fall. Their vocation was always to rule creation: that will now involve putting right what went wrong.

And if you want to see what it would have looked like for them to have responded to that vocation and taken up that task, then look at the person of Jesus. Here at last is a human being fulfilling the human vocation. (More than a human being, as we shall see – but not less. In the end, it took God to live a fully human life – but it was a fully human life that He lived.) Here at last is a human being doing what human beings were intended to do: subduing the earth, stilling the storm, healing the sick, dealing with demonic distortion, raising the dead. Here at last the effects of the angelic Fall were being undone, and creation restored. Here at last was the (beginning of the) solution to the problem of evil.

Far from being part of the solution, however, human beings became part of the problem. Instead of undoing the effects of the angels' rebellion, they joined in that rebellion. And instead of putting things right, they made matters worse. That is why Genesis 3 can blame all the divisions of the world on human beings, even though the world was riddled with such divisions even prior to the human rebellion. Because, had we been faithful to our therapeutic vocation, all things would have been put right. The *continued* occurrence of suffering in our world is therefore the result of the human Fall, even though its *original* occurrence was the result of the angelic Fall. They brought about evil in our world, and we failed to eradicate it. Indeed, we added to its momentum. On this understanding, therefore, all evil and suffering are the consequence of creatures abusing the free will that God gave them, and are not built into the way the Creator chose to set up His creation. All the tragic elements of our world stem from creatures choosing to cut themselves off from God and go their own way instead of His – and not just human creatures, but inhabitants of the spiritual dimensions as well.

That's my suggestion. All I claim for it is that it fits all the relevant facts, and enables us to say the things that need to be said. First, it enables us to say what needs to be said *theologically*, that God is not the architect of suffering. He does not build it into His world. He made His world good, and He made angels and humans free, and it is the way we have used that freedom that 'brought death into the world, and all our woe'.[16]

Secondly, it enables us to say what needs to be said *ethically*. In contrast to the dictum that 'Whatever is, is right', the doctrine of the Fall declares that what is, is *not* necessarily right. It is therefore illegitimate to argue from the way things are to the will of God. We are forbidden to give normative status to the way things currently are. A black widow spider eating the male after mating with him does not legitimate similar behaviour for us! More seriously, we may not argue from the violence of nature that God is not interested in animal welfare and that therefore we need not be either. We may not argue from the fact of spontaneous abortion to the validity of genetic screening. There is no straightforward line to be drawn from the *status quo* to the will of God. Every such attempt falls down the abyss that exists between the world as it now is and the world as it was intended to be in the loving purposes of the good Creator. Our ethics are therefore to be based, not on what is, but on what was to be in the original purposes of God and what is to be in the restored and redeemed creation.

Thirdly, this account of the fallenness of creation enables us to say what we may need to say *scientifically*. If there is any truth to modern science, then we cannot place the blame for the violence and cruelty of the natural world on the shoulders of humanity, because there has been pain and suffering and killing in creation since long before human beings evolved. Now, not all Christians, and, indeed, not all scientists, are convinced that the current evolutionary account of human origins is well grounded. I am not scientifically trained and am not equipped to adjudicate. My point here is two-fold. First, even for those who reject the evolutionary hypothesis, it is still problematic to blame Adam and Eve for what has gone wrong with our world, for in Genesis itself, as we have seen, creation is not perfect prior to their taking the forbidden fruit, and some account has to be given of why that might be. The Fall of the angels hypothesis offers such an account.

Secondly, if we accept that things were not perfect even before the human Fall (as *biblically* I think we must), then the main point of contention between theology and science melts away. The beauty of the Fall of the angels hypothesis is that it fits all the relevant facts – both biblical and scientific. If there was such a Fall, and if it distorted the way in which creation developed, introducing pain and predation into a world that was meant to be harmonious, then we would not expect to find palaeontological evidence of a 'Golden Age' of harmony between species because such an age never occurred. It *should* have done, if the angels had not rebelled. It still *could* have done, if human beings had been faithful to their calling and their Caller. And it *will* do, when the vision of Isaiah 11 is realised and the glorious liberty of the children of God is revealed. But it has not occurred so far, and therefore the absence of evidence for it is no problem for Christian belief.

The Fall of the angels hypothesis allows us to hold that the evolutionary mechanism meshed with the purpose of God to the extent that it produced creatures of sufficient intelligence, creativity, relational ability and moral capacity to reflect His nature and to rule His world. And it enables us to hold that belief *without* requiring us to believe that evolution was God's *chosen* way of working. Richard Dawkins' strongest argument against theistic evolution is that it would be odd for a loving God to choose such a bloodstained and cruel process. Indeed, it would. But if the Fall of angels hypothesis is correct, He did not choose it. Competition and carnivorousness came about as a result of the dislocation of creation consequent upon the angelic rebellion, but they could not thwart the purpose of God to produce beings He could walk with and talk with and become one with and share His life with – beings to die for! I suggest that this position enables us to say what we need to say scientifically.

And lastly, it enables us to say what we need to say *pastorally*, which is that suffering is not the work or the will of God. He may allow it, He may not heal it this side of the grave, He may bring good out of it and meet you within it, but it is never His desire. It is never something He looks at without pain Himself. It is never what He *wants* for us in any ultimate sense. He did not build it in and He's going to root it out. He is against suffering, and He is *for* you.

RESOURCES FOR FURTHER READING, PRAYER AND ACTION

Mike Starkey, *What's Wrong? Understanding Sin Today* (Bible Reading Fellowship, 2001) gives an excellent and highly readable overview of the different theories of the Fall, and proves its excellence by coming to the same conclusion as I do!

Michael Lloyd, 'Are Animals Fallen?', a chapter in *Animals on the Agenda*, edited by Andrew Linzey and Dorothy Yamamoto (SCM, 1998). 'The Humanity of Fallenness', a chapter in *Grace and Truth in the Secular Age*, edited by Timothy Bradshaw (Eerdmans, 1998). 'The Fall', a short article in Paul Barry Clarke & Andrew Linzey (eds), *Dictionary of Ethics, Theology and Society* (Routledge, 1996). *The Cosmic Fall and the Free Will Defence* (a D.Phil. thesis, 1997, available from the Bodleian Library in Oxford.)

N. P. Williams, *The Ideas of the Fall and of Original Sin* (Longmans, Green & Co., 1927) is long, technical and a little dated, and I know of no one today who advocates his position, but this is still the best treatment of the whole issue.

Marguerite Shuster, *The Fall and Sin: What We Have Become as Sinners* (Eerdmans, 2004) is the first major book to be written on the subject since 1927, which says something about how neglected the doctrine of the Fall has been. Her answer to the problem of natural evil is, in my view, a little bizarre, but there are lots of insights along the way.

David Bentley Hart, *The Doors of the Sea: Where was God in the Tsunami?* (Eerdmans, Grand Rapids, Michigan and Cambridge, UK, 2005). This book pleads with Christians not to try and justify appalling events such as tsunamis as being in any sense God's will. It insists that we see them as a consequence of the tragic fallenness of nature.

J. R. W. Stott (ed.), *Free to be Different: Varieties of Human Behaviour* (Eerdmans, 1984) is a defence of human freedom against environmental, genetic and theological determinism by a psychologist (Malcolm Jeeves), a biologist (R. J. Berry) and a theologian (David Atkinson).

Alvin C. Plantinga, *God, Freedom and Evil* (Eerdmans, 1978). A bit of a classic by a renowned Christian philosopher, this book argues the case philosophically for the Fall of the Angels hypothesis, and contains a useful section on how God's foreknowledge is perfectly compatible with human freedom. This is Plantinga at his most accessible, but is still hard work for the philosophically untrained. Worth it, though!

Udo Middelmann, *Pro-Existence* (Hodder & Stoughton, 1974). Good on work in a fallen world.

Tony Campolo, *How to Rescue the Earth Without Worshipping Nature* (Paternoster Press, 1992).

T. Campolo & G. Aeschlimen, *Fifty Ways You can Help Save the Planet* (Kingsway, 1993).

Corrymeela

'People of all ages and Christian traditions, who, individually and together, are committed to the healing of Social, Religious and Political divisions that exist in Northern Ireland and throughout the world.' To enquire further, write to: Corrymeela, 8, Upper Crescent, Belfast, BT7 1NT, or visit their website at www.corrymeela.org.

Christian International Peace Service

An organisation 'working for peace in areas of conflict and tension'. Contactable at: 35 Melton Road, Kings Heath, Birmingham, B14 7DA, UK. Or visit their website at www.chipspeace.org. Keith Lindsey's *Making Peace: Biblical Principles and the Experience of*

CHIPS is a brief guide to what CHIPS has learnt about the practical business of being peace-makers.

National Religious Partnership for the Environment

An American organisation bringing together Christians and Jews to campaign and work for a responsibly managed environment. Contactable at: 49, South Pleasant Street, Suite 301, Amherst, MA01002, or by e-mail on nrpe@nrpe.org.

3 PROVIDENCE

God didn't lose interest in His creation once He'd created it. Nor did He abandon it to its own devices once it had rebelled. Jewish and Christian thinkers have always affirmed that He remains actively at work within the world He made. This doctrine is called 'Providence'. It is such a neglected doctrine in the church today that it might be helpful to begin by contrasting it with two other perennial views of whether there is any rhyme or reason, any plan or purpose behind the patterns of human happenstance – namely fate and chance.

a) Fate

Tom was completely right. I have been so preoccupied with Mum and Dad, and so tired from taking Dad's distressed phone calls, I have hardly been noticing Daniel at all: with the miraculous result that he has been all over me. I made a complete arse of myself today, though. I got in the lift to go out for a sandwich and found Daniel in there with Simon from Marketing, talking about footballers being arrested for throwing matches. 'Have you heard about this, Bridget?'

'Oh yes,' I lied, groping for an opinion. 'Actually, I think it's all rather petty. I know it's a thuggish way to behave, but as long as they didn't actually set light to anyone I don't see what all the fuss is about.'

Simon looked at me as if I was mad and Daniel stared for a moment and then burst out laughing. He just laughed and laughed till he and Simon got out and then turned back and said,

'Marry me,' as the doors closed between us. Hmmmm.

Bridget Jones's Diary by Helen Fielding:
Entry for Wednesday 22 February[1]

The interesting point for our present purposes about the various match-throwing accusations made against footballers and cricketers in recent years is not so much whether they are true, but what difference it would make if they were. I have supported Southampton Football Club all my life, but can hardly name more than two members of the squad, so probably don't qualify as one of their more devoted followers. But if I were, I think I would feel cheated. And if I were a team-mate of someone found guilty of match-throwing, I would feel, well, gutted and sick as a parrot, probably. Because if everything is fixed beforehand, then the whole thing loses credibility, spontaneity, reality, and generally becomes meaningless. Look what happened to professional wrestling in the UK: the more people perceived its results to be predetermined, the less people wanted to watch it. If what we watch on a Saturday afternoon makes no difference to a result that has been fixed beforehand by grubby deals in smoke-filled rooms, then washing the car would seem the more exciting option.

And what's true in microcosm on the sports field is also true in macrocosm, I suggest, in every area of life. If fate is king, if our lives are fixed in advance, if they're pre-set, pre-arranged, predetermined, then it is difficult to see what meaning they could possibly have for us. If the patterns of events, actions and reactions that make up human history are begotten entirely outside the human sphere, then we have no purchase on them. They can hardly be said to be our history. If the script of our lives and our generations and our civilisations is written in every detail by someone or something else, then we are indeed but poor players that strut and fret our hour upon the stage, and then are heard no more. If we contribute nothing of *our own* to the way things turn out, then we don't live life – it lives us. If the river of history just keeps rolling along and we are not tributaries of it, then there is no human history – merely sequence. The cry of the disenfranchised used to be, 'No taxation without representation'. In other words, a person is under no obligation to be taxed unless they have had *some* say, however small, in the decision-making process that has led to that tax, its nature and its level. We might equally say, 'No meaning without contribution'. In other words, our lives have no significance if we have not had *some* say in what goes on within us, through us and around us.

Belief in fate thus takes away any sense of meaning. It also takes away any real sense of *hope*, or, indeed, significant action. If nothing we do makes any difference, then why bother to plan, protest, or be politically active? Belief in fate tends to result in injustice being accepted with resignation rather than resisted with resolve. Belief in fate tends to breed a sense of meaninglessness and helplessness.

So part of the good news is that fate is *not* king. Jesus' message was the Kingdom of God, that *God* is King – and therefore fate is not. The church's message has always been that *Jesus* is Lord – and therefore fate is not. Of course, there are areas of our lives over which we have little control – that is why the concept of fate can seem to mesh with our experience at times. But if our *whole* lives are stories which have been pre-scripted, then they have no meaning for us, because nothing we do can make any difference. If *God* is King, however, if *Jesus* is Lord, then we are light-years away from being insignificant.

For God does not impose His will upon us in a way that brooks no opposition and embraces no contribution. He does not pre-determine everything that happens. The main word that the New Testament uses to depict the activity of the Holy Spirit amongst us is *fellowship* – not invasion, nor manipulation, nor control, but fellowship, partnership. We have a vital contribution to make and a unique rôle to play. All that we do matters. For God is King, and He does not dictate His purposes. To think that He does, is to forget (what we learned from the doctrine of the Fall) that God is not the only one who acts in His world. He has given us the freedom and the ability to choose, decide and act for ourselves in ways that affect things and people and history in real ways, for good or ill. We are not helpless victims of fate – we are active agents who can make a difference in God's world.

b) Chance

Here, instead of the story having been written in advance, there is simply no story. Instead of our contributions making no difference, our contributions are all that there is. Life 'is a tale, told by an idiot, full of sound and fury, signifying nothing.'[2] Or, rather, it is a multitude of conflicting tales, told and retold in inconsistent ways, bearing no meaningful relationship to any objective reality outside our over-heated brains. Many tales but no Tale. There is no overarching Story in which our own stories can find their place and make their mark. As Richard Dawkins put it, 'In a universe of blind physical forces and genetic replication, some people are going to get hurt, other people are going to get lucky, and you won't find any rhyme or reason in it, or any justice.'[3]

Up to a point, of course, Dawkins is right. There is no rhyme or reason to much of human experience. Our world is broken, and its purposefulness is broken along with everything else. The universe that we observe is not a just universe, and will not be until it is remade. There is a degree of luck in what happens to us. When one person gets cancer and another does not, that is not because God *wants* one of them to get cancer, it is because the world is fallen and not as God wanted it and chance has been at work. When one person gets stuck in traffic and misses a plane and another person gets to the airport early and catches it, and the plane then crashes, it is

" Thankyou God it didn't rain at the Church barbeque "

DROUGHT
FAMINE

95

not because God wanted it that way. It is because luck has played its part. When Christians deny that luck plays any part, they are often implicitly (though usually unintentionally) attributing all disaster, suffering and death to the hand of God. But God is good. We need, therefore, to accept that there is an element of chance in the way things turn out.

Indeed, that is only to be expected in a fallen world. If the world puts itself outside the personal, loving purposes of God, then it thereby makes itself subject to forces that are neither personal nor loving.

But to acknowledge that there is an element of chance at work in our world is not to accept that chance is *all* that is at work in our world. Chance is a player, but it is not the whole game. Purposefulness is broken, but not non-existent. It is difficult to see how the broken pieces of purpose could fit together, especially as our lives are amongst the pieces, but that does not mean that it cannot be done. God lovingly and (literally) painstakingly gathers the fragments of purpose and meaning and slowly restores them, reshapes them and uses them. The hymn insists that 'God is working His purpose out'. It does not pretend that those purposes are clearly visible or yet achieved. There is still a fight to be fought with the purpose-defying forces of sorrow and sin. There are still captives to be set free. But it looks forward to the day when that fight is over, and those purposes are finally accomplished and 'the earth shall be filled with the glory of God as the waters cover the sea'. And until that day, it invites us to make our contribution to the working out of God's purposes. 'What can we do to work God's work?' it asks:

> What can we do to hasten the time,
> the time that shall surely be,
> When the earth shall be filled with the glory of God
> as the waters cover the sea?

A. C. Ainger

There *is* a contribution for us to make, but our (feeble and contradictory) contributions are not all there is: 'All we can do is nothing worth unless God blesses the deed.' It is a partnership.

Chance does not rule. God does not leave His creation to the random buffetings of other forces. To imagine that He does is to forget (what we learned from the doctrine of Creation) that all creation is open to Him and He works within it. The events of our lives are therefore not ultimately random and meaningless, for they are capable of being given the direction and purpose of God, our Creator and the Creator of all the other agents we influence and are influenced by. Chance, like any other player, can frustrate and (possibly) delay God's purposes for His world, but it cannot ultimately thwart them. It can sour the present, but it cannot rob us of the future that God has always intended for His creation. The time when 'the earth shall be filled with the glory of God' is 'a time that shall surely be'.

What Christians believe in, therefore, is neither fate nor chance, but Providence.

c) Providence

Providence is the belief that God works within events – messy and obscenely tragic and blasphemously inimical to His will though they may be – to bring about His purposes. 'From one ancestor he made all the nations to inhabit the whole earth, and he allotted the times of their existence and the boundaries of the places where they would live' (Acts 17:26 NRSV). In other words, He is at work historically and demographically. He is at work within the very structures of time and space. He is at work within the patterns of human interaction, habitation and migration to bring about His purposes. And what are those purposes? The particular facet of God's intentions upon which Paul focuses here is 'so that they would search for God and perhaps grope for him and find him – though indeed he is not far from each one of us' (Acts 17:27 NRSV). He is at work to bring human beings into relationship with Himself. He is not only the Good Shepherd, searching for *us*: He also works

97

through every circumstance to try and get us to search for *Him*. He will not dispense with our response, nor compel it, but He will move heaven and earth to try and elicit it. His purposes thus are relational, and His mode of working is international and political.

But His purposes are also moral, and His mode of working individual and personal. As the famous verse, Romans 8:28, puts it: 'we know that in all things God works for the good of those who love him'. And the moral good for which He works is that we should be 'conformed to the likeness of his Son' (v.29), not least in His suffering and death. Notice what Paul does *not* say. He does *not* say that 'only good things happen to those who love God'. He does *not* say that if you go God's way, things will go your way. No, he simply promises that *in and through whatever happens, good and bad alike*, God's purposes can and will be worked out. God does not determine events, and often He detests them, but His purposes will not be thwarted by them, and He is committed to bringing good out of them.[a] And Paul only makes that promise to those who love God, because God will not force us to accept Him, will not force relationship or transformation upon us. If the world can in some sense cut itself off from God and thereby cut itself off from loving purposefulness, so can an individual.

In fate, there is an overarching story, but we cannot make our mark in it. In chance, there is no overarching story. There is therefore no meaning for us in either position. In Providence, not everything that happens is the will of God, but the will of God will be worked out in and through (and sometimes despite) everything that happens. There is an overarching story. There is a purpose for

---

[a] We need to insist here, as in the last chapter, that this does not 'justify' evil or painful events. It does not make them 'okay' – merely in some sense usable. Such events are not 'harmonisable' with the purposes of God – merely harnessable by them. Providence does not 'put right' heinous acts – but it can invest them with a purpose and a meaning other than the evil purpose with which they were originally launched (Genesis 45:5–8, 50:20). Even evil acts can be made carriers of a diametrically different intentionality from that of the diseased mind that engendered them. But that does not stop them from being evil acts, which we would have been better off without (Matthew 26:24.) It does not stop them from besmirching history, even if they are prevented from poisoning eternity.

the whole created order. There is a goal to which God is working that will not ultimately be denied. And we are invited to play our part in realising that purpose, to contribute to that story, to nudge the bits of creation for which we are responsible in the direction of the destiny for which they were designed. And it is in the interplay between God's non-coercive purposes and our unprogrammed response that meaning is to be found.

The next five points will hopefully unpack some of what we mean when we speak of Providence.

1. GOD'S PLANS TAKE ACCOUNT OF OUR CHOICES AND DECISIONS

God's plans are not inflexible. They do not happen regardless of who we are, and how we choose, and how we act, and how we live. They do not ignore or override our decisions and determinations. Of course, His ultimate objectives do not change, but the means He uses to bring about those objectives do adapt to the changing circumstances of our world. His plans not only take account of our choices and decisions: they even incorporate them.

The place where this can be seen most clearly is perhaps the delightful story of Jonah. Jonah was told to go and tell the people of Nineveh that in forty days' time they would be destroyed. No 'ifs or 'buts' – they were to be destroyed.[b] After a few transport difficulties, he arrived and delivered his message. The people of Nineveh listened to him, repented – and were not destroyed. Jonah was incandescent with (what he thought of as) righteous indignation. Because Jonah was a fatalist. He believed that God should do what God had said He would do – regardless of the reactions and responses of the people. He thought that God's plans were like a bullet with your name on, coming to get you – and there's nothing you can do about it.

---

[b] Actually, he was told to 'Go to the great city of Ninevah and preach against it' (Jonah 1:2) – no mention initially of its destruction. However, Jonah 3:10 corroborates Jonah's message that God had indeed threatened to destroy it.

But God's plans don't work like that. God is not a fatalist. His plans are not fixed and unalterable. His plans are adaptive and responsive, and respect our freedom. And God's plans adapted to take account of the people of Nineveh's change of heart. The people's choices had a profound effect on their destiny. Our free choices and decisions and thoughts and actions are taken up into God's plans, and make a difference to them.

The book of Jonah does not teach chance. God is active in His world in real ways, through the human agency of Jonah and through the very fabric of creation – the whale gets Jonah to Nineveh and the plant teaches him a lesson when he gets there. Neither does the book of Jonah teach fate: the destruction of their city does not come to the people willy-nilly. Here is no inexorable destiny, pursuing them whatever they do. They are not like the legendary Oedipus, who was condemned to live out a pre-ordained set of shameful actions, however much he sought to avert it. Fixed, unalterable decrees may have been the way of the Medes and Persians (Daniel 6:8), but they are not generally the way of God.

Nor is the story of Jonah an exception to the general rule. On the contrary, it is typical of God's way of working. The story of Jeremiah's visit to the potter's house in Jeremiah 18:1–10 assures us that the flexibility, adaptability, responsiveness and relationality that we see in the story of Jonah are the constant characteristics of God's action in the world.

> This is the word that came to Jeremiah from the Lord: 'Go down to the potter's house, and there I will give you my message.' So I went down to the potter's house, and I saw him working at the wheel. But the pot he was shaping from the clay was marred in his hands; so the potter formed it into another pot, shaping it as seemed best to him.
>
> Then the word of the Lord came to me: 'O house of Israel, can I not do with you as this potter does?' declares the Lord. 'Like clay in the hand of the potter, so are you in my hand, O house of Israel.'

Now, the image of the potter has often been used to suggest that God does what He likes and there is nothing that we can do about it, but that is precisely the opposite of the message that God gives to Jeremiah:

> If at any time I announce that a nation or kingdom is to be uprooted, torn down and destroyed, and if that nation I warned repents of its evil, then I will relent and not inflict on it the disaster I had planned. And if at another time I announce that a nation or kingdom is to be built up and planted, and if it does evil in my sight and does not obey me, then I will reconsider the good I had intended to do for it.

God's actions do not ignore us. They don't wash over us or sweep us along with them. They take account of us. They are morally responsive purposes and they take account of our obedience or evil-doing. It matters how we live. The decisions we make in response to the myriad moral choices we face, and the answer we give to the passionate call of God all help to fashion the fabric of history. We help tell the story of God's dealings with His world (or they wouldn't be *dealings* at all).

One way of illustrating the responsiveness of God's plans might be to turn to Joyce Grenfell's famous Nursery School Sketches, intriguingly entitled, *George – Don't Do That ...* (We never discover what it was that George shouldn't have been doing.) This comes from a sketch called 'Story Time', and needs to be read in an exaggeratedly up and down, primary school teacher voice:

> Let's have some nice straight backs, shall we? What shall we tell our story about today?
> Rachel, take your shoe off your head and put it on your foot.
> Shall we tell it about a little mouse?
> Or a big red bus?
> About a dear little bunny rabbit! All right, Peggy, we'll tell it about a dear little bunny rabbit.

No, Sidney, he wasn't a cowboy bunny rabbit, and he didn't have a gun.

Why don't you come out from under the table and help us tell our nice story?

All right, stay where you are, but you must stop machine-gunning everybody. I don't want to have to tell you again.

One of our individualists! He does have little personality problems, of aggression, but we feel that when his energies are canalised in the right direction he is going to be a quite worthwhile person. That's what we hope ...

Where did our bunny rabbit live?

No, he didn't live in a TV set.

No, not in a tree.

No, not in a flat.

Think please.

He lived in a HOLE.

Yes, Hazel, of course he did.

Only some of us call it a burrow, don't we?

He lived in a burrow with – who? His mummy bunny rabbit ... and his? ... Daddy bunny rabbit ... and all his? ... dear little sister and brother bunny rabbits. Wasn't that nice.

Yes, it was, Sidney.[4]

Okay, so it's not Dostoevsky. And I don't want to suggest that God is as patronising as that teacher. But the point is that, just as the Nursery School teacher invites the children to contribute to her story, so God invites us to contribute to the story of Creation, and it is this that gives us responsibility and meaning.

2. GOD'S PURPOSES ARE NOT RESTRICTED TO ANY ONE NATION OR GROUP

This is obvious, but it needs to be said. For all Israel's status as the chosen people, the Old Testament nevertheless saw God's providence as embracing all nations. That is clear from the very fact that Jonah was sent on a mission to the pagan city of Nineveh. In fact, some scholars see the book of Jonah precisely as a polemic against the sort of nationalism to which the people of Israel were periodically prone. Be that as it may, the point is made very forcibly by the very last words of the book, when Jonah is upbraided for his annoyance at the repentance of the people of Nineveh and at God's failure to destroy them:

> But the Lord said, 'You have been concerned about this vine, though you did not tend it or make it grow. It sprang up overnight and died overnight. But Nineveh has more than a hundred and twenty thousand people who cannot tell their right hand from their left, and many cattle as well. Should I not be concerned about that great city?

> **Jonah 4:10–11**

(So it's not just all nations, but livestock as well – the whole of creation – that is the focus of God's providential concern. Jesus was later to emphasise the breadth of the Father's providential embrace with His reference to sparrows and lilies (Matthew 6:25–30).)

The same point is made even more forcibly in the prophecies of Amos when God asks, 'Did I not bring Israel up from Egypt?' (Amos 9:7). This is a reference to the Exodus of the people of Israel from slavery in Egypt – probably the most foundational story in Israel's self-understanding and in her understanding of God. Who was Israel? She was the people that God brought out of Egypt. Who was God? He was 'the LORD your God, who brought you out of Egypt, out of the land of slavery' (Exodus 20:2). 'Did I not bring Israel up from Egypt?': Amos' hearers would have given an enthusiastic Yes to this rhetorical question. They would have baulked, however, at what the message of Yahweh went on to say: 'Did I not bring the Israelites up from Egypt, *the Philistines from Caphtor and the Arameans from Kir?*' In other words, God was saying, 'Just as I was involved in your history and your coming to be as a nation, so I have been equally involved in the history and national identity of other nations – even that of your arch-enemy, the Philistines. The difference is that with you, I have shown my working. With you, I have made myself known and sent prophets to explain my ways and to help you recognise my hand when and where and how it has been at work. But do not suppose that my covenant with you means I am not concerned about and involved within and active amongst the other nations. On the contrary, my covenant with you is intended to be the means of blessing all the peoples of the earth.' (A fairly *free* paraphrase of Amos 9:7!) Choosing the hated and despised Philistines as an example was rubbing their noses in it, but it made the point powerfully: if God was involved in the history of *that* wretched people, then there could be no history in which He is not actively present.

Nor are those who do not know or acknowledge God thereby excluded from His providential embrace. Even pagan nations doing terrible things could unwittingly serve His purpose. For example, the benign, but unconverted (Isaiah 45:4–5) Persian, Cyrus, could be the means of restoring Israel to her homeland at the end of the Exile, and could even merit the title of 'shepherd' (Isaiah 44:28). God is not as particular as we might like when it comes to harnessing people and projects to bring about His purposes.

It is but a small jump from here to the teaching of Jesus. For Him, God's love, and the practical expression of that love as provision, are indiscriminate: 'Love your enemies and pray for those who persecute you, that you may be children of your Father in heaven. He causes his sun to rise on the evil and the good, and sends rain on the righteous and the unrighteous' (Matthew 5:44–5). The providence of God, mercifully, is both morally and racially indiscriminate. He is at work in every nation and every circumstance, to provide, to protect, sometimes to punish, always to draw people to know Him and enjoy Him and to become what they were intended and are now empowered to be in the loving wisdom of the Creator.

The only limitation that providence knows is the limitation we place upon His working by refusing that relationship and resisting that restorative impulse. Even then, He does what He can. As so often, C. S. Lewis manages to give narrative expression both to the limitations we can place upon God's lavishly providential longings, and to His gentle and gracious doing of what He can. Aslan (the lion who acts as a Christ-figure in the Narnia novels) is speaking to Polly about the selfish would-be magician, Uncle Andrew:

> 'He thinks great folly, child,' said Aslan. 'This world is bursting with life for these few days because the song with which I called it into life still hangs in the air and rumbles in the ground. It will not be so for long. But I cannot tell that to this old sinner, and I cannot comfort him either; he has made himself unable to hear my voice. If I spoke to him, he would hear only growlings and roarings. Oh Adam's sons, how cleverly you defend yourselves against all that might do you good! But I will give him the only gift he is still able to receive.'
>
> He bowed his great head rather sadly, and breathed into the Magician's terrified face. 'Sleep,' he said. 'Sleep and be separated for some few hours from all the torments you have devised for yourself.' Uncle Andrew immediately rolled over with closed eyes and began breathing peacefully.[5]

3. GOD'S PLANS ARE OFTEN HIDDEN FROM US

One of the glories of the Christian faith is that it introduces us to a God who can be known. Unlike many religions, its God is not unknowable and therefore unpredictable to the point of capriciousness, but knowable and consistent. Indeed, the knowability of God is Paul's starting-point when addressing the pagan but religious people of Athens on the Areopagus (Acts 17:23): 'Now what you worship as something unknown I am going to proclaim to you.' We are not left to guess about the nature of God and of the patterns of His providential activity. He gave Israel His law to express the holiness of His nature and as a blueprint for their life together as a nation (see Psalm 147:19–20). He sent

His prophets to point out and interpret His interventions and actions in the world (see Amos 3:7). He has sent His Son as the culmination of that process of revelation (see Hebrews 1:1–3). He poured out His Spirit 'of knowledge' (Isaiah 11:2) to 'teach you all things and … remind you of everything I have said to you' (John 14:26). And He gave us His apostles to be the authoritative interpreters of His full and perfect self-revelation in Jesus of Nazareth (see John 13:20 and Ephesians 3:5) and thus to be the foundation of His Church (Ephesians 2:20). The apostle Paul uses the word 'mystery', to denote, not a continuing puzzle, but a part of the plan and purpose of God which 'has been kept hidden for ages and generations, *but is now disclosed* to the saints' (Colossians 1:26, my italics; cf. Ephesians 1:9, 3:3 etc). He has revealed the sort of God He is and the sort of purpose He has. We are not left to guess.

And yet. Even allowing for His continuing guidance, His promptings, nudgings and prophetic addressings of us, it is far from clear how our particular stories fit into the great revealed narrative of His purposes for creation. The great motorway of His story is marked reasonably clearly, but the B-roads of our particular lives and vocations are often not shown on the map, and it is usually difficult, if not impossible, to see where they are leading. Nowhere is that more the case than with Job. Job was never told the reason for His suffering. He never knew what was happening or what God was playing at. Even after the torment was over and his prosperity was restored to him, he still never learnt what the 'days of his hard service' (Job 14:14) were all about.

We don't know why God never told him. Maybe, as Alvin Plantinga says, he couldn't have understood the reason even if he had been told it: 'Indeed, it is only *hubris* which would tempt us to think that we could so much as grasp God's plans here, even if He proposed to divulge them to us.'[6] But whatever the reason, it is vital for the book of Job that any purpose within Job's suffering is never disclosed to him. As the commentator H. H. Rowley wisely observes, 'If it had been, the book would have been of little value to others, who must suffer in the dark.'[7] And suffering normally is in the dark. Very seldom can we say at the time, 'Ah yes. I see what God's up to in this thoroughly unpleasant experience I'm going through. That's okay then.' Usually our perplexity adds to the pain of it. Both Scripture and experience thus tell us that the workings of Providence are often opaque.

Consequently, the Scriptures are cautious about tracing the providential purposes of God in the messy mire of history. Even an apostle is guarded about detecting the hand of God: perhaps, says Paul, the reason why Onesimus was separated from Philemon was to facilitate his conversion and to reunite them as brothers (Philemon 15) – 'Perhaps. I don't know. I'm just hazarding a guess.' See the same caution in Esther 4:14: 'Who knows but that you have come to royal position for such a time as this?' It seems obviously providential to the reader, but Mordecai is more circumspect. He does not pretend to understand the ways of God. It seems to fit what he knows both of God and of the current situation, but just because it makes sense to him doesn't mean that it is God's sense, God's working. 'Maybe that's what's going on here. Maybe that's what God's up to. But who knows?' He is cautious in the extreme. And it becomes us equally finite and fallible human beings to be cautious too. It is good to be looking out for the hand of God. It is good to be looking out for the ways God is working so that we may join Him in working those ways. But it is good, too, to be humble about our ability to detect and recognise that hand at work in our world. 'Perhaps' and 'Who knows?' are appropriate catchwords when it comes to discussing such matters, which are too lofty for us to attain to, and too wonderful for us to understand.

4. GOD'S PURPOSES ARE AGAINST EVIL

This is one of the fixed, foundational points of Providence. God is good. Creation is good. God works within creation to root out its evil and to restore its goodness. There is an inescapably moral intentionality to His ways among us.^c

The ways in which God works to counter evil and frustrate it are myriad, and beyond the scope of our minds, let alone the scope of this chapter. But I want to focus on seven 'moments' of God's providential assault upon evil which we may detect in the Scriptures.

a) God permits, but does not commit, evil

Nicholas has broken into the lumber room and is looking at a tapestry picture on an old firescreen that he has found there:

> A man, dressed in the hunting costume of some remote period, had just transfixed a stag with an arrow; it could not have been a difficult shot because the stag was only one or two paces away from him; in the thickly growing vegetation that the picture suggested it would not have been difficult to creep up to a feeding stag, and the two spotted dogs that were springing forward to join in the chase had evidently been trained to keep to heel till the arrow was discharged. That part of the picture was simple, if interesting, but did the huntsman see, what Nicholas saw, that four galloping wolves were coming in his direction through the wood? There might be more than four of them hidden behind the trees, and in any case would the man and his dogs be able to

---

^c Perhaps, however, 'moral' is too weak and misleading a word to describe the character of God's action in creation. It is too weak a word because it tends to conjure up for us an image of a truncated life within straight-jacketing boundaries. In fact, it is about the liberation of creation from the crushingly constrictive and, indeed, destructive effects of alienation, injustice, degeneration and death. And 'moral' is a misleading word if we associate it with a self-righteous dismissal of those who don't measure up, and a supercilious self-distancing from the morally tainted. But 'moral' cannot mean that when applied to the God who ate with the compromised, touched the contagious, defended the adulterous, and allowed Himself to be kissed by prostitutes in public. It cannot mean that when applied to the God who, far from distancing Himself from His world, works within it, and welded Himself to it, and will one day restore it. As we have seen, He is prepared to get His hands dirty by using the evil acts of others, but only to turn them to His and our advantage, only to hijack them for good, only to invest them with a radically different purpose from the one with which they were originally invested. His purposes are not only moral: they even threaten to give morality a good name!

cope with the four wolves if they made an attack? The man had only two arrows left in his quiver, and he might miss with one or both of them; all one knew about his skill in shooting was that he could hit a large stag at a ridiculously short range. Nicholas sat for many golden minutes revolving the possibilities of the scene; he was inclined to think that there were more than four wolves and that the man and his dogs were in a tight corner.[8]

That passage from Saki's delightful short story, *The Lumber Room*, gives a good example of what is one of the oldest tricks in the storyteller's book – namely, letting the audience know something that the character within the story does *not* know. Nicholas could see the four wolves galloping through the wood, but the huntsman (probably) could not. And that is what gives a tension and a power to the tapestry picture. There can hardly have been a single dramatist who has not used this device in one way or another. An obvious example is the pantomime. We, the audience, can see the baddy at the back of the stage, but the goody at the front of the stage can't see him. 'He's behind you', we shout. But by the time the goody has turned round, the baddy has disappeared, so we're into the 'Oh no he isn't', 'Oh yes he is' routine.

And it is this device which underlies the whole book of Job, and gives it such dramatic tension and power. We, the *readers*, know, from the first two chapters of the book, that Job's sufferings are not God's idea but Satan's, and that they are put into effect, not by God, but by Satan. God *permits* them. Of course: He is omnipotent and they happen, so He must have permitted them. But He does not *do* them. He does not *commit* them. They are not *of* Him. The author is deliberately and carefully distancing God from any imputation of direct involvement in, or responsibility for evil and suffering. He is, in other words, guarding the goodness of God.

It seems to me that we should do likewise. We too need to put moral distance between God and evil. We need to be careful in our thinking and our speaking not to suggest that God is the author of suffering. We need to preserve the distinction between what God permits and what He commits. To forget that distinction is to say that God *wills* Auschwitz and Hiroshima and the Gulag and the Laogai and the killing fields and Enniskillen and September 11th – and that we must never say. We must guard with our theological lives the goodness of God. We may and we must feel the strength of the case against that goodness. There is a Job in each one of us and he must be allowed to rail. But the time must come when we put our hand over our mouth and find our hope in the goodness of God. For only an ultimately good God can be relied upon to answer our cries. Only an ultimately good God can be relied upon to care. Only an ultimately good God can be relied upon to put all things to rights. Thus the distinction between what God allows and what He actually does is essential if we are to have a good doctrine of Providence, a good understanding of God's ways with His world.

b) God limits evil

God permits evil, but does not give it an entirely free hand. In the story of Job, He places limits on Satan's activity (Job 1:12, 2:6). The limits are not as stringent as we might like, and certainly not as stringent as Job would have liked! And the limits He placed upon Satan's activity with regard to Job are not universal. Satan is not allowed to lay a finger on Job in Chapter 1, and is required to spare his life in Chapter 2. Many are not protected in those ways. Nevertheless, it encourages us to believe that evil is not given a completely free rein. There are things Satan is not permitted to do, lines he is not able to cross. There are limits to the permission of evil. We do not know exactly what those limits are, and it is not, perhaps, a huge comfort, but the story of Job seems to me to teach that not everything that could happen is allowed to happen. (Rather as Joyce Grenfell's primary school teacher does not permit every contribution to the story that is suggested!)

c) God weights the scales against evil

God ensures that good acts have disproportionately good effects. In the list of commandments in Exodus 20, God says,

> 'I, the Lord your God, am a jealous God, visiting the iniquity of the fathers upon the children to the third and fourth generation of those who hate me, but showing love to a thousand generations of those who love me and keep my commandments.'
>
> **v.5 RSV, v.6 NIV**

This verse is not without its own problems, of course, but notice here the disproportion. Choices have consequences, naturally. And bad choices have bad consequences – not just for those who make the choices, but for others. That's the way we're made. We're not islands entire of ourselves, having no influence upon others, and insulated from all the actions and attitudes of others. We are relational beings. We affect one another. We impact upon one another, for good and ill. The choices of one generation make a difference to subsequent generations. That is part of what is involved in being significant.

But God has promised to give good choices a longer shelf life. Hatred and sin reach down three or four generations: love and obedience reach down a thousand. Just as loaves and fish in His hands feed more people, so lives in His hands influence more generations more positively than do finite lives that defy the Infinite. All events are significant, but some are more significant than others. Good events flowing from predominantly right decisions spring out more energetically and lastingly and have a greater effect upon future generations than do the sterile acts of evil. 'The evil that men do lives after them, the good is oft interrèd with their bones', according to Mark Anthony[9], and at the level of reputation and remembrance, he is often right. But at the level of ultimate reality, it is the other way round. The good that men do not only lives after them, but is incorporated into the new creation (Revelation 21:26) and will live for ever. The evil that men do is not 'interrèd with

111

their bones,' but is restricted in the knock-on effects it can have, and, having had its day, will certainly have no after-life (Revelation 21:27).

d) God works against evil

He does not just lay out the ground rules in goodness' favour. He is also a player in the game on goodness' side. Through command; through conscience; through confronting creatures with the consequences of their choices; through limiting their capacity for evil by capping the duration of life-in-rebellion; through gracious care of the perpetrators and the preservation of their dignity; through calling one man, one family and one nation to spearhead the remaking of creation; through acts of deliverance and in particular through rescuing His people from slavery.

Through guidance, protection and provision; through the trumpet blast and the still, small voice; through the law; through the legal system and the sacrificial system; through training the people in patterns of praise and prayer and confession and thankfulness; through leaders; through acts of judgment, exposing the nature and consequences of evil; through not abandoning His people in exile; through not abandoning them there but giving them assurance of His continuing presence, through encouraging and enabling them to take up important positions within the Empire that had taken them captive, and thus to temper some of the oppressiveness of that régime; through raising up a political leader minded to allow captive peoples to return; through a heart-rent cry maturing into a growing hope crystallising into a positive expectation that God would soon visit His people in the person of His Messiah, rescue her from oppression, end her suffering and restore His creation.

Through becoming a human being and living a human life, and being a pawn in the power games of world leaders, and announcing the Kingdom, and feeding the hungry, and healing the sick, and raising the dead, and bringing to order the disordered, and giving the possessed back control of themselves, and providing leadership to the lost; through absorbing the hatred of His enemies and the violence of the Empire and the cynicism of its officials rather than adding to the momentum of evil by returning hatred and violence for violence, and praying for His killers, and enduring the alienation to end all alienation. And through dying and joining humanity in the utter helplessness of the mortuary slab. And through being raised to a new dimension of life and freedom and scope.

Through being poured out on all flesh, and empowering the church, and encouraging its witness and opening it up across every barrier, and turning its squabbles to missionary advantage, and using it to heal, to break the hold of curse and spell, to challenge the powers, to transform value systems.

Through evil's propensity to fragment, through the law of diminishing returns, through dissatisfaction and reflection on mortality, through the eternity he has placed in the human heart which demands that there must be more to life (quantitatively and qualitatively) than this, through feeble-feeling prayers that seem to reach nowhere, through undramatic acts of goodness that no one seems to notice, through the bravery of those who stand up to the System, through their refusal to forget the fact of the future.

Well, there are a few of the ways in which God works against evil in His world – based loosely on the history of Israel, because, as we noted earlier, it is there that God has shown something of His working.

e) God suffers from evil[d]

God is not thrown by evil. He is not ultimately thwarted by evil. It does not shape Him, or, rather, it does not misshape Him. He is not forced to suffer by any external necessity. He is not forced to become anything that is not essentially true of Him. Evil does not threaten His love or His power. It does not weaken His resolution or His commitment to sustain and renew.

---

[d] I am aware that this is a controversial statement. See the Resources section for books that argue it each way, and see Chapter 5 for an attempt to argue it in a way that might be more widely acceptable.

But neither is He untouched by evil and the suffering it causes. It affects Him – how could it not? Throughout the Scriptures, there are occasional insights into what we might perhaps call, without irreverence, the emotional life of God. After all, we are emotional beings – it is part of our glory – and we are made in the image of God. It would not therefore be surprising if God were in some sense emotional too.[e] And, while allowing for the vividly pictorial nature of the language that Scripture uses, that is exactly what we find. In Genesis 6:6, we are told that, because of the depth of wickedness and violence on the earth, 'God was grieved that he had made human beings on the earth, and his heart was filled with pain.' Or, as Eugene Peterson put it, 'God was sorry that he had made the human race in the first place; it broke his heart' (Genesis 6:6 THE MESSAGE). Paul probably has this verse in mind when He calls upon his readers not to grieve the Holy Spirit of God (Ephesians 4:30). Now, obviously we must be careful about how we apply human language to God, but on the other hand it must mean something. We must not, in our carefulness, empty it of all meaning and power. Such is God's involvement in and commitment to those who are the victims of human evil that He is appalled in quite self-jolting ways by what they suffer. Even allowing for the way in which God, like a mother talking to her child, has to 'lisp' so that we can understand, such language cannot mean less than that, I suggest.

This compassion is well depicted in C. S. Lewis' portrayal of Aslan, the lion Christ-figure in *The Chronicles of Narnia*. In this passage from *The Magician's Nephew*, Digory mentions his sick mother to Aslan:

> 'But please, please – won't you – can't you give me something that will cure Mother?' Up till then he had been looking at the Lion's great front feet and the huge claws on them; now, in his despair, he looked up at its face. What he saw surprised him as

---

[e] It would be odd if we human beings had, in our emotionality, a good capacity of which God was incapable, a language which was foreign to Him.

much as anything in his whole life. For the tawny face was bent down near his own and (wonder of wonders) great shining tears stood in the Lion's eyes. They were such big, bright tears compared with Digory's own that for a moment he felt as if the Lion must really be sorrier about his Mother than he was himself.[10]

Furthermore, one of the most characteristic qualities ascribed to God in the Scriptures is *compassion*, which does not include the word 'passion' within it for nothing. To be compassionate is to suffer with someone. Now, there is a whole theological tradition that is wary of using such language about God for fear of suggesting that God can change in a way that compromises His consistency. That theological tradition's instinct is right to want to defend His consistency. It is vital that we never suggest that God is changeable in the sense of capricious.

But compassion is simply what love is in the face of suffering – there is no inconsistency here. God is love, through and through, and all that changes is the form that that love takes. Love in the presence of suffering takes the form of compassion. Love in the presence of injustice takes the form of anger. Love in the presence of love takes the form of delight. So calling God compassionate, with all the emotion that that implies, in no way threatens His non-capricious consistency, which is part of the gospel.

As we saw in the last chapter, Jesus wept and was disturbed in spirit at the tomb of Lazarus. And He is our window onto God. He is how we may know what God is like. He is not the Father, of course, but He reveals the Father, and the grief and anger in His heart must have some counterpart in the Father's heart.

But finally it is the cross that justifies the (albeit careful) ascription of suffering to God. There we find that God is not free *from* suffering, but free *to* suffer, if, in His love, He so chooses. There we see the *crucified* God.[f] There we see the difference between the true God

---

[f] This phrase comes from the title of Jürgen Moltmann's book, *The Crucified God*, translated by R. A. Wilson & John Bowden (London, SCM Press, 1974).

and the pagan gods. The whole concept of a crucified God was unthinkable to the Greek and Roman world. It was a contradiction in terms. The whole point about the Greek and Roman gods was that they were immortal. They did not dirty their hands with the pains and sufferings of mortals. As the Greek goddess, Artemis, says to the dying Hippolytus in Euripides' play:

> ... I may not look upon the dead,
> Nor stain my sight with the anguish of departing breath ... [11]

How different was the God we meet in Jesus. Not only did He gravitate towards suffering people, not only did He stain Himself by touching the ritually impure and the dying and the dead but He also shared their suffering Himself, knew *in His own lungs* the anguish of departing breath. It was not a stain upon Him to suffer human pains and die a human death – it was the very thing for which He came, and the very highest expression of who He was, and of who God eternally is.

We shall revisit this point when we look at the Cross in Chapter 5, but here notice what a difference it makes to our understanding of God's providential ways. If God is genuinely compassionate, if He suffers all the pains and pangs of life along with us, then only He is in a position to know whether the project of creation will ultimately have proved worthwhile. He is no *deus ex machina* who pops up at the end to sort everything out. He is the God who is there all the way through, fighting evil at every turn, taking its full force into Himself, going through whatever we go through, and turning it to good.

f) God can bring good from evil

If God can bring good out of deicide, then there is no act so evil as to be infertile for good. If God can bring good from creation killing the One through whom it was made, then He can bring good from anything. If He can make the cross of Christ the means of healing and restoring all things, then He can turn any act to our good and to His glory. If the joy of the resurrection follows the agony of the cross, both as its consequence and its culmination, then there is no tomb of agony or hopelessness from which the stone may not be rolled away. If the evil event in which every act of evil is included and incorporated is also made the act by which evil is disarmed and defused, for what can there be no hope? What dungeon can be keyless? The cross and the resurrection therefore both illustrate and underwrite the despair-puncturing, hope-insistent promise of Providence.

We must, however, insist again here that the good that God can bring from evil in no way nullifies the evil. It does not justify it, or make it in any way acceptable. It does not paint it in different colours. It does not make it 'okay'. It does not take responsibility away from the perpetrator: the fact that the betrayal of Jesus was used to bring to climax the purposes and promises of God, does not condone that betrayal (Matthew 26:24). Evil remains evil, however much it may be contained and defused and robbed of its full impact and destiny. We should therefore be cautious and hesitant to speak of the good that can be squeezed out of evil acts. It is offensive to be too quick to turn from acts of enormity to their supposedly beneficial consequences. We must not use the hope of Providence to belittle the suffering of others – or of ourselves. The Resurrection did not cancel out the cross. Jesus still bore the marks of His wounds, glorified though they now were.

But having said that, and *only* having said that, we need to insist too that you do not pay proper tribute to suffering by refusing to accept that any good did or could come from it. That would be to turn evil into a black hole, constantly warping time and space. The good news of the gospel is that time and space will not be forever warped. The good news of Providence in particular is that God is not waiting until the final putting right of all things – He is at work at all times and in all places to put right and to straighten out and to open up and to set free and to wrest history away from all that would defy meaning and hope.

g) God will destroy evil

There is a goal to the purposes of God. Providence is leading somewhere. What God has been doing, often incognito, in the ebb and flow of history, He will bring to completion and perfection, openly and transparently and for all to see. What He did in microcosm on the streets and hills of Galilee in the person of Jesus, He will do for the whole cosmos. What He did for the man with the shrivelled hand in the synagogue (Mark 3:5), He will do for everything (Acts 3:21). Jesus' own phrase for the climax of history was 'the renewal of all things' (Matthew 19:28).

The Bible ends with the elimination of evil, the exclusion of all impurity, shame and deceit from the new creation, and therefore an end to death and mourning and crying and pain (Revelation 20:10; 20:27; 21:4). The great cry of the oppressed – 'How long, Sovereign Lord?' (Revelation 6:10) – will finally be answered. The victory of the resurrection – ending the long reign of sin, renewing a broken world and making humanity whole – will finally be complete. Evil alone, and that which clings to it, will have no future.

5. GOD'S PURPOSES ARE CHRIST-SHAPED, CHRIST-ENABLED AND CHRIST-DISCLOSED

a) God's purposes are Christ-shaped

How do we recognise God's hand in the mass of happenings around us and in our world? How do we know what is His doing and what is not? How do we know when He is at work in the kind of way He wants to work, and when He is at work in ways He would not have chosen to work if things had not gone so wrong? What is the litmus paper of Providence? Answer: Christ. If we want to know whether a particular event or pattern of events bears the hallmark of God's activity, then it is to Christ that we look. He is how we know what God is like; He is therefore how we know what God's activity is like. God's activity has His character, His stamp, His aroma.

Let me give a couple of examples of using this criterion, one screamingly obvious, and the second perhaps more subtle. The first is the so-called Lord's Resistance Army in Northern Uganda. Is this an agent of God's will, as its name would claim? And how would one make such a judgment? Answer: by comparing its actions with the character of God as we see it in Christ. He had twelve legions of angels at His beck and call but would not use them to defend Himself against the legions of Rome. He spoke against armed resistance to Rome and refused to endorse the violent revolutionary agenda of the early 'zealot' movement. He offered the alternative of passive resistance: turning the other cheek and going the extra mile. And He practised what He preached. He refused to be the military messiah many were expecting and hoping for. He refused to cut a swathe through the Roman ranks, orphaning and widowing with every swipe. Far from meting out violence, He submitted Himself to it, absorbing the crushing might of the Empire into His own body, allowing the Roman eagle to gorge itself on His flesh.

'The Lord's' Resistance Army, by stark contrast, has adopted violence as its method, abducting children and mutilating its enemies. The incompatibility could hardly be greater. By comparing its methods with those of Christ, we see that it stands condemned as a grotesque, and quite possibly demonic, contradiction of the ways of God. When one applies that criterion, it becomes immediately apparent that it is not His will they are performing nor His purposes they are advancing.

The second example is evolution. Assuming for the moment that it represents a roughly accurate account of how present species (including ourselves) came to be, what are we to make of it? Is it how God has chosen to create? Is it His chosen mechanism for bringing about creatures of sufficient intelligence and creativity and moral awareness to be bearers of His image? What answer might we give to Richard Dawkins' question as to why a good God would have chosen such a blood-stained method of creating? Again, we must use the criterion of Christ. How do the outworkings of evolution compare with the character of Christ? Very badly, I would suggest. As I argued in the last chapter, the whole movement of the one is in a totally opposite direction from the whole movement of the other. Evolution involves the survival of the fittest, with the weakest being jettisoned: Christ demonstrated the care of God for the weak and the sick and the disabled and those who would otherwise be the victims of the evolutionary process. Evolution depends upon death: Christ came to bring an end to the reign of death. In the system upon which evolution operates, one creature has to take the life of another in order that it might itself live: on the Cross, Christ gave up His life in order that *others* might live.

I suggest, therefore, that all we know about the character of God from the person of Christ forbids us to say evolution was God's *chosen* way of creating, at least in the form that it has in fact taken. He did not deliberately set up a system in which pain and predation prevail. On the contrary, such phenomena are distortions of the harmonious creation that He intended. They are consequences, not of creation, but of Fall. That does *not*, of course, prevent us from saying that God worked through the messy business of evolution in order to bring about His purposes. As we have seen, God is prepared to get His hands dirty by using evil acts and turning them to His and our advantage. We do not have to reject the theory of evolution, nor do we have to deny that it may have been used by God to bring richness and variety and complexity and, indeed, humanity to an already fallen world.

But we do have to say that it is not *of Him*. It was not His original idea. It does not, as it currently operates, have His stamp upon it. It's not the way He would have chosen to work if He had not been opposed. To answer Richard Dawkins' question: why would a good God have chosen to create in such a cruel way? He didn't. He intended a world without cruelty, but there was rebellion within it and consequent distortion of it, and the result was that the processes of creation took on a very different character from the one they should have had. Despite that rebellion and that distortion, God's purposes will not ultimately be thwarted. And He will work, even through the messiness and pain of those jarring processes, to bring creation to completion (in human beings) and, finally, to restoration (in Christ).

Whether or not you agree with the argument of the previous paragraphs, I hope you see how the character of Christ acts as a criterion. As we read the pages of the Gospels, we discover how He dealt with people and situations as He came across them in His earthly life, and we say, 'Ah! That's what God is like. That's the sort of thing that God does. That's the sort of way in which He operates.' And then we use that knowledge of God in the person of Christ as a way of seeking tentatively and humbly to recognise His hand at work in our lives and our experiences.

b) God's purposes are Christ-enabled

Jesus doesn't just reveal God to us so that we can recognise His characteristic ways of working. He and His acts also create the conditions in which God can work in new ways to bring about His purposes for creation. They unlock the power of God and bring it to bear on the created order in general and on human beings in particular. They are not just *instances* of God working, from which we may derive various observations about how He tends to work: they are the very *grounds* upon which He works in certain ways.

The Incarnation is the ground upon which a bridge is established between God and the world of space and time He created. All that He does in and for His creation is thereby placed upon a new and intimate footing. All that He is and does within His world is thus focused and summed up and taken forward in Jesus of Nazareth. By becoming a human being, Jesus (or, more accurately, the Son[8]) has changed the dynamic of the relationship between Creator and creation. He is now the bridge and the (common) ground and the point of intersection and the place of meeting between God and His beloved creatures. By becoming a human being, Jesus has revealed God and made reconciliation possible.

The Cross is the ground upon which He is able to reconcile all things to Himself (Colossians 1:20), and therefore to one another.

---

[8] Strictly speaking, Jesus did not become human: Jesus was the human being the Son of God became.

The future harmony of all things under Christ (Isaiah 11:6–9, Ephesians 1:10), and all that God is doing now to work towards that future harmony, depends upon the alienation and darkness Jesus experienced on the cross. The future free from predation, cruelty and pain that the prophets promised depends upon the pain He endured and the blood He shed. The forgiveness and the welcome God offers depend upon the outstretched arms of the crucified Christ. The purposes of God have been hard won.

The Ascension is the ground upon which the Spirit could be poured out in new ways. In John's Gospel, Jesus tells His disciples that 'It is for your good that I am going away. Unless I go away, the Counsellor will not come to you; but if I go, I will send him to you' (John 16:7). In a way which we will explore further when we come to look at the Ascension in Chapter 6, Jesus' return to His Father releases the Spirit to come to His people and His world in new ways. The Spirit has always been at work in creation, of course. But the prophets looked forward to a time when He would be 'poured out on all flesh' (Joel 2:28ff), bursting through old barriers and sweeping away old partitions. The going away of the Son enabled the powerful new coming of the Spirit.

In the Incarnation, a bridge is established between God and creation. At the cross, the gulf between holiness and murderous sinfulness is bridged. At the Ascension, the bridge is secured on the far side, and the way is clear for the Spirit to flow into creation in new ways. And when creation is at last re-made, the new heavens and the new earth will finally be flooded with the presence, glory and love of God, mediated through the Spirit. We shall explore and explain these points in subsequent chapters. Our point, here, is that all these stages in the healing and transfiguring purposes of God are enabled by the faithful obedience of Christ. They do not happen without Him, and they do not happen without incalculable cost.

c) God's purposes are Christ-disclosed

'Life, you know, is rather like opening a tin of sardines. We are all of us looking for the key', says the spoof vicar in Alan Bennett's *Take*

A Pew.[12] 'The universe is like a safe to which there is a combination. But the combination is locked up in the safe', laments Peter de Vries in *Let me count the ways.*[13] They give voice, as does John in Revelation 5, to the pervasive sense human beings have, that meaning and purpose evade them:

> Then I saw in the right hand of him who sat on the throne a scroll with writing on both sides and sealed with seven seals. And I saw a mighty angel proclaiming in a loud voice, 'Who is worthy to break the seals and open the scroll?' But no-one in heaven or on earth or under the earth could open the scroll or even look inside it. I wept and wept because no-one was found who was worthy to open the scroll or look inside.

> **Revelation 5:1–4**

The scroll stands for the key, the combination – a symbol of the meaning and purpose of all that is. And what is needed is someone who is worthy enough to open the scroll, unfold the meaning. (*Worthy* enough, notice – not 'intelligent' enough, for intelligence on its own leads to mere cleverness. It is the combination of intelligence *and goodness* that leads to wisdom and understanding.) And no-one is found worthy to open the scroll. Not surprisingly, for we are beings of limited intelligence and distinctly limited goodness. We have a limited, and warped, perspective. We are part of the picture and cannot see the whole picture. There is no-one who can unveil the mystery and meaning of existence. No wonder John weeps. To live in a vast and awesome universe, to have a short and fragile life, and to be in ignorance of what they are for, is the ultimate frustration. The twentieth-century's culture and philosophy echo to the sound of the same tears. But:

> Then one of the elders said to me, 'Do not weep! See, the Lion of the tribe of Judah, the Root of David, has triumphed. He is able to open the scroll and its seven seals. Then I saw a Lamb, looking as if it had been slain, standing in the centre of the throne

> ... He came and took the scroll from the right hand of him who
> sat on the throne.

Revelation 5:5–7

The Lamb is the only one who is able to open the scroll, to unfold
and to effect the purposes of God for His world. Only He can unveil
the meaning of creation authoritatively, because it was created
through Him. Only He can unlock the meaning of history validly,
because only He was before it, within it and beyond it. Only He can
propound the purposes of God safely, because truth is only safe in
scarred hands. Only He can realise the purposes of God effectively,
because, in being slain, He has won back a community from every
tribe, language, people and nation to operate that healing rule of
the earth to which we were originally called (Revelation 5:9–10).
Only in the light of Christ can anything be seen in its true colours.
Only in His light will creation yield up its secrets. We will not
understand anything *aright* if we will not learn from Him – not
history, not science, not evolution, not ethics, not ourselves – for 'all
things were created by him and for him' (Colossians 1:16).

SOME PRACTICAL CONSEQUENCES OF THE DOCTRINE OF PROVIDENCE

The doctrine of Providence is not just an academic thing. It does
not just affect our theology. It affects fundamentally the whole
way in which we view ourselves, our actions, our lives and our
world. Here are four practical consequences of the Doctrine of
Providence.

i) We are responsible for our lives and actions

If fate ruled, if everything we did was fixed and determined,
we could not be held accountable for our actions. And if chance
ruled, there would be no one there to hold us accountable. But if
Providence pertains, if God is not the only one who acts in His
world, if He gives us freedom and respects that freedom, then we

can and will be held to account, and our actions therefore have the dignity and significance of being ours.

ii) Fatalistic practices are rendered invalid

CANCER: Honk if you're a late Cancer! Striking to think how, had your mother held on for just a little longer, you would be a Leo – with staggeringly different consequences for your personality, attitude and, even, facial expression. Aren't the stars unbelievable?

LEO: Neptune in Capricorn counsels you to stay at home for the whole of next week eating ice-cream. Call your workplace first thing tomorrow to explain. And feel free to use my name, if necessary. Your boss is bound to be sympathetic.

TAURUS: Apology: last week, Taureans should have been urged to apply 'spit and polish' around the house, and not as it appeared. Thanks to all those who wrote in, enclosing cleaning bills.

From Psychic Psmith, in the *Sunday Telegraph Magazine,*
19 July 1998

Horoscopes (apart from Psychic Psmith's spoof ones, of course!) are a delusion, not because of some arbitrary rule, but because they tend to encourage a view of life that is based on fate. They tend to suggest that we are entirely ruled and determined by forces beyond ourselves, whereas in fact our own choices affect our destiny. Horoscopes tend to suggest that our future is fixed irrespective of our response to God, but in fact how we respond to God is a key factor in the sort of people we become and the sort of lives we live. (Not that if we respond to God our lives will go smoothly and happily – that is never promised – but that if we respond to God our lives will be interlaced with His life and His love and will be fruitful in myriad, lasting ways of which we may be mostly unaware.) Instead of passively being told what is going to happen and how we need to do fairly bland and banal things that would be true of anybody in any situation, we can actually take responsibility for our own actions and our own lives under God.

iii) Prayer can make a difference

If we lived in a universe ruled by fate, intercessory prayer would be pointless because everything would turn out the same whether we prayed or not. And if we lived in a universe ruled by chance, then there would be no one to pray to. But if the purposes of God take account of our choices and decisions and actions, then prayer can have an effect. Prayer, including intercession and petition, finds its rightful place in a providential world-view.

iv) We are never on the scrapheap

If God's plan is fixed in advance, then we might miss out on it. If it is unalterable, then it might pass us by. But if it adapts to take account of our choices and decisions, then it begins where we are – and not where we should be. God's purposes can always embrace us, in whatever state we are in, and however far we are from where and what we should be. However much and for however long we may have misread God's guidance, and however appallingly we may have betrayed Him, His purposes will regroup around us, and include us, and take us forward, and make us fruitful. And that seems to me to be pastorally and personally vital.

The following passage sums up that 'never on the scrapheap' hopefulness. The author, Ronald Rolheiser, is gently critical of an element of the Catholic tradition in which he was raised. The fault of which he writes is, however, one with which most of us will be familiar in our own denominations and backgrounds.

> If the Catholicism that I was raised in had a fault, and it did, it was precisely that it did not allow for mistakes. It demanded that you get it right the first time. There was supposed to be no need for a second chance. If you made a mistake, you lived with it and, like the rich young man, were doomed to be sad, at least for the rest of your life. A serious mistake was a permanent stigmatisation, a

mark that you wore like Cain. I have seen that mark on all sorts of people ... There is too little around to help them. We need a theology of brokenness. We need a theology which teaches us that even though we cannot unscramble an egg, God's grace lets us live happily and with renewed innocence far beyond any egg we may have scrambled. We need a theology that teaches us that God does not just give us one chance, but that every time we close a door he opens another one for us.[14]

And part of that theology will be an adaptive understanding of Providence such as we have been attempting in this chapter.

RESOURCES FOR FURTHER READING, PRAYER AND ACTION

On the issue of whether God suffers

J. Moltmann, *The Crucified God* (SCM Press, 2001). Particularly Chapter 6, arguing that He does.

Tom Weinandy, *Does God Suffer?* (T & T Clark, Edinburgh, 2000), arguing that He doesn't.

Richard Bauckham, 'Only the suffering God can help: Divine passibility in modern theology' in *Themelios*, 9.3 (April 1984), pp. 6–12.

Paul Fiddes, *The Creative Suffering of God* (Clarendon Press, 1992).

On Providence generally

C. S. Lewis, *The Horse and His Boy* (Collins). Lewis manages to convey many of the subtleties of a Christian view of Providence in this narrative. A very different view of Providence is expressed in one of George Macdonald's children's books, *At the Back of the North Wind* (Puffin Classics).

4 INCARNATION

"I thought incarnation was a motor magazine"

Alan Hargrave's book, *An Almighty Passion*, is subtitled 'Meeting God in Ordinary Life' and consists of stories from personal experience illustrating the great doctrines of Trinity, Incarnation, Passion and Resurrection. In the section on the Incarnation, he writes about his family's return to South America for a three-year stay. It did not begin well. There was no one to meet them when they arrived, exhausted, at Lima airport. They eventually got to the friends' house where they were to stay, but their young daughter took an instant dislike to the place and announced that she wanted to go home.

> One morning I go up to her room and discover to my dismay that she has packed her bag. 'What are you doing?' I ask. 'I'm leaving this horrible place and going home!' she exclaims. Her voice is absolutely firm, and her chin set like stone.
>
> I go downstairs and talk to my wife. We are concerned that she may just go out of the front gate and wander off. As we talk

she comes downstairs with her rucksack on her back and heads for the door. We try and tell her that it just isn't possible to go back to England, that we are thousands of miles away. But there is no reasoning with her.

'Right,' she says. 'I'm going' – and she walks out of the door. I look at my wife and decide there is only one thing to do. 'OK,' I say, 'I'll come with you' – and off we set.

We open the front gate. 'Which way?' I ask. 'Left,' she replies, without hesitation. We walk together to the end of the block. 'Which way now?' 'Straight on.' We cross the road and walk another block. 'Left again,' she proclaims without a trace of uncertainty. Another block. 'Right.' Another. 'Straight on.' We walk briskly on. 'Left,' 'Left,' 'Straight on,' 'Right,' 'Straight on.' But after a while the pace starts to slow and her hand grips mine a little more tightly.

After quite some time we arrive at yet another corner. 'Which way?' I ask gently. Her lip begins to quiver and she looks down at the floor. 'I don't know,' she says, and bursts into tears. I kneel down beside her on the path and hug her very tight. … We are both weeping profusely. … We have lost our way. After a lot of struggle, over the next few weeks and months, we will find it again. But it will not involve a journey back to England, or anywhere else for that matter.[1]

It is a parable of the human condition. We none of us actually know where we are going. There is no reasoning with us. We are driven by a sense of dissatisfaction with where we are. And we want to strike out on our own, if only to give ourselves the sense of being in control. The reality is, of course, that we are lost. And we have to go down many blocks, and find ourselves in many a blind alley, before, perhaps, we'll admit it.

It is a parable, too, about God. He doesn't stop us. He didn't stop Adam and Eve. He didn't stop Israel. He didn't stop the prodigal son. He didn't stop the Roman executioners. He doesn't stop us, when we strike out on our own. He doesn't stop us, but nor does

He abandon us. He comes with us. He joins us in our lostness. He does not leave us to our own reckless rebelliousness and its wretched consequences. He comes with us. He waits until we come to the necessary recognition of our condition. He holds us and weeps with us in the pain of our own making. And then slowly He helps us to a different way – a way that deals with our sense of dissatisfaction without giving in to our directionless defiance.

At heart, it is a parable about the Incarnation, because the Incarnation is about God joining us in our lostness. It is about God visiting and redeeming His people (Luke 1:68). It is about God becoming a human being. It is about God becoming flesh and making his dwelling among us (John 1:14). Indeed, the word 'Incarnation' means 'enfleshment'. It comes from the same word as 'carnal' and chilli con *carne* – chilli with meat, with flesh. In Jesus of Nazareth, says the doctrine of the Incarnation, God became utterly human, human in its entirety, human in all humanity's dimensions, including its physicality. In Jesus of Nazareth, God had His own human genotype. It was a human life that He lived and a human death that He died.

It is important to be careful what we mean by this, and what we *don't* mean. First, we don't mean that God became a human being in such a way as to cease to be God. He didn't *turn* into a human being. No, He took humanity up into Himself in the person of Jesus. He took *on* our nature – He did not put *off* His own. He *assumed* all that it means to be human – He did not leave behind any of what it means to be divine. He added the whole essence of humanity – He did not subtract any of the essence of deity. The Word became flesh but did not stop being the Word. We shall see why this is so important when we come to points 2 and 6 in particular.

Secondly, when we say that the Word became *flesh*, we do not mean that He took on human sinews alone. We don't mean that Jesus was some sort of hybrid, comprising a human body and a divine mind. No, He was a complete human being, with a human mind and human emotions and a human psyche and a human subconscious as well as a human body. He had everything that pertains to humanity, and everything that pertains to divinity. He was, and is, fully divine and fully human. At the Incarnation, He remained God, He took on being (completely) human, and, for roughly three decades of world history, He lived among us. Physicists estimate that the universe is approximately fourteen billion years old: how can three decades two millennia ago be of ultimate significance? Only if those three decades saw *God* living a human life. Only if they saw the theatre-owner appearing on his own stage, now turned by the resident company, inexplicably, into a scaffold. And if *that* is the case, then those thirty years are of profound and manifold significance, the surface of which we shall attempt to scratch a little in the rest of this chapter.

1. THE INCARNATION IS THE CENTRE-POINT OF HISTORY

'But when the time had fully come, God sent his Son, born of a woman ...' (Galatians 4:4). The conception and birth of Jesus constitute the arrival of *the time*, the bursting into history of its key moment. It was like the entry of the singers and the explosion of the Ode to Joy in the last movement of Beethoven's Ninth Symphony – the final, joyful eruption of the great theme for which the long introduction has been carefully preparing and to which it has been slowly building. The whole way in which the evangelists present the birth of Jesus reveals that they saw this event as the culmination of God's dealings with His people, and therefore of His purposes for the cosmos.

This truth is reflected in the Western way of dating historical events by reference to the (presumed) date of the birth of Jesus. When Dominican friars meet on Christmas Eve each year, they glory in this truth, as the cantor recites the following florid but powerful passage:

> Be comforted, be comforted, my people, says your God. For in the year 5199 from the creation of the world, when in the beginning God created heaven and earth, in the year 2957 from the flood, ... in the year 1510 from Moses and the going forth of the people of

> Israel from Egypt, in the year 1032 from the anointing of David as king, in the sixty-fifth week according to the prophecy of Daniel, in the one hundred and ninety-fourth Olympiad, in the year 752 from the foundation of the city of Rome, ... Jesus Christ, eternal God and Son of the eternal Father, willing to hallow the world by his most gracious coming, ... and nine months having passed since his conception, was born in Bethlehem of Juda, made man of the Virgin Mary.[2]

Chronologically, of course, it is rather quaint, but its theological instinct is spot on. As Professor John Webster comments:

> What is so remarkable about that passage is the highly elaborate set of references whereby Jesus' birth is dated: by reference to creation, ... to the Exodus, and by using both the Greek ['the one hundred and ninety-fourth Olympiad'] and the Roman ['in the year 752 from the foundation of the city of Rome'] methods of computing time. Such elaboration is no mere rhetorical ornament. Rather, it is making a profound theological affirmation of the universal significance of this one obscure and rather messy birth. All other times are relative to this birth, all other events are relative to this one event. For intersected by this one event, the whole range of human history comes to take on meaning, shape and coherence. By this one event all times are judged: it is their norm, the measure of their worth. And so henceforth human time is not some sort of continuum to be measured by reference to our own experience; rather time becomes time before and time after Christ, ante and post Christum. For in this simple, concentrated event all times fall before the one time, which is God's time with us.[3]

C. S. Lewis makes the same point in his poem, 'The Turn of the Tide'.[4] He pictures a 'deathly stillness' spreading from Bethlehem to Jerusalem to 'the islands and the North', to Rome, to Carthage and the Nile. He imagines the earth sending out a signal to the rest of the cosmos, 'Great Galactic lords' wondering and whispering whether this was the end of their story and their glory. He captures the moment at which the tide was neither going in nor going out, the moment of stillness before momentous change. And then suddenly the tide begins to rush in again, life returns and pulsates into space. The constellations are shaken, the spheres give out their music once more, but this time new and different. Heaven dances, and 'A shiver of re-birth and deliverance on the Earth went gliding.' Leprechauns dance, the Phoenix rises – astronomy and mythology, science and science fiction are orientated towards 'the cry of the One new-born'. It is his way of saying that here, in this event, something decisive has happened to the constitution of the cosmos. This is the hiatus of history and the turning-point of time.

'But how does this happen?' asks John Webster. 'What is the culminating event, the point in time which becomes the axis of all other times? It is the birth of a child. The point to which all times are moving is human, nameable. Here lies the source of order and meaning in human history, the origin and ultimate ground of all that is: Jesus, born of Mary.'[5]

Both Webster and Lewis are grasped by the fact that God has become part of His world. He has entered into its dimensions, its physicality, its chronology, its life, its set of interrelationships and constraints. He is here within it. He has always been present within it, of course, but not as *part of it* before. Something new and dramatic and eternal has happened which is relevant to every particle of matter and every moment of time. And this new, dramatic, eternal, cosmic event is accessible and comprehensible and relatable-to, because it is a human event, a birth, a life event for a peasant girl – and *the* Life Event for all that is. He has become one of us.

2. THE INCARNATION SHOWS US WHAT GOD IS LIKE

'No one has ever seen God. But the only-begotten One, Himself God, who rests on the breast of the Father – He has made Him known' (John 1:18, my translation).[6] If Jesus is God in human form, then we have some idea of what God is like. We are not left to guess. If we want to know what God is like, then it is to Jesus that we need to look. In Him, God actually lived a human life – and we have some handle on a human life. We know what human beings are like, we know how they interact, we have some idea of the range of emotions of which they are capable. So if God did indeed become a human being and live a human life, and if we have access to what happened when He did, then we can have some understanding of who He is and what He is like. In the Gospel stories of Jesus meeting with different people and being placed in different situations, we get to know something of His character – what His passions were, how He related to people, what angered Him, what astonished or delighted Him, how He responded to loyalty, betrayal or attack – and, in so doing, we get to know the character and heart of God.

In the life of Jesus, therefore, we see the life of God. In Jesus' love for us, we do not just experience the love of another fellow finite individual, we experience the love of God.[a] In His welcome, we are embraced by God's welcome. In His forgiveness, we may know God's forgiveness. In His assurance, we have the assurance of God Himself.

'If all this is so', says John Webster, 'Christmas is a festival of protest. The Christmas miracle initiates perpetual protest against inhuman gods; it spells the end of idols.'[7] For by telling us what God is like, the Incarnation also tells us what He is *not* like, what

---

[a] In Romans 5:8, Paul tells us that `God demonstrates his love for us in this: While we were still sinners, Christ died for us.' How can the death of a human being demonstrate the love of God? How can God demonstrate His love for us by getting someone else to die for us? In fact, isn't that immoral? Doesn't that give us a rather repulsive view of God, that He asks someone else to do the messy and painful bit of dying for us? Yes, it would be immoral and it would give a repulsive view of God – if it were indeed someone else who was doing the dying. But if Jesus is God living a human life and dying a human death, then it is not someone else who was dying for us – it is God Himself. Only if Jesus is God incarnate does the logic of Paul's statement work. The same is true of John 3:16. As the Coptic Pope Shenouda III writes, `Does this mean that God loved the world at the expense of Another? No, never! This verse cannot be understood properly unless God and Christ are One ...' (*The Divinity of Christ*, Coptic Orthodox Publishers Association, 1989, p.64).

He is thoroughly *unlike*. Christmas is thus a protest against all 'pictures of the divine which, far from according with his revealed nature, simply project our fears or fantasies and so obscure the real character of the one with whom we have to do.' That is why actual interaction with the Scriptures and the Gospels in particular is so important, not only to our spiritual growth and development, but also to our humanity and emotional freedom. Because we all project our own fears and fantasies onto God. We are all idolaters at heart. We all operate with distorted perceptions of who God is and what He thinks of us. And we need to have them corrected and refined. We have to know that our pictures and perceptions of God, distorted as they are by the pains and fears that we project out of what we might call the *un*well-springs of our own hearts, are precisely idols – not how God is in Himself. We have to see how He revealed Himself to be in the person of Jesus, and to allow that reality to correct *and heal* our distorted images so that they no longer oppress us. Because idols always oppress, whereas God as He is in Himself liberates. We need to have our views about God, and our pictures of God and our assumptions about God challenged, healed and enlarged by the vision of God in Christ. We need to allow the reality of the biblical Jesus into the imaginary world of our own speculation, projection and wishful thinking. We need to replace our invented godlets with the grandeur and goodness of the Christlike God. That is the nature of the pastoral task.

Let me give a couple of examples of how the reality of Jesus can correct and enlarge our view of God. First, the Incarnation teaches us the *humility of God*. We would not, I think, have guessed that God is humble. Humility is not one of the characteristics that we would instinctively have projected upon Him. Humility is not an obvious feature of other gods: the Greek and Roman gods, for example, squabble and jockey for position and power. Nor is humility a natural feature of our own interactions: whether in the office or on the prison block, where we are in the pecking order matters to us. (Of course, these two observations may be related: it is at least arguable that the Greek and Roman gods

135

were projections of our own experience and values. The fact that there are so many of them thus reflects the dividedness of the human community, and the fact that they jockey for position reflects our own self-promotion and pride.) It was only the belief that Jesus was divine and that in Him God had 'emptied himself by taking the form of a slave' (Philippians 2:7 MB[8]) and subjected Himself to a slave's death (Philippians 2:8) that established humility not only on the ethical map (Philippians 2:3), but also on the divine map. The Incarnation does not happen despite God's transcendent greatness, but because of His inherent humility. It is not a temporary exception to His greatness but a permanent demonstration of it. Humility is not something that God took on at the Incarnation, but part of who He eternally is. Indeed, it is because He is essentially humble that the Incarnation came naturally to Him. As Oliver O'Donovan comments:

> Naturally, it is paradoxical to speak of God as humble and self-effacing, but that is simply what the gospel teaches us to do, forcing us to revise all our natural conceptions of God's glory. God does not cease to be glorious and awe-inspiring and majestic because He is humble: it is our mistake to imagine that there is no place for lowliness within true majesty. True majesty is not afraid to stoop, because it cannot be destroyed or lessened by stooping.[9]

Or, as Gregory of Nyssa, the great fourth-century theologian from Cappadocia, put it, 'The greatness is glimpsed in the lowliness and its exaltation is not thereby reduced.'[10]

The second example of how the Incarnation changes our understanding of God is by unveiling, and embodying, the extent of *God's commitment to His world*. If Jesus is God incarnate, then we do not have a remote unknown God – one who keeps us at arm's length, who directs the campaign from a safe distance, like some First World War general. Rather, we have a God who enters into our world, our lives, our sufferings, our moral ugliness and our consequent mortality. We have a God who is not only committed to His world, but *internally* committed to it. He has entered into it, and it has entered into Him. Creator and creation are now bound inextricably together. And within the mess and pain of our still-fallen world, it is the life of God that He lives – the only unwarped presence in a warped environment.[b] And thus, as we reflect and meditate on the person of Jesus, our view of God is transformed – from stranger to lover, from tyrant to servant, from aloof to passionate.

It is essential that we do not begin with a pre-set view of God and then try and make Jesus fit that view. People sometimes speak as if we all know what 'God' means, and the only question is whether Jesus was/is that God. Does He fit our preconceived ideas of who God is, or doesn't He? And we argue one way or the other, Christians answering Yes, and others answering No. But that is to get the whole thing the wrong way round. Because in fact we do not know what 'God' means. There is no consensus, and the word is used radically differently by different people, with the result that the discussion inevitably gets off on the wrong foot. We do not know what God is like. How could we?

The Incarnation says, 'Begin with Jesus'. He is the One we have some sort of handle on, because He has lived a human life. We should begin with Him, and let the sort of person He is and the sort of life He lived and the sort of death He died shape and inform our understanding of God. As we do that, our view of God will become less idolatrous, less a projection of our own fears or our own hopes, our own limited personalities – and more in tune with God as He

[b] The best depictions of the unwarpedness of Christ amidst the warpedness of the rest of humanity must surely be Hieronymus Bosch's striking painting, *Christ Carrying the Cross*, and his subtler *The Crowning with Thorns*. Of the latter, Xavier Bray writes: 'His humble and serene expression contrasts with the ugliness of the tormentors cramped tightly around him. He gazes calmly at us, lost in his own thoughts amid the vile abuse of his aggressors, whose stares of hatred convert them into caricature-personifications of mockery and malice.' (*The Image of Christ*, the catalogue of the exhibition, *Seeing Salvation*, National Gallery Company Ltd., London, 2000, pp. 114–15.)

actually is and has shown Himself to be. To move from how Jesus is presented in the Gospels (which we can know) to an understanding of who God is (which we would not otherwise know) is a safer methodology to follow if the doctrine of the Incarnation is true. Indeed, it is the only safe methodology to follow if the doctrine of the Incarnation is true.[c]

3. THE INCARNATION SHOWS US WHAT IT IS TO BE HUMAN

If Jesus is both divine and human, then He not only shows us what God is like: He also shows us what human beings are *meant* to be like, what we were intended to be like, what we could be like and what, one day, by the gracious graft of God's Holy Spirit, we shall be like. If Jesus is God living a human life, then we have, in Him, the designer's blueprint for how human beings are meant to live. So if we want to know what it would look like to be completely human – human in a way that is unmarred and unscarred by the myriad ways in which we habitually distort our humanity – then it is to Jesus that we must turn. Here at last the glory of humanity is on view. Our assumptions about what it is to be human, what it is to be 'successful', will be radically different if we take Jesus as our model. As John Webster put it, 'if Christmas is a protest against idolatrous pictures of God, it is no less a protest against inhuman pictures of man.'[11]

To illustrate this, let me give two examples of how taking Jesus as our model transforms our view of what it is to be human. They are the same two examples that we used to illustrate how Jesus transforms our view of what *God* is like. After all, we are made

[c] Of course, this raises the questions, 'Why should we start with Jesus? Doesn't that presuppose belief in Him? How would we get to the point of believing in Him?' And part of the answer is that we look and see what beginning with Him would do to our understanding of God and how the human condition would look in the light of such a God. Seeing God as like Jesus, I suggest, removes many of the blockages to belief. But that is only part of an answer, and enough of this book is taken up with footnotes as it is!

in the image of God: transform the concept of divinity and there must be a corresponding change in the concept of humanity. So, first, the example of Jesus lays *humility* before us as an essential characteristic of a fully human mind-set. It would be easy to miss the stunning novelty of this contribution to ethical thinking. When pagan writers compiled lists of the virtues, they included many of the qualities we too take for granted – but humility was always conspicuous by its absence. Indeed, humility was not even reckoned a virtue at all in the pagan world before the Christian gospel came to it. In fact, it was usually regarded as a weakness. Markus Bockmuehl tells us that, in secular Greek, the word for humility was 'rarely used, and then in a derogatory sense to denote servile weakness, obsequious grovelling or on the other hand mean-spiritedness'.[12]

The coming of God as a human being, as a human baby, challenged and changed all that. Humility had, of course, been recognised and valued as a quality in the Jewish tradition, but it is in the humility and self-emptying of Christ in His Incarnation and death that arrogance and self-aggrandisement are most clearly shown up for the unpleasant and de-humanising things that they are. It is in the Incarnation and Cross that we see the humanity of humility.

Secondly, true humanness expresses itself in *commitment to and involvement in our world*, not in passionless detachment from it. There are religious traditions that teach us to respond to suffering by detaching ourselves from the world. The less we invest, the less we can lose. The more self-reliant we are, the less power anyone or anything can have over us. The less passion, the more poise. The less we desire, the less we shall be disappointed. The less we love, the less we shall be hurt. And if we had nothing else to go by, we might consider that to be quite good advice. It makes a lot of sense, on the face of it, to achieve a state in which life cannot hurt us.

But if our blueprint of what it is to be human is a person who entered into our world and entered into our suffering and got strung up on a cross, then our view of what it is to be human and live a human life will be very different. If He is our model, then we must not detach ourselves from the world. We must not try to make ourselves immune to its sufferings and pains, but (where those pains rightly impose themselves upon us) enter into them – there to live the life of Christ, as He entered into our world and there lived the life of God. The Incarnation gives us a vision of how to be human.

4. THE INCARNATION DEMONSTRATES AND BESTOWS DIGNITY ON HUMANITY

If someone not only sets up a company but also invests all they have in it, then you know that they believe in it. If God not only created human beings but also became one, then we may know that He believes in us and values us. What most dignifies us as a species is that God became one of us and lived a human life. God becoming human is the most massive affirmation of the project of creation in general and of the value of humanity in particular. If we are what God could (and chose to) become, then that gives us a dignity and a sanctity of which we would not otherwise dream. As the Dominican liturgy for Christmas Eve put it: Jesus Christ 'was willing to hallow the world by His most gracious coming'.

You occasionally see bits of graffiti or bumper stickers saying things like, 'Woman was God's second mistake.' The Incarnation shows that God's creation of men and women was not a mistake. He made us deliberately. He made us in His image. He made us with a view to becoming one of us. And He will never cease to be one of us. Nothing less than that is the extent of His stamp of approval upon us. (Though, actually, there is more, as we shall see in the chapters on the Cross and the Exaltation of Christ.) People sometimes say that they feel ennobled to belong to the same species as Shakespeare or Mozart or Gandhi: to belong to the same species as the One through whom all things were made is to have unassailable significance.

5. THE INCARNATION EFFECTS A TRANSFORMATION OF OUR CREATURELY PLIGHT

> Christmas … is not simply revelation. It does not simply impart new knowledge of who God is, but effects a transformation of our reality. For in this man, humanity is both remade and given new possibilities. In his birth is our birth: our wasted ways are restored, our endless capacity to undo our own lives is itself undone.[13]

John Webster is here suggesting that the Incarnation doesn't just show us something: it changes everything. It doesn't just reveal God to us (though, as we have seen, it does that): it *brings* God to us and *unites* Him to us. It doesn't just show us what we should be (though, as we have seen, it does that too): it is a vital stage in the process of *making* us what we should be.

A while ago, the Hubble Space Telescope was found to be malfunctioning, notoriously due to the fact that one poor scientist had put a minus sign where there should have been a plus sign in some mathematical (mis)calculation. The telescope was still operating, but it wasn't pointing in the right direction, and it was producing nothing like the clarity or the discoveries of which it was capable. All attempts to repair it from the ground failed. In the end, NASA figured out a way of correcting the fault, and, several years after its original launch, sent up a manned flight to dock with the orbiting telescope and cover it with a new lens, which would refocus it and enable it to carry out the work for which it was designed. This was not a fault that could be put right by remote control. Only by coming alongside and, indeed, into the stricken craft, could the necessary repairs be made and the telescope refocused and redirected. In the Incarnation, the Creator has docked with His malfunctioning creation. It is only in this way that what is wrong can be put right. Only by coming alongside us, and, indeed, becoming one of us, can He enable us to be and to do all that we were created for. When the manned flight *docked* with Hubble, the situation was materially changed and the telescope was instantly in possession of new possibilities. So is our plight changed and our humanity given new possibilities by the Incarnation of God in Jesus Christ.[d]

Ruth Burrows is a nun who has had a difficult and painful life. At the beginning of her remarkable autobiography, *Before the Living God*, she writes of the difference that the Incarnation makes to the experience of suffering:

> There is something awe inspiring in recalling the moment of one's birth. Human birth! I wish I could speak adequately of this deep mystery. I can do nothing but recall the unutterable wonder that God too had a human birth: he came into the world as we come into it; he came to drink with us the bitter cup of humanness. He drank it to the dregs, and *thereby transformed its bitterness*. Bitter it is and yet sweet, for his lips meet ours over the brim.[14]

I have a friend who is a calligrapher, and I have sometimes asked him to write out this passage as a present for new parents, because it seems to me to be rigorously realistic, and yet charged with a sense of the glory hidden within and behind the suffering of a fallen world. There is more to come which we shall explore in subsequent chapters, but the human condition is already transformed by the fact that God has entered it and shared it and taken it to Himself. He has docked with His creation, and creation is thereby in possession of infinite resources. As a sixth century prayer put it: 'When your Word took to himself this frail nature of ours, it was honored with the gift of eternity.'[15]

---

[d] It is not, of course, a perfect analogy. For one thing, we human beings need more than refocusing and redirecting and enabling to achieve our full potential. For another, in docking, the two link but do not become one. And for a third, after the repairs were complete, Hubble and the spacecraft separated, whereas, as we shall see when we consider the Ascension, God will never cease to be human in Jesus. But apart from all that, it's quite a good analogy! (All I can say in my own defence is that the Incarnation is an utterly unique event, so good analogies are actually impossible.)

6. THE INCARNATION MEANS THAT ONLY JESUS CAN RECONCILE US TO GOD

a) To reconcile us to God, He had to be fully human

If He had not been fully human, then the bridge between God and us would have been broken on the near side. However close God had come to us, there would have been a gap, a gulf, that would have prevented traffic from crossing over that bridge in either direction. Some evangelistic pamphlets use the picture of a bridge to explain how the Cross works. They depict God on one side of a chasm and us on the other. And they portray the Cross as the only way in which that chasm can be bridged. All other attempts to bridge the gap are shown to fail. In many ways, it is a helpful explanation of what the cross achieved. However, it is equally useful as an illustration of the Incarnation. If Jesus was not fully human, then the bridge does not reach us, and is therefore of no use to us.

Only if the bridge fits and belongs on both sides of the divide does it actually constitute a bridge. Only if Jesus fits and belongs both as a human being and as God does He actually constitute a means of bringing the two together.

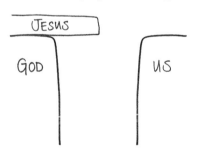

The early church had a slogan which encapsulated this point. They used to say, 'What is not assumed is not healed.' In other words, unless God took on Himself the whole of human nature at the Incarnation, then the whole of human nature is not healed. If part of what it means to be a human being is left out of Jesus, then part of what it means to be a human being is not put right. If Jesus is not fully human, then our full humanity is still cut off from God. But if Jesus is fully human as well as fully divine, then the two are no longer cut off. They can meet in Him. There can be traffic between the two. There can be relationship. Of course there is still the blockage of sin to be dealt with, but at least in the sinless person of Jesus, there is common ground between a holy God and His perishing people.

b) To reconcile us to God, He had to be fully divine

If He had not been fully divine, then the bridge between God and us would have been broken on the far side.

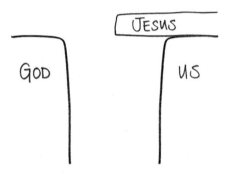

However close to God we attempted to get, we would have fallen short of participating in the divine nature (2 Peter 1:4), which is our intended destiny in the purposes of God. How can someone who is less than divine enable us to participate in the divine nature? To be united to a fellow-creature could not give us union with God. It is a good thing to be united with a fellow-creature. It can mediate to us our worth and our lovedness. It can give us a degree of intimacy and security. But it cannot give us salvation. It cannot bring us to God. It cannot unite us with Him and enable us to participate in the relationship of conversation and love that is the life of God.

But if Jesus is fully divine as well as fully human, then the bridge extends over the whole divide.

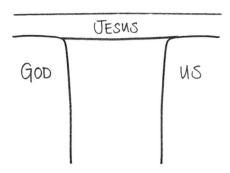

If Jesus is fully divine, then to be united with Him is to be united with God. If He is God, then He can raise us up to participate in the life of God. If He is God, then to be in Him is to be part of the life of God Himself.

That is why the church has always stood firm on the divinity of Jesus. Because a church that lets go of the divinity of Jesus has no gospel. Indeed, a church that lets go of the divinity of Jesus has ceased to be a church. For it can no longer offer access to the Father. It can no longer offer peace with God. It can no longer offer knowledge of what God is like. It can no longer invite us to join in the divine dance. For all these things are available 'through our Lord Jesus Christ' (Romans 5:1). And they are available through Him because He is the common ground, the sacred and sacrificial space where we and God can meet.

7. THE INCARNATION GUARANTEES THAT THE MORE GODLY WE BECOME, THE MORE HUMAN WE BECOME

One of the characters in John Osborne's play, *Look Back in Anger*, shouts out: 'If you can't bear the thought of messing up your nice, clean soul you'd better give up the whole idea of life, and become a saint. Because you'll never make it as a human being.'[16] Many people fear that there is some sort of a choice to be made between godliness and humanity. They fear that the further they go down the godliness route, the more they will have to leave behind their humanity. They fear that the Christian life will turn out to be the cuckoo in the nest of their humanity.

Before I was ordained, I went through a year of severe depression and doubt. It got to the point where I could not even pass a church or a chapel without experiencing a wave of nausea – which is not ideal for someone about to become a full-time church employee! One of the fears that fuelled this depression was the sense that the more consistently Christian I became, the more bits of my humanity I would have to leave behind. I feared that if I gave my life whole-heartedly to God, I would spend my whole time doing 'religious' things, like reading the Bible, praying, evangelism, worship. I didn't doubt that these were good things, but I didn't want to spend my whole time doing them. I wanted to be spending time with friends, listening to music, going to the theatre, frequenting cafés, walking on the fells and generally spending a lot of time eating! And I didn't see how I could justify such activities. I feared that becoming genuinely consistent in my Christian life would require me largely to leave such things behind. And they were what, for me, made life rich and enjoyable and worth living. (They still do.)

The Incarnation guarantees that we do not need to leave such things behind. The fact that Jesus is fully human as well as fully divine defuses those very real fears. For if we follow One who was, and remains, both divine and human, then the more like Him we become, the more godly *and the more human* we shall become. Because our model is fully human, there is nothing human that needs to be left behind. Sin alone needs to be left behind (Hebrews 12:1) because our model is sinless (Hebrews 4:15), and because sin *de*-humanises us. Nothing human needs to be lopped off our life. Of course, we are finite, so choices will need to be made over our use of time, in order to live a life of balance between all the different aspects of who we are. But the liberating point here is that following Christ *adds* to the creative possibilities for human life – it does not subtract from them. Nothing of what it is to be intrinsically human or intrinsically *me* is squeezed out of my life by following the God who became human in Jesus of Nazareth (and who, I am pleased to note, seems to have spent quite a lot of time eating as well!). Far from a consistent Christian life involving a truncated humanity, the very opposite is the case. A life that so focuses on the divine as to exclude the human is a denial of the Incarnation. The Roman author, Terence, is quoted as saying: 'I am a human being: I consider nothing human to be irrelevant to me.' Those who follow the God who became human in Jesus should defer to no one in the enthusiasm with which they adopt the same motto and the same attitude.

Perhaps I might illustrate this by pointing to the Virgin Birth, or, more accurately, the Virgin Conception of Jesus. The accounts of Jesus' conception and birth in Matthew and Luke affirm that Mary was a virgin when Jesus was conceived, and that the place and contribution of a human father were taken by the Holy Spirit. Now, in our experience, if two different kinds of animal are crossed, what you get is a hybrid (and a sterile one at that). If you cross a horse and a donkey, you get a mule, which has some of the characteristics of one and some of the characteristics of the other. So if Jesus had a human mother and a divine father, why is He not a hybrid? Why is He not half-human and half-divine, with some of the characteristics of humanity and some of the characteristics of divinity? How come He is *fully* divine and *fully* human, with all the necessary characteristics of both?

Because, I suggest, God's nature is such that, far from overwhelming everything else, He enables everything to be fully itself. When we contribute to something, we limit it; when God contributes to something, He liberates it. When we relate to someone, we draw out bits of who they are, and we inhibit other bits. I am a particular kind of person with one friend and a slightly different sort of person with another friend. It's not that I'm schizophrenic, nor that I'm (especially) hypocritical: it's just that different relationships bring out some aspects of who I am, and restrict others. That's what it is to be finite. But God, being infinite, restricts us in no way and enables us to be fully ourselves. So when

He relates in this special way with Mary, His contribution doesn't stop Mary's contribution from being fully itself. His presence co-exists with her presence and in no way threatens it. His nature co-exists with her nature and in no way stifles it. And the child that is born to her has both His divine nature and her human nature in their totality, and is no hybrid, mixture, or compromise.[e]

So it is with our human nature. It is not squeezed out by who He is or what He requires. It is not overwhelmed by God's nature. On the contrary, it is respected and embraced and enriched and enabled to be utterly and (sometimes painfully but) fulfillingly itself.

8. THE INCARNATION MEANS THAT THERE IS NO SPLIT BETWEEN THE 'SACRED' AND THE 'SECULAR', THE 'RELIGIOUS' AND THE 'ORDINARY'

The realisation that there is no split between sacred and secular or between religious and ordinary helped to defuse the fears that so tore at me in the year before my ordination. The freeing truth here was that the Incarnation refuses to allow us to divide up life in these ways. Because when God became a human being in Jesus, it was a *whole* human life that He lived. No part of human life is therefore outside God's concern. No part of human life cannot be shot through with the beauty and life of God. No part of human life is outside God's domain. Every part of Jesus' life spoke of God's character, even when He was not speaking explicitly about God: every part of our lives, therefore, can do the same, even when we are not explicitly telling people about Him.

For Jesus was not God only while He was doing religious things like teaching or healing or praying, and human while doing ordinary

[e] I have here used the language of 'natures' but I mean in no way to exclude the Coptic Church's understanding of Christ. Though Coptic Christians believe that Christ had only one nature, their intention is entirely orthodox and they affirm energetically that 'He was Perfect in His Divinity and Perfect in His humanity', a statement in the Common Formula of the Vienna Pro Oriente Conference of 1971.

things like eating, getting dressed and going to the toilet. He was no Jekyll and Hyde figure, sometimes human and sometimes divine. He was consistently and fully both. He was God when He was eating, God when He was sleeping, God when He was defecating. No part of human life is incapable of being taken up into the life of God. There can therefore be no dividing line between that which is God's domain and that which is not: He claims it all. He can indwell it all. God lived an 'ordinary' human life, and it thereby became extraordinary.

Some years ago, some friends of mine and I went for a walk on a hot summer's day. We came across a beautiful little country church, and went in and had a look around. The churchyard was so peaceful and quiet and lovely that we and one or two others sat down in the long grass and ate the sandwiches we had brought with us. The vicar arrived to say Evensong and turned us all out somewhat peremptorily, accusing us of defiling 'God's acre' – an old term for a churchyard. I later wrote to him and probably cheekily pointed out that the cattle on a thousand hills were His – I didn't think He was confined to the odd acre here and there! But the vicar clearly made a distinction between secular things like eating sandwiches and sacred things like graveyards, and ne'er the twain shall meet.

But they do meet, as the Incarnation – and the Lord's supper – make clear. To quote Rosemary Haughton, '... it is only the assurance that we know God fully, clearly, and only, in the human fact of Jesus of Nazareth which makes it impossible to reject any aspect of creation as irrelevant to the Kingdom of God'.[17] Or, as John Davies puts it, 'The closer we get to the sacred, the closer we get to the profane and the worldly. ... The Son of God comes sanctifying the shady and apparently ungodly sides of the world. This world, in spite of all its flaws, can be a dwelling for the divine.'[18] That is the world's hope, and our calling.

9. THE INCARNATION GIVES US A PATTERN FOR BALANCED CHRISTIAN LIVING

When I was going through my period of depression and doubt, one of the things that most frightened me was the suspicion – and this is related to the previous two points – that, if I were to give myself unreservedly to God, I would end up a fanatic. Now, fanaticism left me cold. It scared me rigid. And one of the lessons I learnt through the hard thinking that the experience prompted was that fanaticism is not different in *degree* from Christian faith. It's not having too much of a good thing. It's not Christian faith just taken a little too far. It's different *in kind*. It's a totally different kind of thing altogether. In fact, fanaticism is basically a heresy. For fanaticism emphasises the divine in the equation of our lives at the expense of the human.

Let me illustrate. The (not very funny, but, as it happens, rather apposite) story is told of a Christian man caught up in a flood. The waters came in to the ground level of his house, so he went up to the first floor. A boat came past and offered him a lift. 'No, thank you', he said in a Mr Bean sort of voice, 'I'm a Christian. God will look after me.' The waters continued to rise and he had to climb up on the roof. A helicopter whirled overhead, and a man on a rope was winched down, offering to take the man to safety. 'No, thank you', he replied. 'I'm a Christian. God will rescue me.' Eventually, the waters closed over the top of his house and he was drowned. He arrived at the proverbial pearly gates with a severe case of sense of humour failure. 'I was depending on you', he shouted at God. 'Why didn't you rescue me?' 'Well', said God, 'I sent you a boat and a helicopter – what more did you want?' The man was a fanatic. He expected God to work *directly* – and not, as He usually does, through people. Divine-only aid was all that was acceptable to him. He tried to live as much as possible at the God level, and as little as possible at the human level. But the Incarnation is about God becoming human. Serving God does not therefore mean abandoning our humanity. It does not mean ignoring it or disparaging it or downplaying it. A man in a boat can be just as much the rescue of God as an angel from heaven.

Fanaticism, I suggest, always does downplay the human. For example, you get people who say, 'You shouldn't take out an insurance policy – you should trust God.' I knew a couple whose church had told them that. Their house had subsequently burnt down and they had lost everything. How different from the balanced and sane attitude of Nehemiah, who, when the walls of Jerusalem were under threat of attack, 'prayed to our God and posted a guard day and night to meet this threat' (Nehemiah 4:9). For him, the divine (praying) and the human (posting a guard) went hand in hand. The one didn't render the other unnecessary or inappropriate. The two belonged together and were both essential. Together, they do justice to the dimensions of who we are: people made by, for and in the image of God.

People sometimes say, 'You shouldn't prepare sermons – you should allow God to tell you what to say.' Normally, you can tell when someone has followed this advice – the sermon is usually shallow, unstructured and interminable! Again, the mentality is that the divine is all you need; human study and preparation are somehow rendered superfluous by the Spirit. For the fanatic, the divine is all that matters. The divine must do everything. The divine must sweep all before it. Whereas, in a properly incarnational mind-set, the divine and the human belong together, with prayer and preparation not squeezing each other out.

A third example would be healing. For the fanatic, only healing that is direct really counts as God's work. And for the extreme fanatic, that means that accepting medical or psychiatric help demonstrates a lack of faith. A better model, which reflects the divine-human model we have in Christ, is provided by Burrswood, a home of healing in southern England, where prayer and conventional medicine go hand in hand.

Fourthly, you get the same attitude in the whole area of guidance. The fanatic tends to say 'God told me to ...' as if that makes their course of action immune from questioning. On the incarnational model, however, prayer and prophecy do not dispense with the need for the whole messy, human business of weighing up the alternatives, getting advice, listening to one's own heart and so on. Again, the divine does not swamp the human.

Lastly, when I was a young Christian at university, I remember being told, at a seminar on evangelism, that I should try to twist conversations round to the subject of God. This seems to me to be almost exactly the wrong advice. For what it implies is: 'I'm not interested in what you're interested in. All I'm interested in is God.' And that is a denial of the love of God. To show interest in what someone else is interested in, to listen to them, and take their stories and their interests and their passions seriously – that is to love them. That is to mediate God's love to them. To try and get the conversation away from such things as quickly as possible is not to take them seriously as people, not to mediate God's love to them. It is therefore to deny the gospel, not to proclaim it. And furthermore, it is to say, 'God is all that matters'. Whereas, if the Incarnation is true, the whole of creation matters profoundly to God. He became a human being in Jesus: nothing human is therefore irrelevant to Him.

The opposite tendency is equally distorting. There are those who find their whole security in human measures, and who fail to find their ultimate security in God, where alone it may be found. There are those who prepare their sermons, but fail to pray, fail to allow God to speak to them and shape their message, so that in the end it is only their own sterile words that are heard. There are those who rely on medical science alone, without acknowledging the Source of all healing, or who make their own decisions without any real reference to the God who knows them and loves them and desires the best for them. There are those who fail to pray for natural opportunities to talk to people about God, and who are generally too embarrassed to talk about Him even if the opportunity lands on their plate.

Both these tendencies are limiting and distorting. (They are just tendencies, of course. Nobody falls into one category exclusively. I am not here attacking actual people, merely types of mentality and categories of behaviour.) The Incarnation holds the human and the divine together, and our lives should attempt to do the same. That way, they will reflect something of the beauty and balance of the life of Jesus Himself.

10. THE INCARNATION IS THE MODEL FOR OUR PASTORAL CARE AND PRAYER

All too often the people who make the decisions which affect unemployed or homeless people have never themselves known what it is like to be unemployed or homeless. Can you solve a situation which you have not shared? The Gospel tells us that the Son of God was incarnated among us, that he put himself at the mercy of the place where he belonged. He descended to the bottom of a society which treated him as valueless and redundant – he ended up in the dregs. The Gospel tells us that the Son of God is to be found on the wrong side of human systems of religion, law and public opinion. He is our great priest because he has been the victim, and that is where his followers are called to be.[19]

God does not shout at us through a megaphone from a safe distance. He came down to us, became one of us, lived our life with us, suffered with us, offering up human life to God at every point. Similarly, our pastoral care of one another should not be detached instruction, but embodied identification. It will mean being there with one another and for one another. It will make us not passionless, but compassionate. People in the caring professions are sometimes told that they mustn't get emotionally involved. But that is both impossible and, if we look to Christ as our model, undesirable. Was He wrong to weep at the grave of Lazarus? (John 11:35) Was He wrong to love the rich young ruler who came to Him pastorally? (Mark 10:21) Of course it is right to set up appropriate boundaries around ourselves – and Jesus was quite prepared to say No to some of the demands people made upon Him (Luke 4:42–3). But if the

Incarnation is the model for our pastoral care, then it needs to be whole-hearted and full-bodied and genuinely compassionate.

Through the Incarnation, God entered into human life and lived there a life of total openness to and intimacy with God. We weren't able to live such a life ourselves, so God came amongst us, came as one of us, and lived that life on our behalf. So if we are to take the Incarnation as our model, we shall enter into situations of pain and despair and open them up to God. We shall find ourselves supporting people who are not able to live this episode of their lives in touch with the realities of God – either because they do not believe in Him, or because they are simply too hurt, too sad, too fearful, too depressed or too darn tired to turn to Him. So we have the privilege of coming into their situation and inviting God into it. (Silently and privately, unless they invite us to do so aloud.)

A man once went on a parachute jump for charity. He had never done one before, and, accidentally, he hit his head on the door of the aircraft as he jumped out. The instructor realised that he had knocked himself unconscious and would be unable to pull his ripcord to release the parachute. So he jumped out after the man, managed by plunging head-first to catch up with him, and catch hold of him – and pulled his own ripcord. He was just in time, and they both fell safely to earth. And that is similar to what is involved in pastoral care on the model of the Incarnation. First we need to get alongside the person, and then we need to do for them what they cannot do right now for themselves. We need to make use of the resources that are available, but which they are, for whatever reason, unable to tap for themselves. And the time will come when we need someone else to do the same for us.

11. THE INCARNATION IS POLITICALLY SUBVERSIVE

The front cover of *Private Eye*'s Christmas issue in 1988 carried a reproduction of Bruegel's *The Adoration of the Kings*. There was a balloon coming out of Jesus' mouth, singing, 'I was born under a wandering star'. One of the onlookers is leaning over to another and whispering, 'They're not married, you know', and the other is answering, 'No, but it's a stable relationship'. One of the soldiers is helpfully volunteering the opinion that 'Kevin's a nice name'. And Mary is saying to the kings, 'Do you know the Messiah?', to which they reply, 'Hum it and we'll sing along'.

The Gospels do not say they were kings, of course. Nevertheless, the painters have captured something of the politically subversive nature of the Incarnation by having kings kneeling at His manger. Because if the King of kings and Lord of lords has entered our world, then all other claims on our allegiance are relativised.

We so easily miss the political dimension of Jesus' birth, but it is there in almost every verse. When Mary sings, 'He has brought down rulers from their thrones but has lifted up the humble. He has filled the hungry with good things but has sent the rich away empty' (Luke 1:52–53), what is that if not politically subversive? When Zechariah sang of being delivered from our enemies and from the hands of those who hate us (Luke 1:71), it was fairly clear who he had in mind. As John Davies points out, 'If the Roman police were to hear this song, the next thing for Zechariah would be a spell of darkness in the local cells.'[20] When Herod heard from the wise men about the birth of a new king of the Jews, he felt threatened enough to take brutal action against the babies of the area. For Herod's claim to be king of the Jews was hardly watertight – he wasn't even fully Jewish.

An inscription has been found, dating from 9 BC, eulogising the Emperor Augustus, who was the adopted son of Julius Caesar, and therefore nominated himself 'son of god':

> The providence which has ordered the whole of our life ... has ordained the most perfect consummation for human life by giving to it Augustus ... and by sending in him, as it were, a saviour for us and for those who come after us, to make war to cease, to create order everywhere ...; the birthday of the god [Augustus] was the beginning for the world of the glad tidings that have come to men through him.[21]

So when the angel calls Jesus 'the Son of God' (Luke 1:35), when the shepherds are told that a 'Saviour' has been born to them (Luke 2:11), and that this amounts to 'glad tidings of great joy' (Luke 2:10), the message is clear: it is not powerful Caesar who's the Son of God, it's this insignificant peasant girl's utterly dependent baby, born on the eastern extremity of the Empire. It's not Caesar who's your Saviour, it's this helpless bundle in a cattle trough. It's not Caesar who makes war to cease – how could he? He became Emperor by violence, and the Empire was always sustained with the threat of war – it's this hungry, crying, armyless, vulnerable new-born.

That He was a threat to the Empire very quickly became obvious. It was not for nothing that He ended up on a Roman cross. And the ringleaders of those who proclaimed the kingship of Jesus often followed suit. The second volume of Luke's work (*The Acts of the Apostles*) ends with Paul in Rome, under house arrest, awaiting his execution, but still proclaiming (unwisely but boldly) the good news (not about Caesar but) about Jesus.

One of the traditional readings at Christmas carol services (Isaiah 9) reminds us that we have a God who shatters the yokes that burden people, takes away the heavy bars across their shoulders, breaks the rods of oppressors. We need therefore three things. We need, first, a bigger view of God. Is your God One who tears down tyrants from their thrones and sends the rich away empty? Is He One who scatters the proud? Is He the God of the political world as well as of your personal world? Can He be met with in the Cabinet as well as in the Quiet Time? We have a God who became human, became subject to the laws of physics, and the laws of an occupying force, and the laws of economics, who was pushed round by political whims, who was caught up in the whole human condition – and yet is Lord of it all. If He seems irrelevant to many of our contemporaries, maybe it's because we have confined Him to the 'sacred' and kept Him out of the real world. We need a bigger view of God, if we are to deal with Jesus.

Secondly, we need a smaller view of all other powers. One of the wonderful things about constitutional monarchy such as that that Britain has is that it puts politicians in their place. It prevents them from using the language of total power. Because the top spot is already taken. So they have to settle for and squabble over lesser positions. It is the same with all human power. The top spot is already taken. We may, therefore, give only our *secondary* allegiance to all other claimants, be they the state, the party, the monarch, the wife, the husband, the company, the church, the self. What we owe to our bosses and superiors is a respectful and loving refusal to worship at their shrine, because we are worshipping at the manger.

Thirdly, we need a bigger view of the powerless, the overlooked, the ignored and the despised. The Christmas story is a story of the plan of God being made known to the pawns of history, and the pawns of history therefore becoming great players in the plan of God: the young and morally suspected like Mary; the elderly and marginalised like Zechariah and Elizabeth and Simeon and Anna; the despised like the shepherds. These are the people God used to bring in His Kingdom – the Kingdom that would supplant all other kingdoms (Daniel 7; Luke 1:33; Revelation 11:15), all other claimants. They were ordinary people going about their ordinary tasks, people who heard and acted on what they heard, ordinary people who said Yes. Through them, God shook the Roman Empire to its roots. Through them, God challenges all ruthless perversions of power. Through them, through us, God will one day usher in His reign of peace.

Put quite simply, if Jesus is Lord, then Caesar isn't. And nor is anyone, or anything, else. Thus, whenever any human power has set itself up as demanding our ultimate allegiance and conformity, then the church has always found itself consciously attempting to subvert those claims. Be it Rome, Nazism, Communism or apartheid, the church has had to stand up against the arrogance of its claims and the inhumanity of its actions. I just ask whether there might be comparable injustices and oppressions in our own society and in our own day to which we are blinded by their social acceptability, and which we are called upon to expose and oppose and subvert in faithfulness to the Lordship of Jesus, and in the timeless tradition of the church, when it has lived up to its calling. Thanks to the Incarnation, we know God, and we will not worship any other power. Thanks to the Incarnation, we have seen the blueprint of humanity, and we will resist any oppression or distortion of it.

RESOURCES FOR FURTHER READING, PRAYER AND ACTION

Alan Hargrave, *An Almighty Passion: Meeting God in Ordinary life* (Triangle, SPCK, London, 2002). Alan is one of the warmest and most incarnational people I know, and something of that warmth and wisdom and sheer humanity pervades this book. (I hope that he'll accept this little testimonial in part payment for the time he expended and slipped discs he incurred helping me move house!) See in particular the section on Incarnation.

Bill Hybels and Rob Wilkins, *Losing to Win: How Loss can mean Gain* (Marshall Pickering, London, 1993). This is an extended and practical meditation on Paul's poem on the Incarnation and Cross in Philippians 2:1–11, advocating that we follow the trajectory of the Incarnation and become 'downwardly mobile'.

John Webster, 'The uncontrollable mystery on the bestial floor' in *Evangel*, Spring 1985, pp.10-12.

John Webster, *God is Here!: Believing in the Incarnation Today* (Marshalls Paperbacks, Basingstoke, 1983). Beautifully simple and helpful.

Monica Furlong, *Burrswood: Focus of Healing* (Hodder, 1978).

Or visit the Burrswood website: www.burrswood.org.uk.

John Davies, *Be Born in Us Today: The Message of the Incarnation* (Canterbury Press, Norwich, 1999). A delightful book, drawing on his years of ministry in South Africa, and bursting with fresh insight on the familiar accounts of Jesus' birth. And great for preachers trying to say something new at the Midnight service!

5 ATONEMENT

And then, one Thursday, nearly two thousand years after one man had been nailed to a tree for saying how great it would be to be nice to people for a change, a girl sitting on her own in a small café in Rickmansworth suddenly realised what it was that had been going wrong all this time, and she finally knew how the world could be made a good and happy place. This time it was right, it would work, and no one would have to get nailed to anything.

Sadly, however, before she could get to a phone to tell anyone about it, a terrible stupid catastrophe occurred, and the idea was lost forever.[1]

On the first page of *The Hitchhiker's Guide to the Galaxy*, Douglas Adams gives voice to the prevalent and persistent human sense that the world could and should be a good and happy place, if only we could find out what has been going wrong and put it right. Pretty well everybody feels that the world could and should be a good and happy place. Pretty well everybody knows it isn't. And pretty well everybody has a diagnosis and suggested cure. These are basic elements in just about any world-view.[a]

Adams introduces us, too, to an event that has been proffered as that cure. But he trivialises it as someone being 'nailed to a tree for saying how great it would be to be nice to people for a change'.[b] And he looks around for a solution that avoids the cost and scandal of the cross – 'no one would have to get nailed to anything'. Many cross-less cures have been offered. Much liberalism suggests an educational solution. Marxism promulgates a revolutionary solution. Various ethical traditions advocate a moral solution. Various religious traditions propose an escapist solution. Capitalism advances an economic form of Darwinism. And many (though not as many as used to) hold out the hope of a scientific solution to the problems of famine, over-population,

---

[a] N. T. Wright (following and amending Middleton and Walsh, *The Transforming Vision* (IVP, 1984)), suggests that the basic world-view questions are: 'who are we, where are we, what is wrong, and what is the solution?' (*The New Testament and the People of God*, SPCK, London, 1992, p. 123.) (He later added a fifth question, 'what time is it?' (*Jesus and the Victory of God*, SPCK, London, 1996, p. 138). I think I would want to add a sixth: 'where are we going?' This does not seem to me to be entirely covered by the first five.) Adams here focuses on questions three and four, though without giving any answers – the literary device of the idea being lost forever gets him out of having to attempt that!

[b] Unfortunately, this doesn't work historically. The Romans didn't nail people to trees for saying how great it would be to be nice to people. In fact, they didn't nail people to trees for any religious or spiritual ideas. They nailed people to crosses if they were perceived to be some sort of threat. They nailed people to crosses if they made a play for people's primary allegiance. They nailed people to crosses if they were subversive of the Empire and its values and practices. There must be a better historical reason for Jesus' death than Him telling people to be nice to one another. Jesus' teaching must have been at least capable of a more subversive interpretation than that, or He would never have been crucified. For a treatment of the historical question, 'why did Jesus die?' see chapter 12 of N. T. Wright's *Jesus and the Victory of God*.

illness and, maybe, ultimately death itself.

All of these approaches have some insight to share on the human condition, directly or indirectly. Many of them can contribute to the amelioration of our society and the improvement of our lot. Conversely, all of them can, directly or indirectly, exacerbate it. None of them, says the Cross, is *ultimately* radical enough. What is needed ultimately, says the Cross, is not education, nor revolution, nor self-improvement, nor detachment, nor competition, nor experimentation, but salvation. The root of the human malaise is not educational, social, moral, metaphysical, economic or scientific – these are all symptoms. The root of the human malaise is relational. (Such a diagnosis seems to me to resonate with the recognition (noted in Chapter 1) that it is relationships that are the most valuable and defining aspect of our lives – the very heart of our humanity, and our inhumanity.)

As we saw in Chapter 2, it is alienation from the God by whom and for whom we were made that is the cause of all our other alienations. Nothing that fails to address that root alienation can therefore claim to be the cure for the gone-wrongness of our species and our world. We need nothing less than atonement – to be at one with the Love from which we sprang. We need, like the prodigal, to come home, to know the running, embracing, forgiving, accepting, re-clothing, celebrating, dancing love of the Father.[c] And when we have come home, then, as Romans 8 affirms, creation can come home as well. And for that, Someone did have to get nailed to something.

In that act, the putting-right of creation reaches its climax. The history of salvation has been building up to this point. The doctrine of the Fall shows that we are fallen and therefore need saving. The doctrine of Creation shows that we are essentially good and therefore worth saving. The doctrine of the Incarnation shows that there is One who is both divine and human and is therefore able to save us. And now we come to the Cross of Christ which is where it

[c] I owe these descriptive words to Julia Harvey.

162

all happens. Here at the Cross, atonement is made – we are made at one with our Life-giver, Lover and Lord. Here at the Cross, we are forgiven and accepted and welcomed home. This act of injustice, cruelty and deicide is the low point of human history – and the self-definition of God. It is the fundamental unveiling of who God is and of who we have become. And somehow it is the bringing of those two together.

1. THE DEATH OF CHRIST SHOWS UP THE SERIOUSNESS OF SIN

I want to suggest three ways in which the Cross reveals to us the seriousness of sin. First, if, when God became a human being, and lived a human life of perfect love and goodness, we humans killed Him, then it shows how diabolically twisted we have become and how desperately we are in need of the salvation He holds out to us with open and lacerated arms. As the Scottish theologian, Tom Smail, put it:

> When we can get our hands on God, this is what we do to him. When the divine love that we see in Jesus comes among us, not only do we fail to imitate it, we turn upon it; not only are we not like him, but all the priorities by which we live turn us against him.[2]

Or, to quote the Russian theologian, Alexander Schmemann:

> No, this is not some misunderstanding, this is not some kind of accident. Christ is crucified because His goodness, His love, the blinding light that pours from Him, is something the people cannot stand. They cannot bear it because it exposes the evil they live by, which they conceal even from themselves.[3]

So, as Lesslie Newbigin said:

> ... essentially what happened was that the human race came face to face with its Creator and its response was to seek to destroy him.
>
> That utterly crucial and central moment in universal history is the ground on which we are compelled to say that all of us, the good and bad together, are sinners ...
>
> It is at that point where we are judged and condemned without distinction. The cross cannot be used as a banner for one part of humanity against another. It is the place where we are all, without distinction, unmasked as the enemies of God. But it is also the place where to all, without distinction, there is offered the unlimited kindness and love of God.[4]

Once again, the pictures of Hieronymus Bosch, portraying the unwarped Jesus surrounded by distorted humanity, make the point dramatically. What we did to God in Christ shows how warped we have become.

Secondly, if God needed to die in order to put us right, then there must be a lot wrong with us. If you call your doctor and she says, 'Take two aspirin and don't call me in the morning,' then whatever you have is probably not too serious. If, however, she sends you straight into hospital for an eight-hour operation, then it probably is. The kind of treatment that is needed reveals the seriousness of the diagnosis. The fact that it took the Cross to deal with human deformity means that that deformity must have been profound and intractable. If the Cross is the objective ground of our forgiveness, then we may take it that there is objective reality to our guilt, or other (less painful and degrading) ways might have been found to address our predicament.

Thirdly, the cry of dereliction declares the extent of the alienation from God which sin brings about. He who had always been conscious of the glory He had with the Father before the world began (John 17:5), whose intimacy with the Father was such that He spoke to Him as children would address their father ('Abba'), He who knew that His prayers were always heard (John 11:42) and that His knowledge of God was unique and complete (Matthew 11:27) – this same Jesus cries out from the cross, 'My God, my God, why have you forsaken me?' (Matthew 27:46). The Holy One of God utters the cry of sterile, sinful humanity. From the first human self-assertion against the person and purpose of the Life-giver, when He came looking for relationship and the human couple *hid* (Genesis 3:8), we have been aware of our alienation, aware of being cut off from the source of meaning and fulfilment and joy, of no longer being irrigated in the depths of our being (eg Psalm 42:1–2). Express it how we will, the human experience is shot through with elements of exile. That cry of dereliction lies behind all human cries, as that alienation lies behind all human ills. Coming so incongruously from the lips of Jesus, the cry of dereliction sums up the desolation that is the essential consequence of sin.

All this, of course, flies in the face of psychological fashion. It goes against the grain of contemporary ways of understanding ourselves. The current tendency is to soft-pedal guilt, to ignore it, deny it or explain it away. The (usually unexamined) assumption is that guilt feelings are negative things, unnecessary and unhealthy things, unreal things, and that we are better off learning not to be so hard on ourselves, to 'forgive' ourselves – which implies that we are the only ones we have hurt, and that forgiveness is a DIY activity. And of course there is such a thing as neurosis. There are such things as excessive or inappropriate guilt feelings. But the cross (and history[d], and conscience) insists that that is not all there is. There may be inappropriate guilt feelings but there are also thoroughly appropriate guilt feelings that we repress at our peril. Push them underground, and, like anything else we repress, they'll find (really unhealthy) ways of resurfacing.

Our culture has been called 'the culture of the victim'. But the

[d] As M. Scott Peck reminds us: 'Evil is not the figment of some medieval theologian's imagination. Auschwitz and My Lai and Jonestown are actual places and actually happened. Human evil is real.' *What Return Can I Make?* With Marilyn Von Walder and Patricia Kay (Arrow Books, London, 1990), p. 64.

Cross refuses to let us see ourselves *only* as victims. It refuses to let us repress the fact of our guilt, where it is a fact. It calls us to 'acknowledge and confess our manifold sins and wickedness; and that we should not dissemble nor cloak them before the face of Almighty God, our heavenly Father.'[5] For ultimately to deny or try to forget our guilt is to repress something that is true and significant about ourselves. It is not the whole truth, but it is the truth. And we are not actually being ourselves if we downplay it. That is why the liturgies of the Church make confession so central a part of everything we do together as Christians – that we may be ourselves, and be set free continuously to be more truly ourselves.

The Cross says, 'Your choices do matter. Your behaviour does affect not just you and those around you but the world and Him who made it. Look at the nails, look at the spear, look at the scourge – see how they reveal the reality and the seriousness of your guilt. For *this* is what it took to put things right – *this* is what it cost Him to prise you apart from all that mars you.' We often speak too glibly about hating the sin and loving the sinner, as if it were easy to tell, and tear, the two apart. But the extricability of sin and sinner is not a general truth – it is one of the hard-won consequences of the cross.

We may not be able to follow the complete logic or mechanics of the cross, but we find ourselves constrained by the fact that God found it necessary to die for us. And if He found it necessary to die for us, we may take it that our rationalisations and our excuses fail to cover up the reality of our guilt, or to bridge the abyss of our alienation. This realisation leads to a healthy taking of responsibility for our actions and our inactions. It leads us to own them as our own. Only thus can we avoid the perversion of self-righteousness. It is pretence, not confession, that leads to self-righteousness. As M. Scott Peck, the American psychiatrist, says:

> The poor in spirit do not commit evil. Evil is not committed by people who feel uncertain about their righteousness, who question

their own motives, who worry about betraying themselves. The evil in this world is committed by the spiritual fat cats who think that they are without sin because they are unwilling to suffer the discomfort of significant self-examination.

Unpleasant though it may be, the sense of personal sin is precisely that which keeps our sin from getting out of hand. It is quite painful at times, but it is a very great blessing because it is our one and only effective safeguard against our own proclivity for evil. St Thérèse of Lisieux put it so nicely in her gentle way: 'If you are willing to serenely bear the trial of being displeasing to yourself, you will be for Jesus a pleasant place of shelter.'[6]

Acknowledging our sinfulness leads away from self-righteousness. It also leads away from despair. For the Cross not only exposes our sinfulness – it also deals with it. It not only maps the abyss – it also bridges it. Only in the knowledge of the sufficiency of God's cure may we have the courage to attend to the seriousness of His diagnosis. Only Christianity can face the full horror of human evil and its consequences, because only Christianity has the Cross. Only the Christian gospel can absorb the appalling depths of human depravity within the continuing proclamation of God's love. We may only look Auschwitz in the face, if we keep looking Calvary in the face. To quote the words of one who experienced the concentration camps, 'There is no pit so deep that He is not deeper still.'[7]

2. THE DEATH OF CHRIST DEMONSTRATES THE DEPTH OF GOD'S LOVE

'You see, at just the right time, when we were still powerless, Christ died for the ungodly. Very rarely will anyone die for a righteous person, though for a good person someone might possibly dare to die. But God demonstrates his own love for us in this: While we were still sinners, Christ died for us' (Romans 5:6–8). We looked at this verse in the previous chapter and saw how it only works if we assume the divinity of Christ – otherwise it is God demonstrating His 'love' for us by getting *someone else* to die for us, which would not demonstrate *God's* love at all. John Stott expresses this point helpfully:

> If God had sent a man to us, as he had sent the prophets to Israel, we would have been grateful. If he had sent an angel, as he did to Mary at the annunciation, we would have counted it a great privilege. Yet in either case he would have sent us a third party, since men and angels are creatures of his making. But in sending his own Son, eternally begotten from his own Being, he was not sending a creature, a third party, but giving himself. The logic of this is inescapable. How could the Father's love have been demonstrated if he had sent someone else to us? No, since love is in its essence self-giving, then if God's love was seen in giving his Son, he must thereby have been giving himself.[8]

Notice here the point we have just made about the seriousness of sin: Paul has no compunction about calling us 'powerless', 'ungodly', 'sinners', 'enemies' (Romans 5:10), and, by implication, unrighteous and bad. He feels no need to soften his account of the human condition, because he knows (and goes on to say) that it is all covered by the Cross. Our sinfulness is not deeper than the love of God, nor is it wider than the Cross of Christ.

Notice, too, the statement of historical purpose. The crucifixion happened 'at just the right time'. It was not a hastily put-together Plan B. God's putting-right of creation did not surf the unpredictabilities of the historical flow: it was planned and prepared, and brought about at a time and place of God's omniscient choice.

And notice, finally, the assumption that must lie behind Paul's statement here. The Cross can only be a demonstration of God's love if it achieves something. If a father runs back into a burning building in order to rescue his child, that is a demonstration of his love. But if he jumps off a high building, shouting 'Look how much I love you!' it would demonstrate only his confusion and folly. Only if there is a rescue that is attempted (and preferably accomplished) can there be a love that is demonstrated.

Those accounts of the Cross, therefore, which portray it as a revelation of divine love but which *deny* that it contributes anything objective towards our salvation therefore cut off the branch they are sitting on. As so often, they are right in what they affirm and wrong in what they deny, and need to be supplemented by other approaches. Only if the Cross accomplishes something we could not have done for ourselves – 'when we were still powerless' – can it demonstrate God's own love for us. John, like Paul, holds together that which we so often tear apart – the subjective and the objective, the love demonstrated and the atonement achieved: 'This is love: not that we loved God, but that he loved us and sent his Son as an atoning sacrifice for our sins' (1 John 4:10).

3. THE DEATH OF CHRIST IS AN EXAMPLE FOR US TO FOLLOW

a) Non-retaliation

> For it is commendable if you bear up under the pain of unjust suffering because you are conscious of God. But how is it to your credit if you receive a beating for doing wrong and endure it? But if you suffer for doing good and you endure it, this is commendable before God. To this you were called, because Christ suffered for you, leaving you an example, that you should follow in his steps. 'He committed no sin, and no deceit was found in his mouth.' When they hurled their insults at him, he did not retaliate; when he suffered, he made no threats. Instead, he entrusted himself to him who judges justly.

> **1 Peter 2:19–23**

Evil develops a momentum of its own. When we retaliate, we add to that momentum. It's like those early computer tennis games, where you had to hit a ball back against your opponent, and the more times you hit the ball back, the more momentum it picked up, and the faster it went. So it is with the 'rally' of evil: the more we retaliate, the more momentum the whole process develops, and the more the situation accelerates out of control. It is easy to see this when we look at the Middle East conflict, for instance. One side commits some atrocity, the other hits back, the first retaliates against that retaliation, and so on, as more and more people get hurt, more and more people get sucked into the spiral of violence, and the possibility of peace retreats further and further into the distance. Jesus shows us a saner alternative, and that is to absorb the anger, to absorb the insults, the mockery, the violence. That way, the cycle is broken, the rally is not kept going. Evil loses its momentum – or at least doesn't gain it from us. That is what He preached in the Sermon on the Mount. That is what He practised on the Cross. And that is what the apostle urges us to imitate in our own experiences of ill-treatment and injustice.

b) Humility and unselfishness

When Paul is looking for an example of the humility and unselfishness that alone can make unity possible, it is to the Incarnation and the Cross that he turns:

> Do nothing out of selfish ambition or vain conceit, but in humility consider others better than yourselves. Each of you should look not only to your own interests, but also to the interests of others. Your attitude should be the same as that of Christ Jesus:

> Who, being in very nature God,
> did not consider equality with God
> something to be grasped,
> but made himself nothing,
> taking the very nature of a servant,
> being made in human likeness.

And being found in appearance as a human being,
he humbled himself
and became obedient to death –
even death on a cross!

Philippians 2:3–8

In Chapter 4, we looked at the humility of God as revealed in the Incarnation. Now we see the extent of that humility, the depths to which it was prepared to sink – 'all the way to death on a cross' (Philippians 2:8 M B). And on the Cross we see writ large the unselfishness of God, the *for-othersness* of God, the extent to which God was prepared to look to our interests rather than to His own. As Karl Barth puts it:

> God shows Himself to be the great and true God in the fact that He can and will let His grace bear this cost, that He is capable and willing and ready for this condescension, this act of extravagance, this far journey. What marks God out above all false gods is that they are not capable and ready for this. In their otherworldliness and supernaturalness and otherness, etc., the gods are a reflection of the human pride which will not unbend, which will not stoop to that which is beneath it. God is not proud. In His high majesty He is humble. It is in this high humility that He speaks and acts as the God who reconciles the world to Himself.[9]

There are many appropriate responses to this revelation of the character of God, including wonder, praise, gratitude, awe. But one essential response, insists Paul, is imitation. We are to go and do likewise. We are so to inculcate that attitude into ourselves, that it will naturally find beautiful embodiment in our own attitudes and actions. 'Your attitude should be the same as that of Christ Jesus' – the Jesus of the Incarnation and the Cross.

c) The creative giving up of power

> 'Put your sword back in its place,' Jesus said to him, 'for all who
> draw the sword will die by the sword. Do you think I cannot call
> on my Father, and he will at once put at my disposal more than
> twelve legions of angels? But how then would the Scriptures be
> fulfilled that say it must happen in this way?'
>
> **Matthew 26:52–54**

I am a big fan of Handel's music, and in particular his operas. I am
trying to 'collect' all forty or so of them, and I'm about half way
through. One of my favourites is *Berenice*, which I saw in a superb
production by the Cambridge Handel Opera Group. Its plot is
typically tortuous in its romantic and political machinations. It's
one of those 'A loves B, B loves C, C loves A but has been promised
to D' kind of plots. Add to that the fact that A is Queen of Egypt,
and Rome wants her to marry some Roman bigwig in order to
cement an alliance between Rome and Egypt against Rome's
current enemy, Pontus, and what you end up with is romantic,
political and diplomatic gridlock.

All the characters have their own goals, their own desires, their
own fears, their own interests which are mutually contradictory
and totally irreconcilable. Indeed, things seem to be heading
inexorably towards war, until one relatively minor character,
Arsace, renounces his claim on Selene, despite having been
promised her by the Queen. This act of relinquishing his power and
giving up his rights breaks the whole log-jam, and slowly the knot
unties as others relinquish their rights too. And in the final scene,
valid claims are waived, deceptions are forgiven, and harmony is
restored. Handel was a Christian, and so it is no coincidence that
he was attracted to plots such as this, which reflect in some small
way the self-abnegation of God on the Cross.

Nigel Biggar, the ethical thinker, has written that the lesson we
must learn 'about the just exercise of political power, about the

use of power to heal and build relationships, is that nothing quite becomes it so much as the giving it up ... So if we would exercise power justly, in such a way as to promote the flourishing of human community, then we must practise the art of surrendering it.'[10] Jesus had the power to protect Himself and promote Himself, but He forswore the use of it. Rome always used her legions to defend her interests: God declined so to use His. To follow the example of the Cross means to sit loose to power, to practise the art of surrendering it, and to determine to use such power as we have justly, wisely, creatively and sacrificially.

d) The valuing of the powerless

> For the message of the cross is foolishness to those who are perishing, but to us who are being saved it is the power of God. For it is written: 'I will destroy the wisdom of the wise; the intelligence of the intelligent I will frustrate.' Where are the wise? Where are the scholars? Where are the philosophers of this age? Has not God made foolish the wisdom of the world? ... Brothers and sisters, think of what you were when you were called. Not many of you were wise by human standards; not many were influential; not many were of noble birth. But God chose the foolish things of the world to shame the wise; God chose the weak things of the world to shame the strong. He chose the lowly things of this world and the despised things – and the things that are not – to nullify the things that are, so that no-one may boast before him.
>
> **1 Corinthians 1:18–20, 26–29**

If God, at His moment of clearest revelation and self-definition, took the form of a dying slave (Philippians 2:7–8), then what does that do to the ways in which we value (or fail to value) one another? Paul tackles that question head-on in 1 Corinthians 1, and it makes for radical reading. The world looks at the Cross and sees failure, foolishness, weakness, shame and disgrace. What it *should* see, says Paul, is the power and wisdom of God (v.24). Similarly, the world looks at the Christian Church and sees a bunch of low-class, low-grade, uneducated no-hopers. What it *should* see is a community of people chosen and valued by God. The Cross and the Church therefore constitute a challenge to the world's way of looking at things, a challenge to the world's values and assumptions and attitudes. What the world despises, God cherishes.

And that means that, if we are to let the Cross shape our way of seeing, we may look dismissively upon no human person at all, however lowly, however shamed. We like to be with attractive people, intelligent people, witty people, important people, entertaining people, influential people, those who don't require time and effort to get to know. That's why we name-drop our connections. That is why our society is so obsessed with celebrities. God, however, is not impressed by such meaningless criteria. He likes to be with hurt people, despised people, ignored people, sinful people, crushed people, real people. That was His teaching (Luke 14:12–24). That was His practice in life (Luke 15:1–2) and in death (Luke 23:32). That was reflected in the make-up of the early Church ('Not many of you were wise by human standards; not many were influential; not many were of noble birth'). That is the standard by which we must calibrate our own values and assumptions.

I received this circular letter from a friend who had been a dentist in The Falkland Islands. Bill Mahood was approaching 70 when he became a Christian, and his letter was a reflection on what he had learnt as a result:

> Reading another letter from a very dear friend in the Falklands brought to mind dear Mabel, an old servant in the Hospital there, who had had a very hard upbringing and whom many looked on as being rather mentally deficient. Regrettably, this dear friend was burned to death in the fire which destroyed the old Hospital, on 10th April 1984. Dear Mabel died as she lived. In the seven-page account of the fire in Sir Rex Hunt's book, My Falkland Days, she gets not even a line – only 'and Mabel Neilson'. To this

day she lies in the cemetery in Stanley in an unmarked grave.

This made me think of another great friend, Craig Stewart, a Down's syndrome man of about 30 years at the time. I met him when working in the L'Arche community[e] in Vancouver and, like many such people, he could teach us much of love and of being loved, and thus teach us much about proper relations. I cherish the thought of these people, wonderful in their own way, great friends, great people to know, but not recognised by this world, whose values seem to have gone so awry.

I often look at Mabel's letters which I shall always keep close to me. Wherever I was, Mabel wrote – to Australia, Canada, South Africa, England, the centre of Mabel's world. She must have spent hours writing these letters. Or I think of taking Craig for a walk and the first thing he did was to put his hand into mine. He didn't want to know how much money I had, how many degrees, nor indeed my failures in life.

What of Jesus? Wasn't He rejected and put to death by those in power? While no great Christian, I have a firm belief that the Mabels and Craigs of this world can show us something of the depth of God's love for us, and that we are of some worth in the world.

Well, he claims to be no great Christian, but he has learned one of the great and central truths of the Cross, which is that it transforms the way we judge and estimate and evaluate ourselves and others, and it puts those who were at the bottom of the pile on the top.

---

[e] The L'Arche communities were founded by Jean Vanier as places where those with learning difficulties and volunteers live together in community. There are now L'Arche communities all around the world. In many ways, L'Arche attempts to embody just this reversal of values of which the Cross speaks. As Jean Vanier himself put it: 'I live with people who cannot speak, who are rejected, seen as "mad" and all too often kept away from the Good News of Jesus.' (Jean Vanier, *A Door of Hope* (Hodder & Stoughton, 1996), p.7.) But he and his co-workers have time for them, live with them, learn from them.

4. THE DEATH OF CHRIST WAS 'IN OUR PLACE'

> He himself bore our sins in his own body on the tree, so that we might die to sins and live for righteousness; by his wounds you have been healed.

1 Peter 2:24

This verse is of course referring to the great Servant song in Isaiah 53:

> Surely he ['my servant'] took up our infirmities
>   and carried our sorrows,
>   yet we considered him stricken by God,
>   smitten by him, and afflicted.
> But he was pierced for our transgressions,
>   he was crushed for our iniquities;
> the punishment that brought us peace was upon him,
>   and by his wounds we are healed.
> We all, like sheep, have gone astray,
>   each one of us has turned to our own way;
>   and the Lord has laid on him
>   the iniquity of us all.

Isaiah 53:4–6

Looking back in the light of the Crucifixion and Resurrection, in the light of all that Jesus had taught them about His death both before and after it happened[11], and in the light of their own experience of forgiveness and receiving the Spirit and the new situation – new age, even – that this brought about, the early Church found that this passage from Isaiah helped them to understand what was going on in the ministry (Matthew 8:17) and death of Jesus.[f] He went to

---

[f] Joachim Jeremias wrote that 'No other passage from the Old Testament was as important to the Church as Isaiah 53' (*The Eucharistic Words of Jesus*, OUP, 1955, p. 228). Morna Hooker disagreed (*Jesus and the Servant*, SPCK, London, 1959). See the judicious but creative summary of the issues in N. T. Wright's *Jesus and the Victory of God* (SPCK, London, 1996, pp. 588–91, 597–604).

His death, not just as an individual – or why would His death be of more significance than the execution of any other victim of injustice? He went to His death as the Servant, the representative of Israel, and therefore of humanity, and therefore of the cosmos. He went to His death as '*My* servant' – as the *divinely chosen and accepted* representative of Israel, humanity and the cosmos. And as our representative, He died for us, on our behalf, in our place, taking upon Himself the fact and guilt of our sin. This joyful conviction inspired the praise, teaching and mission of the early Church.

It even shaped the way in which they heard and told the story of Jesus' death. In particular, they saw Barabbas as the archetypal sinner, the first person who could say, 'Jesus died in my place.' To quote Tom Wright:

> Luke describes the event in such a way that we can hardly miss the point. Barabbas is guilty of some of the crimes of which Jesus, though innocent, is charged: stirring up the people, leading a rebellion ... Either Barabbas or Jesus must die; either the one who stands for violent revolution, which Jesus has opposed from the beginning, or the one who has offered and urged the way of peace. Jesus ends up dying the death appropriate for the violent rebel. He predicted that he would be 'reckoned with the lawless' (22:37) [a quotation from Isaiah 53:12], and it has happened all too soon.
>
> Luke's readers are by now used to seeing Jesus in company with tax-collectors and sinners. ... We were not, perhaps, quite prepared for it to end like this. It is one thing for Jesus to go in and eat with a man who is a sinner (19:7). It is a considerable step beyond that for him to go off and die the death of the violent rebel.
>
> But this is in fact the climax and focus of the whole gospel.

This is the point for which Luke has been preparing us all along. All sinners, all rebels, all the human race are invited to see themselves in the figure of Barabbas; and, as we do so, we discover in this story that Jesus comes to take our place, under condemnation for sins and wickednesses great and small. In the strange justice of God, which overrules the unjust 'justice' of Rome and every human system, God's mercy reaches out where human mercy could not, not only sharing, but in this case substituting for, the sinner's fate.[12]

So effective is this substitution that all our moral muck and grime are extricated from us and absorbed by Him. He takes our place. He takes our sin. Paul goes so far as to say that He *becomes sin* for us, so that we might become the righteousness of God (2 Corinthians 5:21). That is the great exchange that He effected for us. No wonder He felt Himself to be forsaken by God: because all that cuts us off from meaning, and purpose, and hope, and beauty, and life and love, was now cutting Him off instead.

All of this means that, in some sense that we shall never fully understand, we need no longer be the person who did the things we did. We can be instead the untarnished, untainted, unashamed, and unimplicated people we were created to be. Our life histories can be washed and our beings unburdened. No one, perhaps, has depicted this unburdening more simply and powerfully than John Bunyan:

Now I saw in my dream that the highway up which Christian was to go was fenced on either side with a wall, and that wall was called Salvation. Up this way therefore did burdened Christian run, but not without great difficulty, because of the load on his back. He ran thus till he came at a place somewhat ascending, and upon that place stood a cross, and a little below in the bottom, a sepulchre. So I saw in my dream that just as Christian came up with the cross, his burden loosed from off his shoulders, and fell from off his back, and began to tumble, and so continued to do, till it came to the mouth of the sepulchre where it fell in, and I saw it no more.

Then was Christian glad and lightsome, and said with a merry heart, 'He hath given me rest, by his sorrow, and life, by his death.'[13]

Some have objected that this substitution is immoral, for it involves God punishing an innocent person (Jesus) for the sins of guilty people (us). It is not immoral, however, as long as we remember two points. First, Jesus is fully human and is therefore able to represent us. He is so fully identified with us as to be able to act as our representative. If the Indian Government had an issue with the German Government, and rounded up a group of Spanish tourists and imprisoned them in protest at what the German Government had done, that would be arbitrary and inappropriate, because they are an innocent third party to this dispute. If, however, the Indian Government called in the German ambassador and made representations to him or her, then that would be an acceptable way of dealing with the dispute, because the ambassador is there precisely as a representative of the German Government.[8] Jesus is fully human, fully identified with us in our fallen humanity by the Incarnation and in our sinfulness by the Cross. He is therefore not an inappropriate representative of us.

Secondly, we need to remember that Jesus is fully divine, and therefore God is not punishing an innocent third party but taking the sin and the guilt and the alienation and the death onto Himself – not onto someone else. As we saw earlier, *Christ* dying for us is God loving us. At the Cross, God takes our sin and guilt *onto Himself,* and there disposes of it. Our cut-offness and alienation is absorbed into the being of God, and thus dissolved. The cry of

---

[8] This illustration is adapted from a similar one used by Professor O'Donovan in his lectures on the Thirty Nine Articles, which were written up (without the inclusion of this illustration) in his *On the Thirty Nine Articles: A Conversation with Tudor Christianity* (Paternoster Press, 1986) – in my view, one of the finest theological books of the past twenty years.

dereliction is taken up into God Himself – experienced, expressed and overcome.[h]

There are, of course, problems with this picture of what happened on the Cross. That is hardly surprising, given that it was an utterly unique event. It is worth noting, however, that there are vital truths lost if we jettison it. In his profound little book, *Does Jesus Know Us? Do We Know Him?*, the great twentieth-century Roman Catholic theologian, Hans Urs von Balthasar, makes the point that, as Jesus was sinless, there would be areas of human experience that were completely unknown to Him unless He had taken our sins upon Him:

> Even if Jesus "in every respect has been tempted as we are, yet without sinning" (Heb 4:15), does he not still lack the one vital thing, knowledge of how the sinner feels? He can try to imagine it, just as a healthy person can imagine how a sick person feels, but there remains a fundamental difference between imagination and experience.[14]

He therefore argues that there are parts of human experience that Jesus could only know by taking our place and making them His own. 'Only now, having passed through the dark terrain, the chaos of human sin, has Jesus gained complete knowledge of man.'[15] Only by taking our sin upon Him does Jesus know the full human condition from the inside. And only that which is assumed can be

---

[h] How can God take our sin upon Himself without being morally compromised? It is vital, of course, that He is not morally compromised. The uncompromised goodness of God is part of our message (1 John 1:5). The fatal problem with pantheism is its implication that, if all things are in God, then there is evil in God as well as good. Why is the same not the case with the Cross? If He takes sin upon Himself at the Cross, why is there not evil within the being of God? I do not know. However, the issue of ritual impurity may provide a useful analogy. When Jesus touched people who had leprosy, He should have become ritually impure. What happened instead was that the leper became whole. There is an exchange between the two, but, Jesus being who He is, the impurity doesn't 'stick' on Him. It may be the same with the Cross. He takes our sin upon Him, but, being who He is, and dying as He did, it does not 'stick' within the person and nature of God. The point is that sin is not just assumed at the Cross – it is dealt with and disposed of. It dissolves on contact with the undiluted holiness of God.

healed. Therefore Balthasar gladly proclaims the mystery of this substitution: 'God's infinite love for fallen man is the same as that of his Son, whose love for us was so great that he took our guilt upon himself in order to restore our relationship with the Father.'[16]

5. THE DEATH OF CHRIST RECONCILED JEW AND GENTILE, TO CREATE ONE NEW HUMANITY

So then, remember this! In human terms, that is, in your 'flesh', you are 'Gentiles'. You are the people who the so-called 'circumcision' refer to as the so-called 'uncircumcision' – circumcision, of course, being something done by human hands to human flesh. Remember that at that time you were separate from Christ, excluded from citizenship in Israel and foreigners to the covenants of the promise, without hope and without God in the world. But now in Christ Jesus you who once were far away have been brought near through the blood of Christ. For he himself is our peace, who has made the two one and has destroyed the barrier, the dividing wall of hostility, by abolishing in his flesh the law with its commandments and regulations. His purpose was to create in himself one new humanity out of the two, thus making peace, and in this one body to reconcile both of them to God through the cross, by which he put to death their hostility. He came and preached peace to you who were far away and peace to those who were near. For through him we both have access to the Father by one Spirit.

Ephesians 2:11–18, v.11 NTW[17]

In Genesis 3, we see that when people cut themselves off from God, they are thereby no longer at peace with each other (Adam blames Eve, Cain kills Abel), with the natural order (childbirth becomes excruciating, work becomes toil), or within themselves (they feel ashamed and cover themselves). The theological division is the root cause of all the other (sociological, ecological and psychological) divisions. Healing the theological division should therefore have an impact on all the other divisions, and that is what we find. If the Cross reconciles us to God, it also reconciles us to one another. If two people are in harmony with God, then they are *objectively* in harmony with each another, however deep their hostility might in practice be. Like so much in the Christian life, it is then a matter of their relationship becoming what it intrinsically is.

Paul insists that the great historic division between Jew and non-Jew has finally been overcome in Israel's Messiah. The Cross not only operates vertically, as it were, but horizontally. And it was Paul's passion that this should be lived out in the Christian communities he founded or wrote to. The Church was to declare to the world, and to the unseen forces that shape and misshape it, that it is possible to live in harmony across the barriers and divides that we put up against one another. And that harmony is to be found in Christ, because of what He did on the Cross. If He reconciled us to God, then He reconciled us to one another, and we are to be a reconciled community spreading a message of reconciliation. The Church, if it is to be faithful to the Cross, must live in defiance of the hostilities and enmities that so lace and lacerate our world.

It's not often that one remembers word for word the opening of a sermon one heard twenty years ago. (And I like to think that doesn't matter much: after all, I can't remember many meals I had twenty years ago, either, but they did me good at the time! But maybe I'm being professionally defensive.) However, I do remember the opening words of a sermon our Pastoral Theology lecturer gave when I was at theological college. He began by saying, 'On the first Good Friday, the veil of the temple was ripped from top to bottom. And the Church has spent the last two thousand years trying to sew it back up again!' He meant in particular the ways in which the Church has often in practice denied people the access to God that Jesus won on the Cross, but I think it also applies to the ways in which we cut ourselves off from each other.

The Church, which is meant to be an example, a proof of the way in which division and faction and conflict and suspicion can be overcome, has far too frequently fragmented along lines of doctrine, geography, race, language, class, age and taste. Jewish Christians and Gentile Christians still often congregate separately. One church I worked for has a Ghanaian fellowship that meets in its building on Sunday afternoons, separately from the mainly white, mainly young, mainly urban professional congregation that meets there on Sunday evenings. There are many reasons for such practice, and I am not blaming anyone for it: it is easier to associate with people of similar background and tradition. I am simply pointing out that it fails to demonstrate the achievement of the Cross. As Tom Wright put it, commenting on this passage from Ephesians, 'If our churches are still divided in any way along racial or cultural lines, he [Paul] would say that our gospel, our very grasp of the meaning of Jesus' death, is called into question.'[18]

Some statistical studies have shown that churches grow faster if they are socially and racially homogeneous. Churches that are basically middle-class or basically working-class or basically young grow faster than ones which are mixed. Maybe. It's just not what the church is for. We are meant to be a model of how, when you come into relationship with God through what Christ did on the Cross, you begin to have your other relationships healed as well. Our future is to be a great multitude that no-one could number, from every nation, tribe, people and language, standing before the throne of God, and before the Lamb who has won us for God and welded us to one another – and it is the task of the Church to be a pointer to that reality here and now. To attempt less is to hide the Cross, and to sew back up the veil.

6. THE DEATH OF CHRIST EMBRACED THE WHOLE UNIVERSE

For God was pleased to have all his fullness dwell in him, and through him to reconcile to himself all things, whether things on

183

> earth or things in heaven, by making peace through his blood,
> shed on the cross.
>
> **Colossians 1:19–20**

It is not just we who are reconciled at the Cross, but all things, heaven and earth, the whole shebang. Everything that mars the created order has been dealt with in principle on the Cross. As H. E. W. Turner put it, 'Redeemed man also lives in a redeemed universe, and a world in which the Cross and Resurrection have taken place can never be the same again.'[19] It may look much the same, and be subject at present to the same old forces of entropy and decay, but a new word has been spoken over it, and a new future secured for it. Creation has been welded to its Creator by the Incarnation and the Ascension, it has been delineated from all that makes for its violence or dissolution by the Cross, and its future has been revealed to it in the resurrection of Jesus. Its groans (Romans 8:22) have been heard just as surely as were the cries of the people of Israel in Egypt (Exodus 3:7), and those groans have been transformed by the suffering of the Cross from death-pangs into labour-pains. And, as a result of Jesus' death-pangs, a new and healed creation will be brought to birth. This is what Oliver Quick called the 'Gospel of the New World'.[20]

Stephen Hawking recalls how a research student at Cambridge discovered 'objects in the sky that were emitting regular pulses of radio waves. At first Bell and her supervisor, Antony Hewish, thought they might have made contact with an alien civilisation in the galaxy! Indeed, at the seminar at which they announced their discovery, I remember that they called the first four sources to be found LGM 1–4, *LGM* standing for "Little Green Men".' Sadly, they turned out to be the rather more prosaic but still exciting phenomena of rotating neutron stars, and constituted, writes Hawking, 'the first positive evidence that neutron stars existed'.[21] Some have suggested that, if there do turn out to be little green men, then maybe Christ would be incarnated as a little green man and die to redeem that race. While wanting in no way to place restrictions on what God could or could not do, we can say, from the perspective of Paul's theology, that there would be no need. Calvary availed for the cosmos. The scope of the Cross was co-extensive with the scope of the Fall. There is nothing, now that the Cross has happened, that cannot be redeemed. There is nothing that cannot now be put right. There is nothing – evil apart – that cannot be set on an eternal footing. There is nowhere you can go where you fall off ground that has been reclaimed by the Cross. The Cross has said it all, to quote Matt Redman – and the Cross has done it all.

7. THE DEATH OF CHRIST REVEALS THAT GOD CAN SUFFER

Two gentlemen wearing dog collars found themselves sitting beside one another on a plane. One of them, worryingly thinking that a theological bone of contention would be a good conversational opening gambit, said to the other, 'Do you believe in infant baptism?' To which the other one replied, '*Believe* in it? I've seen it done!' Similarly, a good reply to the question, 'Do you believe God can suffer?' would be, '*Believe* it? I've seen it happen!' The Cross shows it happening, and therefore challenges all pictures of God as being remote, uninvolved, unconcerned, uncommitted, uncaring, hermetically sealed, immune or self-protected. As we saw in Chapter 3, He is not *forced* to suffer. But He did and does choose to love us, and, in a fallen world, to love is to suffer. His suffering is therefore free and not forced – but it is real, or, when we look at Christ, we do not see God as He is in Himself.[i] He is free to suffer because He is free to love.

[i] That is why, so far as I know, pretty well all Christians agree that God in Christ suffered on the cross. What that means for the old Greek metaphysical principle that God is 'impassible' (ie not subject to suffering) is hotly debated. Some try and reconcile the Cross with impassibility: others simply dismiss impassibility as an incompatible hang-over from Greek philosophy. Even those who try to hold on in some sense to the impassibility of God nevertheless believe in a God who 'could really and not just fictitiously suffer' (*Whatever Happened to the Human Mind?* by Eric Mascall, SPCK, London, 1980, p.84). Traditionally, Christian theology has always denied that the Father suffers: today, many theologians are questioning that. But even those who hold to this tradition agree that suffering in some sense intruded into the Godhead. Otherwise, Jesus would, arguably, not reveal God to us, and the Cross (and Gethsemane) would mislead.

When Buckingham Palace was bombed during the Second World War, the Queen (later to become the Queen Mother) is reported to have remarked that now she could look her people in the face. She was not the cause of their suffering, but somehow she felt that her leadership would only have credibility if she shared in it. I suggest that something similar is true of the governance of God. He is not the cause of our suffering, but His Godhood only has credibility if He shares in it. That is why Bonhoeffer (who knew a little about suffering, having been imprisoned under the Nazis and awaiting execution) suggested that only the suffering God could help.[22] The same instinct is powerfully expressed in Edward Shillito's poem, 'Jesus of the Scars'. It was written just after the First World War, when people were grappling with the horror through which they had just lived:

> The other gods were strong; but Thou wast weak;
> They rode, but Thou didst stumble to a throne;
> But to our wounds only God's wounds can speak
> And not a god has wounds, but Thou alone.[23]

That is why, says Shillito, *this* God, this God we meet on the Cross of Christ, is relevant to us with our wounds, our vulnerabilities, our pains, our hurts. This God reaches parts other gods cannot reach.

8. THE DEATH OF CHRIST SHOWS GOD SIDING WITH US

a) God sides with us in our sinfulness

We have already seen that the death of Christ was in *our place*. The place of judgment was ours. The place of alienation was ours. Gabbatha (John 19:13) and Golgotha (John 19:17) were both *our* places. Yet He made them His own. As Jürgen Moltmann put it, 'the symbol of the cross in the church points to the God who was crucified not between two candles on an altar, but between two thieves in the place of the skull, where the outcasts belong, outside the gates of the city'.[24] Whatever we have done, and whatever we have become, however hateful to others or to ourselves, however repugnant to God's holiness, He sides with us on the Cross. So total is His identification with us that Luther could write:

> Our most merciful Father, seeing us to be oppressed and overwhelmed with the curse of the law, and so to be holden under the same that we could never be delivered from it by our own power, sent His only Son into the world and laid upon him all the sins of all men, saying: Be thou Peter that denier; Paul that persecutor, blasphemer and cruel oppressor; David that adulterer; that sinner which did eat the apple in Paradise; that thief which hanged upon the cross; and briefly, be thou the person which hath committed the sins of all men; see therefore that thou pay and satisfy for them.[25]

He has sided with us in our denials, our blasphemies, our oppressions, our adulteries, our sins.

b) God sides with us in our sinned-againstness

God is, of course, used to being sinned against. Every sin there has ever been is a sin against Him in that it is against His will and His command: it is a rejection of His authority and lordship, it is an affront to His goodness and a claim on His compassion. But nowhere have His creatures sinned against Him more directly than when He entered His creation as one of them, vulnerable to spit, fist and spear.

In the account of His arrest, trial and crucifixion, we see Him lining up with others in their sinned-againstness, in many ways the archetype of innocent suffering, for His innocence alone is unmixed. We see Him lining up with the betrayed, lining up with victims of injustice, lining up with the excluded, lining up with the voiceless. As Rowan Williams says in his book on the trial of Jesus:

In Luke 22:67, Jesus is asked by the council to tell them if he is the Messiah. 'If I tell you,' he replied, 'you will not believe me, and if I question you, you will not answer.' In other words: I have nothing to say that you will be able to hear or to which you will be able to respond. Luke's Jesus places himself with those whose language cannot be heard ... God's transcendence is in some sense present in and with those who do not have a voice, in and with those without power to affect their world, in and with those believed to have lost any right they might have had in the world. God is not with them because they are naturally virtuous, or because they are martyrs; he is there simply in the fact that they are 'left over' when the social and moral score is added up by the managers of social and moral behaviour. Or, to put it a bit differently, God appears in and through the fact that our ways of arranging the world always leave someone's interest, welfare or reality out of account.[26]

The points at which the life-history of Jesus overlaps with our life-histories, His pains with our pains, are easy enough to identify with. But what about those of our experiences which have no direct counterpart in what Jesus Himself experienced? This question was brought home to me by a pastoral conversation I had with someone who had been the victim of multiple abuse. 'I can see what the Cross does for my abusers', she said, 'but what does it do for me?' It obviously wasn't adequate (or indeed sensitive) to say, 'Well, you have probably been on the giving side of sin as well as the receiving side, so the Cross might come in handy at that point!'

Just then, I managed to dredge up from the murky depths of my memory a piece of (what I had hitherto regarded as) dusty academic theology from my ordination training. The doctrine of *recapitulation*, as it is called, is associated with the second century theologian, Irenaeus, and suggested that the life-history of the Messiah 'recapitulated', or summed up within itself, the life-histories of all creatures: 'For He it is who sailed [in the ark] along with Noah, and who guided Abraham; who was bound along with Isaac, and was a Wanderer with Jacob.'[27] The first task of the doctrine of recapitulation, writes Douglas Farrow, 'is to signify that no realm whatever lies beyond the pale of his domain, that there are no autonomous times or spheres over which he is not the Lord – and because the Lord, also the redeemer'.[28] If the doctrine of recapitulation is accepted, therefore, there can also be no *experience* that lies beyond the pale of His domain, no *experience* He cannot redeem.

Be that as it may, Isaiah 53:4 tells us that 'Surely he took up our infirmities and carried our sorrows'. Jesus was not just the Sin-Bearer, siding with the sinful: He was also the Pain-Bearer[j], siding with the sinned-against. The Cross is therefore the affirmation of the reality of our sin, as we saw earlier in the chapter, *and the affirmation of the reality of our sinned-againstness*. To the victim of abuse, or indeed any kind of injustice, for whom to be believed is such a life-giving experience, such an affirmation could be an important step in the process of breaking the hold that the past can wield over them. But of course the Cross does not leave it there. The Cross is not just an affirmation of the reality of both sinfulness and sinned-againstness: it is also the promise of the dissolution of that sin, and the ultimate healing of that hurt.

We need, of course, both aspects of this divine *siding*. It's rather like holding a hyperactive hamster in your cupped hands – you have to keep shifting the hand with which you hold it as it runs from one to the other. So with God. He has to keep shifting the basis upon which He holds us – now standing with us in our sinfulness, now standing with us in our sinned-againstness. The two aspects held together mean that whatever we do or whatever is done to us, we are held. We find divine ground under our feet and divine resources at hand wherever we are, in every diverse circumstance of our lives.

---

[j] 'Pain-Bearer' is a term put to liturgical use by Jim Cotter. See, for example, his *Prayer at Night: A Book for the Darkness* (Cairns Publications, Sheffield (1983), 1988), p. 52.

We, too, have to try and mirror that double siding in our turn. As God stands with us in our sinfulness, so we have to be prepared to stand with others in theirs. That is why the church has always sought to have a presence in prisons – to embody God's siding with those who have offended. But of course prisons are but the tip of the iceberg. When I was at school, there was a boy who was known as something of a bully, and eventually a point of critical mass was reached and the whole school turned against him. I remember him one break-time, down one end of a long hall, being confronted by an angry crowd. Only his brother stood with him. It is one of the things of which I am most ashamed in my life that I did not go and stand with him. Jesus would have done. We know that from the Cross.

And as God stands with us in our sinned-againstness, we have to be prepared to stand with others in theirs:

> Father Dimitrii Klepinin was a Russian priest who, along with the famous Mother Maria Skobtsova, worked in Paris in the German occupation, providing French Jews with forged papers to assist their escape. Then he was captured. 'Fr. Dimitrii was interrogated for four hours. He made no attempt to exculpate himself. Later, at Lourmel, Hofmann was to describe how he was offered his freedom on the condition that he helped no more Jews. Fr. Dimitrii had raised his pectoral cross, shown the figure on it and asked, "But do you know *this* Jew?" He was answered with a blow to the face.'[29]

Rowan Williams goes on to comment:

> Both Mother Maria and Father Dimitrii died in the camps. Eyewitnesses recalled the way Father Dimitrii was mocked: 'One of the SS began to prod and beat him, calling him *Jude*.' ... Then in the mockery Father Dimitrii meets as he is herded off to the camps himself, he in turn is recognized as a 'Jew', as someone who has, so to speak, earned the right to be counted with the crucified and with the Jewish kindred of

the crucified. If the symbol of the crucified does not make this sort of recognition (and this sort of being recognised) possible, it has become an empty sign.[30]

Such siding is costly, as God Himself found. In the film, *Dead Man Walking*, a nun befriends a man on death row for rape and murder. In one desperately awkward and poignant scene, she visits the parents of the murdered girl. They ask her:

'What made you change your mind? ... What made you come round to our side?'

To which the nun replied:

'I wanted to come and see if I could help you all, and pray with you. But he asked me to be his spiritual adviser, to be with him when he dies.'
'And what did you say?'
'That I would.'
'But we thought you'd changed your mind. We thought that's why you were here.'
'No.'
'How can you come here? How can you do that? How can you sit with that scum?'
'Mrs. Percy, I've never done this before. I'm trying – I'm just trying to follow the example of Jesus who said that every person is worth more than their worst act.'
'This is not a person – this is an animal ... Matthew Ponseler is God's mistake, and you want to hold the murderer's hand. You want to be there to comfort him when he dies ... Sister, you're in waters way over your head ... My parents raised me to respect a religious person. Sister, I think you need to leave this house right now ... You can't have it both ways. You can't befriend that murderer and expect to be our friend.

To which the mother adds,

> 'You've brought the enemy into this house, Sister. You've got to go.'

To side both with the sinful and with the sinned-against is our near-impossible calling if we are to be the community of the crucified.

9. THE DEATH OF CHRIST DEFUSES POST-MODERN FEARS

People today are suspicious of anything that claims to be *the* answer, *the* truth, *the* system, *the* solution – and understandably so. So often the people who have made such claims have ended up advancing them by force. The Church had its Inquisition. Fascism had its Auschwitz. Communism had its Gulag Archipelago. Islam had its Taliban. And they have made us wary of totalitarian systems of thought, lest they end up in totalitarian systems of government. Believe anything too strongly, and you'll end up imposing it on others – that's what we fear. 'All ideologies reek of the death camps', as one post-modern writer put it. Hence the dearth of ideologies around at present. In the British political scene, New Labour has jettisoned its socialist baggage. The Conservative Party has toned down its Thatcherism. Pragmatism rules.

Yet the price is high, for with no 'big picture', there can be no meaning. If there is no overarching story into which our life-stories fit and to which they can contribute, then our life-stories are isolated, discreet, unrelated and therefore ultimately meaningless units. Our generation has thought itself faced with the choice between meaninglessness and meaning + division + oppression, and, by and large in the West, it has chosen meaninglessness. The post-modern world thinks it is better off without meaning if meaning is likely to be imposed upon it.

But the Cross of Christ defuses that (very understandable) fear. For Jesus did not impose His agenda upon others. He believed that God gave us freedom, and that we should therefore respect that freedom in others. He allowed the rich young man to go away sad (Luke 18:23). He allowed His followers to give up on Him (John 6:66), to betray Him, to desert Him and to deny Him. He allowed Himself to be arrested, tried and crucified. He restrained those who would use force in His defence. Far from slaughtering the Romans as the Messiah was supposed to do, He allowed the Romans to put Him to death. Far from imposing His agenda on others, He allowed others to impose their agenda upon Him.

A world-view that is based upon a crucified Messiah, therefore, cannot logically impose itself by force.[k] Here is a world-view, then, that can offer meaning without force, meaning that is constitutionally opposed to violence (both because of the Cross, and, as we shall see in a later chapter, because of the Trinity). This is where the weak God, the stumbling God, the wounded God comes into His own. Such a God made us and respects us, gave us freedom and respects that freedom, allowed us to rebel against Him, to reject Him and to kill Him. Such a God is Love, and knows the nature of love, that it cannot be forced. The Cross insists that we give others the same freedom that God has given to us all.

As we saw in Chapter 3, only the Lamb who has been slain is able to open the scroll that stands for the meaning of existence. Only a world-view that is based on such a God can thus defuse the justifiable fears of our contemporaries. Truth is only safe in scarred hands. Far from forfeiting our freedom, we find our freedom in Him. And far from being divisive, we find that all tribalism is dissolved, and all divisions undone, around His throne.

> You are worthy to take the scroll
> and to open its seals,
> because you were slain,
> and with your blood you purchased for God

---

[k] I say 'cannot logically impose itself by force' because of course there have been shameful attempts to impose a 'Christian' society by force. The point here is that, as Rowan Williams observes, 'If it [the cross] becomes the badge of a group causing or colluding with the suffering of others, it is no longer the cross of Jesus' (*Christ on Trial*, p. 42).

> members of every tribe and language and people and nation.
>
> **Revelation 5:9**

And if it is true that God does not impose His truth or Himself upon us, then clearly ...

10. THE DEATH OF CHRIST MUST BE APPROPRIATED FOR OURSELVES

If it is one of the lessons of the Cross that God will not force us, then obviously we need to accept for ourselves what He has made available by the Cross – there is no other way we can receive it. If He is to act as our representative, then He has to be accepted as such by both parties: God has accepted Him as such, and now it remains for us to 'elect' Him as our representative. If what God does is not to force us but to woo us, then we need to say our Yes to Him. If He will not violate our freedom, then we need to make our free response to all that He has done.

Nor does He leave us to make that response by ourselves. As we shall see in Chapter 7, He gives us His Spirit to enable us to make a free response. And here we just note that He Himself has given us ways of appropriating, ways of receiving what He has done for us on the Cross. I draw attention briefly to four.

a) Repentance

> 'Therefore let all Israel be assured of this: God has made this Jesus, whom you crucified, both Lord and Christ.' When the people heard this, they were cut to the heart and said to Peter and the other apostles, 'Brothers, what shall we do?' Peter replied, '*Repent* and be baptised, every one of you, in the name of Jesus Christ for the forgiveness of your sins. And you will receive the gift of the Holy Spirit.'
>
> **Acts 2:36–38, my italics**

If the Cross shows us the seriousness of our sin, then accepting the Cross necessarily involves a turning away from that sin. If the Cross reveals the depth of God's love, there must be a turning to God and a pleading with Him to induce a like love in our loveless hearts. If the Cross gives us an example to follow, it must alert us to and turn us from the ways in which we have failed to live out that way of being human. When we see what sin is like when it is full grown, as we do at the Cross, there must be a decisive repudiation of such a cancer, and a prayer that God cut it out of us, or we shall be ever infected with it and have our life slowly eaten away by it.

As Rowan Williams says, 'While it is essential to see the passion of Jesus as something that freely works, independently of our effort, to renew and heal us, that very healing and renewal come to their fullness only as we absorb in heart and mind what it is in us that calls out for healing.'[31] That, of course, is a lifelong process, but, like any journey, it begins with a single step.

b) Faith

> God has appointed him as the means of propitiation, a propitiation accomplished by the shedding of his blood, to be received and made effective in ourselves by faith.
>
> **Romans 3:25** JBP[1]

If God does not impose His reconciliation upon us, then it has to be 'received and made effective in ourselves' – and faith is the primary means by which that is done. As the great Congregationalist theologian, P. T. Forsyth, put it, 'I would begin by recalling the educational principle, that as no lesson is really taught till it is learned, so revelation is not revelation till it get home, till it return to God in faith.'[32] And though the Cross was more than just

---

[1] For 'propitiation' as a concept appropriate to Paul's thought at this point, and in Christian theology generally, see N. T. Wright's commentary on Romans in Volume X of the New Interpreter's Bible series, Abingdon, 2002: see especially pages 434–35, 476, & 520.

revelation – a fact upon which Forsyth himself insisted – the same goes for 'all other benefits of His passion'.[33] Faith of course involves more than (though it includes) intellectual assent. What happened on the Cross needs to be believed in, relied upon, tested out, lived out. Indeed, as Forsyth wisely remarks, 'The difficulty in believing in an Atonement is in great measure due to the fact that the belief needs self-surrender.'[34]

c) Baptism

> 'Therefore let all Israel be assured of this: God has made this Jesus, whom you crucified, both Lord and Christ.' When the people heard this, they were cut to the heart and said to Peter and the other apostles, 'Brothers, what shall we do?' Peter replied, 'Repent *and be baptised*, every one of you, in the name of Jesus Christ for the forgiveness of your sins. And you will receive the gift of the Holy Spirit.'
>
> **Acts 2:36–38, my italics**

Baptism is one of the apostolically prescribed ways of *responding to* the cross and Resurrection, because it is one of the God-given ways of *entering into* an event that happened 2,000 ago. We cannot enter into the cross historically, but we can enter into it *sacramentally*. 'Were you there when they crucified my Lord?' asks the old Negro Spiritual, and the baptised Christian can answer, Yes, I was there. I was on that cross. I was crucified with Christ (Galatians 2:20). 'Or don't you know that all of us who were baptised into Christ Jesus were baptised into his death? We were therefore buried with him through baptism into death in order that, just as Christ was raised from the dead through the glory of the Father, we too may live a new life' (Romans 6:3–4).

Baptism bridges the centuries and accomplishes what would otherwise be impossible – our participation in an historical event. It expands the 'event horizon' backwards. To continue the analogy from modern physics, baptism is a sort of time warp that makes it possible for us to be present in a remote, past event, and for that past event to be effective for us in the present.

d) The breaking of bread

Is not the cup of thanksgiving for which we give thanks a participation in the blood of Christ? And is not the bread that we break a participation in the body of Christ? Because there is one loaf, we, who are many, are one body, for we all partake of the one loaf.

1 Corinthians 10:16–17

When we meet to break bread together, we remember the Lord (1 Corinthians 11:24–25), we proclaim His death (1 Corinthians 11:26), but we also participate in it. Breaking bread together is a chronology-transcending, community-uniting, life-changing event. For in it, we are 'riveted to our redemptive events'.[m] In it, we 'enter into the movement of his self-offering'.[n] The analogy that comes to the mind of a cricket enthusiast such as myself is that of a bowling machine, by which I don't mean one of those somewhat frightening contraptions which fire cricket balls in your general direction at a high velocity. I mean the type of machine into which bowlers can be harnessed, which forces their arms to go through exactly the right motion for effective bowling. Harnessed in this way, the trainee bowler can only perform the motion correctly. And the idea is that, having done it correctly five hundred times a day for six months, they will then do it correctly when finally allowed out of the harness and onto the playing field. Breaking bread together is

[m] I'm afraid I do not know the source of this quotation. I first heard it in a sermon by my parish priest, Leslie Chadd, many years ago – and, like much of his preaching, it stuck in my mind.
[n] This helpful phrase comes from the report on Eucharistic Doctrine by the Anglican–Roman Catholic International Commission. See The Final Report, CTS/SPCK, London, 1982, p. 14.

rather like that. It trains us in the 'movement of his self-offering'. By entering into His sacrificial, self-giving death, we learn to live sacrificial, self-giving lives. In other words, as we enter into His self-offering, His self-offering enters into us.

Breaking bread together is therefore the time travel by which we are present in that which is past. It is the conference call by which we are linked to all our fellow time travellers. And it is the training ground where we calibrate our lives with the model and pattern of the Cross. We only fully live in so far as we model ourselves on His death. And we only have a future thanks to that event in the past.

FURTHER RESOURCES FOR READING, PRAYER AND ACTION

John Davies, *The Crisis of the Cross* (Canterbury Press, 1997).

Tom Smail, *Windows on the Cross* (Darton, Longman and Todd, 1995).

John Stott, *The Cross of Christ* (IVP, 1986).

Rowan Williams, *Christ on Trial: How the Gospel Unsettles Our Judgment* (Zondervan, 2000).

On Impassibility

Paul Fiddes, *The Creative Suffering of God* (The Clarendon Press, 1990).

Jürgen Moltmann, *The Crucified God* (1973) (SCM Press, 1974).

T. F. Torrance, *Space, Time and Incarnation* (OUP, 1969), pp. 74 ff. Torrance rejects the impassibility of God.

Thomas Weinandy, *Does God Suffer?* (Continuum International Publishing Group, T & T Clark, 1999). Weinandy defends the impassibility of God.

On post-modernism

Brian Walsh and J. Richard Middleton, *Truth Is Stranger Than It Used to Be: Biblical Faith in a Postmodern Age* (Gospel and Culture) (SPCK, 1995).

On the breaking of bread

Tom Wright, *Holy Communion for Amateurs* (Hodder & Stoughton, 1999).

6 RESURRECTION AND ASCENSION

THE RESURRECTION

Some years ago, the Episcopal Church in the United States was revising its prayer book. Soon after publication, the person who chaired the Revision Committee received a letter from the American equivalent of 'Disgusted of Tunbridge Wells' ('Incandescent of Idaho' perhaps), saying, 'If Jesus Christ knew what you've done to the liturgy, He'd turn in His grave!' That was one objection they didn't feel they had to take terribly seriously! It has always been a central tenet of Christianity that Jesus Christ is no longer in His grave. It stands or falls on the truth or falsity of the Resurrection.[a] As St Paul argued, 'If Christ has not been raised, our preaching is useless and so is your faith' (1 Corinthians 15:14). Lenin is in his mausoleum. You can still visit Abraham's grave. The Buddha is still in his tomb in Kusinagara. Elijah is believed to have bypassed death by being taken up into heaven by a whirlwind. But only of Jesus is it claimed that he went *through* death and out the other side.

It is possible, however, to move too quickly to the 'happy ending' of the Resurrection. The danger is that we minimise the momentousness of what Jesus endured, and that we minimise

---

[a] I don't intend to address here the subject of the historicity of the Resurrection. For a recent detailed and thorough treatment of this issue, see N. T. Wright's *The Resurrection of the Son of God* (SPCK, 2003).

the full horror of what others endure too. That way, we miss out on the full meaning of the Cross, for we fail to notice the heavy cost of our redemption; we miss out on the full meaning of the Resurrection, for we fail to notice the depths of what we have been redeemed from; and we fail to do justice pastorally to those who are most in need of our understanding and support. We must never use the Resurrection as a way of invalidating the suffering or grief of others (or ourselves).

We must take our time over the transition between Cross and Resurrection. There wasn't a day between them for nothing. I therefore propose to linger a little over the three days in turn, before moving on to consider the meaning that the Resurrection of Jesus has for us.

Good Friday

On the first Good Friday, Jesus identified with humanity in all its moral deformity and spiritual warpedness. He stood with us in our sinfulness. He took upon Himself our guilt and its consequences. And the chief and final consequence of sin is death (Romans 6:23, James 1:15). He did not shrink from taking even that upon Himself. (Well, He did shrink from it in the Garden of Gethsemane, but He did not shirk it.) He took our sin upon Himself – and consequently He died. The cup was not taken from Him – He drank it to the dregs. No cavalry appeared over the hill. There was no last-minute reprieve or stay of execution. He had given up His spirit (John 19:30) and breathed His last (Luke 23:46). His haemorrhagic fluid had separated out (John 19:34). He was fully dead. In the words of the Apostles' Creed, He 'descended to the dead'.

Holy Saturday[b]

We tend to think of Good Friday as the low-point, to be followed by the high-points of the Resurrection and Ascension. But in a sense, the tomb is even lower than the Cross. Holy Saturday is even lower than Good Friday. On Good Friday, He still had power. He could have come down from the cross. On Holy Saturday, He was powerless. From the moment of His death to the morning of His resurrection, He identified with humanity at the lowest point of our fallenness. He identified with us in our deadness, in our complete helplessness, in our utter dependence upon God for any future whatsoever. He lay beside us on the mortuary slab. He shared with us in the lifelessness that is otherwise the terminus of our earthly journey. His love did not just bring Him to walk with us along the sunny lanes of Galilee: it brought Him to lie inert alongside us on the sunless shelf of the grave. Had He not done so, His identification with us would have been partial. As von Balthasar insists, 'The fact of being with the unredeemed dead, in the Sheol of the Old Testament,[c] signifies a solidarity in whose absence the condition of standing for sinful man before God would not be complete.'[1]

The Russian Orthodox hymn for Holy Saturday puts these words onto the lips of Jesus:

'Do you not understand, do all of you not understand, that I had two friends on earth, Adam and Eve. And when I came to them I did not find them on the earth which I had given them. And

---

[b] Holy Saturday refers to the day between Good Friday and Easter Sunday, though many people call it Easter Saturday – wrongly.
[c] 'Sheol' is the word usually translated 'Grave' in modern translations of the Bible. It functions as the personified place of the dead.

loving them, I descended to where they were, into the darkness and horror and hopelessness of death.'[2]

He came to join them there, but not to leave them there. For His presence transforms. The old monastic service of Compline has a prayer which begins:

O Lord Jesus Christ, Son of the living God, who at this evening hour didst rest in the sepulchre, and didst thereby sanctify the grave to be a bed of hope to Thy people ...

The grave is no longer a place of despair, but a bed of hope. It need no longer be a terminus, but a tunnel. To quote Pope Gregory the Great, by sharing our deadness with us, 'God has made this abyss into a way.'[3] Christians of all traditions have seen the difference that this makes. The great Puritan writer, Richard Baxter, was comforted by the thought that 'Christ leads me through no darker rooms than He went through before.'[4] In Chapter 4, we saw that our plight was transformed when God linked Himself to human life in the Incarnation. We heard Ruth Burrows recall:

... the unutterable wonder that God too had a human birth: he came into the world as we come into it; he came to drink with us the bitter cup of humanness. He drank it to the dregs, and thereby transformed its bitterness. Bitter it is and yet sweet, for his lips meet ours over the brim.[5]

What we observe now is that He also had a human death. He went out of the world as we go out of it. No moment of our fallen humanness is more bitter than death, but that too is transformed, for He has been there, He has lain there, and therefore we need fear no evil there. John Saward draws on Balthasar's work to give powerful expression to this hope:

> Dying and death, the very deadness of Sheol, have been made his own by God the Son, in his human soul, out of loving obedience to the Father. Even upon the absence of God, he has printed the sign of the Son, the filial sign of the Cross. The prison has been made a way: the wasteland of dereliction has been transformed into a royal highway, a track through the trackless waste, the road to the Father's house and heart.[6]

That transformation, however, depends not just upon Jesus having lain with us in the tomb, but also upon His having burst out of the tomb. The grave can be a way and a track and a highway, not just because Jesus lay in it, but also because the Father raised Him to a full and free life the other side of it. And what He did, He did for us.

Easter Day

Many of our Easter hymns and songs and sermons celebrate the fact that Jesus is alive. Few capture just *how* alive. It is possible to read the accounts of the Resurrection appearances in Luke's Gospel and come to the conclusion that, if He can walk through walls, then it must be a fairly insubstantial and non-physical existence that He has, the other side of the grave. That, I suggest, is to miss the point. Jesus Himself, in Luke 24:37ff, insists that He is no ghost, and eats fish in the disciples' presence to prove His (transformed) physicality. It is not that He is so insubstantial that He can walk through walls. It is that He is *so* substantial and *so* real that walls are insubstantial and unreal in comparison. Walls are so much less 'solid' than Jesus' resurrection body that they can offer no resistance to Him.

It is perhaps poets who help us to grasp this. John Updike insists on the realness of the Resurrection in (four of) his *Seven Stanzas at Easter*:

> Make no mistake
> if he rose at all
> it was as his body;
> if the cells' dissolution did not reverse, the

molecules reknit, the amino acids rekindle,
the church will fall.

It was not as the flowers,
each soft Spring recurrent;
it was not as his Spirit in the mouths and
        fuddled eyes of the eleven apostles;
it was as his flesh: ours.

...

Let us not mock God with metaphor,
analogy, sidestepping transcendence;
making of the event a parable, a sign painted in the
        faded credulity of earlier ages;
let us walk through the door.

The stone is rolled back, not papier-mâché,
not a stone in a story,
but the vast rock of materiality that in the slow
        grinding of time will eclipse each of us
the wide light of day.[7]

...

The Resurrection is of course the first 'bit' of the new creation, the
present tip of a future iceberg. Here C. S. Lewis portrays the solidity
and reality of the new creation:

> ... the light, the grass, the trees ... were different; made of some different
> substance, so much solider than things in our country that men were
> ghosts by comparison. Moved by a sudden thought, I bent down and
> tried to pluck a daisy which was growing at my feet. The stalk wouldn't
> break. I tried to twist it, but it wouldn't twist. I tugged till the sweat stood
> out on my forehead and I had lost most of the skin off my hands. The
> little flower was hard, not like wood or even like iron, but like diamond.
> There was a leaf – a young tender beech-leaf, lying in the grass beside it.

I tried to pick the leaf up: my heart almost cracked with the effort, and I believe I did just raise it. But I had to let it go at once; it was heavier than a sack of coal. As I stood, recovering my breath with great gasps and looking down at the daisy, I noticed that I could see the grass not only between my feet but also through them. I also was a phantom.[8]

And the inhabitants of the new creation, he calls, by contrast, 'the solid people'. On what authority does he so depict them? On the authority of the one resurrection body of which we have any knowledge – that of Jesus Himself. Solid, real and pulsatingly alive.[d]

1. A) THE RESURRECTION AFFIRMS AND IN NO WAY NEGATES THE REALITY AND NEGATIVITY OF DEATH

Jesus' Resurrection did not cancel out His crucifixion. He still bore the marks of the nails in His Resurrection body. It is not now as if the crucifixion had never been: on the contrary, the crucifixion is now forever present in Him and part of Him. He remains forever affected by what happened, eternally shaped by it – could we go so far as to say 'defined by it'?[e] He is the 'Lamb slain from the foundation of the world' (Revelation 13:8 NKJV).

---

[d] The play and film about Lewis' life, *Shadowlands*, was so named because of his insistence that it is this world that is the shadowlands: it is the next world, the coming new creation (already arrived in the resurrection of Jesus), that is the real land and the real life. What we learn from the Resurrection of Jesus is that we are shadows of our future selves, as N. T. Wright puts it in his *New Heavens, New Earth* (Grove Books, 1999), p. 12.

[e] It seems to me that the scars on Jesus' resurrection body provide a good model for how we should deal with suffering. We should not try to 'get over' suffering. We should not attempt to get back to how things were and how we were before we went through it. It should not become as nothing to us. On the contrary, we should seek to come through it, marked by it, changed by it, but no longer distorted or inhibited by it. In the scars of Jesus there is the promise that our suffering cannot thwart our glorification – indeed, it can even be commandeered by God as the means to that glorification. (For a brief but profound meditation on the scars of Jesus, see Nicholas Wolterstorff's *Lament for a Son* (Eerdmans, 1987) (Hodder and Stoughton, London, 1989), pp. 92–94.)

And what is true of His Resurrection will also be true of ours. The promise of our future resurrection does not make death an irrelevance. It does not make it okay. It does not make it something to be contemplated with equanimity. It is a *defeated* enemy, but it is still an *enemy* (1 Corinthians 15:26), and we continue to experience it as such. We are told not to grieve as those who have no hope (1 Thessalonians 4:13): we are not told *not* to grieve. We must not belittle the horror of death and of bereavement, for to belittle death is to belittle the achievement of the Resurrection. We must acknowledge fully the weight upon us of the shroud that envelops all peoples (Isaiah 25:7), its capacity to blight and poison existence. John of Damascus saw this well:

> Truly terrible is the mystery of death.
> I lament at the sight of the beauty
> created for us in the image of God
> which lies now in the grave
> without shape, without glory, without consideration.
> What is this mystery that surrounds us?
> Why are we delivered up to decay?
> Why are we bound to death?[9]

Nowhere is this deep theological and personal abhorrence of death given more moving expression than in Nicholas Wolterstorff's remarkable book, *Lament for a Son*. When his son, Eric, died in a mountaineering accident, he wrote down his reflections and feelings and questions and thoughts in a book pleading with Christians not to minimise death in the name of the resurrection. I quote extensively, for I feel that it is a point that needs to be heard.

> Elements of the gospel which I had always thought would console did not. They did something else, something important, but not that. It did not console me to be reminded of the hope of resurrection. If I had forgotten that hope, then it would indeed have brought light into my life to be reminded of it. But I did not

207

think of death as a bottomless pit. I did not grieve as one who has no hope. Yet Eric is gone, here and now he is gone; now I cannot talk with him, now I cannot see him, now I cannot hug him, now I cannot hear of his plans for the future. That is my sorrow. A friend said, 'Remember, he's in good hands.' I was deeply moved. But that reality does not put Eric back in my hands now. That's my grief. For that grief, what consolation can there be other than having him back?

… What do you say to someone who is suffering? Some people are gifted with words of wisdom. For such, one is profoundly grateful. There were many such for us. But not all are gifted in that way. Some blurted out strange, inept things. That's OK too. Your words don't have to be wise. The heart that speaks is heard more than the words spoken. And if you can't think of anything at all to say, just say, 'I can't think of anything to say. But I want you to know that we are with you in your grief.'

Or even, just embrace …

But please: Don't say it's not really so bad. Because it is. Death is awful, demonic. If you think your task as comforter is to tell me that really, all things considered, it's not so bad, you do not sit with me in my grief but place yourself off in the distance away from me. Over there, you are of no help. What I need to hear from you is that you recognise how painful it is. I need to hear from you that you are with me in my desperation. To comfort me, you have to come close. Come sit beside me on my mourning bench.

I know: People do sometimes think things are more awful than they really are. Such people need to be corrected – gently, eventually. But no one thinks death is more awful than it is. It's those who think it's not so bad that need correcting.[10]

1. B) THE RESURRECTION WAS A DEFEAT OF THE AWFUL REALITY OF DEATH, AND GIVES HOPE

Having said all that we have just said, we are in a better position to hear, in all its depth and without distortion, the New Testament's joyful proclamation of death's defeat in the Resurrection of Jesus. Only those who have faced the full horror of death can know the full joy of resurrection. And the first disciples certainly fall into both categories. 'We *had* hoped …', say two of them as they walk disconsolately along (Luke 24:21, my italics). But suddenly hope becomes not so much past as present and future. Hope bursts upon them in the form not of a proposition but of a Person.

The New Testament celebrates that hope. It almost flaunts it: '"Where, O death, is your victory? Where, O death, is your sting?"' (1 Corinthians 15:55). Exuberant joy and gratitude gush from the New Testament writers at what Jean Vanier calls 'the most stupendous cosmic reality in the history of our universe'.[11] The same exultant tone is to be heard throughout the history of the Church, as the hope of the Resurrection sinks in afresh in each generation.

The pastoral task is to hold these truths together – to insist that the Resurrection defeated death, without denying its dreadful reality. It is to remember that death is a *defeated enemy*, and to give weight to both words. Our theology, our pastoral care, and our funeral services need to allow space for grief and to give voice to hope. We need to pray for wisdom to know on which aspect of the Resurrection's rich reality to draw when dealing with dying or bereavement, whether ours or others'. The Methodist New Testament scholar, Richard Hays, seems to me to display that wisdom well in the following account of a pastoral situation in which he was involved:

> I have never forgotten a conversation I had with a young woman in my church years ago. I will call her "Stephanie". Her eighteen-year-old sister (whom I will call "Lisa") had been killed in a car accident. All the members of the family were saying things like

"Lisa is so much happier now in heaven; she was always such an unhappy child here" or "God must have wanted her to be with him" or "I just know that Lisa is watching us now and telling us not to be sad." Stephanie was infuriated by such sweet, pious talk, for it seemed to deny both the reality of Lisa's death and its tragedy. Yet Stephanie felt guilty, because as a Christian she thought she ought to believe the pious things her family was saying. Thus, it came as a liberating word to her to learn that Paul speaks of death as a destructive "enemy" that will be conquered only at the end of this age. First Corinthians 15 enabled her to acknowledge soberly that Lisa was now really dead and buried in the ground, while at the same time realising that she could hope to hold Lisa in her arms again, in the resurrection.[12]

'In a culture that evades telling the truth about death,' Hays concludes, 'the teaching of the resurrection comes as a blast of fresh air.' Just as in the last chapter I suggested that we can only face the depth of our sinfulness once we know that we have been forgiven, so here I suggest that we can only speak the truth about death once we know that it has been relativised by the Resurrection of Jesus.

2. A) THE RESURRECTION IS THE VINDICATION OF JESUS

The Resurrection is the vindication of Jesus as Messiah

At the beginning of *The Life of Brian*, three men arrive by camel at a softly-lit stable. They enter, and see a woman sleeping beside a newly-born baby in a manger. The following dialogue ensues between the wise men and Brian's mother (who looks and sounds suspiciously like Terry Jones and his other alter ego, Mrs Scum):

Brian's mother: Who are you?

The wise men: We are three wise men.

Brian's mother: What?

The wise men:	We are three wise men.
Brian's mother:	Well, what are you doing creeping in on a cowshed at two o'clock in the morning? That doesn't sound very wise to me.

Her tone changes completely, however, when they mention the gold, frankincense and myrrh they have brought as gifts. They explain their mission.

Brian's mother:	So you're astrologers, are you? Well, what is he then?
The wise men:	Hmm?
Brian's mother:	What star sign is he?
The wise men:	Uh, Capricorn.
Brian's mother:	Capricorn, eh? What are they like?
The wise men:	He is the Son of God, our Messiah, King of the Jews.
Brian's mother:	That's Capricorn, is it?
The wise men:	No, no, no, that's just him.
Brian's mother:	Oh, I was going to say. Otherwise, there'd be a lot of them.

There *was* a lot of them in first-century Israel. It was not as if Jesus was the only candidate. Many came claiming to be the Messiah, and most ended up being killed by the Romans, or being killed by their followers, or killing themselves to prevent capture by the Romans. Tom Wright puts it helpfully:

> We know ... of about a dozen or more messianic or would-be messianic movements around the time of Jesus, and we have no indication that any of them said anything at all about their leader being still around after his death. Hezekiah, the great revolutionary in the 40s BC, was killed by Herod the Great: his followers didn't claim he'd been raised from the dead. Judas, his

son, led a messianic movement after the death of Herod; after his death, nobody claimed to have seen him alive. An ex-slave called Simon was proclaimed king in around 4 BC, and when the Romans killed him no movement arose to commemorate him. A shepherd called Athronges was crowned by a group of followers at the same time, and he went the same way. In the decade or two after Jesus' death there were three or four other messianic leaders; they were either cut down by troops or crucified, and nobody said they had risen from the dead three days later. During the war a generation after Jesus' time there were two more great revolutionary king-figures, another Simon and a descendent of Hezekiah and Judas called Menahem; Simon was captured by the Romans and executed, and Menahem was killed by a rival group of Jews. Nobody claimed to have seen them alive, and eaten in their company, a few days later. Two generations after that Simeon ben-Kosiba was hailed as Israel's Messiah. He led a glorious three-year guerrilla resistance movement, before finally being caught and killed by the Romans. No sect arose claiming to have been witnesses that God had raised him from the dead.

But within a short while of the crucifixion of Jesus of Nazareth, his disciples, who had been defeated and bedraggled just before, appeared in public in front of their countrymen claiming that they had seen Jesus, that they had spoken with him, that God had brought him through death and out the other side into a new dimension of life over which death no longer had any authority. And they saw this without a shadow of doubt as the vindication of his claim – that his death really had been the turning-point of history, the moment around which all other moments must now regroup themselves.[13]

In every other case, their messianic claim was disqualified by their defeat and death. Their followers might rally around a son or relative of the deceased leader, or they might simply disperse. What never happened was that they continued to believe in the messiahship of their dead leader. Except in the case of Jesus. Why was He an exception? His followers said it was because God had vindicated His cause by raising Him from the dead.

Paul, for instance, says that Jesus 'was born of the seed of David according to the flesh, and declared to be the Son of God with power according to the Spirit of holiness, by the resurrection from the dead' (Romans 1:3b–4 NKJV). We need to remember that the phrase 'Son of God' would not have meant 'Second Person of the Trinity' to a first-century reader. Indeed, it would not necessarily have implied divinity at all. The phrase would have meant one of three things. It could have referred to angels (Job 1:6). It could have referred to Israel (Exodus 4:22). Or it could have referred to Israel's King (2 Samuel 7:14), and, in particular to Israel's *great* king, the one who is and sums up Israel in himself – Israel's Messiah. So what Paul is saying is that Jesus was declared with power to be the Messiah, to be Israel's great embodiment and King, by the Resurrection. The Resurrection says, 'Yes, He was that faithful King for whom Israel had been longing throughout long periods of faithless and exploitative kingship, that liberating leadership for which she had been yearning during her time of exile and her years of oppression.'

Without the Resurrection, Jesus would not have been recognised as fulfilling that hope. He certainly didn't look like the sort of Messiah they were expecting. As Tom Wright reminds us, 'The Messiah had a task: to rebuild or cleanse the temple, to defeat the pagans, to rescue Israel and bring God's justice to the world. Anyone who died without accomplishing these things, particularly anyone who attacked the temple and died at the hands of the pagans he should have been defeating, leaving Israel unredeemed and the world still unjust, was obviously not the true Messiah. This is why it took something utterly extraordinary to make anyone suppose that Jesus was in fact the Messiah. Paul is clear: It was the resurrection that marked Jesus out as "son of God" (Romans 1:4). The resurrection reversed the verdict that all thoughtful first-century Jews would have passed on Jesus at the time of his crucifixion.'[14]

The Resurrection is the vindication of Jesus as divine

There has been a tendency in recent years for supermarkets to provide services for which, in previous years, we would have had to go to a specialist shop. You now no longer need to go to a chemist to get a prescription – you can just go to the supermarket's chemist counter. In rather the same way, Jesus caused quite a stir by claiming to be able to forgive sins directly, without going through the official dispensary (eg Mark 2:1–12). The reason why this caused a stir is because everyone knew that only God could forgive sins (Mark 2:7) and that you had to go to the temple to receive that forgiveness. That, among other things, is what the temple was for (1 Kings 8:33–4, 38–9). Yet here was an itinerant, untrained rabbi going round dispensing it with no official authority. (He claimed that his healing ministry was evidence that His ministry of forgiveness came with God's authority, but that was clearly a moot point at the time.)

Another of His implicit claims was that He was the strange figure of Daniel 7 – the 'Son of Man' – who was given authority, glory and power by the Ancient of Days, and was worshipped by people of all races, nations and languages. Another was that He would be the judge on the last day (Matthew 25:31–3), and that the result of that great judgment would depend ultimately upon people's response to Him (Matthew 25:40, 45, Mark 8:38).

Now, it is important to notice that these are all implicit claims. Jesus did not go round the Palestine of His day claiming explicitly to be God. What He did do is make claims and display assumptions and perform acts which only make sense if He were. Only God could forgive sins, yet here was a man proclaiming people's forgiveness. God would be the Judge at the end of history, yet here was a man who claimed that rôle for Himself. And, perhaps most fundamental of all, it was known – and indeed fought for and died for – that God alone was to be worshipped, and yet here was a man who accepted the worship of others (eg Matthew 8:2, John 9:38[f]), and implied that

---

[f] Contrast how Jesus accepted worship with how Peter (Acts 10:25–6) and an angel (Revelation 19:10) recoiled from it.

He would in due course be worshipped by people of every race and language.

The question, of course, is, 'What does *God* think about this chap going about making these claims?' Some of the people followed Him and believed in Him:[8] others took offence at Him and considered Him a blasphemer. But what really matters is God's view of Him, and how are we to know that? The Resurrection gives an answer to that question. If God were going to raise one human being ahead of the general resurrection at the end of history, He would hardly raise a blaspheming self-promotionalist. The Resurrection is God's seal of vindication on the ministry and claims of Jesus. As Tom Torrance puts it in his important book, *Space, Time and Resurrection*:

> ... in the resurrection the Father owns Christ as his Son, which has the effect not only of confirming all that Jesus had taught and done, and indeed had claimed, up to the crucifixion, but of acknowledging that his [ie Jesus'] activity in life and death was his [ie the Father's] very own.[15]

2. B) THE RESURRECTION IS THE VINDICATION OF THE CROSS

The early church claimed that the Cross was the solution to all that was wrong with the cosmos. It claimed that on the Cross, Jesus had finally and forever dealt with that which has laced our history with violence, that which makes us a threat to and at threat from the rest of creation, that which makes it impossible for us to live harmoniously with one another, that which cuts short and makes meaningless our lives, that which alienates us from the Love for which we were made. Sin had been dealt with on the Cross, they claimed. It is easy to overlook the extraordinary nature of that claim. Oliver O'Donovan asks:

---

[8] Not at this stage as being divine, probably – the claims were too implicit for that.

> On what authority did those early disciples announce that the death of Christ, the apparent defeat of all their hopes, was, in reality, a victory? Certainly, its victorious character was not evident to the onlooker ... If there were no divine act of vindication, such an interpretation of Jesus' death would be, simply on theological grounds, preposterous. Presumably, one may say of any death one likes that it has 'infinite significance as the redemption of the universe and as the inauguration of a new creation', but unless God actually accepts that redemption and inaugurates the new creation, one is simply indulging in fantasy.[16]

Thus the Resurrection is the 'divine act of vindication'. The Resurrection provides the authority on which they claimed the Cross to be a victory. The defeat of death was the proof that sin had been dealt with, for sin is the root cause of death, so if death has been defeated, then sin must have been dealt with. That is the logic behind the claims of the early Christians, and it is the underlying logic behind Paul's assertion that 'If Christ has not been raised, your faith is futile: you are still in your sins' (1 Corinthians 15:17). The Resurrection vindicates the claims, and underwrites the achievements, of the Cross.

Thus, as Michael Ramsey insisted, 'The Crucifixion is not a defeat needing the Resurrection to reverse it, but a victory which the Resurrection quickly follows and seals.'[17] The Resurrection is the *fruit and disclosure* of the victory of the Cross rather than a reversal of the defeat of the Cross. Much Christian art portrays Christ in glory on the Cross in order to remind us of the underlying reality of victory beneath the veneer of defeat – a reality that can only be seen in the light of the Resurrection. Were it not for the Resurrection, we would have to conclude that the Cross was just another in a long line of tragic miscarriages of justice. But in the light of the Resurrection, we find ourselves having to say that the Cross was not merely a miscarriage of justice where an innocent man was wrongly declared to be guilty – it was also the place where guilty men and women are rightly and justly declared to be innocent (Romans 3:26).

2. C) THE RESURRECTION IS OUR VINDICATION

The Messiah is a representative figure. What is true of Him becomes true of those who are 'in Him'. Was He crucified? Then we too have been crucified with Christ (Galatians 2:20). Did He die? Then, in some sense, so did we (Romans 6:8, Colossians 3:3). Was He raised from the dead? Then we too have been raised with Him (Colossians 3:1). Will He appear again? Then we also will appear with Him in glory (Colossians 3:4). Was He vindicated by the Resurrection? Then we too are vindicated by His Resurrection. As Paul asserts, 'He was delivered over to death for our sins and was raised to life for our justification' (Romans 4:25). Tom Torrance again:

> If the death of Jesus on the Cross is to be regarded as the sentence of divine judgment inflicted on him for our sakes, and on us in him, the resurrection is to be regarded as the obverse of that, itself the sentence and judgment of God … If the Cross is God's No against us in judgment on our sin which Christ endured for our sakes – 'My God, my God, why hast thou forsaken me?' – the resurrection is God's Yes to us in affirmation of Jesus as Son of Man and all that he has done for us in our nature and on our behalf.[18]

So when we look at the Resurrection of Christ and hear God's great Yes to all that Christ is and has been and has done, then we hear also, within that Yes, God's resounding Yes to us and His vindication of us against any blot upon us, or corruption within us or claim against us – His vindication of us now, ahead of time, ahead of the Last Judgment; and we hear now what we are going to hear then, which is God saying Yes, and Welcome, because we are in Him, and what is true of Him is now true of us.

3. THE RESURRECTION IS THE BEGINNING OF THE END

Jon[athan Miller]	How will it be, this end of which you have spoken, Brother Enim?
All	Yes, how will it be?
Peter [Cook]	Well, it will be as it 'twere a mighty rending in the sky, you see, and the mountains will sink, you see, and the valleys shall rise, you see, and great will be the tumult thereof ...
Alan [Bennett]	And will there be a mighty wind, Brother Enim?
Peter	Certainly there will be a mighty wind, if the word of God is anything to go by.
Dudley [Moore]	And will this wind be so mighty as to lay low the mountains of the earth?
Peter	No, it will not be quite as mighty as that, that is why we have come up on the mountain, you stupid nit – to be safe from it. Up here on the mountain we shall be safe. Safe as houses.
Alan	And what will happen to the houses?
Peter	Well, naturally, the houses will be swept away and the tents of the ungodly with them and they will all be consumèd by the power of the heavens and on earth, and serve them right.
Alan	And shall we be consumed?
Peter	Con-sum-èd? No, we shall not be con-su-mèd. We shall be up on the mountain here, you see, while millions burn, having a bit of a giggle.
Jon	When will it be, this end of which you have spoken? ...
Peter	In about thirty seconds' time, according to the ancient pyramidic scrolls and my Ingersoll watch.

Jon	Should we compose ourselves, then?
Peter	Good plan, Brother Pithy. Prepare for the end of the world. Fifteen seconds …
Alan	Here, have we got the tinned food?
Dudley	Yes.
Peter	Ten seconds …
Jon	And the tin opener?
Dudley	Yes.
Peter	Five – four – three – two – one – zero!
All (chanting)	Now is the end, perish the world!
	Pause.
Peter	It was G.M.T.,[h] wasn't it?
Jon	Yes.
Peter	Well, it's not quite the conflagration I'd been banking on. Never mind, lads, same time tomorrow. We must get a winner one day.

People have always been fascinated by the ultimate destiny of our world. Not just nutters, as satirised in that classic sketch from *Beyond the Fringe*[19], but every thinking person wants to know where we are headed and what lies in store for the world of which we are a part. And we want to know the cosmic goal, for the very good reason that *unless* we know, we cannot understand. Unless we know how a play or a film or a novel *ends*, then there is every chance that we shall fundamentally misunderstand it. If someone only saw the first half of *The Crying Game*, for instance, or missed the last ten minutes of *Body Heat* or *The Shawshank Redemption*, their impression of those films as a whole would be disastrously misleading. So it is with our understanding of the world. Unless we have some conception of where we are headed, then we shall have little idea as to what life is *for*.

[h] Greenwich Mean Time

219

In first century Jewish eyes, the Resurrection was expected at the end of history. Everyone would be raised from death, judged, and the new age would begin.[i] As the Pentecostalist New Testament scholar, Gordon Fee, put it, 'from his Jewish roots Paul understood the resurrection of the dead to be the final event on God's earthly calendar, the unmistakable evidence for the full arrival of the End.'[20] The Resurrection of Jesus made him rethink the whole projected scenario. Because if Jesus had been raised from the dead, it meant that the Resurrection had already begun, the End had already arrived. It had not arrived in its fullness, obviously, because people still died, and the world was not put to rights, and Israel was still subjugated,[j] and God was not all in all. But here in the *middle* of history – not at the end – the Resurrection had begun, the Spirit was unleashed, and the new age had been inaugurated:

> However, the End had only begun; they still awaited the final event, the (now second) coming of their Messiah Jesus, at which time they too would experience the resurrection/transformation of the body. They lived 'between the times'; already the future had begun, not yet had it been completely fulfilled. This already/not yet perspective, in which they believed themselves already to be living in the time of the End, even though it was yet to be consummated, is the eschatological[k] framework that

[i] Of course, there was a variety of beliefs within first century Judaism. Some (such as the Sadducees) did not believe in the resurrection at all. Some believed that only the righteous would be raised, others (on the basis of Daniel 12:2) that all would be raised and then judged. What no one was expecting was that one person would be raised ahead of the general resurrection, in the middle of history.

[j] See Acts 1:6.

[k] 'Eschatos' is the Greek word for 'last'. Eschatology is the study of the last things, our understanding of where we are headed, what is our destiny, and where we are now in the unfolding of that destiny. I once told a friend I was giving a lecture on 'The Resurrection and Eschatology'. She looked puzzled and said, 'What has Houdini got to do with the resurrection?' It was then my turn to look puzzled, until I finally twigged and said, 'Ah. Not escapology – eschatology!' It's an important difference. Christian eschatology is not escapist. It is not about us escaping from this material world and freeing ourselves from the shackles of the body. It's about God healing and transforming this material world and ridding it of all that mars it (Revelation 21:1–5) and giving us new bodies. See Chapter 9.

determines everything about them – how they lived, how they thought, and how they understood their own place in the present world, which was now understood to be on the way out.[21]

Such a framework can help us to live a balanced life in the present. On the one hand, we must not live as if nothing has changed, nothing has happened, the new age has not arrived, the Spirit has not come, there is no power available to drive forward the Church's ministry and mission, its healing and its care. We must not try and follow our own agendas, in our own strength. We must not live as if the Spirit is not forming us into one body, ripping down the barriers that have hitherto divided the human community. We must not live in denial of the unity that the Spirit works to bring. On the other hand, we must not pretend that the new age has arrived in its fullness. We must not promise people what is not on offer until the final restoration of all things. We must not lead people to expect that their lives will be free from suffering, that their devotional lives will be ones of constantly experienced intimacy with God, that their prayers will always be answered as they want them to be, that Christians will always be healed, that there will not be times when they feel 'utterly, unbearably crushed' (2 Corinthians 1:8 NRSV). Such a perspective can give a healthy balance to our lives, so that we neither miss out on the glories of the Kingdom now, nor are disillusioned by expecting now what is not available until the Kingdom comes in its fullness.

And the Resurrection gives us a glimpse of our destiny as human beings, and the destiny of creation. It shows us where history is headed. It shows us that history does indeed have a goal. History is not just a set of random stories being told by different people that doesn't amount to anything coherent, as post-modernism would have it. It is going somewhere. It has direction. It has a destination. God is at work within it, and is committed to bringing it safely to the harbour of His final purpose for it.

The Resurrection shows us – it doesn't just leave us hoping, it *shows us* – that God will ultimately triumph, that creation will not be discarded but will ultimately be reaffirmed and renewed and restored, that death will finally be overcome, that the relationships for which we are made and because of which life is worth living do not come to a cul-de-sac in the grave, that meaning will not forever be mocked by our finitude, that evil and suffering will not forever blight our world, that our physicality is not a temporary encumbrance but an essential part of our glory, that injustice and oppression and disease and decay and death and sorrow and unkindness and brokenness are finite whereas Life and Love and Beauty and Glory and Joy are eternal. This is not the domain of the nutter: it is part of the framework of hope and the structure of sanity.

Many people like to turn to the end of a novel and see what happens at the end, long before they actually read through to that point. It is, of course, a thoroughly reprehensible way of reading a novel! But it is exactly what we are encouraged to do with the book of history. Look and see what's going to happen at the End, because then you'll know how to live in the present. The book of history is a different sort of book – one in which we know the beginning and the end, and it is our job to make up the intervening chapters as we go along. We are given, in the Resurrection of Jesus, a vision of what creation will look like when it is finally healed, a vision of what we will look like when we are fully ourselves, and a knowledge of what will *last*. It is our job now to live in such a way as to point in the direction we know we are headed, to be more and more the sort of people we know we shall be then, to align ourselves with the coming Kingdom and not with the passing age.[1]

---

[1] For a fuller and more sophisticated version of this book analogy, see N. T. Wright, *The New Testament and the People of God* (SPCK, 1992), pp. 140–144.

4. THE RESURRECTION ASSURES US THAT JESUS WILL BE JUDGE

> In the past God overlooked such ignorance, but now he commands all people everywhere to repent. For he has set a day when he will judge the world with justice by the man he has appointed. He has given proof of this to everyone by raising him from the dead (Acts 17:30–31).

The coming Messiah was expected to be God's appointed Judge. He would be King (Psalm 2), and part of the job of kings was to judge – wisely and fairly. That was the aspect of kingship in which Solomon excelled, of course (1 Kings 3:9, 11, 16–28), and it was an aspect of what Israel hoped for in her coming great king:

> He will not judge by what he sees with his eyes,
>> or decide by what he hears with his ears;
> but with righteousness he will judge the needy,
>> with justice he will give decisions for the poor of the earth.
>
> **Isaiah 11:3–4**

It was an aspect of what was observed in the ministry of Jesus. He had a reputation for integrity, impartiality (Matthew 22:16) and insight (John 2:24–5), such that people wondered whether He might be the Messiah (John 4:29), and asked Him to solve their legal disputes (Luke 12:13). So observable were His judicial qualities that, when asked for a sign, He did not point to His miracles but claimed a wisdom greater than that of Solomon himself (Matthew 12:42). And He even claimed that He would be the one by whom all the nations would be judged (Matthew 25:31).

But it was the Resurrection that vindicated these claims, and sealed His claim to be Judge. The Resurrection proclaimed Him to be the Messiah. The Messiah was to be King and Judge. Thus the Resurrection was proof that God had appointed Him to judge the world with justice (Acts 17:31). The appropriate response is repentance (Acts 17:30) – and relief that the One who will judge us is the one who loves us enough to die for us (Romans 5:8) and was raised to life for our vindication and acquittal (Romans 4:25).

5. THE RESURRECTION OF JESUS IS A PICTURE AND PLEDGE OF OUR OWN

'If we have been united with him in a death like his ...' says Paul – and we *have* been: that's what baptism is all about (Romans 6:4) – '... we will certainly be united with him in a resurrection like his' (Romans 6:5 NRSV). Or, as he says elsewhere (1 Corinthians 15:20), the resurrection of Jesus is the *first-fruits* of the coming harvest. The Jewish people in Old Testament times would celebrate the feast of the first-fruits by offering the earliest produce of the year to God. They knew that it was safe to celebrate, because it had started to be gathered in. The first bit of the crop held the promise that the fields were fertile, the harvest had already started, the full crop was on its way. And that is how Paul saw the resurrection of Jesus. It is, as we have already seen, the End bursting into the middle. It is the Resurrection beginning early. And it assures us that the full crop, the general resurrection, is on its way. We know that God can do it, because He has already done it to Jesus. And we know that He *will* do it, because what He did to Jesus, He did for us. The Resurrection is the pledge of our own resurrection.

His resurrection is a picture of our own. We shall be united with Him in a resurrection *like His*. In the glorious, glorified, uninhibited, unrestricted and transfigured body of Jesus we see what God wants to do for us and for every created particle – namely, make it translucent to the glory of God.

Paul draws out some of the implications of the resurrection body of Jesus for envisaging our own resurrection bodies, in his extended reflection on the issue in 1 Corinthians 15. What will our resurrection bodies be like? They will be bodies in which our mortality is a thing of the past (1 Corinthians 15:53). They will be bodies in which our physicality is taken up and transfigured (1 Corinthians 15:44). They will be bodies in which our diversity is preserved and enhanced (1 Corinthians 15:39–42a). All the rich variety of human shapes, types, colours, gifts, characters, minds, humours, interests, gestures, laughs, mannerisms and peculiarities will be taken up and polished up – purged of all sin and healed of all hurt.

This flies in the face of one of the major world-views in Paul's day, namely Platonism. For Platonism, diversity was a problem. Indeed, even the fact that some people become plumbers whereas others become carpenters was seen as part of the problem of evil. For Platonists, diversity was a problem because their goal was to return to the One.

For Christians, however, our goal is to return to the Three-in-One. The Trinity is our model, not the One, and in the Trinity you have diversity *within* the unity of God. Unity is therefore not incompatible with diversity. On the contrary, you have diversity within the very being of God Himself. Yes, we want unity, but a unity that completely embraces the entire diversity of God's creation. He made it diverse in the first place, and He wants it diverse for ever. So neither physically nor in any other way will we be squeezed into a mould when we are remade. Neither physically nor in any other way will our uniqueness be reduced. On the contrary, it will be enhanced, for it is sin that makes us behave with sheeplike conformity (Isaiah 53:6), and we shall no longer be constrained by sin.

As a Christian community, therefore, we need to learn to delight in diversity. We must not expect everyone to conform to our way of being Christian, to our way of worshipping, to our way of praying. There are God-given parameters, of course, but there is also room for everyone to be the unique person God made them to be, within those parameters. I remember speaking to a man who was Pastoral Director at a seminary. When he was a student at the same seminary, the then Pastoral Director took him to the window of his office, pointed at the nearby Heinz factory, and said, 'They're doing very much what we're doing in this seminary – turning out identical products!' To which the future Pastoral Director said, 'At least they have 57 Varieties!' There are as many varieties as there are people, and that variety will be preserved and enhanced at the Resurrection. In the mean time, we must enable and encourage every individual to be themselves, in submission to Christ and in relationship with others. We must resist the tendency of the world to squeeze us into one mould – one acceptable clothing style, one attractive body type and so on – against the grain of our own uniqueness.

A while ago, I was at a party and got talking to a delightful concert pianist. He asked me what I did, and I told him – which usually provokes some sort of a reaction! And in his case, he started attacking the idea of an after-life. 'Life is so rich', he argued, 'that we don't need something else to look forward to. To look forward to another life is to fail to appreciate this one.' I listened for a while, and then I asked him what he would say to my brother, who had a stroke in his late forties, was left unable to speak and had limited movement of his limbs. He thought for a moment, and then said, 'I think I would lie.' Which was, paradoxically, very honest of him. But I explained that I don't have to lie. I believe that my brother will be given a new body: one which responds to his impulses and gives expression to who he is, one that enables him to communicate, move, touch, feel, dance, one that no longer frustrates his intentions or limits his options, one that throbs with vitality and character. And that is not just wishful thinking: it comes on the authority of the Resurrection of Jesus in human history, in flesh and blood, and in defiance of all that would consign us to dust. That doesn't make his present condition 'okay'. Far from it. But it does set it in the context of ultimate hope.

6. THE RESURRECTION OF JESUS IS THE PLEDGE – AND BEGINNING – OF CREATION'S RENEWAL

This point is linked to the last. The future restoration of the universe is closely related to our future resurrection – a point made by Eric Mascall:

Because we are by our nature physical beings linked by our bodily metabolism both with one another and with the rest of the material world ('Whatever Miss T. eats', Mr de la Mare has reminded us, 'turns into Miss. T.'), our resurrection will involve nothing less than the transformation of the whole material order. This is, in fact, what orthodox Christian theology, following the teaching of the Bible, has always held. The resurrection of the body is intimately linked with the ultimate transfiguration of matter as such.[22]

Romans 8 makes the clearest link between our future resurrection and the healing of the physical universe. It is not just human beings who are crying out in pain (Romans 8:23), crying out for justice (Revelation 6:10), calling on Christ to come and put all things right (Revelation 22:20): *creation itself* is groaning in its friction and conflict and mortality and decay (Romans 8:22), and is longing for its liberation (Romans 8:21). And that liberation will come as and when the children of God are revealed in all their full status as adopted sons and daughters (Romans 8:23). Because human beings were created to rule creation – in obedience to and in reflection of the loving and liberating rule of God – it is only when human beings take up that responsibility at last and properly perform that rôle that creation will be 'liberated from its bondage to decay and brought into the glorious freedom of the children of God' (Romans 8:21).

We saw in the first chapter that creation is good, that it has value in its own right, that it has purpose. We saw that same goodness and value and purpose affirmed when God entered into His creation, became part of creation, took creation up into Himself. Here in the Resurrection, we see creation reaffirmed. When He rose up from the dead, He did not leave creation behind. He did not leave His physicality behind. He remained committed to it. It remained part of Him. In Him, a little bit of creation has been brought through death and out the other side, forever beyond the reach of death and decay. In Him, a little bit of creation has been healed and glorified and transfigured.

And that little bit of creation is the first-fruits of a cosmic harvest. Those few cells are the bridgehead for every other particle. We know that creation will be redeemed because the process has already begun in the resurrection body of Jesus. Disharmony, and division, and disease, and disability, and death and decay have had notice served upon them. We look forward not to salvation *from* the world, but to the salvation *of* the world.

7. THE RESURRECTION TELLS US THAT OUR PHYSICAL NEEDS MATTER AND CALLS US TO ATTEND TO THE PHYSICAL NEEDS OF OTHERS

I worked for a year as flight dispatcher for an air ambulance service in Newfoundland and Labrador. And one of the little fishing villages dotted along the Labrador coastline used to call their doctor 'the man for the body', and their minister 'the man for the soul'. But that might suggest that God isn't interested in the body – just in the soul. And nothing could be further from the truth. If He had not been interested in the body, He would hardly have gone to the trouble of raising the body of Jesus, and He would hardly go to the bother of raising *our* bodies. The Resurrection demonstrates that God's concern is for the totality of the human person – and indeed the totality of the created order.

Platonism saw the body as a temporary and somewhat distasteful encumbrance which we shall shed when we die, whereas the Resurrection demonstrated that it will be an essential and permanent aspect of who we are as human beings. We were made physical – and God saw that that physicality was *good*. He took physicality into Himself at the Incarnation, and He did not jettison it when He was raised from the dead. As we shall see when we come on to the Ascension, it remains part of who He eternally is. Our physicality is God-given: it is good, it is essential and it will be remade the other side of the grave. We do not want to be unclothed, says Paul in 2 Corinthians 5:4, but to be *re-*

clothed; not to be divested of our physicality but to be reinvested with a renewed physicality, free from the mortality of our present existence.

And therefore it is an essential part of our service of one another to attend to one another's physical, as well as spiritual, moral and emotional needs. That is the assumption of the whole New Testament. It was the practice of Jesus who insisted upon feeding the crowds as well as teaching them. He had a healing ministry as well as a teaching ministry. He taught that failure to attend to the physical needs of others is a matter of eternal significance (Luke 16:19–31, Matthew 25:31–46). It was the practice of the apostles, healing the sick and paralysed, and organising famine relief (Acts 11:27–30, Romans 15:26 etc). And it was the teaching of the New Testament writers that it is hypocritical to see a brother or sister without clothes or food and to ignore those physical needs (James 2:15–16).

Theory and practice here go hand in hand. We have a world-view shaped by the Resurrection of Jesus, which sees the physical as an essential aspect of who we were created to be. And we have a community that seeks to address the physical needs both of its members and of the world around. The Church, when it has been true to itself, has always done the same. It is no coincidence that it was the Church that founded the hospital (and, more recently, the hospice) movement. If we are to be faithful to the vision of human nature and human destiny that we have been given in the Resurrection of Jesus from the dead, the physical needs of others will make sacrificial inroads into our time, our money and our imagination as a Christian community.

8. THE RESURRECTION IS POLITICALLY SUBVERSIVE

Christian faith is often portrayed as 'pie in the sky when you die'. It is therefore often dismissed as being the 'opium of the people'. Give people hope for a better life after this one, and it'll keep them politically acquiescent now. But that is profoundly to misunderstand the Christian faith and to leave the Resurrection out of account altogether. For the hope of Resurrection is not pie in the sky when you die. For one thing, it is not 'in the sky': it is a radical transformation of heaven *and earth*. It is the remaking of this world, not our removal from it. It is *on earth* that God's Kingdom is to come and His will be done. Nor is it just 'when you die'. For the Resurrection has already begun. The new age has already started. The Kingdom has already been inaugurated. It is therefore just as much about bread now, working conditions now, fair trading arrangements now, justice now, as it is about pie then.

Of course, there is a future dimension to our hope. Of course, the Kingdom is not yet here in its fullness. Of course, we see only through a glass darkly. And of course, the end of death, crying, mourning and pain is still to come. But we are called to work now, so far as we can, for the sort of world that is going to be ushered in then. We are called to be Resurrection people, Kingdom people, harmony people – looking and working towards that new age by all that we are and by all that we do. The new day is dawning, and we are called to be people of the light now.

I want to suggest three reasons why the Resurrection is politically subversive. First, *the Resurrection is politically subversive because it proclaims Jesus to be Son of God*. As we saw in Chapter 4, the title 'Son of God' was not a vacant one at the time. It was one of the titles of Caesar. So when Paul says that Jesus has been declared with power to be Son of God by resurrection from the dead (Romans 1:4), he was on a collision course with Caesar. No wonder that, when we last see him in the book of Acts, he is under house arrest in Rome. As N. T. Wright remarks:

> There can be no question that the title would have been heard by many in the greco-roman world, from very early on, as a challenge to Caesar. And there is certainly no question that some of the early writers, including Paul, intended it in this way ... Calling

Jesus 'son of god' they constituted themselves by implication as a collection of rebel cells within Caesar's empire, loyal to a different monarch.[23]

Because the Resurrection has vindicated Jesus as Messiah and as divine Lord, Christians may give their ultimate allegiance to no one else. And this will bring us into conflict with all totalitarian systems. It will impel us to challenge all abuse of power, all dehumanising government, all lordship that usurps and warps the loving lordship of Christ. From Peter and John before the Sanhedrin to Archbishop Jamani Luwum before Idi Amin, the church has, when it has been faithful to its resurrected Lord, challenged all oppressive leadership – and has paid the inevitable price.

Secondly, *the Resurrection is politically subversive because it happened within, and is God's claim upon, the real world*. This is essential, for unless the Resurrection happened within the real world, it is of no relevance to the real world. We are back here to the old principle that 'what is not assumed is not healed', usually applied to the Incarnation, but true, by extension, of the Resurrection as well. Unless the Resurrection happened within the real world, it could not have been the healing of the real world. That is the significance of the title of Tom Torrance's book, *Space, Time and Resurrection*. Unless it happened within the coordinates of space and time – the same coordinates within which we live, and struggle, and flourish, and die – then it does not impinge healingly upon us. It does not touch us and it cannot give hope. If it happened outside the coordinates of this world, then it constitutes no threat to those who claim this world for their own.

But if the Resurrection was an event in time and space, an event by which God began to heal creation by reclaiming it for His own liberating rule – and how else could it be healed? – then it constitutes an inherent threat to all exercise of political power that is not compatible with the freedom, love and care that characterise the rule of God. Calling Jesus 'Son of God', as the Resurrection impelled them to do, was thus:

> ... a refusal to retreat, a determination to stop Christian discipleship
> turning into a private cult, a sect, a mystery religion. It launched
> a claim on the world: a claim at once absurd (a tiny group of
> nobodies cocking a snook at the might of Rome) and very serious,
> so serious that within a couple of generations the might of Rome
> was trying, and failing, to stamp it out. It grew from an essentially
> positive view of the world, of creation. It refused to relinquish the
> world to the principalities and powers, but claimed even them for
> allegiance to the Messiah who was now the lord ...[24]

The Resurrection thus belongs first and foremost to the realm of
public truth rather than of private belief, of fact rather than opinion,
of history rather than psychology, of politics rather than pietism.

Thirdly, *the Resurrection is politically subversive because it gives us
a glimpse of the kind of world we are going to be, and encourages us to
work towards that now.* In other words, the Resurrection shows us
that God is capable of, and committed to, putting things right. He is
set upon the righting of wrongs, including, and culminating in, the
wrong that is death. To work and pray for the righting of wrongs
now is therefore to act in harmony with the momentum of history.
It is to align oneself with the coming Kingdom. It is to go with the
grain of God's activity. It is to place oneself on the (ultimately)
winning side. The Resurrection therefore (literally) encourages us
to fight the effects of the Fall, and to try and reshape the present to
resemble the future.

> Hoping for the resurrection fuels revolutionary aspirations, at
> bottom, because it affirms the goodness of the created order and
> God's desire to put it right; hope for pie-in-the-sky challenges
> the goodness of the created order, suggesting that it's not worth
> doing anything about the way things are at the present, since the
> longed-for redemption will occur in a different sphere altogether.[25]

The Resurrection gives us the blueprint of a restored Creation and
calls us to try and implement that blueprint through our actions

and our prayers. To change the analogy, the Resurrection is like the lid of a jigsaw puzzle which gives us a picture of what the puzzle is meant to look like when it is completed. And having that picture helps us to start piecing it together now.

9. THE RESURRECTION GUARANTEES THAT 'OUR LABOUR IN THE LORD IS NOT IN VAIN'

At the end of his great chapter on the Resurrection, Paul draws his final conclusion from the great fact of the resurrection of Jesus. 'Therefore, my dear brothers and sisters', he says, 'stand firm. Let nothing move you. Always give yourselves fully to the work of the Lord, because you know that your labour in the Lord is not in vain' (1 Corinthians 15:58). Or as Mother Teresa often used to put it, 'Nothing done in love is ever lost.' But that is only true if there is going to be a resurrection. It is not true otherwise. All sorts of things done in love are lost, all sorts of loving actions fail to achieve what we want them to achieve. Only the Resurrection guarantees the truth of what she says there. It is only true if the fragments of our lives and of our bodies are gathered up so that nothing be lost, like the bits of bread and fish after the feeding of the five thousand (John 6:12).

The Globe Theatre in London is a reconstruction, as accurate as they could make it, of Shakespeare's theatre. The paving slabs on the floor outside the theatre have names on them. When they were trying to raise money to put up this remarkable edifice, people could have their names chiselled on the paving slabs in exchange for a tidy sum. A number of cathedrals do the same. So you can go to the building you have helped put up, when it is finally done, and see your contribution embedded in the beauty of the building.

So it will be with the Resurrection. All the things that we do, all the work that we do for the Kingdom, every loving act, every right choice, every sacrificial deed is going to be there, as part of that rebuilt cosmos. Nothing is going to be left behind. Nothing is going to be wasted. Even if that work has not proved 'successful' in this life, it's still going to be taken up in some way into the new creation. It's not going to be lost. It's not going to be left behind. It's going to be there making its mark in the renewed and restored creation. We don't bring about the Resurrection: God does. But when He does, all that we are and all that we have done that is not incompatible with the Kingdom of God will be there, shot through with the love and the glory of God.

A while ago, there was a programme on the radio about a community of nuns that was dwindling in number and slowly dying out. Some of the nuns were interviewed and asked the predictable question, 'How do you feel about the death of the Order?' And they replied, 'Well, when the last one of us dies, the work will be complete. Maybe it has served its purpose in the providence of God.' They seemed to have no sense that because the work was coming to an end, their contribution had therefore been in vain. On the contrary, they seemed to have learned the lesson of the Resurrection, that their work in the Lord could never be in vain, however finite and futile it might appear.

THE ASCENSION

In some old baronial halls, stately homes and hunting lodges, one sees deer's heads on the walls, complete with antlers, which are probably annoying from the point of view of dusting, but useful for Christmas decorations. It has frequently been observed, but always strikes me afresh, that the stag must have been going at quite a rate to have got its head through the wall like that! The same could be said of the famous chapel dedicated to the Ascension in Walsingham, which features two plaster feet sticking out from beneath the ceiling – Jesus must have had quite a G-force to have achieved such vertical take-off speed in the space of two metres!

But, of course, the plaster feet are just a pictorial representation of something impossible to represent. Christians have never imagined that the Ascension was a spatial journey like the spatial journeys that the space shuttle makes. When the Russian cosmonaut returned to earth and declared that he had not seen heaven, his observation did not trouble the faith of any modern Christian. Nor is it just modern Christians who are untroubled by such a failure to locate heaven within our space-time universe. The great fourth-century theologian, Athanasius, for instance, said that 'When Christ sat on the right hand of the Father, he did not put the Father on his left'.[26] In other words, to say with the Apostles' Creed that 'He ascended into heaven, and is seated at the right hand of the Father' is to make a theological, not a geographical, point. Nor, to go even further back, did the writers of the New Testament imagine that they were speaking of a spatial journey when they spoke of the Ascension. N. T. Wright assesses their language thus:

> Just as we speak of the sun 'rising', even though we know that the earth is turning in relation to the sun, so ancient Jews were comfortable with the language of heavenly ascent without supposing that their god, and those who shared his habitation, were physically situated a few thousand feet above the surface of the earth ... To speak of someone 'going up to heaven' by no means implied that the person concerned had (a) become a primitive space traveller and (b) arrived, by that means, at a different location within the present space-time universe. We should not allow the vivid, indeed lurid, language of the Middle Ages, or the many hymns and prayers which use the word 'heaven' to denote, it seems, a far-off location within the cosmos we presently inhabit, to make us imagine that first-century Jews thought literalistically in that way too. Some may indeed have done so; there is no telling what things people will believe; but we should not imagine that the early Christian writers thought like that.[27]

No, with Oliver O'Donovan, we 'do not think of the incarnation and ascension as journeys through space from one location to another, like a journey between the earth and the moon ... These events are transitions between the universe of space and time that God has made and his being which is ... beyond it.'[28] We have to use spatial language such as 'up' and 'ascended' because we are creatures of space and time and cannot think without the help of such dimensions, but that does not mean that we think of heaven as being literally 'up there'.

But once we have disposed of the rather crude and simplistic attack of sceptics such as the Russian cosmonaut, we are left with the question of what the Ascension *means*. Does it matter? Does it have anything to teach us? I suspect that it does not impinge greatly on the minds or imaginations of most modern Western Christians. It is a hugely neglected doctrine and a hugely unattended festival, and that is a pity, for it is a moment of our salvation that is rich with significance and good news.

1. THE ASCENSION MARKED THE END OF CHRIST'S EARTHLY APPEARANCES

'I am going to the Father, where you can see me no longer' (John 16:10). There was a time, as Jesus had predicted, when the disciples stopped seeing Him, when the Resurrection appearances ceased. (Jesus' appearance to Paul years later on the road to Damascus, was an anomalous exception, as Paul himself recognised (1 Corinthians 15:8).) Why did they cease? Because Jesus was no longer around in the way that He had been around. As C. S. Lewis saw, 'a phantom can just fade away; but an objective entity must go somewhere – something must happen to it.'[29] And the Ascension affirms that something *has* happened to Jesus' body. It has gone somewhere. It has gone to the Father. It has left this universe of space and time and gone to the very presence of God, who transcends what He has made.

2. THE ASCENSION WAS THE 'CORONATION' OF CHRIST

In my vision at night I looked, and there before me was one like a son of man, coming with the clouds of heaven. He approached the Ancient of Days and was led into his presence. He was given authority, glory and sovereign power; all nations and peoples of every language worshipped him. His dominion is an everlasting dominion that will not pass away, and his kingdom is one that will never be destroyed.

Daniel 7:13–14

In context, the Son of Man is a representative figure (standing for faithful Israel), who suffers at the hands of the beasts (standing for the pagan nations), and who is finally vindicated the other side of suffering by coming on the clouds of heaven before the Ancient of Days, and is given authority, glory and power. The affinity between this passage and the Ascension is palpable. Jesus called Himself 'Son of Man'. He suffered and died at the hands of a pagan empire. He came before God, 'and a *cloud* hid him from their sight' (Acts 1:9). He was vindicated and glorified and worshipped by *all* nations – Gentiles as well as Jews – and given an everlasting Kingdom. In the light of Daniel 7, we may say that the Ascension was Jesus' vindication,[m] Jesus' exaltation, Jesus' coronation, Jesus' enthronement.

> The highest place that heaven affords
> Is his, is his by right,
> The King of kings and Lord of lords,
> And heaven's eternal Light.[30]

And this of course brings into even sharper focus a point that we made about the Resurrection, namely that it is politically subversive. The Ascension was Part Two of the vindication and exaltation of Jesus. Part One was to raise Him to life: Part Two was to raise Him to heaven. The top spot is therefore taken. Jesus is on the throne, and therefore the beasts are not. Nebuchadnezzar is not. Belshazzar is not. Herod is not. Pilate is not. Caesar is not. The Prime Minister is not. The Queen is not. The President is not. The World Bank is not.

---

[m] For the Ascension as Jesus' vindication, see also John 16:10.

The Market is not. I am not. That is extraordinarily good news, for it means that the governance of the universe is in the utterly safe, scarred hands of Jesus: He alone will use power exclusively in the service of love. It is extraordinarily good news for it means that the days of the beasts and their distorted and destructive power and pathetic propaganda are numbered. But it is also extraordinarily subversive, for it prohibits us from giving our worship or ultimate allegiance to anyone or anything but Him. And the beasts don't like it when we refuse to worship them.

3. THE ASCENSION WAS THE EXALTATION OF CHRIST, AND THEREFORE OF HUMANITY

If the Son of Man was, indeed, a representative figure, and if we allow Him to represent us, then what is true of Him becomes true also of us. And that is exactly what we find with reference to the Ascension. 'Because of his great love for us, God, who is rich in mercy, made us alive with Christ even when we were dead in transgressions – it is by grace you have been saved. And God raised us up with Christ and seated us with him in the heavenly realms in Christ Jesus' (Ephesians 2:4–6). In Jesus' Resurrection, we were 'made alive with Christ': in Jesus' Ascension, we were 'raised up with Christ'. His vindication is our vindication. His exaltation is our exaltation.

If we look for the basis of human dignity, then we may look for it in the fact that we were created in the image of God, to rule and care for creation. We may look for it in the fact that God Himself took human flesh and lived a human life. We may look for it in the fact that God valued us highly enough to die for us. We may look for it in the resurrection body of Jesus, and see something of the glory and potential of being human. But, perhaps most significantly of all, we may look for it in the fact that human nature has now been taken into the realm of God, into the presence of God, onto the very throne of God in the Ascension of Jesus:

Thou hast raised our human nature
 In the clouds to God's right hand;
There we sit in heavenly places,
 There with thee in glory stand;
Jesus reigns, adored by Angels;
 Man with God is on the throne;
Mighty Lord, in thine Ascension
 We by faith behold our own.[31]

There is a human being on the throne of heaven. One of our own. One like us (in every respect bar our sin). One who is not unacquainted with our difficulties and struggles and pains. One in whom we have a stake. Think how affirmed and encouraged the Polish people felt when one of their own countrymen was elected to sit on the chair of St Peter. How affirmed then are we by having one of our number to sit upon the throne of heaven. But it is greater than that. Because He is our representative, and He is on the throne of heaven, therefore *we* sit in heavenly places, *we* stand in glory, *we* share in His reign. His enthronement is *our* enthronement. There is no higher place for us to aspire to.

This, of course, has ethical implications. The more dignified and exalted humanity is seen to be, the more it matters how each and every member of the species is treated. As John Davies notes:

> He is taking his human nature into the realm of the Father. Henceforth, our humanity is represented within the community of God; heaven will never be the same again. Henceforth, any insult to the humanity of any person, any treating of a human being as expendable rubbish, is strictly a blasphemy; it is an insult to the nature which God has eternally taken upon himself.[32]

4. THE ASCENSION TELLS US THAT THE BRIDGE IS STILL SECURE BETWEEN GOD AND US

In Chapter 4, I applied the 'bridge' diagram, which is usually used of the Cross, to the Incarnation, and suggested that Jesus could only be the bridge between God and us if He were both fully divine and fully human.

Many people tend to imagine that in Jesus, God became human, lived a human life and died a human death, and that He then left off being human and went back to being God, rather like one of the old Apollo rockets, which would jettison its spent stages when it no longer needed them. NO. When He took upon Himself humanity in the Incarnation, at the moment of conception, that was for ever. He is never going to let go of that. He is never going to let go of *us*. As an old prayer put it, 'The Son of God for love of our fallen race didst most wonderfully and humbly choose to be made man, *as never to be unmade more,* and to take our nature, *as never more to lay it off.*'[33]

Therefore the bridge is forever secure on both sides, because He is never going to let go of His humanity and He is never going to let go of His divinity. He is eternally welded to us and committed to us. So the only bridge over which we may return to God will never collapse. We shall never lose our access to God, because of the Incarnation and the Ascension.

5. THE ASCENSION ENABLED THE SPIRIT TO BE POURED OUT ON ALL FLESH

In the Old Testament, the Spirit was active in the bringing into being of creation (Genesis 1:2) and in the empowerment of particular leaders, artists and warriors for particular tasks. But the prophets promised the people a day when the Spirit would be poured out on all flesh, on all ages and classes, and would enable them to hear, to glimpse and to reflect the reality of God to one another (Joel 2:28).

Jesus was a man uniquely endowed with the Spirit. The Spirit was specially operative in His conception (Luke 1:35). The Holy Spirit descended on Him like a dove at His baptism (Luke 3:22). He is described as 'full of the Holy Spirit' and 'led by the Spirit' (Luke 4:1). He travelled around 'in the power of the Spirit' (Luke 4:14). He was 'anointed' by the Spirit (Luke 4:18). He cast out demons 'by the Spirit of God' (Matthew 12:28). All this was true of Him uniquely. But He spoke of a time when the Spirit would come to His disciples too (John 16:13), and our point here is that He said that that could only happen after, and as a result of, the Ascension. 'I tell you the truth: It is for your good that I am going away. Unless I go away, the Counsellor will not come to you; but if I go, I will send him to you' (John 16:7).

Why is the Ascension the necessary prerequisite for the outpouring of the Spirit? I don't know. But it seems as if somehow the Ascension secures the bridge on the far side. To use a different analogy: if a diver plunges into the sea to retrieve from the seabed something that has been lost, it is an important moment when they find what has been lost and take hold of it – but the rescue is not complete until they return with it to the surface. Similarly with the rescue of humanity. It is a vastly significant moment when God takes hold of our lost humanity in the Incarnation – but the rescue is not complete until He exalts it to the realm and the reign of God at the Ascension. It is then that the bridge is finally secured on both sides, and can bear the weight of traffic.

It seems as if somehow the bridge is meant not just as the means for us to return to God, but also – and as the necessary precursor to that – for the Spirit to cross over from God to us, in new, liberated and liberating ways. Jesus is a ladder that is meant for two-way traffic (John 1:51): first the Spirit to us, and then us to the Father. This is but speculation, but Jesus makes clear that there is some sort of link between His going and the Spirit coming. It is to the Ascension, then, that we must be grateful for the coming of the Spirit.

6. THE ASCENSION TELLS US THAT GOD IS ETERNALLY AND INTERNALLY COMMITTED TO HIS WORLD

Jesus did not leave behind His humanity when He ascended to the Father. Therefore there will always be atoms, molecules and cells within the very being of God. So God cannot now abandon His creation without abandoning Himself. There is creation within Him. It's part of Him. He is utterly identified with it. He is *bound* to His world and cannot walk away from His relationship with it.

And that is good news for a world that is fearful for its own survival. In the days of the Cold War, we were afraid that we might destroy our world by nuclear catastrophe. Now, that danger has receded somewhat, and the more urgent danger is environmental, that by our greed and our exploitation we might so damage our world as to render it uninhabitable, or at least less diverse, less beautiful and less congenial. Thus there is the fear that for whatever reason, the time will come when our place will know us no more. And to that fear, the internal commitment of the eternal and life-giving God as made known in the Ascension of Jesus, speaks its message of hope.

7. THE ASCENSION GIVES US A JOB TO DO

With Jesus no longer physically with us, God's primary means of working in His world is now through us. To that task he commissions us at the Ascension, and for that task He equips us at Pentecost. In His final charge to His disciples, He makes a statement, issues a command and gives them a promise. The statement is that 'All authority in heaven and on earth has been given to me' (Matthew 28:18). It is an uncompromising claim. He does not say that '*Some* authority has been given to me, and some to Moses and some to the Buddha and some to Mohammed and some to Haile Selassie', but makes the audacious claim that '*All* authority in heaven and on earth has been given to *me*' – a claim which the Resurrection and

Ascension between them make good, and which the Cross makes safe. Only in the wounded hands of the One who gave up power can such authority be safely placed.

He then issues a command which is as all-encompassing as the statement: 'Therefore go and make disciples of all nations, baptising them in the name of the Father and of the Son and of the Holy Spirit, and teaching them to obey everything I have commanded you' (Matthew 28:19–20a). *All* authority has been given to Him: we are to make disciples of *all* nations. We may not limit ourselves to those nations which don't have perfectly good religions already – we are sent to make disciples of *all* nations. And we are not told to go to all nations and give them the benefit of western civilisation and education, but simply to give them Jesus, His teaching, His sacraments, and the new (trinitarian) understanding of God that He (and the experience of the Spirit) occasioned.

Finally, the promise: 'surely I am with you always, to the very end of the age' (Matthew 28:20b) – 'all authority … all nations … all things I have commanded you … always'. The universality of our mission springs from the universality of His authority, and is utterly dependent upon the universality and constancy of His presence. If His statement is true, then nothing can prevent Him from keeping His promise. How He keeps that promise is the subject of the next chapter.

FURTHER RESOURCES FOR READING, PRAYER AND ACTION

The Resurrection

N. T. Wright, *The Resurrection of the Son of God* (SPCK, London, 2003). An offputtingly huge, but surprisingly readable and powerful cumulative argument for the bodily resurrection of Jesus.

Also, his popular-level book on the Resurrection, entitled *Surprised by Hope* (SPCK, 2007). You could try, too, his controversial little book, *For All The Saints? Remembering the Christian Departed* (SPCK, London, 2003).

A. M. Ramsey, *The Resurrection of Christ* (Bles, 1945).

T. F. Torrance, *Space, Time and Resurrection* (1976) (T & T Clark, Edinburgh, 1998). A difficult, but important, book on the Resurrection and the Ascension in the light of modern science.

An Easter Sourcebook, edited by Gabe Huck, Gail Ramshaw and Gordon Lathrop (Liturgy Training Publications, Chicago, 1988).

Steve Chalke, *Faithworks: Actions speak louder than words* (Kingsway Publications, 2001).

Steve Chalke and Tom Jackson, *Faithworks: Stories of Hope* (Kingsway Publications, 2001). These two books take up my plea, on the basis of the Resurrection, to take people's physical needs seriously in our service of them. They urge churches to get involved in service of the communities in which they are set, and give many suggestions and examples as to how this could be attempted.

The Ascension

Peter Toon, *The Ascension of our Lord* (Nelson, Nashville, 1984).

Doug Farrow, *Ascension and Ecclesia: On the Significance of the Doctrine of the Ascension for Ecclesiology and Christian Cosmology* (T & T Clark, Edinburgh, 1999). Heavy-going, but important.

Rowan Williams, 'Ascension of Christ', *A New Dictionary of Christian Theology*, edited by Alan Richardson and John Bowden (SCM Press, London, 1983).

Joseph Ratzinger, 'Ascension of Christ', *Encyclopedia of Theology*, edited by Karl Rahner (Burns and Oates, London, 1975).

7 SPIRIT

" Ooooh.. sounds
like a Christmas bottle
of Malt. "

There was an old man who cried 'Run!
For the end of the world has begun.
The one I fear most
Is the old Holy Ghost.
I can cope with the Father and Son!'

And so it is, in some ways, I suspect, with us. Jesus was a human being and we can therefore relate to Him. 'Father' and 'Son' are personal terms. We may or may not have had good experiences of our fathers (or our sons for that matter), but we know that they are *people* not things. But 'Spirit'. Worse still, 'Ghost'. It all sounds a bit spooky and scary. 'Spirit' strikes us as an impersonal word. And therein lies the problem. We see the

Spirit as something.[a] But the Spirit is not a thing – He is a personal being.

1. THE SPIRIT IS A PERSONAL BEING

At the beginning of this book, we saw something of the huge significance of believing that there is a Person behind the universe, a Person at the heart of reality. The need to be loved, the need to be valued, to have meaning and purpose are all ultimately unmeetable needs, unless there is a Person there who loves us, values us and has purposes for us. It would be very odd, therefore, if the Spirit who, as we shall see, was instrumental in bringing creation into existence and is the agent of its renewal, were less than personal Himself.[b] Instead of being the *Holy* Spirit, He would simply be the amoral, impersonal, unrelational, non-purposive, unknowing, uncaring 'life-force'. As it is, however, 'the actions attributed to the Holy Spirit are personal actions, the doings of a divine person', says Tom Smail.[1] Gordon Fee enumerates:

> That Paul understands the Spirit as person is confirmed … by the fact that the Spirit is the subject of a large number of verbs that demand a personal agent: The Spirit searches all things (1 Cor 2:10), knows the mind of God (1 Cor 2:11), teaches the content of the gospel to believers (1 Cor 2:13), dwells among or within believers (1 Cor 3:16; Rom 8:11; 2 Tim 1:14), accomplishes all things (1 Cor 12:11), gives life to those who believe (2 Cor 3:6), cries out from within our hearts (Gal 4:6), leads us in the ways of God (Gal

[a] Jane Williams sees this as a particular problem in the West: 'The extent to which the Spirit failed to find an imaginative role in Western art is clear in all those pictures of two men and a bird. Compare that with Rublev's mysterious and lovely Trinity of equal persons grouped around the table.' (*Trinity and Unity*, a booklet in the Affirming Catholicism series (Dartman, Longman & Todd, 1995), p. 6.) Rublev was a supreme artist of the Eastern Orthodox tradition, which she sees as having a less inadequate view of the Spirit.

[b] As von Balthasar says, 'I give myself over, in belief, into the sacred and healing Mystery of the Spirit. Surely not into an impersonal power, for there can be no such thing in God, but rather into an incomprehensible Someone, who is someone Other than the Father and the Son (John 14:16).' (*Credo: Meditations on the Apostles' Creed*, translated by David Kipp, T & T Clark, Edinburgh, 1990, p. 76.)

5:18; Rom 8:14), bears witness with our own spirits (Rom 8:16), has desires that are in opposition to the flesh (Gal 5:17), helps us in our weakness (Rom 8:26), intercedes in our behalf (Rom 8:26–27), works all things together for our ultimate good (Rom 8:28), strengthens believers (Eph 3:16), and is grieved by our sinfulness (Eph 4:30). Furthermore, the fruit of the Spirit's indwelling are the personal attributes of God (Gal 5:22–23).[2]

Not only is the language used of the Spirit personal language, but, as Tom Smail points out, the pronouns used of the Spirit are personal pronouns.

Thus he concludes that 'in his dealings with us, the Holy Spirit acts personally towards us'.[3] The image of wind that is used of Him (John 3:8, Acts 2:2) is simply a way of picturing His invisibility, power and unpredictable, uncontrollable sovereignty – not His impersonality. The tongues as of fire which came upon the disciples as the Holy Spirit came upon them (Acts 2:3) suggest His purification of them for the tasks to which they were called, which implies that the Purifier is both purposive and moral – both of them characteristics of personhood. The Holy Spirit may be more than personal, but He is not less than personal – or He would (in that respect at least) be less than us. Nor is He less than divine.

2. THE SPIRIT IS A DIVINE PERSON

In Chapter 4, we saw that only if Jesus is divine can He reveal God to us and reconcile us to Him. The same is true of the Spirit. Only if the Spirit is divine can He be instrumental in revelation and salvation. And certainly Scripture, which sees Him as involved in both those works of God, assumes His divinity. Paul calls the Spirit 'the Lord' (2 Corinthians 3:17), which is how the Greek translation of the Old Testament translated the name 'Yahweh'. He says that the Spirit 'gives life' (2 Corinthians 3:6), which is something only God can do. He writes that 'The Spirit searches all things, even the deep things of God. For who knows the thoughts of another human being except that person's own spirit within? In the same way no-one knows the thoughts of God except the Spirit of God' (1 Corinthians 2:10–11) – an analogy which, as Tom Smail notes, 'clearly implies the identity of the Spirit with the God whom he reveals'.[4] And, of course, Jesus Himself labels speech against the Holy Spirit 'blasphemy' (Matthew 12:31–32).

Despite the wealth of biblical evidence for the divinity of the Spirit, a movement arose in the fourth century, called the Macedonian heresy, which denied that the Spirit is divine. St Basil led the orthodox defence of the Spirit's divinity, and was accused of a little underhand liturgical innovation to impress the divinity of the Spirit on the worshipping public by stealth. Those who denied the divinity of the Spirit tended to say the Gloria as 'Glory to the Father, through the Son, in the Holy Spirit.' In response to the Macedonian heresy, Basil preferred to say 'Glory to the Father, *with* the Son, *together with* the Holy Spirit.' His opponents accused him of making it up to suit his theological agenda. He claimed that it was not an innovation. It had just as ancient a pedigree.[5] Both are perfectly acceptable theologically. 'Glory to the Father, through the Son, in the Holy Spirit' expresses the trinitarian grammar more exactly – the Father is the terminus of our praise, the Son is its conduit, and the Holy Spirit is its milieu and its motor. 'Glory to the Father, with the Son, together with the Holy Spirit' emphasises the equality, the equal divinity and the equal praiseworthiness of all three persons of the Trinity – and it is (roughly) this version that, with Basil's advocacy, 'stuck' and is in liturgical use today. What is important is that the divinity of the Spirit was accepted and established, for, without it, the person of the Father and the saving work of the Son would be inaccessible – and unknown – to us.

3. THE SPIRIT IS A DISTINCT DIVINE PERSON

If, when you asked your doctor for a second opinion, he went out of the room, returning in a Groucho false nose and glasses to give you exactly the same diagnosis, you would feel that it had hardly been a second opinion. Similarly, when Jesus promised His disciples 'another Counsellor to be with you for ever – the Spirit of truth' (John 14:16–

17), it would hardly be *another* Counsellor if it were really Jesus in another form. And when Jesus says of the Spirit that 'He will bring glory to me by taking from what is mine and making it known to you' (John 16:14), it would be self-promotional – and indeed non-sensical – unless the Spirit were distinct from Jesus Himself.

> Through the work of the Spirit, Jesus will receive a glory from outside himself that nevertheless has its ultimate divine source in the Spirit, who shares his divine being and yet is … distinct from him. Jesus finishes his work and returns to the Father, but the Spirit leads his people in every generation into the unfolding riches and manifold implications of what he has done, and thus brings him new glory. The personal distinctness of the Spirit's work over against the work of the Son is the source of the freedom and spontaneity of our response to Christ.[6]

The Spirit is distinct from the Father and the Son. The Spirit is divine. How that can be, and what the implications are, will be the subject of the next chapter.

4. THE SPIRIT GAVE LIFE AND GIVES NEW LIFE

In Genesis 1, 'the Spirit of God was hovering over the waters' (v.2), or, in Eugene Peterson's version, THE MESSAGE, 'God's Spirit brooded like a bird above the watery abyss.' This is of course a paraphrase but it captures well the way in which the Spirit is the agent of creation, bringing the universe to birth, bringing the cosmos into being. And then, in Genesis 2, 'the LORD God formed the man from the dust of the ground and breathed into his nostrils the breath of life, and the man became a living being' (v.7). The Spirit is instrumental in the coming to be of the cosmos, and in particular in the emergence of humanity. He broods the universe into being, and He breathes human beings into life.

But it is not just life, original life, the fact of our existence, that came to us by the Spirit. It is also our re-creation, our re-making, our new life. It is the Spirit who gave new life to Jesus after His death and entombment (Romans 8:11). Tom Wright picks up the imagery well in his *Easter Oratorio*:

On the seventh day God rested
    in the darkness of the tomb;
Having finished on the sixth day
    all his work of joy and doom.
Now the word had fallen silent,
    and the water had run dry,
The bread had all been scattered,
    and the light had left the sky.
The flock had lost its shepherd,
    and the seed was sadly sown,
The courtiers had betrayed their king,
    and nailed him to his throne.
O Sabbath rest by Calvary,
    O calm of tomb below,
Where the grave-clothes and the spices
    cradle him we did not know!
Rest you well, beloved Jesus,
    Caesar's Lord and Israel's King,
In the brooding of the Spirit,
    in the darkness of the spring.[7]

It was a brooding that came to term in the new life of Easter morning.

And what the Spirit did for Jesus, He will do for us and for all things. Just as God breathed into the body of Adam and he became a living being, so Jesus breathed on His disciples to give them new life, saying, 'Receive the Holy Spirit' (John 20:22). It's a deliberate echo of our original creation. It's a pictorial way of saying, 'I gave you life in all its fullness, and you've spoiled it and squandered it and diminished it and misused it and circumscribed it and forgotten the point of it. You've become unresponsive and lifeless. You are dust, and, without the water of the Spirit to animate and vivify and refresh you, you are drying out to dust again. But I am breathing on you my life, I'm giving you my Spirit, I'm remaking you, I'm committed to you, and death and non-existence will not triumph over you.' And not just us, but the whole of creation. Romans 8 makes clear that the whole creation is headed for liberation and renewal, thanks to the power, the prayer – and the labour-pains – of the Spirit. Which is a good excuse to quote Gerard Manley Hopkins:

The world is charged with the grandeur of God.
 It will flame out, like shining from shook foil;
 It gathers to a greatness, like the ooze of oil
Crushed. Why do men then now not reck his rod?
Generations have trod, have trod, have trod;
 And all is seared with trade; bleared, smeared with toil;
 And wears man's smudge and shares man's smell: the soil
Is bare now, nor can foot feel, being shod.

And for all this, nature is never spent;
 There lives the dearest freshness deep down things;
And though the last lights off the black West went
 Oh, morning, at the brown brink eastward, springs –
 Because the Holy Ghost over the bent
  World broods with warm breast and with ah! bright wings.[8]

The earth is fallen and smeared, and we have become alienated from it, by our sin and by our sophistication. Its preservation, its continuing beauty, the possibility of cultural renewal, and the sure and certain hope of the dawning of a renewed world are all alike dependent upon the loving, pained but patient brooding of the Spirit. The Spirit is the one who gives life (John 6:63; 2 Corinthians 3:6).

5. THE SPIRIT IS THE LIBERATOR

The Spirit of the Lord is on me,
because he has anointed me
to preach good news to the poor.

He has sent me to proclaim freedom
> for the prisoners
and recovery of sight for the blind,
to release the oppressed,
> to proclaim the year of the Lord's favour.

Luke 4:18–19

Because the Spirit is the giver of life and the giver of new life, involved both in creation and in recreation, He is at work in the present to bridge the gap between the two. Because pain and poverty, disability and debt, injury and injustice had no place in His original plans for creation and will have no place in the restored creation, the Spirit is actively working against them now. Because the poor are often excluded from the benefits and opportunities that society affords, the mission of the Spirit specifically embraces them.

And what He anointed the Messiah to do, He will empower the Messiah's people to do also. When we do our evangelism in such a way as not to exclude those who couldn't or wouldn't read for pleasure, and those who feel awkward in a social setting, and those who feel educationally out of their depth, then we are remembering to preach good news to *the poor*. When we help run an Alpha course in prison or help support a prisoner when they are released, when we write our Amnesty International letters, or visit the housebound, or take a group of disadvantaged children to the beach, or run a Deaf Awareness course at our church, we are proclaiming freedom for the prisoners. When we pray for people's healing, or pay for someone to have a cataract operation in a Third World country, or to have glasses prescribed for them, when we support a charity that gives community training on how to prevent river blindness, when we provide service sheets and hymn-books and Bibles in Braille, when we offer to read for someone who is blind, we are proclaiming that recovery of sight is part of the Messianic agenda. When we write letters to our MPs about the injustices of world trade, when we buy fairly-traded products, when we stand up for someone at work who has been unfairly treated, we are proclaiming that the Spirit will not rest until the oppressed are released. When we urge the G8 countries to cancel those Third World debts that are unpayable and are crippling tiny economies, we are proclaiming that Jubilee Year (Deuteronomy 15 and Leviticus 25) that the Spirit sent Jesus to announce. In these and a myriad of other ways, we are carrying out the Messianic Manifesto, and allowing ourselves to be blown as the Spirit wills.

In fact, the Spirit is behind so many of the aspects of the Church's mission and ministry that we so often tear apart. He is behind our worship, our prayer, our ministry of healing, our social action, our evangelism, our campaigning for justice, our art. As Tom Smail observes:

> On the one side are charismatic Christians who constantly seek the anointing of the Holy Spirit, but who have yet to show how willing they are to become involved in God's liberating activity in the world. On the other there are social, activist Christians, who want to liberate the oppressed, without receiving the messianic Spirit, who alone will enable them to do so effectively. Oh for the day when the charismatics become the liberators and the liberators become charismatic, because Jesus was both![9]

That was written in 1988, and I see hopeful signs that these delineations are being broken down, and that the whole church is beginning to embrace the whole agenda of Jesus and the Spirit.

6. THE SPIRIT ENABLES US TO BELIEVE

'No-one can say, "Jesus is Lord," except by the Holy Spirit' (1 Corinthians 12:3). We cannot simply choose to believe in God the same way we can choose to join a squash club. And by 'cannot' I don't mean that God won't let us, but that we are just not capable of it. Sin doesn't pass through us, leaving us untouched. It affects us. It changes us. It distorts us. It warps us. And it warps every part of us

– including our will. This was the substance of the famous dispute between St Augustine and a British monk called Pelagius, in the fourth century. Pelagius, quite rightly, took a dim view of sin, and, quite wrongly, felt that all we needed to do was to pull ourselves up by our own moral bootlaces. He thought that we were perfectly free not to sin. We just needed to stop being so wimp-like and get on with it. Augustine knew himself – and humanity – too well to go along with that. The point is, as he recognised, that we *cannot* pull ourselves up by our own moral bootlaces. We cannot simply do what is right. Sin has too much of an after-effect and too much of a hold over us for that. We need God's healing and restorative grace if we are to make any moral progress as human beings whatsoever. And we cannot even ask for that grace, cannot even want it, unless God helps us to want it. We cannot even want to return to God without the help of God. Because our will is fallen, broken and imperfect. Like every other aspect of who we are, our will is not working properly. No part of us is what it should be, and no part of us can get along quite satisfactorily without the help of God.

Thankfully, no part of us, and no part of the process of coming back to God, need be unaided. God reaches out to help us in every place and at every turn. As Oliver O'Donovan writes:

> It is not enough to say, 'God has done his part; now you must do yours.' For [anyone] to believe in what God has done and to respond to it, itself requires a miracle of God. There can never be a point in my salvation at which God simply stops and leaves it to me. The existential act of belief in Christ needs to be evoked in us by God himself. That is what the Holy Spirit does. He is God within me, prompting me to believe in God manifest in Christ, enabling me to approach God the Father.[10]

Notice the trinitarian shape of this process: the Spirit helps me to believe in the Son, who enables me to approach the Father. Only by the work of the Son and the Spirit can we come to the Father. Only thanks to their work is our alienation from Love not eternal. But thanks to that work, our reconciliation is both possible and, as Tom Smail points out, secure:

> If it is through the Spirit that we come to believe the gospel and to appropriate corporately and personally all that the Father has done for us through the Son, none of this is a possibility for or an achievement of our own inherent spirituality; rather, it is a gracious work of God within us. The knowledge of God, the entering into a new relationship with God in Christ, our being renewed into the likeness of Christ, the outcome of our evangelism – all these depend not on human ability or elaborate techniques, but on the promised and uncontrollable activity of the Spirit of God, who, like wind, blows where he wills and is at no one's bidding or command. What matters is not the strength of our spirituality, but the grace of the Spirit of God.[11]

Which is just as well.

7. THE SPIRIT WILL NOT OVERWHELM US BUT WANTS TO WORK WITH US

One of the words that John uses for the Spirit, *Paraclete*, is difficult to translate. Oliver O'Donovan unpacks it helpfully as 'one who stands beside us to help, not one who seizes the controls and runs our lives without consulting us'[12] – which seems to me to help defuse some of the fears that we have about whether our freedom and personality and selfhood would not be swamped by the power and purpose of God, if we were to give Him an inch. As Derek Prince insists:

> The first point which needs to be emphasised is that, in the life of the believer, the Holy Spirit never plays the dictator. When Jesus promised the gift of the Holy Spirit to His disciples, He spoke of Him in terms such as 'Helper', 'Comforter', 'Guide', or 'Teacher'. The Holy Spirit always keeps Himself within these limits. He never usurps the will or the personality of the believer. He never

in any sense forces or compels the believer to do anything against the believer's own will or choice.[13]

The Incarnation itself did not happen without what von Balthasar terms 'the handmaid's discreet Yes'.[14] As Tom Smail comments, 'The gift of the Spirit is in no sense imposed upon [the Virgin Mary] but is gladly received by her.'[15] And the characteristic word that is used of the Spirit's engagement with us is 'fellowship' – not domination, nor invasion, nor control. It is a relationship, a dialogue,[c] a partnership. 'Fellowship' is an interactive term that respects us for who we are, but recognises that we need the help and the perspective and the power of God if we are to grow as human beings and as those through whom God is working to bring about the healing of the cosmos. Far from threatening who we are, the Spirit enables us to be more fully ourselves. Far from impinging on our freedom, it is the Spirit who enables us to be free.

We need to hold points 6 and 7 together. The Spirit enables us to believe (point 6), but does not force us to believe (point 7). The Spirit aids us but does not overwhelm us. In the process of coming to faith, as Tom Smail helpfully encapsulates it, we do not have to decide by ourselves, but we do have to decide *for* ourselves.[16]

We've all known managers who either leave you completely in the dark and fail to consult you on decisions that affect you and your area of responsibility, or, alternatively, land you in it, expect miracles yesterday and fail to give you any support, encouragement or resources to help you accomplish the impossible. The latter, of course, is known as the OTY technique. This is well defined by Annie Rey,

[c] W. H. Auden wrote: 'Our relation to the Word of God is a dialogue between creature and creator ... Again, on God's side, not an exercise of force. As St Augustine said, "He who made us without our help will not save us without our consent."' ('Words and the Word', in *If Christ be not risen*, St Mary's, Bourne Street, London, 1986, p.69.) Of course, the fact that it is a fellowship does not make it a fellowship between equals. And the fact that it is a dialogue does not mean that there is not an essential rôle for obedience on our part. After all, His perspective is total and ours is minuscule. He is perfect and we are warped. And He made us without our help. (Not that we would have been a lot of help!)

from her years of corporate experience. The OTY technique involves: a) Making contact with assorted people who have ambitious ideas, limited experience and no money. b) Promising them: personal attention, extensive training, copious funding, concessionary rates and favoured status. c) Receiving an email from Accounts telling you that none of the above is possible. d) Forwarding the whole project to an underling, marked 'OTY' (over to you). e) Washing your hands of the whole thing, because, after all, staff need to be empowered!

But, in His dealings with us by His Spirit, God takes neither of these approaches. At no point does He bypass or usurp our will, making our decisions for us. And at no point does He abandon us to our own (lack of) resources. Like a good parent, God neither takes over and does it for us, nor leaves us to flounder and fail frustratedly by ourselves. Like a good manager, He genuinely empowers us to do what we would not be able to do without His help and support.

This has two significant implications. The first is that there is no abdication of responsibility in the Christian life. We don't just hand over the controls and allow some sort of Freudian father-figure to make all our decisions for us. That is not who God is, and that is not how He works. He made us to be other than Himself, to be free, to be so other as to be able to relate to Him – and that is what He re-makes us to be. He continues to respect the freedom that He has given. The second implication is that He is to be the model for our management, parenthood, marriage, and indeed, all our dealings with others. We must not seek to dominate, to invade, to control, to take over people's personalities, to run their lives for them, to make their decisions for them. Our model, on the contrary, is the *fellowship* of the Holy Spirit. And He does not overwhelm.

8. THE SPIRIT MAKES US GOD'S CHILDREN AND ASSURES US OF THAT STATUS

But when the time had fully come, God sent his Son, born of

a woman, born under law, to redeem those under law, that we might receive adoption as God's children. Because you are his children, he sent the Spirit of his Son into our hearts, the Spirit who calls out, "Abba, Father". So you are no longer slaves, but God's children; and since you are his children, he has made you also heirs.

Galatians 4:4–7

How are we children of God? By being in Christ, who is *the* child of God. Only because of that. We sometimes speak of everyone being a child of God, and there is a sense in which that is correct (Acts 17:28).[d] Nevertheless, Scripture usually reserves the term, not for that which we all have incipiently by virtue of being human beings, but for that which we inherit abundantly by virtue of being in Christ. He is the eternal Son of the Father – intimately and eternally loved by His Father. And when we are in Christ, the same becomes true of us. It becomes true of us that we too are children of the Father, we too are intimately and eternally loved by the Father. We are adopted as children of the Father, and as members of the community that addresses God as 'Our Father'. That is (part of) what it means to be 'in Him'.

And how do we get to be 'in Him'? By the work of the Spirit, 'because those who are led by the Spirit of God are children of God. For you did not receive a spirit that makes you a slave again to fear, but you received the Spirit of adoption. And by him we cry, "Abba, Father"' (Romans 8:14–15). (Actually, my edition has 'by whim we cry, "*Abba*, Father"', but I take that to be a misprint! It is the very opposite of what Paul means. Adoption is not by our *whim*, but by the Spirit's work.) As Jane Williams says, 'The Spirit's job is to make us able to stand in Jesus' own place in relation to the Father.'[17] Because of the Spirit, we are in the Son. And because we are in the Son, we are children of God.

---

[d] Because we are all children of God in this sense, becoming children of God in the fullest sense makes us who we truly are. It doesn't make us into something different.

All children need reassurance. I saw a cartoon recently, which pictured a family sitting round a table, and the father saying, 'I'm afraid that, with the economic down-turn, we're going to have to let one of you go!' All children need to be reassured that they will never be 'let go'. And that is what the Spirit does for us: 'The Spirit himself testifies with our spirit that we are God's children' (Romans 8:16). He testifies that we stand in Jesus' own place in relation to the Father. We are *that* loved. We are *that* secure. We belong *that* much. And the Spirit embeds that assurance within us, applying a filial lovedness to our deepest and neediest places. Leonardo Boff draws out the significance of this:

> The most frightening and unbearable feeling is rejection, knowing that we are not accepted. It is like being a 'stranger in the nest', experiencing psychological death. When I say 'Father', I seek to express the conviction that there is someone who accepts me absolutely. My moral situation matters little, I can always trust that there awaits a parental lap to receive me. There I will not be a stranger but a child, even if prodigal, in my Father's house.[18]

9. THE SPIRIT BUILDS US INTO THE CHURCH AND GIVES US GIFTS TO SHARE WITH THE REST OF THE CHURCH

If we are children of God, then we are brothers and sisters of each other. There is no avoiding this! There is an inescapable horizontal dimension to any authentic Christian faith. To be in relationship with Jesus Christ is to be in the Church, because Christ's body is the Church. His family is the Church. There is nowhere else to be. You cannot be in relationship with the Father without being thereby in relationship with His other children. So by bringing us into the place of the Son, the Spirit brings us into the Church.

But He does not send us empty-handed into the Church. Like children arriving at a birthday party, we come with a present to contribute.

> Now to each one the manifestation of the Spirit is given for the common good. To one there is given through the Spirit the message of wisdom, to another the message of knowledge by means of the same Spirit, to another faith by the same Spirit, to another gifts of healing by that one Spirit, to another miraculous powers, to another prophecy, to another distinguishing between spirits, to another speaking in different kinds of tongues, and to still another the interpretation of tongues. All these are the work of one and the same Spirit, and he gives them to each one, just as he determines.

1 Corinthians 12:7–11

The Spirit gives to *each one*, however unimpressive and ungifted we may feel. No one is left out when the Spirit is handing out gifts. And therefore, if anyone cuts themselves off from the community or isn't attended to by the community, the community is the poorer for it.

It seems to me that these gifts, which should be a cause of joy amongst us, can sometimes be a cause of self-flagellation. We look at other people's gifts and envy them, or disparage them, or use them to belittle our own. I remember Alan Stibbs, a great biblical expositor of a previous generation, lamenting the fact that he had never been instrumental in anyone's conversion. He loved God and longed to introduce people to Him, but had never been used in that way. But maybe that was okay. Maybe that was because God had given him the gifts of teaching and preaching but not of evangelism. Maybe his primary gift was to build people up in knowledge and love of God through his unfolding of the Scriptures, and it was primarily up to others to do the vital work of evangelism. We must never use someone else's gifts to make ourselves feel bad about what God has given us. (Nor indeed use our own gifts to make others feel bad about theirs.) We need to learn to rejoice in other people's gifts, for they are of course gifts *to me* (amongst others!).

The way in which the Spirit gives different gifts to different people is good news for two reasons. First, it makes us less tempted by pride. Not *un*tempted, of course, but less tempted. If we had all the gifts, we would be insufferable! As Rowan Williams said in a sermon recently, if someone claims to have all the gifts, don't thank God for them – worry about them![19] But secondly, and more positively, the way in which the Spirit gives different gifts to different people makes us dependent upon one another. It makes us mutually interdependent, so that we live in harmony, with each one holding a different line in the music, and each line fitting together, and contributing, and together experiencing that integration which has too often been fragmented by pride on the one hand, and the feeling that we have nothing to contribute on the other.

10. THE SPIRIT INSPIRES CREATIVITY

> Then Moses said to the Israelites, "See, the Lord has chosen Bezalel son of Uri, the son of Hur, of the tribe of Judah, and he has filled him with the Spirit of God, with skill, ability and knowledge in all kinds of crafts – to make artistic designs for work in gold, silver and bronze, to cut and set stones, to work in wood and to engage in all kinds of artistic crafts. And he has given both him and Oholiab son of Ahisamach, of the tribe of Dan, the ability to teach others. He has filled them with skill to do all kinds of work as engravers, designers, embroiderers in blue, purple and scarlet yarn and fine linen, and weavers – all of them able to do all kinds of work and design."
>
> **Exodus 35:30–35**

The Christian community should be an artistic community. For human beings were made in the image of the Creator, and are therefore intrinsically creative. When we are creative, we testify, wittingly or unwittingly, to the existence, beauty and diversity-loving nature of the Creator. So when that image is renewed (Colossians 3:10), our creativity will be renewed too. And, while creativity can be displayed anywhere, in the office, in the home, in the garden, in the park, on the football pitch – for we must not divide the 'sacred' off from the 'secular' – we would also expect it to adorn our life together in the Christian community. Art and crafts and designs and fabrics and music and drama and poetry and dance all beautified the liturgy of the temple, and they should beautify our praise of God and our life together today.

The Church has always taken this side of its calling seriously. It has always been one of the most important patrons of the arts. Michelangelo and Raphael were employed to decorate church buildings. Bach was employed to compose a cantata each week to adorn the Lutheran liturgy. Vivaldi was a priest who composed music for the orphan girls of the Conservatory of the Ospedale della Pietà – thus combining the church's liturgical, educational, artistic and compassionate ministries. The Church's patronage of the arts has reduced considerably in our lifetime. There are many reasons for this regrettable decline: the Church is not as rich as it once was, for one. We need to be praying that the Lord would again fill people with the Spirit of God and with skill and ability as creators, we need to be exploring and developing our own creativity, and we need to be giving so that the Church can again reflect the beauty and creativity of God in its life together.

11. THE SPIRIT IS THE SOURCE AND SURETY OF CREATURELY AND CULTURAL DIVERSITY

I lived for several years in London, and if you happen to be at one of its railway stations during the morning rush hour, you will see what strikes me as a worrying sight. You will see thousands of people going to work, wearing the same sort of clothes, the same kind of blank expression, dashing like lemmings to the office. And, if you're anything like me, you'll wonder whether they have a different thought, value or aspiration between them. Or whether they all go home to their 2.4 children in their nice suburban house, and think, act, feel and vote the same way. Now, I freely confess that this observation tells you much more about me than it does about them. And what it tells you about me is that I fear uniformity. I think most people do. I think most people fear, when they join anything, that it will end up making (or attempting to make them) the same. That, I suspect, is why most people are hesitant about 'organised religion'. They fear that it will indeed organise them, hammer out their distinctiveness and smother their identity. They fear that they will end up looking, sounding and thinking the same as all the other Christians, and it's not a wildly appealing prospect.

We are torn. We want to belong to something bigger than ourselves – for therein lies the possibility of community and meaning. But we fear that we will have our own individuality and identity swamped by that bigger conglomerate. And that fear is at the root of many an international conflict. All separatist movements have that fear somewhere near the centre of their mix of motives. It is the potential for violence within such understandable fears that prompts Roy Clements to ask:

> Is there a power that can unify the divided nations of the earth without subjugating them in the process? Is there a way of making people one, without at the same time making them all the same? I suggest to you that there is. It is precisely that sort of unity which the Holy Spirit brings. And he declared his intention in the matter right at the beginning, on the Day of Pentecost, by the miracle he performed: 'Utterly amazed, they asked, "Are not all these men who are speaking Galileans? Then how is it that each of us hears them in his own native language?"' ([Acts] 2:7–8)
>
> God could have given this crowd a universal tongue. He could have enabled them all to understand one language, but he did not need to do that because they already understood such a language, namely Greek. There would have been little difficulty for Peter to make himself understood in Greek ... but instead each person in the crowd heard them not as foreigners but as if they were members of their own clan or tribe or nation.[20]

Luke is at pains to draw attention to the staggering diversity of cultures represented. In a passage that proves a nightmare to many an unprepared public reader trying to wing it, the onlookers ask one another:

> 'How does it happen that every single one of us can hear the particular language he has known from a child? There are Parthians, Medes and Elamites; there are men whose homes are in Mesopotamia, in Judaea and Cappadocia, Pontus, Asia, Phrygia, Pamphylia, Egypt, and the parts of Libya near Cyrene, as well as visitors from Rome! There are Jews and proselytes, men from Crete and men from Arabia, yet we can all hear these men speaking of the glorious works of God in our native language.'
>
> **Acts 2:8–11** JBP

Not in Greek, the *lingua franca* of the ancient world, not in some spiritual Esperanto, but *in our own languages* – which is a massive affirmation of who we are, and where we come from, and the cultural diversity we represent. And a massive assurance that we will not lose our uniqueness and our difference in the unity that the Spirit is attempting to create. Roy Clements again:

> These pentecostal tongues were a pointer to the way in which the Holy Spirit was going to break down social barriers and create an unprecedented kind of internationalism. Unlike the imperialisms of men, the Spirit had no ambition to homogenise the peoples of the world into a uniform Christian culture. On the contrary, he intended to bridge cultures and to overcome the alienation they create without eroding the diversity they represent.[21]

Why? Because God likes diversity. We saw that when we looked at Creation – He made it and He considers it good. We saw it when we looked at the Resurrection – He made it and He will remake it. And we see it again now as we look at the work of the Spirit:

He seeks a unity without uniformity. It is his distinctive mark. When God freezes the water, he makes a snow storm in which every flake is different. When we human beings freeze water, we make ice cubes! The Holy Spirit wants to make us a people who rejoice in our differences, just as the disciples rejoiced to proclaim Christ in different languages on the day of Pentecost. It was a sign that the church of Jesus Christ is not intended to exhibit the martial unison of regimental khaki, but the multi-tonal harmony of a symphony orchestra.[22]

Tragically, the Church has often failed to tolerate diversity, let alone rejoice in it. I once gave the substance of this book as a course of lectures at Bishop James Settee College, a theological college for Cree Indian pastors in Saskatchewan, Canada. They told me that the first missionaries had been highly sensitive, culturally, and had become fine Cree speakers, but that the second generation had set up church schools where Cree children were forbidden to speak their own language. The result was that a whole generation had grown up that could not speak its own language, and the Cree tongue is in danger of dying as a result – together with its art-forms and thought-forms (for each language enables you not only to *say* things in a unique way, but even to *think* things in ways that could not otherwise be thought). And to think that that was done in the name of Christ, whose Spirit works to purge and to polish, to enhance and to encourage the rich diversity of our cultures and of our cosmos. I say 'purge' because of course not all cultures can merely be affirmed in their entirety. In fact, no culture can be affirmed in its entirety. Most cultures have some element of misogyny or xenophobia or violence embedded within them, which the Spirit would not condone. But the point is that the Spirit fights against such things because they are wrong, not because they are different. All that is not inextricably entwined with what is wrong will be preserved and enhanced.

12. THE SPIRIT SHOWS US MORE OF GOD

Indeed, He is the only reliable interpreter of God. (Which is a bit humbling – but vitally important – for a theologian in particular to remember!) Paul explores the absolute necessity of the Spirit to our knowledge of God, in 1 Corinthians 2:9:

> However, as it is written:
> 'No eye has seen,
> no ear has heard,
> no mind has conceived
> what God has prepared for those who love him.'

God's plans and purposes cannot just be read off from looking at history. We cannot even know them as they relate to us. We cannot know what our own fulfilment would look like. We cannot know our own future, and therefore we cannot know how to live in the present. The intentions of God are inaccessible to human imagination or intellect – '… but God has revealed it to us by his Spirit' (v.10). The Spirit makes known to us what otherwise we would have no inkling of. 'The Spirit searches all things, even the deep things of God. For who knows the thoughts of another human being except that person's own spirit within?' (v.11a) If I were to get up into the pulpit one Sunday morning and say absolutely nothing, the congregation might be hugely relieved and no less edified than usual – but it would have no idea what I was thinking. They could have a guess, but it would just be a pure guess. And if we cannot tell what another human being – someone we know and can see – is thinking, how do we stand a chance of knowing the thoughts of God?

Without the Spirit, we cannot. 'In the same way no-one knows the thoughts of God except the Spirit of God' (v.11b). Only God can interpret God and make God known. Unlike us, the Spirit, being God, is not going to get God wrong. We are therefore utterly and gratefully dependent upon the Spirit (and the Son – see v.16) for reliable access to the deep things of God. One of the vital aspects of the Spirit's work is to show us more of God.

13. THE SPIRIT LINKS US TO JESUS

a) The Spirit points us to Jesus

'When the Counsellor comes, whom I will send to you from the Father, the Spirit of truth who goes out from the Father, he will testify about me' (John 15:26). The rôle of the Spirit is to testify about Jesus, to glorify Jesus, to point people towards Jesus, to shed light upon Jesus. As Jim Packer put it, 'When floodlighting is well done, the floodlights are so placed that you do not see them; you are not in fact supposed to see where the light is coming from; what you are meant to see is just the building on which the floodlights are trained ... This perfectly illustrates the Spirit's new covenant role. He is, so to speak, the hidden floodlight shining on the Saviour.'[23] (If, therefore, we find the Spirit the most difficult of the persons of the Trinity to relate to, there is a sense in which that does not necessarily matter – as long as He is doing His work within us of pointing us to Jesus, and through Him to the Father.)

b) The Spirit takes the things of Jesus and gives them to us

'He will bring glory to me by taking from what is mine and making it known to you. All that belongs to the Father is mine. That is why I said the Spirit will take from what is mine and make it known to you.'

John 16:14–15

So the Spirit points to Jesus. He takes the things of Jesus, which are in fact the things of the Father, and gives them to us. That is how He shows us more of God – by reminding us (John 14:26), and making intelligible and relevant to us, and bringing home to us the things of Jesus. The Spirit is not an independent means of access to the Father. The Spirit does not reveal new things to us that are utterly unrelated to God's primary and final revelation of Himself in Jesus. Tom Torrance underlines this point helpfully:

> It was not of course the Spirit but the Word who became incarnate, and so the Spirit does not bring us any revelation other than or independent of the Word who became incarnate in Jesus Christ.[24]

He may draw our attention to a neglected aspect of how God has revealed Himself in Jesus. He may give us new insight into that ancient self-revelation. He may bring new treasures out of the treasury, but He is not going to open up a new treasury. So we may not set up the Spirit as an alternative source of revelation over and against the revelation of God in Christ. And we may not appeal to the Spirit as justification for a new belief about God that is not rooted in what we see of God in Jesus. Otherwise, we could say what we like about God and claim the Spirit as our authority. There would be no control over our language, our theology or our practice. And, as Oliver O'Donovan reminds us:

> From time to time there have arisen movements of revival in the church which, in their enthusiasm to stress the reality of God's presence in our midst, have succumbed to a temptation to rejoice in the revelations, prophecies, miracles and powers which the Holy Spirit manifests in the church, but not to rejoice, or not very much to rejoice, in the witness which he bears to Jesus of Nazareth as the exalted Son of God. The Montanists of the second and third centuries used to say that with the coming of the Spirit history had entered a new age, the age of the Spirit, which went beyond the age of the Son and brought a superior revelation ... New truth was now made known to the church, which had not been made known by Jesus; new powers were given to the church which Jesus had not given; the gift of Pentecost went beyond the gift of Christmas, Easter and Ascension.[25]

Whereas, in fact, 'Pentecost is not *added* to the sequence, Christmas, Easter, Ascension, as a further and additional moment of divine revelation, but rather stands apart from them, casting light back on them and interpreting them.'[26] The Spirit does not bypass the Son, but provides a road to the Father that passes full-squarely through the Son. This trinitarian chain – the Spirit points us to, and sheds light upon, and interprets, and glorifies the Son, who reveals and glorifies the Father – provides us with a control and a check on all that we may want to say about God. Without this trinitarian chain, theology would cease to be a discipline. With it, it is (at least potentially) a matter of controlled, responsible, accountable, humble and scientific speech.[e]

14. THE SPIRIT INSPIRES THE SCRIPTURES

Above all, you must understand that no prophecy of Scripture came about by the prophet's own interpretation. For prophecy never had its origin in the human will, but prophets, though human, spoke from God as they were carried along by the Holy Spirit.

2 Peter 1:20–21

No matter how accurately and organically and wonderfully Jesus may have revealed God in the first century, that avails us nothing in the twenty-first century unless there is some reliable record, and some reliable interpretation, of what went on. Unless we have a fundamentally accurate account of what happened when God visited and redeemed His people, then we have no access to knowledge of God. Unless we have an account that embodies the promised Spirit's work, reminding us of what Jesus taught us (John 14:26) and making known to us the things of Jesus (John 16:14–15),

[e] For an account of theology as a scientific discipline, responding as science does (and accountable as science is) to an objective reality outside of itself, see Tom Torrance's *Reality and Scientific Theology* (Edinburgh, 1985), and *Theological Science* (OUP, 1969).

then we have no 'inside information' on God, and we are left to guess. If only God can interpret God, then only if the Spirit inspires the Scriptures do we have God-given knowledge of God.

But if it's true, if the Spirit did inspire them, then what we have within the Scriptures is God's interpretation of God's revelation of God. It is the trinitarian chain again – God's interpretation (through the Spirit) of God's revelation (in the Son) of God (the Father). Just as 'There can never be a point in my salvation at which God simply stops and leaves it to me',[27] so there can never be a point in the process of *revelation* at which God simply stops and leaves it to us.

Of course, human beings were involved. Once again, the Spirit did not simply do the whole job for us: He inspired the human authors to remember and report and interpret 'as they were carried along by the Spirit'. Their personalities were not bypassed. Their thought-forms, and art-forms, and literary conventions, and vocabularies, and characteristic modes of communication were taken up and used to give authentic voice to the self-communication of God. Notice how, in 2 Peter 1:21, once again, it is a fellowship, a dialectic, an interaction between the Spirit and the prophets. The Spirit is not a dictator, and inspiration is not dictation. The humanity of the authors is taken up, not over-ridden. Their personalities are harnessed, not suppressed. They are carried along, not swept aside.

But what emerges in and through those human words is God's interpretation of God's revelation of God. If that were not so, the Incarnation would be, from a revelatory point of view, largely in vain. Would God go to all the trouble of becoming incarnate as a first century Palestinian embryo so as to make Himself known (John 1:18), and then fail to give us any knowledge of what He was like when He shared our space and time? A while ago, my computer was infected with a virus, which corrupted not just the software, but the hardware as well. The computer became unusable. I took the hard drive to a computer expert, who tested it and told me that there was nothing he could do about it. All the information was still in there somewhere, but there was no way of accessing it. And so it would be with the Incarnation, unless we have knowledge of it in the Scriptural witness.

I recognise, of course, that we still have to understand it. I do not pretend that, by what I have said so far, I have dissolved any of the difficulties that the biblical texts present, or any of the disputes that they have engendered. I acknowledge that I have merely set up the arena, and have not even begun to play the game. And I can hardly deny that Christians disagree as to the implications of belief in the divine inspiration of Scripture.

All I claim – and it is crucial – is that the common Christian confession of the Spirit's inspiration of Scripture agrees on seeing Scripture as the fixed point to which we keep bringing our inadequate understandings and our debilitating disagreements – *and have them corrected* by what we find there.[f] As we do so, we shall have our views challenged and enlarged, and our questions reshaped by the surprising, sometimes joltingly unexpected content of the texts. Agreement on the inspiration of Scripture does not answer all our questions, but it does include us all in the same process. It does at least get us all playing the same game.

And out of that common pursuit may come a deeper understanding that gets behind our differences and our divisions, and renders them irrelevant. As George Caird wrote:

> For each new step of faith we take
> thou hast more truth and light to break
> forth from thy Holy Word.[28]

Notice two things about this statement. First, notice that there is always more truth and light to be quarried. We must never be satisfied with the understanding we have. We must always be pressing on to a greater knowledge and love of God. We must not be fearful of

---

[f] A friend of mine, Chris Green, used to say that we need to treat Scripture as a trampoline, not as a springboard. If we keep coming back to Scripture, as in the trampoline image, we can gain height. If we leave it behind like a springboard, we find ourselves in deep water!

learning new truths, having our view of God enlarged, expanded, and made less idolatrous by the Spirit of God. But secondly, notice that it is *from thy Holy Word* that these new truths are to come. Just as we may not set up the Spirit as an alternative source of revelation, bypassing the revelation of God in Christ, so we may not set up the Spirit in opposition to the witness He has given in Scripture to that revelation. Any new truth we think we have received from the Spirit must be in harmony with, and answerable to, how God has shown Himself to be in Jesus, as authoritatively recorded in Scripture.

15. IN THE HOLY SPIRIT, THE FATHER AND THE SON GIVE THEMSELVES TO US AND MAKE THEIR HOME WITHIN US

'Those who love me will obey my teaching. My Father will love them, and we will come to them and make our home with them.'

John 14:23

This amazing statement is sandwiched between two discussions of the Spirit (John 14:16–17 and 25–26). So the implication is that, when the Spirit comes to Jesus' disciples, He does not leave the other persons of the Trinity behind. When we open ourselves to the Spirit, we don't just get the Spirit, we get the entire package. Three for the price of one! We get the whole triune, eternal, infinite God taking up residence within us – living with us, interacting with us on a permanent, moment-by-moment basis. Our need for love is near-infinite – and Infinite Love comes and inhabits our needy, arid interiors.

The Jewish people were used to the fact that God had chosen to dwell amongst them. First in the tabernacle, and then in the temple, He was present in the midst of their life together. The early Church discovered that they had inherited that privilege. They were the new temple, in which God lives by His Spirit (Ephesians 2:22, 1 Corinthians 3:16). God was present in the midst of their life together. Not only that, but they came to realise that they *individually* were temples of the Holy Spirit as well (1 Corinthians 6:19). Here in John 14, Jesus unpacks that further. It is not just the Spirit who comes to live within us like some impersonal force to empower us, but the whole trinitarian relationship takes place within us. When we become the place wherein the Holy Spirit makes His dwelling, as the hymn says,[29] we become thereby the place where the Father is glorified by the Son, and the Son by the Spirit, where the Spirit is loved by the Son and the Son by the Father. We become, in other words, the place where the eternal relationship between the persons of the Godhead lovingly rages. We become the receptacle, the furnace of trinitarian passion, and we carry it around with us. Of course, it does not always, or indeed often, feel like that. But then we are seldom in touch even with our own deepest emotions, so we should not be surprised to be largely unaware of the even deeper reality of God's subtle presence within.

'But will God really dwell on earth? The heavens, even the highest heaven, cannot contain you. How much less this temple I have built!' (1 Kings 8:27) How much less the constraints of the human heart. It is indeed, as Tom Wright said of the Incarnation, like putting a hurricane into a bottle.[30] And yet there is nothing destructive about this hurricane within – or, at least, nothing destructive of who we intrinsically are. As Hans Urs von Balthasar says,

> In Christianity this indwelling is a serious and radical feature, without needing to explode and annihilate the finite self; on the contrary, here, in the most mysterious way, the self comes to fulfilment beyond itself in God.[31]

Tom Torrance makes the same point, and tries to spell out something of the (relational) nature of that fulfilment: 'through the Spirit God is able to take possession of his creatures, to sustain them from below, and to be present within them in such a way as to lift them up to the level of participation in God where they are opened out for union and communion with God far beyond the limits of their creaturely existence.'[32]

273

This indwelling of the triune God does not explode us, but it does expand us. We come to fulfilment *beyond ourselves*: we are to live *beyond the limits of our creaturely existence*. In the first chapter, I quoted Flannery O'Connor's statement that 'the Christian novelist lives in a bigger universe.' But we don't just have a bigger universe without – we also have a bigger world within. One of the Pink Panther cartoons has a somewhat surreal episode in which the Pink Panther is standing against a blank background. He looks at the background, and then folds it in half! Then he folds it in half again, and again, and continues folding it (probably more times than it is mathematically possible to fold!) until he can hold it between finger and thumb. Then he puts it in his mouth and swallows it. After a moment or two, it starts unfolding inside him, doubling in size with a jerk each time until the whole background is pink, with a face and a tail! Take the Holy Spirit inside you, and you get the Holy Trinity inside you – and that will expand you, open up the possibilities for your nature and your existence, and draw you into that relationship which is the taproot of all being. We do not just become the place wherein the Holy Spirit makes His dwelling: we become the place wherein the Holy Trinity does His praying.

16. THE SPIRIT HELPS US TO PRAY

> Likewise the Spirit helps us in our weakness; for we do not know how to pray as we ought, but that very Spirit intercedes with sighs too deep for words. And God, who searches the heart, knows what is the mind of the Spirit, because the Spirit intercedes for the saints according to the will of God.
>
> **Romans 8:26–27** NRSV

I dread being asked to speak on the subject of prayer. More than any other subject, it exposes my own limitations and superficialities. And I don't think I am alone. All of us, I suspect, feel like largely clueless beginners when it comes to prayer. So it is a comfort that

Paul felt the same way. He who was capable of the most sublime prayers (Ephesians 3:14–21, Romans 11:33–36) was most conscious of 'weakness' in this area, and said that 'We do not know how to pray as we ought'. That is simply a facet of our finitude. We do not know what to pray for, because we cannot know what is best. We do not have all the information, we do not know people's hearts, we do not have God's perspective, we do not have His wisdom, we do not have His love. But that should not stop us from praying, for two reasons.

First, *prayer is something we join in, not something we have to create from nothing.* Lesslie Newbigin tells a story which illustrates this point:

> An Anglican friend was on holiday in Crete and went to church one Sunday morning. He did not know that he was going to have to stand for three hours. The priest observed that after about an hour and a half he was beginning to become a little restive, and he beckoned to the deacon. He whispered some words and the deacon went out and ten minutes later returned and went to where my friend was standing and told him, 'There is a poached egg in the vestry.' My friend replied, 'But the liturgy?' To which the deacon responded, 'The liturgy is eternal. The egg will get cold!'[33]

Lesslie Newbigin comments, 'Worship is not primarily our thing. To say that it starts at 10.30 and finishes at 12.00 is absurd. It is our dropping in to the eternal worship of the Holy Trinity.'

In the highest heaven, in the world-wide church, and in the tardis-like temple of my own heart,[g] an eternal conversation is carrying on between the persons of the Trinity. As John V. Taylor put it:

---

[g] The tardis was a time-machine in the long-running science fiction series on BBC television, Dr Who. 'Tardis' stands for 'Time and relative dimensions in space', and the point for our present purposes is that it was bigger on the inside than it looked from the outside. That is probably always true of the human heart, but even more so of the heart that has opened itself up to the indwelling of the triune God.

Each time of prayer is an attempt to open ourselves up more fully to that direct communion with the Father which Jesus knew, and to realise more deeply our relationship to him as adult sons and daughters. That communion is the primary gift of the Go-Between God [Taylor's name for the Spirit] and he alone can make it happen.[34]

As Jane Williams said, the Spirit makes us stand where Jesus Himself stands in relation to the Father, and that means that we are located in the middle of that communion, that conversation. We shall be looking at this in more detail in the next chapter, but here let's just note the implications for our prayer. It means, as I say, that prayer is not something we have to screw ourselves up to create from nothing, like staring at a blank screen as one attempts to write a book! (Said with feeling!) It is more like a child sitting and eating at the dinner table with the rest of the family and joining in its conversation. And the mistakes we make in prayer are very similar to the mistakes we make as children learning the art of conversation. Sometimes we are too intimidated to say anything at all. Sometimes – more usually, I suspect – we talk so much that we aren't joining in a conversation, we're turning it into a monologue. If prayer is primarily joining in the trinitarian trialogue, then we need to tune in to that trialogue. In short, we need to listen. We need, occasionally, to shut up.[h] Why silence? To quote Tom Wright:

Because there comes a time when the chattering of my voice stops me hearing what I am saying.

[h] Occasionally. I am not suggesting that words have no place in prayer. Far from it. We are verbal creatures, and we worship the Word. And when asked to teach His disciples how to pray, Jesus said, 'When you pray, say ...' (Luke 11:2). Both Balthasar (*Prayer* p. 77) and Bloom (*Living Prayer* p. 110) counsel against making silence the only, or even the main, form of prayer. But words are not fully comprehensible, or fully sane, if there is no break from them. And a conversation is not a conversation unless there is some attempt to listen.

Because there comes a time when the babble of my voice stops me hearing what I am *thinking*.
Because there comes a time when the prattling of my voice stops me hearing what *God* is saying.[35]

A story told by Metropolitan Anthony Bloom makes the same point:

> A woman who had been using the Jesus Prayer[i] for fourteen years complained that she had never had any sense that God was there. But when she had it pointed out to her that she was talking all the time, she agreed to take her stand silently for a few days. As she was doing it she became aware that God was there, that the silence that surrounded her was not emptiness, absence of noise and agitation, but that there was a solidity in this silence, that it was not something negative, but positive, a presence, the presence of God who made himself known to her by creating the same silence in her. And then she discovered that the prayer came up quite naturally again, but it was no longer the sort of discursive noise that had prevented God from making himself known.[36]

There is a time for noisy, joyous praise, of course, but there is also a time to be quiet. There is – or should be – as big a range of modes and emotions in prayer as there are in the rest of life. Bigger, probably. Real prayer is listening in on that conversation that is going on within us by virtue of the fact that the Spirit has come, and the Father and the Son have come and made their home within us – listening in on that conversation, and then joining in. It is not talking, talking, talking, and hoping that God might get a word in edgeways occasionally, on our terms and our agenda. It is the bore who insists that you fit into their conversation, if they let you

---

[i] The Jesus Prayer, much beloved of the Orthodox tradition, consists simply of the words, 'Lord Jesus Christ, Son of [the living] God, have mercy upon me [a sinner].' For how the Jesus Prayer has been found a helpful way of praying beyond the Orthodox tradition, see *The Jesus Prayer* by Simon Barrington-Ward (The Bible Reading Fellowship, Oxford), 1996.

277

into it at all. The person with social skills is the person who listens, allowing the others to have their say, and who contributes in a way that is appropriate to the conversation already taking place. That is the art of prayer – it's just the art of good conversation, that's all, but it happens to be done with the eternal God.[j]

The other style of prayer which allows God to pray within us rather than imagining that we have to make it up for ourselves is praying in tongues. This is a controversial area, and not all Christians agree that it is a legitimate form of prayer for today. But it is there in the New Testament with no suggestion that its legitimacy was limited to the first Christian generation. Tongues have the virtue of allowing God to set the agenda rather than insisting upon setting our own. It's rather like writing God a blank cheque. You would only give a blank cheque to someone you trusted, and praying in tongues is a sign of loving trust that God would only pray within you what is for your good. Why tongues? Tom Wright again:

> Because sometimes I find myself faced with someone who is obviously in great need, and I haven't a clue what that need is;
> Because when I don't know what to pray for, it's just as well that the Spirit knows and can do it in me;
> Because there are people who need me to pray into the heart of their situation, but only God knows what that heart looks like …
> Tongues are a sign that God the Holy Spirit prays within us, so that we are caught up into the conversation between the members of the Trinity.[37]

---

[j] There are of course huge differences between a conversation with God and an ordinary human conversation. God is not so easily and obviously accessible as a human conversation partner. Very seldom – in fact, never in my experience – does He speak in an audible voice, the way a human being does. Our relationship with God is much more opaque than our human-level relationships – we see through a glass darkly (1 Corinthians 13:12) and will not see face to face until the renewal of all things. But that doesn't mean that our relationship with God now is not real, that it isn't a conversation and that it doesn't require some of the same skills as a conversation. It just means that it is difficult – which we all know!

Whatever forms and techniques of prayer we use, we have the promise of the Spirit's help, and the dual experience of rapidly coming to the end of our own resources in prayer and of having those resources renewed is the experience of God keeping that promise. It is an experience that C. S. Lewis relates in his poem, 'Prayer':

> Master, they say that when I seem
> To be in speech with you,
> Since you make no replies, it's all a dream
> – One talker aping two.
>
> They are half right, but not as they
> Imagine; rather, I
> Seek in myself the things I meant to say,
> And lo! the wells are dry.
>
> Then, seeing me empty, you forsake
> The Listener's rôle, and through
> My dead lips breathe and into utterance wake
> The thoughts I never knew.
>
> And thus you neither need reply
> Nor can; thus, while we seem
> Two talking, thou art One forever, and I
> No dreamer, but thy dream.[38]

The second encouragement to prayer that Romans 8:26 gives us is its assurance that *pain and perplexity offered to God are prayer*. The whole passage from which this verse on prayer comes is about groaning. It's about suffering. It's about creation groaning (Romans 8:22) in its frustration (v.20) at not being at peace with its self, its intended rulers and its Maker. It groans in its out-of-jointness, its friction, its dividedness, its decay (v.21). So when we come before God in pain at some aspect of the world's pain, when we weep before God because of what someone we love is going through, or because of what we have seen on the News, or because of what we feel within ourselves, we are acting as the priests of creation. We are being the focal point of creation's pain. We are representing the world to God, which is our calling as human beings. We are not asked to bring the world's pain to God with a knowledge of what needs to be done. We are not asked to bring the world's pain to God with a clear sense of how to pray. We are not asked to bring the world's pain to God without protest and anger. We are not asked to bring the world's pain before God with equanimity and acceptance. We are just asked to bring it before God.

And as we do that, even if it is angry and inarticulate and pained and bewildered, we are promised that the Spirit will groan with us; indeed, that our groans will *be* the Spirit praying within us, in and through our pain and the pain it represents. Our pain is dissatisfaction with fallenness. God too is dissatisfied with fallenness. There is a sense in which the Spirit prompts that very dissatisfaction, and then gathers it up, joins in with it, takes it into the divine conversation, makes it prayer and makes it count.

How does He make it count? Well, notice the context in which Paul places this astounding little verse on prayer. He has been outlining the future hope of the cosmos, to be liberated from its bondage to decay and brought into the glorious freedom of the children of God (v.21). He has been speaking of how, in the mean time, it groans as if in labour (v.22). And then he talks about prayer. Our prayer, he implies, is one of the means by which God bridges the gap between the present and the future. Prayer is one of the ways in which we can hasten the liberation of the cosmos. When we pray, we bring in the future. When we pray, we are let in on the conversation of the eternal God, and that conversation is calling a new creation into existence. That is the privilege and the power of prayer. However paltry our prayers may seem, however little we may feel God when we pray them, however much they may seem to get no further than the ceiling, that is what they are achieving. Through the funnel and the filter of the Spirit, our prayers are the agents of cosmic renewal.

17. THE SPIRIT IS GOD'S PROMISE THAT HE WILL REMAKE HIS WORLD

The creation waits in eager expectation for the children of God to be revealed. For the creation was subjected to frustration, not by its own choice, but by the will of the one who subjected it, in hope that the creation itself will be liberated from its bondage to decay and brought into the glorious freedom of the children of God. We know that the whole creation has been groaning as in the pains of childbirth right up to the present time. Not only so, but we ourselves, who have the first-fruits of the Spirit, groan inwardly as we wait eagerly for our adoption, the redemption of our bodies.

Romans 8:19–23

It is no coincidence that Romans 8 is both the chapter in which Paul deals most extensively with the Spirit, and the chapter in which Paul deals most extensively with the renewal of creation. For, as we saw earlier, it is the Spirit who gives life and it is the Spirit who gives new life. So if the Spirit has been poured out, following the victories of Cross, Resurrection and Ascension, then He is at work, and He is not going to stop until His work is complete, and creation is restored.

The Spirit is the *first-fruits* of our remaking, and therefore of the remaking of all things. As we saw in the last chapter, the Jewish people would celebrate the first-fruits of the harvest, because they knew that they betokened the full harvest to come. So with the gift of the Spirit. The fact that He has already been poured out is the guarantee that He will one day bring creation to new birth and flood it with His presence and His glory. And we need that guarantee, because, without it, the hope of a new world is simply a chimaera. If it depends on us, then it looks like being indefinitely postponed. As Jane Williams has written:

If Jesus is just an example to us, then we have had it. The example of goodness has always existed in human beings, here and there, and most of us have proved perfectly able to resist its lure. But Trinitarian theology assures us that God does not come among us, die, rise and then sit up above and watch how we get on. On the contrary, that desire on God's part to be with us is constant, as it has always been. The Holy Spirit continues to work with us and in us and for us to bring God's creation to fulfilment.[39]

Only if the recreation of the world is in the hands of the Creator Spirit can we rest assured that it is on its way. Only the Spirit who brooded over the void can brood over the bent world and bring it assuredly to new birth.

18. THE SPIRIT WORKS TO MAKE US HOLY

We live in the period between the 'already' of the first-fruits and the 'not yet' of the full harvest, between the 'already' of the resurrection of Jesus and the 'not yet' of the general resurrection, between the 'already' of our own rebirth and the 'not yet' of the world's rebirth, between the 'already' of our adoption (Romans 8:14–17) and the 'not yet' of our adoption (Romans 8:23). The Spirit has inaugurated the new age, but has not yet brought it to fulfilment. The Spirit is at work within us, but He has not yet finished with us. We are not what we once were, but we are not yet what we shall be. We are being changed from one degree of glory to another (2 Corinthians 3:18), but that process of change will only be completed on the great day when we and all creation are remade (1 Corinthians 15:51).

The call upon us now is to live, as much as may be, the life of the healed cosmos. We are to live now, as far as we can, the life that will be lived out when all has been made new. We are to live together now, as far as is possible, in that harmony that all things will share when the times have reached their fulfilment (Ephesians 1:10). It is still night, but the day is coming, and we are to live 'as in the daytime' (Romans 13:13). We are to be pointers to that better world.

We shall struggle and we shall fail, for we still live in the 'not yet'. The world around us has not yet been remade and we ourselves have not yet been fully remade. We shall need to 'pick ourselves up, dust ourselves down, and start all over again'. We shall need to be forgiven, and then to allow God's Spirit to cut our ties to the old order of things, and reorientate us towards the approaching dawn, towards the deep, dear freshness of a world that oozes the love of its (re-) Creator. We shall frequently be frustrated, for, despite our prayers, healing will often be unforthcoming, and usually be incomplete, and always be temporary, until the healing of all things.

But the Spirit will work within us, to make us the people we were created to be. He will work within us to narrow the gap between what we are and what we are to be. He will beautify us so that more and more, bit by bit, we cede ourselves to sanity, and give our tired world a picture of its coming transfiguration. That is the beauty of holiness, and it is the work of the Holy Spirit.

FURTHER RESOURCES FOR READING, PRAYER AND ACTION

On the Spirit

Gordon Fee, *Paul, the Spirit and the People of God* (1996) (Hodder & Stoughton, 1997).

Tom Smail, *The Giving Gift: The Holy Spirit in Person* (Hodder & Stoughton, 1988).

On working with the Spirit for liberation

David Sheppard, *Bias to the Poor* (Hodder & Stoughton, 1983).

The Jubilee Debt Campaign: www.jubileedebtcampaign.org.uk

Christian Blind Mission: www.cbmi.org

Christian Solidarity: www.csw.org.uk

Amnesty International: www.amnesty.org

FairTrade Foundation: www.fairtrade.org.uk

On Christianity and the Arts

Francis Schaeffer, *Art and the Bible* (Hodder & Stoughton, London, 1973).

Edith Schaeffer, *Hidden Art* (Norfolk Press, London, 1971).

Jeremy Begbie (ed.), *Sounding the Depths: Theology through the Arts* (SCM Press, London, 2002).

On the Inspiration of Scripture

Colin Gunton, *A Brief Theology of Revelation. The 1993 Warfield Lectures* (T & T Clark, Edinburgh, 1995).

Tom Torrance, *Reality and Evangelical Theology: The Realism of Christian Revelation* (1999) (Wipf and Stock Publishers, 2003).

8 TRINITY

Schoolmaster: Now you're sure you've got the Catechism all buttoned up, Foster?

Foster: I'm a bit hazy about the Trinity, sir.

Schoolmaster: Three in one, one in three, perfectly straightforward. Any doubts about that see your maths master.[1]

Foster is probably not the only one to be confused about the Trinity. This area of belief is notoriously difficult and mysterious, not to say mystifying. Thomas à Becket, when he was Archbishop of Canterbury, stipulated that one Sunday every year should be devoted to the doctrine, because he was horrified at how little it was understood. It doesn't seem to have done the trick, to judge from what the guide book at Fountains Abbey says: 'Here in the Chapter House the monks gathered every Sunday to hear a sermon from the Abbot except on Trinity Sunday, owing to the difficulty of the subject.'[2] Many modern clergy would empathise. And the Athanasian Creed (somewhat unhelpfully named, as it wasn't written by St Athanasius!) positively revels in the doctrine's incomprehensibility:

> But the Godhead of the Father, of the Son, and of the Holy Ghost, is all one: the Glory equal, the Majesty co-eternal. Such as the Father is, such is the Son: and such is the Holy Ghost. The Father uncreate, the Son uncreate: and the Holy Ghost uncreate. The Father incomprehensible, the Son incomprehensible: and the Holy Ghost incomprehensible. ... And yet ... there are not three

> incomprehensibles, nor three uncreated: but one uncreated, and one incomprehensible.[3]

As the schoolmaster says, 'Perfectly straightforward'!

But if it is so difficult to understand, so confusing and so baffling, that raises the interesting question, 'Why was it ever formulated in the first place?' Requiring people to believe something that even Abbots cannot explain is hardly a good sales pitch, so why did anyone come up with it? Let me respond to that question with four others (or, possibly, one question asked from four different angles).

First, why would we expect the infinite, eternal God to be easily grasped by our minds, which are finite, haven't been around for very long, won't be around much longer (unless God remakes them) and which we know to be affected by our moods, hormones, (limited) experiences and indeed digestion? After all, we don't apply that criterion in science. We don't say, 'Quantum Mechanics is so hard to understand, it can't be right!'

Secondly, would we not, in fact, expect the God who made the rich, complex, incomprehensible and yet surprisingly knowable world to have a corresponding richness, complexity, diversity and delightfully explorable depth? Indeed, if His mind conceived the complexities of creation, is He not likely to be less fathomable than they?

Thirdly, does the doctrine of the Trinity not have precisely the ring of something that comes from beyond human understanding rather than something that was engendered by it? Those who formulated this doctrine seemed to have been constrained to do so by the very nature of the Reality with which they were dealing. If the map they drew is unexpected and baffling to us, might that not be because the terrain they were attempting to map was unexpected and baffling to them?

And fourthly, if we found the revelation of God's nature easy to understand and assimilate and accept, might that not mean that it was adding nothing to what we already knew and believed? If it all seemed perfectly straightforward, (as it apparently did to Alan Bennett's schoolmaster,) might that not mean that it did nothing to us, that it expanded our categories in no way, that it added nothing to our understanding? Isn't the experience of finding something difficult often a way of expanding our minds, bursting open our regular ways of thinking, forcing us into fresh insight? If it doesn't stretch our minds, it probably won't stretch *us*. In which case, we will simply be left as we were – which is lacking the information, wisdom or goodness to solve our problems (individually and socially), or to find meaning, or to live appropriately.

So, open to the possibility that it was Reality, and not a desire to 'baffle your friends', which constrained the early Church to formulate the doctrine of the Trinity, let us see what exactly it was that led them to map the contours of that Reality in such a way.

How did the early Church come to believe in the doctrine of the Trinity?

1. THEY CAME TO BELIEVE THAT, IN JESUS, GOD WAS VISITING HIS PEOPLE

Jesus, of course, did not wander around Galilee claiming to be God. But He did make the sort of assumptions which only make sense if

He were. He did speak and act in ways that would only escape being nonsensical or blasphemous if they were the words and works of God Himself. Where the Old Testament prophets used to introduce their message with the formula, 'This is what the LORD says', Jesus' standard formula was simply, 'Truly, (truly,) I say to you'; where the prophets saw their authority as being derived, Jesus saw His as being innate.[a] He assumed that He had the right to alter (and intensify) the teaching of Moses, upon which Israel had founded its law and its identity and its national life (Matthew 5:21f). He claimed that in His ministry, Israel was experiencing something of greater significance than the temple, which was where God met with His people (Matthew 12:6). He claimed to be of greater significance than the most successful of prophets (Matthew 12:41) and the wisest of kings (Matthew 12:42); One whom even David called 'Lord' (Matthew 22:41–46) and One who had priority even over Abraham, the founding father of the Jewish family and faith (John 8:58). He assumed that He had the right to forgive people's sins, which, as the Pharisees pointed out – and Jesus did not gainsay them – is something only God can do (Mark 2:1–12). He assumed that He would be the One to judge all humanity at the end of time (Matthew 25:31f) – again, the rôle that only an omniscient and wise God could properly perform.

N. T. Wright summarises the elements that seem to have contributed to Jesus' divine self-understanding:

[a] 'It is true that he described his doctrine as being not his but the Father's who had sent him. Nevertheless, he knew himself to be such an immediate means of divine revelation as to be able to speak with great personal assurance. He never hesitated or apologized. He had no need to contradict, withdraw or modify anything he said. ... He asserted that his words were as eternal as the law, and would never pass away.' (From John R. W. Stott, *Basic Christianity*, (IVP, 1958), pp. 30–31.) The Jewish scholar, Jacob Neusner, sees the point clearly: 'Here is a Torah-teacher who says in his own name what the Torah says in God's name ... For what kind of torah is it that improves upon the teachings of the Torah without acknowledging the source – and it is God who is the Source – of those teachings? I am troubled not so much by the message, though I might take exception to this or that, as I am by the messenger ...' (*A Rabbi talks with Jesus*, Doubleday, New York, 1993, pp. 30f.).

His messianic vocation included within it the vocation to attempt certain tasks which, according to scripture, YHWH [the sacred name for God, often written as Yahweh] had reserved for himself. He would take upon himself the role of messianic shepherd, knowing that YHWH had claimed this role as his own. He would perform the saving task which YHWH had said he alone could achieve. He would do what no messenger, no angel, but only the 'arm of YHWH', the presence of Israel's god, could accomplish. As part of his human vocation, grasped in faith, sustained in prayer, tested in confrontation, agonized over in further prayer and doubt, and implemented in action, he believed he had to do and be, for Israel and the world, that which according to scripture only YHWH himself could do and be. He was Israel's Messiah; but there would, in the end, be 'no king but God'.[4]

But such was the authority of His presence and the beauty of His life, and so much was His ministry marked by healing power, that His disciples could not dismiss Him as being deluded. Besides, they had heard divine testimony to Him at His baptism and on the mountain. And of course the Resurrection clinched it. If God were going to raise one human being to life in advance of the general resurrection, He would hardly make it one who was deluded or deceiving. And therefore, despite saying the Shema[b] every day – 'Hear, O Israel: The Lord our God, the Lord is one' – and despite living in a fiercely monotheistic culture which prohibited any representations of God, they came to believe that in Jesus, God was visiting and redeeming His people.

2. THEY REALISED THAT JESUS WAS DISTINCT FROM THE FATHER

One of the most striking features of Jesus was His prayer life. For

---

[b] The Shema is a Jewish prayer/creed consisting of Deuteronomy 6:4–9, 11:13–21 and Numbers 15:37–41, quoted by Jesus in Mark 12:29f.

one thing, He gave quite a lot of time to it. In addition to the daily rhythm of private prayer (morning, afternoon and evening, and benedictions before and after meals), the weekly rhythm of public prayer in the synagogue (Luke 4:16) and the annual rhythm of festivals in the temple (John 2:13, 5:1, 7:10, 10:22), He would often get up early in the morning and escape to 'a solitary place' to pray (Mark 1:35). Sometimes, He would spend the night in prayer (Luke 6:12), and His whole public ministry grew out of and drew upon the forty days He spent fasting and praying in the wilderness (Luke 4:1–13, Matthew 4:1–11). If we ask ourselves why Jesus' ministry was so fruitful and effective, we should not look to His divinity alone (Mark 9:29).

But it was not just the regularity, discipline and priority of His prayer life that would have impressed His disciples. It was also the fact that it was so natural a part of His ordinary life. He could easily slip into addressing God in praise (Matthew 11:25–26) or thanksgiving (John 11:41). But perhaps the most notable quality of His prayer life was its intimacy. His use of the Aramaic word 'Abba' as an address to God was not absolutely unique, but it was highly distinctive. And it was not used only by children to their fathers, but it was a term of intimacy and family love. All this adds up to a relationship with God of such rare attractiveness that it is not surprising that the disciples wanted it for themselves (Luke 11:1).

The point for our present purposes, however, is that *He prays to His Father*. He does not pray to Himself. It is a *relationship* that He has in prayer – not a monologue. And for the disciples who came slowly but disturbingly to the conclusion that Jesus was divine, a number of questions began to trouble them: how can this be? How can He be divine and yet be distinct from the Father? How can He be God and yet converse with God? How can there be a conversation going on within God Himself? They had been given hundreds of extra pieces of the jigsaw, which would eventually enable them to come to a much bigger picture. For the moment, it probably seemed just to add to their confusion.

3. AFTER PENTECOST, THEY BEGAN TO EXPERIENCE A PRESENCE WITHIN AND AMONG THEMSELVES WHICH THEY RECOGNISED TO BE DIVINE

When the disciples received the promised Holy Spirit at Pentecost, they experienced a Power amongst them and within them, which seemed to be working to dismantle the ancient divisions. The very fact that the Galilean disciples were understood across the language barrier – and everyone heard them 'speak in our tongues the wonderful works of God' (Acts 2:11 AV) – was symptomatic of what was to come. Jesus had included within His (symbolically significant) twelve apostles both a collaborator, such as Matthew, and a zealot – or at least someone with the nickname 'zealot' – such as Simon (Luke 6:15); and where He had included Israelite outcasts at His table and within His movement, the early church found the boundaries of its mission being pushed out even further to include, first, the hated and polluted Samaritans (Acts 8), then a God-fearing Gentile and a member of the occupying army to boot (Acts 10), and finally out-and-out pagans (Acts 13:46f, 14:27, 19:19, 25–27).

The way in which Luke tells the story in *The Acts of the Apostles* makes it clear that this was entirely the work of the Spirit, and not the result of the apostles' theological insight. They had to be pushed into acceptance of non-Jews, kicking and screaming. Peter, for example, was only persuaded by the combination of the Spirit talking to him, and the Spirit coming upon a room full of Gentiles (Acts 10:10f, 19, 44). Since the mysterious coming-upon-them of the Spirit at Pentecost, the same Spirit seemed to be building them together into a family, on the basis of faith in Jesus, irrespective of gender, class and even of race – the final frontier. In the Spirit, God was undoing all the divisions that had come about with the Fall and with Babel – and was creating a new society.

If the Spirit was bringing about the reconciling work of God, implementing the achievement of the Cross and helping people to understand that achievement, emboldening their witness, impelling their prayer, inducing their holiness and enabling them to share in the life of God, then the Spirit must be divine too. Only the Creator God could heal creation of its constitutional brokenness. Only God could take us up into the life of God. Only God could reconcile us to God. But this only complicated an already perplexing picture. Yet more pieces of the jigsaw were being placed on the table.

4. THEY KNEW THAT THE SPIRIT WAS NOT THE SAME AS JESUS OR THE FATHER

The fact that Jesus went away and then the Spirit came could easily have led the early Christians to conclude that the Spirit was simply Jesus in another guise. They would still have had to place Jesus on the map of God somehow, but at least they wouldn't have had to find a different place for the Spirit as well. But easy(ish!) though that would have been, it is not the route that they took. They took the more disturbing and disruptive route of mapping God as trinity, and they seem to have made things difficult for themselves in this way because, in John's Gospel, Jesus had made it clear that the Spirit was not the same as the Father and not the same as Himself. In John 14:16, Jesus says, 'I will ask the Father, and he will give you another Counsellor to be with you for ever – the Spirit of truth.' So the Counsellor is not the same as the Father – for the Father is the Giver whereas the Counsellor is the Gift.

But neither is the Counsellor the same as Jesus – He is *another* Counsellor, not the same one. The satirical magazine *Punch* once carried a three-part cartoon, in the first drawing of which a military dictator in military uniform is standing on the balcony of the presidential palace addressing the people. 'In fulfilment of my promise at the time of the coup, I am now handing over to civilian rule', he announces. In the second cartoon, he leaves the balcony. And in the third, he returns wearing a suit! When Jesus promises us *another* Counsellor, we don't expect the same one in different dress. Besides, in the immensely influential episode of Jesus' baptism, they had encountered all three Persons together.

So they went the route of having to find a distinct place for the Spirit too in their understanding of God. But how? What were they to make of all that had happened? Where did it leave their thinking about God? What did they have to say about Him now – after all that they had learnt about Him and seen of Him in Jesus, and after all that they had experienced of Him by the Spirit? They might have concluded that there were in fact three Gods, but there is no evidence that they so much as toyed with this suggestion. They were Jews, they were monotheists, they repeated twice a day that 'The LORD our God is one LORD' (Deuteronomy 6:4, NIV margin), it was deeply ingrained in them that there was and had always been and could only ever be one God. And they instinctively knew that everything would be lost if they abandoned that fundamental belief. Their unified concept of reality would be shattered and they would be left with the anxiety of paganism. The harmony, integrity and security that comes with belief in one God must never be compromised.

So, instead, they were forced to conclude that God was richer and stranger than they had previously suspected. There were not three gods. There was one God – but He was three-fold. The great advance of monotheism was preserved – there is a Person at the heart of the universe, a Person who loves us and values us and has purposes that include us, a Person who created us to be persons and to whom we may relate person-to-Person. That resonated with their deep sense of who they were as human beings. It made sense of who they knew themselves to be. They were personal because God is personal. They were valuable because God valued them. They felt the need to be infinitely loved because they *were* infinitely loved. They felt the need for purpose in life because the Life-Giver *has* purposes into which we can fit and to which we can contribute. This they had always known.

But now they discovered a further dimension to God, that He is not only personal – He is also *relational*. There is relationship going on within the very being of God. There is a relationship that has eternally been going on between the Father, the Son and the Spirit.

That intimacy that they saw in Jesus' relationship with the Father, that tenderness and delight in one another which characterised the extraordinary scene of Jesus' baptism – that love had always been there. And so they came to draw the 'map' of God something like this:

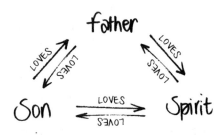

God is relational. God is Relationship, the Relationship from which everything else flows. Just as a human couple (ideally) have children out of the overflow of their love for each other, and in order that their children might be born into that love and grow up in it and share it, so God created the universe in order that we might enter into and share that love which is the one abiding fact of existence.

And once they had seen that, they realised that it resonated with the deepest crannies of human experience and identity. What is most valuable to us as human beings? In the end, it is relationships. Not possessions, not achievements, not knowledge, nor power. It is relationships. And it is relationships that matter most to us because we were not only made *for* relationship, but *by* Relationship. We were made in the image of God – and God is relationship. So that is who we are, that is what we are for, that is where we may find fulfilment.

We touch here on the most basic of all truth. This is the fundamental fact of all that is. You can divide up a molecule. You can split an atom. You may even be able to split the quark. But you can never divide up the love that the Father has for the Son, and the Son for the Spirit, and the Spirit for the Father, and the Father for the Spirit, and the Son for the Father, and the Spirit for the

Son. That is indivisible. That is the surest thing there is. That is the starting-point – and the goal – of all things. Here we stand on holy – but utterly firm – ground. And the view from here is stunning.

WHAT ARE THE IMPLICATIONS OF SEEING GOD IN THIS WAY?

a) The doctrine of the Trinity means that God is Love

Belief in God as Trinity enables us to say that God is Love. If God were simply One, and that is all that we could say about Him, then He might be loving, but He wouldn't be Love. He might love us, but He wouldn't be Love in Himself. We would then have to draw the map of God something like this:

Indeed, if this is our map of God, if God is just One and not Three, then God would not even be loving intrinsically, for until He created the world, He would have had nothing to love. For 'most' of eternity He would not have been involved in a loving relationship. He would be dependent upon the world to provide an object for His love. (Nor would He be Father intrinsically, for He wouldn't always have had a Son.) As Brian Hebblethwaite put it, 'we can no longer rationally think of God as love when relational – in christian terms, trinitarian – thinking goes by the board.'[5]

But if God is Trinity, if God is Three as well as One, if (something like) *this* is our map of God –

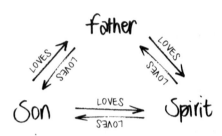

– then God is not only lov*ing*, He is Love, because there is and has always been and will always be a giving *and a receiving* of love within His very being. He is not dependent upon the world to provide Him with something to love – the Father has always had the Son and the Spirit to love, the Son has always had the Father and the Spirit, the Spirit has always had the Father and the Son. That dynamic of love is who God has always been. As Jane Williams writes, 'God is constituted, not by being "one is one and all alone and ever more shall be so", but by being in relation. God relates, even before we exist to be related to.'[6] That is simply and intrinsically and eternally who He is. It is not accidental that Christianity is big on love. Love has an exalted place in Christian ethics because love has an exalted place in a Christian understanding of God. He is love. That is the foundational insight that emerges out of – and is enabled by – the doctrine of the Trinity.

b) The doctrine of the Trinity means that we are on the divine map

Unlike the unitarian map of God in which we are separated from Him by a long line, we are actually located *within* the trinitarian map of God. Where are we on it?

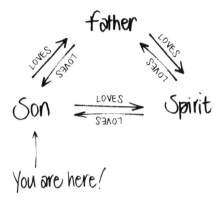

If we are in Christ, then we are in God, and we share in the life and the love of God. We are taken up into the divine relationship, we are included within the trinitarian conversation, we belong within the eternal community. As 2 Peter 1:4 puts it, we 'participate in the divine nature'. That is where we already are if we are 'in Him': and to be drawn ever more intimately into that Love is our calling. That is the extraordinary privilege of being a Christian, of being part of the Church.

And because that is where we are on the map of God, because we are located in the Son, because, as Jane Williams put it, the Spirit enables us 'to stand in Jesus' own place in relation to the Father'[7], therefore what is true of the Son becomes (in an important sense) true also of us. It becomes true of us that we are eternally rooted in the love of the Godhead. It becomes true of us that we are eternally loved. It becomes true of us that we are eternally held in the love of the Father. We are eternally held in the unbreakable bond of love that is at the root and at the heart of all things. Ours is the utter security of being held in this eternal relationship of love. The Father speaks over us what He speaks over the Son, 'You are my beloved, in whom I am well pleased.'

As we shall see below, we do not *become* the Son. We are not dissolved into the Son. We do not become God and are not dissolved into God. We remain who we are. We remain – indeed, fully become

– ourselves. We remain the bride and not the bridegroom. We remain in relationship with God. But it is an internal relationship, not an external relationship. As Peter Adam put it, 'we are included in the love with which God loves himself.'[8] We are welcomed into the mutual embrace of the persons of the Godhead. We are invited to join in their conversation. We are recipients of – and contributors to – their life and their love. The Spirit enables us to stand where Jesus stands. His humanity, taken up into the Godhead, is our place, is the space He has created for us, is where we belong. And belong, we surely do. As the Spirit helps us to stand where Jesus stands, so Jesus shares with us His history, His future, His height, His depth, His purity, His lovedness and His love.

As we saw in the last chapter, it is not just that we are taken up into this relationship (2 Peter 1:4): it is also true that this relationship is taken into us (John 14:23). When the Spirit comes into us, the Father and the Son come too and make their home with us. They become resident within us. We become the place wherein the Holy Spirit, and therefore the whole Godhead, makes His dwelling. We are thus enlarged and enriched, and become walking temples, earthen vessels that carry around with us the love that engendered all things. May we be so full of Him that, when we are jolted by this life's pressures and pains, it is that love that sloshes over onto those around.

c) The doctrine of the Trinity means that God will not keep us at arm's length

I suspect that the doctrine of the Trinity was felt to meet two threats to which every human being is subject, two threats, each of which, if fully implemented, would destroy us. I notice that a great deal of what we do is concerned with meeting and overcoming these threats, and that this is a matter both of instinct and of conscious contrivance. I suspect that the doctrine of the Trinity was felt as something like a promise or guarantee that these two threats would be finally overcome. … The two threats are the threat of isolation, on the one hand, and the threat of absorption, on the other. Each is a potential murderer.[9]

So said H. A. Williams in a sermon one Trinity Sunday. Here we shall look at the threat of isolation, and in section d) we shall consider the threat of absorption. Isolation or alienation is not having intimacy. It is being excluded. It is being the one left on the edge of the playground that no one wants to play with – multiplied cosmically. It is being kept away from relationship, or at least from any depth of relationship. It is being kept away in particular from that relationship by which and for which we were created. The fear here is that we shall never experience that intimacy for which our hearts crave and which even the closest of family or marriage relationships fail ultimately to assuage.

When we are young, we need closeness. We need the reassurance of the maternal touch. We need to be held. We need to be hugged. We need to be kissed. Our generation has learned, both from psychology and experience, what happens when children are not loved in these ways. But, though there is a proper independence from parents that increases as we get older and may take the form of adolescent rebellion at a particular stage of our development, we never grow out of the need for intimacy. And without it, we wither. My vicar wouldn't just greet his congregation as they left after the service, but would also meet them with affection and care as they entered the church beforehand. The moment of contact – a hug or kiss for those he knew well – might be the only moment of physical and personal warmth a parishioner would receive all week. Ours is a society that experiences a famine of intimacy in its relationships with one another, and suspects that there is none to be had cosmically or eternally, that there is nothing 'out there' but cold, pitiless indifference.[c]

The doctrine of the Trinity defuses that fear, for in God our deep

---

[c] This belief is of course just as open to the charge of projection as the belief that 'out there' there is a heavenly Father who loves us. It may be the projection of our bad experience or our fear.

need to be close will be met. We shall be close, not only to Him, but also, therefore, to one another. The doctrine of the Trinity shows us that it is possible to be unimaginably close, totally united, totally at one – without ceasing to be ourselves. And it invites us into that Relationship in which the Participants, far from keeping one another at arm's length, enter into one another and interpenetrate one another and delight in one another, and know one another in love.

To be a Christian is to have embarked on a never-ending journey of knowing and being known. It will ease us out of our protective shells. It will encourage us to reveal a little more of who we are. Sometimes we shall get hurt in that process, and sometimes we shall hurt others. And we shall never, in this life, achieve that degree of intimacy that will satisfy our souls.

But when we have been remade, and our self-protective prickliness has been shed and our fearfulness dissolved and our selfishness removed, we shall know fully even as we are fully known (1 Corinthians 13:12), and we shall be taken up, fully and consciously and unreservedly, into that relationship with the persons of the Trinity and with one another for which we were made. We shall know that intimacy to which the closest of marriages is but the palest of pointers.

As H. A. Williams says, 'The threat of being isolated is overcome because the One God is described as being eternally in relation. ... For where there is relatedness there can be no aloneness.'[10]

d) The Trinity means that we will not 'dissolve' into God

At the same time, however, there is the opposite danger, the danger of our being absorbed, absorbed into what promises to extinguish our individuality. ... If I feel that religion is a threat to my individuality, then, if I am a person of any integrity, my religion must consist of opposing religion tooth and nail. ... Marriages often break down because one partner feels that the other is trying to absorb him or her.[11]

The fear here is that I shall get smothered by the relationships I am in, that I shall lose who I am in the force of someone else's personality, that I shall forget who I am in the understanding of who *we* are. This, as Harry Williams observes, is true of our relationships with one another, perhaps especially in marriage. But how much more true is it of our relationship with God? If we can feel threatened by the force of another human being's personality, how much more likely are we to feel threatened by the force of the Infinite God's character? If part of the particular difficulty of our relationships with our parents is that they gave us life, and that we owe our being and our genetic make-up and some strains of our character to them, and therefore feel in particular danger of being smothered or swamped by them, then how much more might we fear being swamped by the One who brought not just us into being, but our parents and our siblings and our environment and our cosmos? Will my individuality and personhood and me-ness not get absorbed into God as a drop of water loses its individuality in the sea? That is the fear.

And it is a fear that some religious traditions do nothing to calm. By and large, religions that see God as 'the One', tend to see our destiny precisely as absorption into that One. This is illustrated well by the Buddhist story of the salt doll.

A doll of salt, after a long pilgrimage on dry land, came to the sea and discovered something she had never seen and could not possibly understand. She stood on the firm ground, a solid little doll of salt, and saw there was another ground that was mobile, insecure, noisy, strange and unknown. She asked the sea, 'But what are you?' and it said, 'I am the sea.' And the doll said, 'What is the sea?' to which the answer was, 'It is me.' Then the doll said, 'I cannot understand, but I want to; how can I?' The sea answered, 'Touch me.' So the doll shyly put forward a foot and touched the water and she got a strange impression that it was something that began to be knowable. She withdrew her leg, looked and saw that her toes had gone, and she was afraid and said, 'Oh, but where is my toe, what have you done to me?' And the sea said, 'You have given something in order to understand.' Gradually the water took away small bits of the doll's salt and the doll went farther and farther into the sea and at every moment she had a sense of understanding more and more, and yet of not being able to say what the sea was. As she went deeper, she melted more and more, repeating: 'But what is the sea?' At last a wave dissolved the rest of her and the doll said: 'It is I!'[12]

The religious traditions that see absorption as our destiny tend to see our individuality as a hindrance to peace both within ourselves and with others and with all things, and therefore train us to suppress it.

But the religion of the Three-in-One holds out a very different prospect. In the Trinity, the Father, the Son and the Spirit are so united that they are utterly One, *and yet they never cease to be themselves*. On the contrary, they are themselves in their relationship with one another. They never dissolve into an amalgam of divinity. They never cease to be three. They never cease to be Father, Son and Spirit. They never lose who they are in their intimate interactions with one another. Their oneness is no threat to their threeness. Their intimacy is no threat to their individuality.

So we need not fear that we shall lose our individuality when we are taken up into God. We shall have to shed our selfishness and our self-assertiveness and our self-promotion, but never our selfhood. God made us and wants to remake us, not to unmake us. He wants to relate with us, not to devour us. We shall remain distinct, as Father, Son and Spirit remain distinct. We shall remain ourselves – in fact, more ourselves than ever. We shall not lose ourselves in God – we shall find ourselves in Him, and in that relationship that is Him. As Harry Williams said, 'the doctrine of the Trinity provides us with an image in which the ... threat of absorption is met and vanquished. The persons of the Godhead are for ever distinct and unconfused. The Son and the Spirit cannot be absorbed into the Father. From all eternity to all eternity they are what they are'[13] and so shall we be.

e) The doctrine of the Trinity gives us a model for our relationships

Once again, it is the baptism of Jesus that gives us perhaps the richest glimpse of the inner life of the Trinity. And when all three Persons 'appear' together, what do we find them doing? We find them glorifying one another. The Father expresses publicly His love for the Son: 'You are my Son, whom I love; with you I am well pleased' (Mark 1:11). The Spirit marks Jesus out as the One on whom the favour of God rests. Jesus submits willingly to the call and the plan of the Father and accepts the anointing of the Spirit to empower Him to carry out that plan. There is mutual expression of love and trust, mutual submission and mutual glorification.

Or take the 'high-priestly' prayer of Jesus in John's Gospel. What is His prime concern the night before His death? It is the same business of mutual glorification.

> Father, the time has come. Glorify your Son, that your Son may glorify you. For you granted him authority over all people that he might give eternal life to all those you have given him. Now this is eternal life: that they may know you, the only true God, and Jesus Christ, whom you have sent. I have brought you glory on earth by completing the work you gave me to do. And now, Father, glorify me in your presence with the glory I had with you before the world began.
>
> John 17:1–5

How we see them relate to one another in these Gospel-glimpses is how they have related to one another for all eternity.

And we are made in the image of this mutually-glorifying God, which means that we need to learn to delight in glorifying one another. We need to become free enough to affirm and glorify and express our love for one another – privately and publicly. That way, we mirror the triune God and become who we were made to be, and flourish and make possible the flourishing of others.

I grew up in a loving family, in which I never doubted the love of my parents and brothers. To know oneself to be so loved is the greatest of blessings and I am deeply grateful to God for my wonderful family. Now, the main form of humour in our family was the insult – we would insult each other joyfully and without malice or offence! My father was a very witty man and came out with a number of choice comments. On one occasion, my mother said, 'You never wear that shirt I gave you, David.' To which my father retorted, in a typically male fending-off sort of way, 'I'm waiting for a special occasion.' 'Well, you'd better hurry up', said my mother, 'or I'll be dead.' To which my Dad replied, 'That'll be the special occasion!' As I say, we knew ourselves to be loved – in fact, such robust banter could only have been funny if we had been entirely sure of that love. But it is probably true that most of us could afford to be more affirming and encouraging, and more expressive of our love for those with whom we are in relationship. We could afford to be more creative and imaginative and generous and liberal in the way we give voice to one another's worth. We could afford to be more glorifying of one another, without running much risk of mawkishness and sentimentality! The mutual glorification of the persons of the Trinity is to be our model, and that sets the bar rather high.

f) The doctrine of the Trinity changes our values

If God were One and not Three, if He did not exist eternally in relationship, if He were a unity and not a triunity, then what would His worshippers value? I suggest that they should value independence and self-sufficiency. For those would be the qualities most pertaining to a God who had spent 'most' of eternity in splendid isolation with no one to love or relate to. But because God is Three Persons in One God, because He has always existed in – or, indeed, *as* – a relationship of love, what His worshippers should value is relationship and love.[d] This poses a fundamental challenge both to the way we do our personal relating, and to the way in which we might go about thinking through socio-economic policies from a Christian perspective. Let me give an example of each area. First, our personal relating.

Martin is a successful, middle-aged businessman. He is something of a self-made man. He enjoys his work, works hard at it, is good at it and does well out of it. He is sociable and fun to have around, and he's popular at the golf club. He has been married to Penny for twenty years, and they have a good marriage, if a little conventional and lacking in both tenderness and passion. (If you have seen *A Fish Called Wanda*, you'll know what I mean when I say that it is more like the relationship between John Cleese and Maria Aitken than the one between Kevin Klein and Jamie Lee Curtis. Not a lot of Russian is spoken in this marriage!) Martin does have one sadness. He always longed to have children. If he were being honest, he'd admit that, in particular, he always longed to have sons to teach to play golf, to play golf *with*, to be proud of. They do have a son, Billy, who's sixteen. But Billy has Down's Syndrome, and will never play golf. He will never take over the business. And if Martin were to dredge his heart, he'd find disappointment there.

Billy is away at a special school. He likes it there because he doesn't get teased, the way he used to at his old school. He's a cheerful boy, always laughing and delightfully affectionate. He

---

[d] I say 'should' in both cases because a) not all Christians do have a set of values appropriate to the triune God they worship, and b) many who have a unitarian view of God have a thoroughly relational view of life. Jews and Muslims, for instance, often have a higher estimation of family and society than many (especially Western) Christians do (I owe this point to Carrie Thompson). That is partly, I suspect, because none of us lives in a way that is fully consistent with our beliefs, partly because our values are largely shaped by the cultures in which we live as well as by the beliefs we profess, but also, I suggest, because of the continuities between the God that Jews and Muslims believe in and the triune God. For many reasons, they do not recognise Him as being triune, but that is what He is nonetheless, so it is not surprising that it is relational values that they have learned from their interaction with Him. As I say, this is a Christian view, and not one that Jews and Muslims would themselves recognise. It might, however, be a fertile area for inter-faith dialogue (trialogue?) to explore.

is always hugging his teacher or his friends. His display of love is uninhibited and unembarrassed. His only real sadness is the fact that his father is so reticent towards him, and has so little time for him. He couldn't articulate this, but he senses that his father is ashamed of him. And that is the only real blight on his happiness.

So Martin contributes to the economy. He is good company. Society views him with approval. Billy it views as little as possible. It sends him away to a special school partly because it wants the best for him, but partly also because that saves its 'normal' children from having to make an effort with him. It saves him from holding their children back. Society gives a very mixed message about Billy's value. On the one hand, it has made great strides in provision for 'disabled' people, opening up access and offering training. On the other hand, it sanctions (and, in some cases, encourages) the killing of people like Billy before birth.

Now, if God were not triune, it seems to me that Society would be right in its relative estimation of Martin and Billy, because Martin is the self-sufficient one. He is the independent one. He is the beneficent one. But if God is triune, if God is Relationship, if there is a *receiving* as well as a giving within God, then it is relationship and love that we will most admire, not independence and self-sufficiency and contribution. And here it is Billy who, for all his lack of sophistication and articulation, is the better at being human. For he gives himself, and does not hold back. He does not resent his dependence, and is a joyful receiver. And he loves with abandonment. Not many of us are his equal in these ways. See how the doctrine of the Trinity subverts our usual ways of making judgments and the assumptions behind our values.

It is not just in the area of personal relating, however, that the doctrine of the Trinity makes such a difference. It is also in the area of public policy. (The two obviously overlap. We have already seen how the example of Billy has implications for public policy on abortion and schooling.) All too often, socio-economic policies are economic first and social second. All too often, we make policy on the basis of what is best for the economy, and then pay the social and environmental consequences.

The Relationships Foundation is a socio-economic think-tank set up to try and do this the other way round. It tries to formulate policy proposals on the basis of what is best for relationships, for marriages, for families, for communities – and then find a way of funding them. It tries not to let economic factors trump all others. That was why it launched the 'Keep Time for Children' initiative and why the associated 'Keep Sunday Special' campaign opposed Sunday trading – not because it was trying anachronistically to impose the strictures of Old Testament theocracy onto a modern secular state, but because it believed that Sunday trading would have deleterious relational consequences. It would mean the closure of many small shops, which can be focal points for small communities. And it would mean that working parents might not have the same day off, which could be highly damaging to marriages and families. All this would be sacrificed to the financial advantage of the big supermarkets. Regardless of one's view of this particular issue, it seems to me to be right to attempt policy-making this way round. The original inspiration for the Relationships Foundation came mainly from the Old Testament, but I believe that it receives ontological undergirding in the doctrine of the Trinity.[e]

The doctrine of the Trinity is no mere academic doctrine. It is about God. It is about the nature of the Person who made our world. It is about the Person whose image we bear. It therefore has incalculable implications for who we are and how we live. Part of the excitement of theology is attempting to be faithful to the nature of God as He has shown Himself to be, in every area of the life He has given us. And part of the excitement of the doctrine of the Trinity in particular is the challenge to exalt in, and to live out, the fact that what we came from and what we are for is relationship. I relate, therefore I am. And we relate, therefore we are.

g) The doctrine of the Trinity means that hierarchy and equality are compatible

The Persons of the Trinity are equal. Unlike the animals in *Animal*

---

[e] By 'ontological undergirding', I mean undergirding in the very structures of being.

Farm, none of them is 'more equal' than the others. None of them is more fully divine. This was a vital truth that was hammered out in the fourth-century debates on the nature of the Godhead. A priest called Arius had suggested that Jesus was not quite divine. He was the most exalted of creatures, and it was through Him that God had created all other creatures. But He fell on the creature side of the Creator/creature divide, and there was a time when He didn't exist. Arius' bishop, Alexander, and Alexander's chaplain, the great Athanasius, knew that this was wrong. If Jesus was not God, He could not reveal God to us, and He could not lift us up to God, and all was lost. There was no good news, if Jesus were not fully divine.

So at the Council of Nicaea in AD 325, Athanasius and his supporters tried to formulate a statement which would safeguard the gospel. Where Arius trumpeted the view that 'There was when He was not' – in other words, there was a time when the Son did not exist – the Council of Nicaea insisted that He was *'eternally* begotten of the Father'. Where Arius and his followers argued that Jesus was just a creature, the Council proclaimed that He was 'begotten, *not made'.* Where Arius believed that Jesus was a lesser being than the Father, Nicaea asserted that He was *'of one being* with the Father.' He was every bit as divine as the Father. 'God from God' said the Nicene Creed. And Arius could just about live with that: 'well, yes, in some senses, Jesus is God', said Arius. 'He's God-ish!' But the bishops realised that that was not good enough. Only if the Son is fully God can He reveal God to us and reconcile us to God. So they added the phrase, 'True God of true God', to which Arius said, 'I'm out of here!' Roughly. So the full equality of the Father and the Son was insisted upon in the Nicene Creed, which is accepted by nearly all the major Christian denominations.[f]

Later the same dispute arose about the Spirit. What came to be known as the Macedonian Heresy denied the full divinity of the Spirit. But Athanasius and a theologian called Basil stood firm. The

[f] It was later added to at the Council of Constantinople in AD 381, but all the key phrases from Nicaea were kept. (The exact relationship between the creeds of Nicaea and Constantinople is unclear.)

same points needed to be made. If the Spirit were not divine, then the Scriptures were not divinely inspired and we have no access to the mind of God. And if the Spirit were not divine, He could not raise us up into the life of God. As we saw in the last chapter, Basil rewrote the Gloria to emphasise the complete equality of the Persons of the Godhead: 'Glory to the Father *and* to the Son *and* to the Holy Spirit.' Without that equality, there could be no revelation, no salvation, God would not be Love, we would not be on the divine map, we would be kept at arm's length, relationship would not be so prized, our values would not be so challenged, and Love would not be our origin. The equality of the Persons of the Trinity is bedrock.

And yet. What are we to make of the fact that Jesus said, 'The Father is greater than I' (John 14:28)? What are we to make of the fact that Paul said, 'the head of Christ is God' [1 Corinthians 11:3)? Was Arius right all along? No. These verses are only a problem for us if we project our own bad experience of human fatherhood, and human headship, and human leadership onto God. It is only because of our own warped mind-sets that we think of a boss as being more important than any other employee. And rather than project our own bad experiences of human bosses onto God, what we need to do is to allow God's kind of headship and fatherhood to challenge and correct ours.

There is hierarchy within the Godhead, and yet all the Persons of the Trinity are equal. We need to allow the hierarchy-within-equality of the Trinity to teach us that hierarchy and equality are perfectly compatible. Being a boss is nothing to do with being 'superior'. You can – and you should – have equality of status within a structural hierarchy. My bishop is not more important than I am: we have different rôles within the organisation. His is to lead – leadership is his particular form of service. And if he does that job well, then that doesn't oppress me – it liberates me for my own ministry. And I owe him a loyalty and a respect that is not entirely symmetrical. Similarly, my father is not more important than I am: but I do owe him a filial respect that is not symmetrical with the paternal respect that he owes me. My father is in some sense 'greater than I', but he is not more important, nor more valuable, nor more human than I. In the same way, the Father is greater than the Son, but He is not more important, more divine, more majestic, more worthy of our worship than the Son or the Spirit. They are co-equal and co-eternal, and of one substance with one another.

We need thus to be thorough-going egalitarians without being 'levellers'. We should insist upon the full and unnegotiable equality of the cleaner and the Managing Director, without having to oppose having a Managing Director at all. We should remember, when we are in positions of leadership and authority, that we are no more valuable or important than any of those we lead, and our interests should weigh no more heavily with us than theirs. In fact, we need to see our leadership as a form of service to them, and therefore true leaders will, if anything, take the interests of the led more seriously than their own.

There is nothing wrong with hierarchy. It can liberate. The problem is with the way in which it is often used to put down and to crush. It is not surprising that many have come to reject the concept of hierarchy altogether, as synonymous with self-interest and domination. But in the Trinity, we have a counter-example. We know that hierarchy does not have to be oppressive. It can be compatible with equality. It can take the form of service and affirmation and glorification and love. So let us seek to model our parenthood and our management and our organisations on that structured equality, that egalitarian hierarchy in whose image we are made.

h) The doctrine of the Trinity means that our Source and our Destiny are Love

Most views of who we are as human beings and what we are for and how we best operate are based on struggle. We are beings who have emerged out of conflict and are marked by violence. Many primitive religions have a creation myth in which creation takes place out of the carcass of a slain dragon. There is some battle between the gods and the forces of chaos, or between gods and other gods, out of which the material world emerges. The dead body of the dragon or the defeated god is the matter from which the stars and planets are formed. This is the pagan myth of primal violence. As Walter Wink says, 'The implications are clear: humanity is created from the blood of a murdered god. Our very origin is violence. Killing is in our blood.'[14] The universe had a violent engenderment, and it is *essentially* characterised by violence.

Modern paganism has the same basic belief. Of course, it doesn't believe that we come from a murdered dragon, but it does believe that our origin is violence. When Darwinism is turned from being a biological hypothesis – with which I have no quarrel – into a philosophy of life, it sees human beings as the creatures of conflict, defined by billions of years of power struggle in which the weakest go to the wall. Marxism sees human beings as being engaged in class struggle.[g] To the Marxist we are essentially competitive beings in a necessarily violent world.

If that is who we are, then that is how we must live. So the myth of primal violence leads easily to the myth of redemptive violence. We use violence to solve our problems, because that is who we are. That's our way. We see this clearly in modern popular culture. Terminator, Popeye, the Power Rangers and Neo from the Matrix films all use violence, but that's okay because they are the good guys. (As Walter Wink observes, 'Violence does not teach Bluto to honor Olive Oyl's humanity, and repeated pummelings do not teach Popeye to swallow his spinach *before* the fight!'[15]) Tragically (and relatedly?) we see it too in international relations. In the two

---

[g] I don't deny that there is truth to both the Darwinian and Marxist analysis of who we are. There is such a struggle going on in the natural order and in human interaction. The question is, are we essentially antagonistic, or are we that way as a result of the Fall? Is that who we are, or just what we have become? The doctrine of the Trinity, like the doctrine of the Fall, insists that, though this is what we have become – and to that extent Darwin and Marx are correct – it is not who we are. It is not who we were made and meant to be. And conflict is not the ultimate truth. It is not our origin. It's not our homeland. It's not our base font. It's not the primordial matrix from which we sprang. What we came from and what we are for is the eternal love of the Father, the Son and the Spirit.

Gulf Wars and the Bosnian War and Operation Enduring Freedom in Afghanistan, the West used force as a problem-solving device. I am not saying that the use of force is always prohibited to the Christian and I am not saying that all these campaigns were necessarily unjustified. What I am suggesting is that the ease and the speed with which we reach for the military option, and the lack of imagination given to finding any other kind of solution, strongly suggest that our civilisation's basic world-view is fundamentally pagan.

If however, we see our Origin and our Destiny not as violence and struggle, and if we see 'the primordial reality from which all things come, and to which all things are intended to converge' not as conflict, but as 'the communion of love given and enjoyed, the bliss of the Holy Trinity'[16], then we will have a very different vision of what it is to be human. This will, in turn, engender very different instincts from the instinct to lash out, both in our personal lives and in our international relations. In radical distinction from – and protest against – a world-view based upon primal violence and redemptive violence, we have a world-view that grounds itself upon primal love and redemptive suffering. And we need to live accordingly.

i) The doctrine of the Trinity means that we should try to be fully trinitarian in our spirituality

God is trinitarian. Human beings are made in the image of God. If, therefore, we focus on one member of the Trinity to the neglect of the others, we will live out an imbalanced humanity. Most of us do have one Person of the Trinity to whom we most easily relate. If we examine our prayers, we will probably notice that we usually have One of the Three in mind as we pray. And if we look at the life of the church we attend, we shall probably find that it too tends to major on one Person of the Trinity. And we needn't be too worried about that. The other two aren't going to be offended! But the one we pray to will want to introduce us to the other two, so that we have a fuller, richer and more rounded view – and experience – of God.

So it is a good spiritual discipline to try consciously to address in prayer the Person(s) of the Trinity with whom we are less immediately comfortable. It makes sense to find prayers or hymns or songs that are addressed to the Person(s) of the Trinity we tend to neglect (or indeed that are explicitly trinitarian in structure), and to use them to bring a trinitarian balance to our spirituality. It is a good idea *occasionally* to go to a church with a very different style from that of the church we usually attend, so as to expose ourselves to a different aspect of the nature of God – and the chances are it will be the very aspect of the nature of God that we are most missing in our own understanding, worship and service of Him. We may find it difficult. We may be confirmed in the view that it is not 'our cup of tea'. But I hope we may already have discovered from our discussion of the doctrine of the Trinity generally that what we find most difficult can be that from which we have most to learn. And there is always more to learn. As Leonardo Boff quite rightly says:

> Indeed, we can delve more deeply for all eternity without ever reaching the end. We go from one level of knowledge to another, forever expanding the horizons into the infinite of divine life without ever sighting a limit. God is thus life, love, and overwhelming communication, into which we ourselves are plunged. This vision of mystery does not cause anguish but expands our heart. The Blessed Trinity is mystery now and will be for all eternity. We will get to know it more and more, without ever exhausting our desire to know and to be delighted with the knowledge that we are gradually acquiring. We know in order to sing, we sing in order to love, and we love in order to be joined in communion with the divine Persons – Father, Son, and Holy Spirit.[17]

RESOURCES FOR FURTHER READING, PRAYER AND ACTION

General

Alister McGrath, *Understanding the Trinity* (Zondervan, 1990). Easy to read, and very helpful.

Donald Macleod, *Shared Life: The Trinity and the fellowship of God's people* (Scripture Union, 1987). Also easy to read and helpful.

Viv Thomas, *Paper Boys: A vision for the Contemporary Church ... from delivery to dance through God as Trinity* (Authentic Media, Milton Keynes, 2004)

T. F. Torrance, *The Christian Doctrine of God: One Being, Three Persons* (T & T Clark, 1996). Not at all accessible, tiny print, long and slightly repetitious, but masterly!

Dorothy L. Sayers, *The Mind of the Maker* (Harper Collins, 1987).

Tom Smail, *Like Father, Like Son: The Trinity Imaged in our Humanity* (Eerdmans, 2006). A masterful look at what it means to be made in the image of God if God is triune. It offers a Trinitarian audit of our humanness.

John D. Zizioulas, *Being as Communion: Studies in Personhood and the Church* (St.Vladimir's Seminary Press, 1997). Highly technical, but a modern classic from an orthodox perspective.

Relating to Particular Sections

Arthur W. Wainwright, *The Trinity in the New Testament* (1962) (SPCK, London, 1975). More technical, but gives the basis for what I say in the section entitled, 'How did the early church come to believe in the doctrine of the Trinity?'.

Jane Williams, *Trinity and Unity* (Darton, Longman and Todd, 1995). Short and accessible, and contains a brief discussion of 'Trinitarian Feminism'.

CARE is a Christian organisation that tries to act on the relational values grounded in the Trinity by seeking to combine the practical, caring initiatives with campaigning at national and local level on social and ethical issues. CARE seeks to bring Christian insight and compassion to matters of family, education, media, citizenship and bioethics – producing resources including a prayer guide to support these aims. You can contact CARE at 53 Romney Street, London, SW1P 3RF. Tel: 020 7233 0455 or by visiting the website: www.care.org.uk.

Elaine Storkey, *The Search for Intimacy* (Hodder & Stoughton, 1995). Fits in particularly with Section c). It has a useful section on 'Intimacy as Imaging God', and some challenging application in the section on 'Intimacy and the Church'.

Michael Schluter & David Lee, *The R Factor* (Hodder & Stoughton, 1993).

The R Option (The Relationships Foundation, 2002). For more details of the Foundation's work, contact www.relationshipsfoundation.org.

Rowan Williams, *Arius* (Darton, Longman & Todd, London, 1987). Useful, but quite technical, background for Section g). (You could just read the postscript at the end – all the fun without the hard work!)

Peter Adam, *Living the Trinity* (Grove Books, 1982). A superb and highly accessible and practical guide, which does what it says on the tin. Fills out what I was trying to suggest in Section i). Highly recommended. (Grove Books is now based in Ridley Hall Road, Cambridge, CB3 9HU. Its website is: www.grovebooks.co.uk.)

9 THE FINAL VICTORY OF GOD

The following comes from James Finn Garner's *Politically Correct Bedtime Stories*:

One day, Chicken Little was playing in the road when a gust of wind blew through the trees. An acorn was blown loose and hit Chicken Little squarely on the head. Now, while Chicken Little had a small brain in the physical sense, she did use it to the best of her abilities. So when she screamed, 'The sky is falling, the sky is falling!' her conclusion was not wrong or stupid or silly, only logically underenhanced. ...

Henny Penny stuck her head out from her garden and said, 'Chicken Little! Why are you carrying on so?'

Chicken Little said, 'I was playing in the road when a huge chunk of the sky fell and landed on my head. See? Here's the bump to prove it.'

'There's just one thing to do,' said Henny Penny.

'What's that?' asked Chicken Little.

'Sue the b——s!' said Henny Penny.

Chicken Little was puzzled. 'Sue for what?'

'Personal injury, discrimination, intentional infliction of emotional distress, negligent infliction of emotional distress, tortious interference, the tort of outrage – you name it, we'll sue for it.'

'Good gracious!' said Chicken Little. 'What will we get for all of that?'

'We can get payment for pain and suffering, compensatory damages, punitive damages, disability and disfigurement, long-term care, mental anguish, impaired earning power, loss of esteem …'

'Person, oh, person!' said Chicken Little joyfully. 'Who are we going to sue?'

'Well, I don't think the sky per se is recognized as a suable entity by the state,' said Henny Penny.

'I guess we should go and find a lawyer and learn who is suable,' said Chicken Little, her diminutive brain working overtime.

'That's a good idea. And while we're there, I can ask whom to sue for these ridiculously bony legs of mine. They've caused me nothing but anguish and embarrassment my whole life, and I should be compensated somehow for all that.'[1]

The fear of the sky falling on one's head, which Chicken Little shares with Vitalstatistix, the chief of Asterix's Gaulish tribe, is basically a fear that we come from chaos and shall return to chaos. It is a fear that the aeon of order and coherence and consciousness and civilization will prove fleeting. It is a fear that if the universe came about by chance then there is nothing that can be guaranteed to preserve it in being. It is a fear that, as the tide came in, washing us up onto the shores of existence, so the tide will go out, taking us out with it into the sea of oblivion. I have suggested throughout this book that paganism is an anxiety-ridden world-view, and this is its final fear, that we are cosmically and existentially and relationally of no fixed abode. We do not belong, and we shall not abide.

Peter Cook's monologue, 'Sitting on the Bench', provides another example of the same basic fear:

I am very interested in the Universe – I am specialising in the Universe and all that surrounds it. I am studying Nesbitt's book – The Universe and All That Surrounds It, an Introduction. He tackles the subject boldly, goes through from the beginning of time

317

right through to the present day, which according to Nesbitt is October 31, 1940. And he says the earth is spinning into the sun and we will all be burnt to death. But he ends the book on a note of hope, he says 'I hope this will not happen'.[2]

If the universe is all that there is, if creation is not held in the hand of a Creator and held in being by His love, then that kind of wishful thinking is the only kind of cosmic hope there could be.

But if there is Someone outside of creation, who made it and loves it and sustains it and is committed to it, then there is hope *for* it. Just as the universe does not contain its own meaning within itself, neither does it contain its own hope. It is dependent upon God for its very survival, let alone its transformation. In that dependence, however, it may find a sure and certain hope. Its origin was not chaos, so its destiny will not be chaos. Its beginning and origin were the creative purpose of God, so it is to the accomplishment and fulfilment of those purposes that the universe is headed.

Currently, those purposes are difficult to detect. They cannot simply be read off from looking at creation or looking at history. For creation is not now the way God intended it to be, and history is full of events that are not what He purposed. But the Jewish and Christian claim has always been that one day those purposes will be clear and complete and perspicacious and unambiguous. And history will have reached its climax, and creation will finally be as God purposed it. This is what is meant here by the final victory of God. There is One who can guarantee the preservation – and the healing – of the world He has made. And He will.

What more may we say about this final victory?

1. THE FINAL VICTORY OF GOD WILL BE IN TIME

The final victory of God will be in time – by which I don't mean 'in the nick of time' like the US cavalry arriving just in time to rescue some beleaguered army outpost, but 'in the sequence of time, in the process of time', which is where we live as human beings. It will be *within* time, part of the space-time continuum which we currently inhabit. The final victory of God will not take place in a completely different sphere altogether – that would be for God to give up on creation. It will not be outside the structures of space and time, but *within* them, as their dénouement, their climax and their completion. The final victory of God will take place within space and time – as their culmination and transformation.

Paul tells us that 'our salvation is nearer now than when we first believed' (Romans 13:11). In other words, there is a linear progression of time on which our past conversion ('when we first believed'), the present moment ('now') and God's final victory ('our salvation') are all located. History does not go round in circles[a], and it will not simply peter out – it is going somewhere. It has a goal. It has direction. It has meaning and purpose. It is not going to be bypassed by what God finally does: it is going to be brought to fulfilment by what God does.

That has been a theme throughout this book – that we are physical beings, 'dwellers all in time and space', and that this is *good*. It was not a mistake. It is what God intended. He is the God of history and of geography. The economy of God can be plotted on space-time coordinates. I've referred to Tom Torrance's two books, *Space, Time and Incarnation*, and *Space, Time and Resurrection*, and what those titles are intended to say is that the workings of God are embedded in the real world, our world, the material world. They are not tangential to it, they are not intended to draw us out of it. The Incarnation and the Resurrection are actions of God *within* the real world because *that* is the world that has gone wrong. It is the real world that has been defiled by sin and defaced by suffering. It

---

[a] Lesslie Newbigin notes that most cultures measure time in a circular fashion, like the Chinese rotation of Years of the Dog, Rat, Pig etc. It is, he says, only cultures influenced by the Bible that measure time on a linear scale, ie 2004 is followed by 2005 – we don't go back to a previous year and start again. And we measure time from the event that ensures creation has a future – the Incarnation of Jesus Christ. He made this point on one of the occasions on which he gave an overview of the Bible. One set of these lectures was written up into *A Walk Through the Bible* (Triangle, SPCK, 1999), though this actual point was not included.

is the real world that needs putting right. It is the real world that needs the operation of God within it if it is going to be redeemed.

God is, of course, beyond space and time (or He would be unable to renew space and time – He would be in need of renewal Himself). He is not bound by them. He transcends the space-time continuum. He did not emerge from it. But He did create it. He is committed to it. He did enter into it. He does work within it and for it – to ransom and redeem it, to heal it and transfigure it, and to make it permeable to the transcendent and the eternal. That is what is going on in the final victory of God.

To say or think otherwise, to deny the whole physicality and historicity of our creatureliness and of God's work amongst us would be to turn the Judeo-Christian world-view into a different religion. It would be to turn it into 'Gnosticism'. Gnosticism believed that God didn't make the world. It was a rather bad, semi-divine being called the *demiurge* who made creation. And the proper God, the good God, didn't much like creation. He wouldn't have made it, Himself. He wouldn't have soiled His hands with such nasty stuff as matter. He didn't enter into it – not really. And His aim, the Gnostics claim, is to rescue us from it into some state of spiritual enlightenment gained by means of special knowledge (which is why they were called '*gnostics*', from gnosis, the Greek word for knowledge).

Now, of course, Gnosticism was a much more sophisticated system of thought than that, but the important point about it for our present purposes is that it downplays history. Because God didn't make this world and doesn't like it, He isn't particularly interested in what happens within it. So Gnosticism isn't too fussed about whether the Resurrection happened, and in many ways would rather it didn't. It isn't too keen on miracles, for that would mean that God was getting His hands dirty in the world of space and time. It particularly dislikes the Virgin Conception because that would involve God in the messy histories and genetics of a material world. And it doesn't look forward to any healing of time and space in the future: it looks for an escape from physicality and history in the present, an ultimate bypassing of the coordinates of the created order.

It is easy to see, even from a thumbnail sketch of Gnosticism such as the above, that the Church and (until relatively recently) academic theology have been heavily influenced by this philosophy. It gave us a negative view of the body, and of physical activities such as dancing and sex. It taught us to sit loose to historical events such as the Virgin Conception and the Resurrection. It led us to offer people escape from this world, rather than to attempt to transform this world. It taught us to neglect people's physical needs and to abandon the public arena and the political world. And it influenced both the 'liberal' and the 'orthodox' wings of the Church – in different, but equally damaging ways. No wonder people sense that the Church is irrelevant, if it comes to them with that message. No wonder they feel that it has nothing to say to the real world in which they live, to the real problems with which they wrestle. No wonder they feel it's a bit negative and life-denying, bloodless and gutless and remote.

For Gnosticism is ultimately anti-life, in that it wants to take us away from this life, to life in a different sphere. Christianity, however, is utterly, intrinsically, and unashamedly pro-life. From the 'very good' of Genesis 1 to the 'Come, Lord Jesus' of Revelation 22, it affirms our physicality and our history. The prayer of Revelation 22, note, is *'Come*, Lord Jesus.' Not *'Take'*. We are not saying, like the heroine of some Mills and Boon romance, 'Take me away from all of this!' We are not to pray for God to remove us from this wicked world. We are to pray for Him to return to it, to transform it, to remake it and renew it – and us.

2. THE FINAL VICTORY OF GOD IS, AT LEAST FROM OUR PERSPECTIVE, FUTURE

It may be *nearer* now than when we first believed, but it is not yet. The apostle Paul wrote to Timothy, warning him of two false teachers who 'say that the resurrection *has* already taken place, and they destroy the faith of some' (2 Timothy 2:18). It would frankly be very depressing if the resurrection had already taken place, if there were nothing more to be looked for, if this is as good as it is going to get, if there is going to be no defeat of death and injustice. Paul insists that that is not the case. There is going to be a resurrection, and it's still to come. There is going to be a judgment. We are going to live with Christ and reign with Him. There is a future dimension to the promises and purposes of God. There is a 'not yet' as well as an 'already' to the victory of God.

That doesn't mean that what Christ accomplished on the Cross was only partial. On the contrary, it was full, perfect and sufficient, as the *Book of Common Prayer* insists. The victory of the Cross was complete – but it has yet to be fully implemented. And that full implementation of the victory of the Cross is what we mean by the final victory of God. And it is future.

A story is told of an earnest young Christian who asked a bishop on a train whether he was saved or not. The bishop replied, 'That depends on whether you mean *sótheis*, *sózomenos* or *sóthésomenos* – 'I have been saved', 'I am being saved' or 'I will be saved'. It was a pompous but correct reply. There is a past, present and future dimension to our salvation. And the answer to the question, 'Have you been saved?' must be 'Yes and No'. God has acted decisively on my behalf, and on behalf of the whole created order, in the Cross of Jesus. And I have, by the work of His Spirit within me, aligned myself with that action on my behalf. But the fullness of what the Cross achieved has yet to be fully implemented in my life or in our world. For that, we await the last day, and God's final victory.

3. THE FINAL VICTORY OF GOD WILL INVOLVE A SEPARATION BETWEEN GOOD AND EVIL

Unlike those Eastern religious traditions which see God as beyond good and evil, and therefore see good and evil as matters ultimately of appearance, the Christian tradition has always seen God as utterly good and in no way evil, and has therefore always seen good and evil as matters of decisive importance. If, then, God is good, the final victory of God will be the final victory of good. If the dividing line between good and evil is maintained by belief in this God, then His final victory will reveal finally where that dividing line passes. The light of God's goodness will expose and dispel the darkness of evil.

Matthew's Gospel makes this point most repeatedly. Three parables, which he alone records, tell of this final separation. The parable of the weeds in Matthew 13:24–30 speaks of wheat and weeds growing together, until they are finally separated at the harvest. The parable of the drag-net in Matthew 13:47–52 speaks of all kinds of fish wriggling around together in the fisherman's net, until the boat reaches the shore and the fishermen sort out the good from the bad. The parable of the sheep and the goats in Matthew 25:31–46 paints the picture of sheep and goats grazing together by day, but being separated out by the shepherd at night-time to be allocated their different sleeping quarters. The implication is clear. Good and evil seem inextricably intertwined in our experience both of the world and of ourselves. It is hard to imagine our world ever being different from how it is now. It is hard to imagine it free from all that currently mars it. And it is hard to imagine ourselves free from the tension and ambiguity that come from knowing a mixture of good and evil motives and desires within ourselves.

It is hard to imagine it, but we long for it. (Or, at least, a part of us does – the best part of us.) We long to see our world free from injustice and oppression and violence and disease and tragedy and rejection and abuse. We long to be free from the propensity to unkind words, unwise actions and untameable, shameful thoughts. We long for things to be morally uncompromised and clear. 'The servants asked him, "Do you want us to go and pull up the weeds?"' (Matthew 13:28 GNB). There were contemporaries of Jesus who were prepared to draw the line between the good and the bad very clearly. Romans and collaborators were bad: zealous Jews were good. And the line drawn was to be a battle line. There have been those all through Church history who have sought to draw the line clearly between those who are 'in' and those who are 'out', to have a thoroughly pure church, with no blurred edges.

But the Sower says, 'No, because while you are pulling up the weeds, you may root up the wheat with them. Let them both grow together until the harvest' (Matthew 13:29–30). If you are too zealous to maintain the purity of the church now, you may turn people away who are genuinely attempting to go the right way. You may pull up wheat along with tares. You have to be patient and wait, and leave such separation to the Son of Man and His angels (Matthew 13:41). The rooting-out of evil is delayed in order to give us time to be extricated from evil and cleave to God, or at least to give us time to get that process under way, so that when evil is finally destroyed, we are not destroyed along with it. Peter wrote in response to those who complained about the delay of the Final Judgment, 'The Lord is not slow in keeping his promise, as some understand slowness. He is patient with you, not wanting anyone to perish, but everyone to come to repentance' (2 Peter 3:9).[b]

It is delayed, but it will come. God is too committed to His creation to leave it forever tarnished and touched with tragedy. There will be a sorting out. 'The Son of Man will send out his angels, and they will weed out of his kingdom everything that causes sin and all who do evil' (Matthew 13:41). 'The angels will come and separate the wicked from the righteous' (Matthew 13:49). 'All the nations will be gathered before him, and he will separate the people one from another as a shepherd separates the sheep from the goats' (Matthew 25:32). Our world and our experience – and our nature – are not always to be

---

[b] If the final sorting-out of good and evil is delayed in order to give us time to repent and thus change categories, then won't there be more people born as a result of the delay who won't have had that opportunity? In fact, wouldn't the Last Day have to be indefinitely postponed in order that the next generation should have time to repent, and then the next, and so on? I suspect that this question rises in our minds partly because we have too individualistic an approach to the matter. Maybe the reason why God delays the Last Judgment is not just to give individuals the chance to repent, but also cultures. He wants, as we shall see, every tribe and language and people and nation to be represented in the new creation – and perhaps He is delaying the renewal of all things until that is accomplished.

mixed. They are not always to be ambiguous and compromised and tainted. Good and evil are not like Yin and Yang – equal and opposite and eternal elements in the woop and warf of creation. They are not on all fours with each other. They are not on an ontological par. They do not both belong in creation. They are not like love and marriage, they don't go together like a horse and carriage: you *can* have one without the other. And we shall.

4. THE FINAL VICTORY OF GOD WILL INVOLVE JUDGMENT AND THE DESTRUCTION OF EVIL

I do not, of course, know what God's options are, but (!), with regard to evil, it seems to me that there are four logical possibilities. First, He could let things carry on just as they are, with the current mix of good and evil, pleasure and pain, joy and misery. Secondly, He could force people to be good, whether they like it or not. He could take back their freedom and simply *make* them do only what is right. He could rewire us. Thirdly, He could simply destroy creation and start again. Or, fourthly, He could judge the world. He could respect our freedom and the choices we make, whether they are the choices He wanted us to make or not, but hold us to account for those choices. He could root out evil from His world, and, along with the evil, all those who refuse ultimately, fixedly and irrevocably to let go of that evil.

Again, it is (thankfully) not for me to decide between these options – I am simply trying to follow the logic of His revealed decisions – but the first option seems to me to be incompatible with love. It seems incompatible with His commitment to creation, to allow it to be forever spoiled, to be forever torn apart by suffering and pain, to allow injustice to continue to triumph with impunity. It seems incompatible with His love and His justice to hear the martyrs cry out, 'How long, Sovereign Lord?' (Revelation 6:10) and to reply, 'For ever. There will never be redress. There will never be justice. There will never be peace. You're just going to have to learn to live with it.'

And the second option seems to me to be incompatible with His love too, for it would render His desire for our love unfulfillable, for love has to be freely given or it is not love. If He came amongst us and died for us in order to restore us to that fellowship with Himself for which He created us, then He would have failed. He would have corrected our behaviour at the cost of our freedom, humanity and love. He would have turned us into automata. He would have gone back on the whole project of creation.

The third option would also be a failure. To destroy creation would be finally to give up on it. This is an option on which He turned His back at the Flood, and which He promised never to revisit. It would be a defeat and it would be a waste. For there is much about our world that is beautiful. There is much of human behaviour that is noble, and much of human achievement that is profoundly impressive. Much better, surely, to preserve what is good, and to purge what is bad – in other words, to judge.

And that is what He has promised to do. He will not only separate the wheat from the weeds: He will also burn up the weeds (Matthew 13:30). He will not only separate good and evil: He will also eradicate evil from His creation. He 'will weed out of his kingdom everything that causes sin and all who do evil' (Matthew 13:41). Those who will not go through the narrow gate that He has provided are left with nothing but the road that leads to destruction (Matthew 7:13–14)[c] – not because He is vindictive, but because He is committed to His world, and because He is the Author of Life and therefore to cut oneself off from Him is ultimately to cut oneself off from life.

Judgment, then, though a dreadful prospect, is part of the good news of God. It is good news because it means that pain and suffering and injustice and oppression will not go on for ever. It is good news because it means that God still longs and looks for our company and has not given up on a relationship with us. It

[c] See also Psalm 73:19, 27; Isaiah 1:28; Hosea 13:3; Malachi 4:1; John 3:16; 1 Corinthians 1:18; 2 Corinthians 2:15; Philippians 1:28, 3:19; Hebrews 10:39; 2 Peter 3:7.

is good news because it means that God is not going to give up on our world. It is good news because it means that we are free and responsible beings whose decisions are divinely respected and make an ultimate difference. It is good news because it means we have a God who will not force us to do His will or go His way. It is good news because it means that we live in a universe that will ultimately be moral. And it is good news because it is the means by which God will purge creation of all that mars it, all that defaces its beauty, and all that prevents us from being fully and freely the creatures God made us to be. It will thereby be the gateway to a new heaven and a new earth in which justice dwells (2 Peter 3:13), because God Himself has taken up residence amongst us, and death and mourning and crying and pain have passed away (Revelation 21:1–4).

5. THE FINAL VICTORY OF GOD IS SOMETHING TO LONG FOR

> For I am already being poured out like a drink offering, and the time has come for my departure. I have fought the good fight, I have finished the race, I have kept the faith. Now there is in store for me the crown of righteousness, which the Lord, the righteous Judge, will award to me on that day – and not only to me, but also to all who have longed for his appearing.
>
> **2 Timothy 4:6–8**

Christians have often shied away from longing for the appearing of Christ, partly to avoid being associated with the 'end-of-the-world' brigade who are always predicting the End and getting it wrong, and partly to avoid the charge of being 'so heavenly minded as to be no earthly use'. Both fears are understandable, but misplaced. The first is misplaced because the right response to abuse of a doctrine is not to abandon it, but to use it properly. The final victory of God is too important a doctrine to leave to the cults. And the second fear is misplaced because it is thorough immersion in the struggle for justice and thorough involvement in the pain of others and thorough love of our world that leads us to long for an end to injustice and suffering, and for this world to be healed. And it is the hope of a world finally restored that encourages and strengthens us for the fight now.

> And when the strife is fierce, the warfare long,
> Steals on the ear the distant triumph-song,
> And hearts are brave again, and arms are strong. Alleluya![3]

So it is not escapist to long for His appearing. On the contrary. It is the by-product of engagement and compassion. It is those who are fighting injustice now who most long for the new heaven and the new earth to be finally established. It is those who care most about the suffering of our world who most long for that suffering to be a thing of the past. It is those who are most involved in campaigning against the pollution and despoliation of the planet who have most to look forward to when humanity is finally at peace with its environment and its Creator. It is those who are hardest at work in the spreading of the gospel who most look forward to the day when 'no longer will they teach their neighbours, or say to one another, "Know the LORD," because they will all know me, from the least of them to the greatest' (Jeremiah 31:34). It is those who are most committed to the work of prayer who most eagerly look forward to seeing Him 'face to face' (1 Corinthians 13:12). It is those who are bearing the heat of the battle who most long for victory.

> The golden evening brightens in the west;
> Soon, soon to faithful warriors cometh rest:
> Sweet is the calm of Paradise the blest. Alleluya![4]

(Not that that Day will bring an end to creative challenge, just to division and diminishment.) Notice that Paul's longing for the appearing of the righteous Judge comes in the context of his having fought the fight and finished the race. The context is one of struggle, of utter involvement in the world as an agent of God's Kingdom. And the weariness and the excitement of that struggle give birth to a passionate longing for the completion and fulfilment of all that Paul has been working for and praying for throughout his ministry as well as a longing for God himself.

Do we long for the appearing of Christ and the putting right of the world's wrongs? Or have we made our peace with the current compromised state of the world? Have we become so inured to the injustices of our world (because our lifestyles are so dependent upon them?) that we harbour no hatred for them in our hearts? The amount that we long for the appearing of Christ is probably the amount we oppose evil. If we want to know how much compassion we have, we merely have to ask ourselves how much we long for the coming of the One who will heal all hurts and bind up the broken-hearted.

6. THE FINAL VICTORY OF GOD WILL DRAW TOGETHER ALL THINGS

a) The final victory of God will gather up all things

> And he made known to us the mystery of his will according to his good pleasure, which he purposed in Christ, to be put into effect when the times will have reached their fulfilment – to bring all things in heaven and earth together under one head, even Christ.
>
> **Ephesians 1:9–10**

If you ask a theologian a difficult question, you may well get the answer, 'It's a mystery!' which is a shorthand (and religious-sounding) way of saying, 'I haven't a clue!' But, for Paul, a mystery was something that *had been* unknown, *but which God has now revealed in Jesus the Messiah.* (So don't be fobbed off with the 'It's a mystery!' line!) What is this former secret which Paul here shares with us? It is that all things are going to be gathered up, brought together, conjoined under the headship of the Messiah. Everything is going to be brought into a (personal, organic) structure that can hold everything in its rightful and delightful place, so that it can thrive and flourish and contribute to the thriving and flourishing of every other thing. Unlike the world as it is at the moment, where many things can only survive at the expense of others – when the times have reached their fulfilment and God's purposes have been achieved and God's victory is complete then the world is going to be a place where no creature is a threat to any other creature. Because they will all be in right relationship to the Messiah, they will all be in right relationship with one another.

Just as Jesus, after the feeding of the five thousand, told His disciples to gather up all the fragments of bread 'that nothing be lost' (John 6:12 AV), so He is going to gather up all the broken fragments of creation so that nothing that can possibly be saved is lost or left behind. Mother Teresa used to say that 'Nothing done in love will ever be lost.' So it is not just things but the seemingly insignificant and fruitless little acts of kindness and of goodness that are also to be gathered up. They will not be for nothing. They will not ultimately be lost.

Oliver Cromwell had a huge and beautiful window of stained glass in Winchester Cathedral smashed into thousands of pieces, presumably because it contained pictures that he considered idolatrous. And when his forces had gone, someone swept up all the pieces, waited until Cromwell's death, and then got them out and tried to reassemble the window. Unfortunately, it proved too difficult a jigsaw, and they simply put them back higgledy-piggledy so that it now looks like a piece of modern art! God will do the same with the broken pieces and people of creation, only He will also be able to put them together, so that they all fit into the overall picture, and so that the light of God may shine through them as it was always intended to.

When the Church holds together Jew and Gentile in community, when it defies the world's hostilities, when it cares for the broken, and ensures that no one is lost or neglected or feels they are nothing, it acts as a pointer to that gathering up of all things under the gracious and attentive headship of Christ.

b) The final victory of God will put right all things

> Peter answered him, 'We have left everything to follow you! What then will there be for us?' Jesus said to them, 'I tell you the truth, at the renewal of all things, when the Son of Man sits on his glorious throne, you who have followed me will also sit on twelve thrones, judging the twelve tribes of Israel. And everyone who has left houses or brothers or sisters or father or mother or children or fields for my sake will receive a hundred times as much and will inherit eternal life. But many who are first will be last, and many who are last will be first.'
>
> **Matthew 19:27–30**

In Jesus' words, the final victory of God is 'the renewal of all things' or 'the regeneration' or 'the new genesis'. Creation is old and tired and finite and distorted and corrupt. It needs renewing. We too are finite and our resources run out, and we exhibit a misshapen humanity. We need renewing. And Jesus holds out the prospect of a renewing of all things. That is when wrongs will be righted, hurts will be healed, sacrifices will be made up for, distortions will be straightened out, that which is the wrong way round will be put the right way up, that which is finite will put on eternity, that which is tired will be reinvigorated, and that which is dull will shine with a new effulgence. (Notice that this renewal of all things is linked to judgment, for we cannot be fully ourselves until that which is irrevocably negative and parasitic – evil – has ceased to interact destructively with us, and we cannot be made new without being purged.)

Peter uses a similar expression when he speaks of how Jesus 'must remain in heaven until *the time of universal restoration* that God announced long ago through his holy prophets' (Acts 3:21 NRSV, my italics). The word Peter uses for 'restoration' is the same word that Luke (who also wrote Acts) uses for the healing of the man with the withered hand (Luke 6:10). What Jesus did for that hand, says Peter, He will do for all things. That is the great act of cosmic renewal that is coming. What we must set our sights upon is the great healing and putting right of all things.

My favourite twentieth-century novel is the magical 'autobiographical' folktale, *Year of Miracle and Grief*, by the Siberian writer, Leonid Borodin, who did hard labour in the Gulag for having belonged to an anti-communist organisation called The Social Christian Union. It contains – indeed, it is – an extended discussion of the nature and the difficulty of forgiveness. A mother and her son are talking:

'You remember when I broke the gramophone? You wouldn't let me go out afterwards. Then in the evening I asked you to forgive me, and you forgave me. Why?'

'Because you hadn't done it on purpose.'

'In that case, why did you say I couldn't go out?'

'Oh my goodness!' laughed my mother. 'After all, you did break the gramophone.'

I thought very hard. 'Yes, and afterwards we had to do without a gramophone. But you forgave me. Why?'

'I don't understand what you're getting at. Later on we bought a radiogram. That was better than a gramophone, wasn't it?'

'Mama,' I said, trying to explain clearly, 'the gramophone was beyond repair, it had ceased to exist. That means I'm guilty towards it for the rest of my life, doesn't it?'

'Guilty towards whom?' asked my mother, frowning and losing patience.

'The gramophone!'

Mama felt my forehead and looked anxiously at me. 'Are you ill, or are you just acting the fool?'

'But please understand, Mama, that time you said "I forgive you", the gramophone went on being broken. And after you'd forgiven me it didn't get mended and it didn't start playing again. How could you forgive me if nothing had been put right?'[5]

Behind this discussion lies, I suspect, the problem of forgiveness in post-Communist Russia. No number of trials and no amount of reparation can 'put right' the nightmare of the Soviet era. So how can Russians find the power to forgive, when nothing has been put right? The particular insight of Borodin here seems to be that all forgiveness draws upon the future restoration of all things. Even that will not make what happened 'okay'. Even the universal restoration will not erase the Gulag. It will remain a scar on human history. But it will be a scar that no longer festers or inhibits or disfigures. It will have been defused of its ability to embitter. And in the light of the coming renewal of all things, we may have the courage and the power to forgive in advance. Without that hope, I do not see how we could, with the gramophone still broken.

c) The final victory of God will harmonise all things

Paul tells us that all things have been reconciled by the Cross of Christ (Colossians 1:20). The harmonisation of all things was won by the Cross and will be fully realised at the restoration of all things. And the prophets give us a vision of what that reconciliation will look like:

> The wolf will lie down with the lamb,
>   the leopard will lie down with the goat,
> the calf and the lion and the yearling together;
>   and a little child will lead them.
> The cow will feed with the bear,
>   their young will lie down together,
>   and the lion will eat straw like the ox.
> Infants will play near the hole of the cobra,
>   and young children put their hands into the viper's nest.
> They will neither harm nor destroy on all my holy mountain,

for the earth will be full of the knowledge of the Lord
as the waters cover the sea.

Isaiah 11:6–9

The cartoonist Bestie, on one of his cards, depicts a lioness pouncing on a pumpkin, and one watching lion is saying to another, 'She's trying to make vegetarianism exciting!' The point here is that it is not just Jew and Gentile that are reconciled by the Cross. It is not just human divisions that will be overcome at the renewal of all things. It is not just human relationships that will be healed. It is all things. The whole created order will be established upon a new basis.

> The purpose of the Incarnation [writes T. F. Torrance] was to penetrate into the innermost centre of our contingent existence, in its finite, fragile and disrupted condition, in order to deliver it from the evil to which it had become subjected, healing and re-ordering it from its ontological roots and entirely renewing its relation to the Creator.[6]

That was the purpose of the Incarnation. That was the achievement of the Cross. And that will be the effect of the final victory of God.

d) The final victory of God will fill all things with His presence

'They will neither harm nor destroy on all my holy mountain, *for the earth will be full of the knowledge of the Lord as the waters cover the sea*' (Isaiah 11:9, cf. Habakkuk 2:14). God's ultimate intention for creation is that it will be flooded with the presence, the knowledge and the glory of God. His plan is that creation will be as translucent as was the body of Jesus on the Mount of Transfiguration, that it will shine with the glory of God as a stained glass window shines with the light of the sun. There will be as much glory around us and upon us and shining through us as there is water covering the ocean beds. That 'weight of glory'[7], to use C. S. Lewis' phrase, will be our environment, the air we breathe, the world we live in, and the characteristic of our very selves. Consequently:

> On that day holy to the Lord will be inscribed on the bells of the horses, and the cooking pots in the Lord's house will be like the sacred bowls in front of the altar. Every pot in Jerusalem and Judah will be holy to the Lord Almighty ...
>
> **Zechariah 14:20–21**

That sort of specialness, that sort of purity, that sort of set-asideness and holiness, that depth of significance will be the norm. Everything – every pot and every trinket – will be charged to that degree with the splendour and glory of God. Christians have sometimes argued over how many sacraments there are. After the final victory of God, every particle will be a sacrament – shot through with God's Spirit and pregnant with the possibility of relationship with our Maker.

e) The final victory of God will marry heaven and earth, Christ and His people

People often find that engagement is a time of looking forward, of anticipation – but also of some frustration. (Probably especially for Christians!) Once you have made the decision, you want to get on with it. You want to be together. You want that interlacing of lives and bodies for which soul and body yearn. But it is not yet. And that is the frustration of being a Christian in the overlap of the ages. We are betrothed to Christ. We are committed to Him and He to us. We long to be together and to know as we are known. We look forward to a relationship of face to face intimacy. But it is not yet. John gives us a glimpse of what it will be like:

> Then I heard what sounded like a great multitude, like the roar of rushing waters and like loud peals of thunder, shouting:
>
> 'Hallelujah!
> For our Lord God Almighty reigns.

> Let us rejoice and be glad and give him glory!
> For the wedding of the Lamb has come,
>> and his bride has made herself ready.'

Revelation 19:6–7

At last the waiting and the frustration will be over. At last we shall enjoy that degree of intimacy which we crave. At last we shall *know* Him in the fullest sense and in the most joyful way.

But it is not just we and Christ that will be conjoined – it will also be our respective realms. Earth and heaven will no longer be veiled off from one another. There has always been traffic between the two (Genesis 28:12, John 1:51), but unless our eyes are opened in some special way, heaven remains opaque to us and beyond our ken. But at the final victory of God, the two shall interpenetrate one another and be shot through with one another. Earth shall be the dwelling place of God, as heaven has always been:

> I saw the Holy City, new Jerusalem, coming down out of heaven from God, made ready like a bride adorned for her husband. I heard a loud voice proclaiming from the throne: 'Now God has his dwelling with mankind! He will dwell among them and they shall be his people, and God himself will be with them.'

Revelation 21:2–3 REB

A Christmas blessing begins, 'Christ, who by his incarnation gathered into one all things earthly and heavenly, fill you with his joy and peace'.[8] At the Incarnation, Christ gathered all things earthly and heavenly into one; at His coming again, He will open them up to one another, that they may be as permeable to one another as are the Persons of the Godhead.

7. THE FINAL VICTORY OF GOD WILL DEMONSTRATE THE RIGHTEOUSNESS OF GOD

> Great and marvellous are your deeds,
>> Lord God Almighty,
> Just and true are your ways,
>> King of the ages.
> Who will not fear you, O Lord,
>> and bring glory to your name?
> For you alone are holy.
> All nations will come
>> and worship before you,
> for your righteous acts have been revealed.

Revelation 15:3–4

The tragic story is told in Wales of a dog called Gelert. His owner, Prince Llewelyn, left him in charge of a baby in a pram (in the days before Social Services). When Prince Llewelyn returned home some time later, the baby was missing from its pram, and Gelert had blood all around his mouth. In shock and grief, the Prince killed Gelert with his sword. Soon after that, however, they discovered the baby alive and well in another part of the garden, with the body of a dead wolf beside it. Clearly what had happened was that the wolf had attempted to eat the baby, and Gelert had attacked the wolf to defend the baby. And he'd been killed for his pains. You can still go and see Gelert's grave today.[d] Things looked pretty bad for Gelert, until they found out the whole story, and then he was vindicated. (Unfortunately, too late.)

The same is true with God. If you just looked around at the world, you wouldn't necessarily jump to the view that it was created by a loving and good God. It doesn't look like the sort of place that God

---

[d] It has been suggested that this story was made up to entice tourists to visit (and spend their money in) a village that was off the beaten track, which is a relief emotionally, but doesn't make such a good story!

337

would want to make. It looks like a place of pain and cruelty and injustice. You couldn't read off from it the righteousness of God. But when you begin to find out more of the story, it begins to look rather different. When you hear about the doctrine of the Fall and realise that the way the world is now is not the way God intended it to be, that alters your perspective somewhat. When you hear that God entered into the mess and the pain of creation and experienced it from the inside, that has an effect too. When you hear that He made a direct assault on the cause of all that is wrong by taking sin upon Himself and dying on our behalf, things begin to look quite different. When you hear that He burst through death and out the other side, and offers to take us with Him, that makes a difference as well. In fact, the more you hear of the story, the more reason you have to believe that God, despite appearances, is in fact good.

And when the vast multitude looks back at cosmic history from the vantage-point of its completion, knowing the *whole* story, and how it ended, they burst out in song, 'for your righteous acts have been revealed' (Revelation 15:4). On that day, it will be abundantly clear why He has acted in the way He has, and that He is utterly righteous in the ways He has acted – *and* in the ways He has not acted. We shall see then what we cannot see now, which is the interaction between His action, His inaction and His love. The end of history will reveal the righteousness of God.

8. THE FINAL VICTORY OF GOD WILL PRESERVE, HEAL, RECREATE, RENEW AND TRANSFORM US

a) It will renew our otherness

By our 'otherness', I mean our distinctness from one another and from God – our individuality. When all things are gathered up under the headship of Christ, we shall not lose who we truly are. It is possible – indeed, it is God's intended destiny for us – to be other than Him, and yet in perfect union with Him.

I once went to a seminar given by the great Orthodox theologian, John Zizioulis, at which he said that the Fall was the rejection of otherness. When the serpent tempted the man and the woman to eat the forbidden fruit, it promised that, if they did, they would be 'as God' (Genesis 3:5 TYNDALE). They would cease to be other than God, as God had made them to be. There would be no distance and no difference between them and Him. In fact, the very opposite happened. Far from collapsing the distance between them and God, their disobedience immeasurably increased it. But if the Fall was the (attempted) rejection of otherness, the undoing of the Fall must involve the preservation of that otherness – the preservation of our who-we-were-made-to-be-ness, our not-God-ness, our us-ness, and therefore of our ability to relate to Him and to be loved by Him.

b) It will renew our embodiedness

> Now we know that if the earthly tent we live in is destroyed, we have a building from God, an eternal house in heaven, not built by human hands. Meanwhile we groan, longing to be clothed with our heavenly dwelling, because when we are clothed, we will not be found naked. For while we are in this tent, we groan and are burdened, because we do not wish to be unclothed but to be clothed with our heavenly dwelling, so that what is mortal may be swallowed up by life. Now it is God who has made us for this very purpose and has given us the Spirit as a deposit, guaranteeing what is to come.
>
> **2 Corinthians 5:1–5**

Politicians seem to be particularly good at mixed metaphors. Edwina Currie is reported as saying, 'There's no smoke without mud being thrown around.' The Northern Irish politician, Revd Ian Paisley, apparently announced that 'We are not going to stand idly by and be murdered in our beds!' And a British Trade Union leader reported that the management 'stabbed us in the back by blowing the talks out of the water before they even got off the ground'![9] The apostle Paul is the past master of the mixed metaphor, however, and he's at it again in this passage. Images of tents, houses, labour-pains, clothes and down payments chase each other down the verses.

But the point Paul is trying to make in and through these mixed metaphors is basically clear. We do not want to be *un*clothed: we want to be *re*-clothed. We do not want to be *dis*embodied: we want to be *re*-embodied. None of what we learned in Chapter 1 about the essential goodness of the material world and of our own physicality needs to be unlearned here. It is good to be physical beings. Our embodiedness, though hurt and marred and restricted in all sorts of ways by factors of fallenness – injury, disease, deformity, age, decay and weariness – is fundamentally part of who we were made to be, and of who we shall be remade to be. All that will be left behind will be our groaning, our burdens and our mortality. This, says Paul, is the very purpose for which God made us. He will not be finally frustrated. And the Guarantor of all this, says Paul, is the Spirit – of course, because He is the Life-Giver. If we have Him living within us, how may we not be re-awoken into whole new dimensions of life?

Whole *new* dimensions, note. Not just back into the old ones. Our embodiedness will be transformed as well as preserved and healed. There will be new dimensions to explore, new capabilities to exploit, new glory to revel in, new beauty to radiate. We shall be more than physical, to be sure – but not less.

c) It will renew our relatedness

First, our relatedness to God will be healed and transformed. Now it is through a glass darkly – fitful, ambiguous, partial. Then it will be face to face (1 Corinthians 13:12). Then we shall see Him as He is, and know Him even as we are known. No selfishness or shoddiness or shame shall cloud our vision, the way it does now. Our minds shall be unwarped, our hearts uncalloused, our souls undistorted, so we shall be free to see God (Matthew 5:8).

Secondly, our relatedness to others will be preserved, but forgiven and unembarrassed. There is a series of books, entitled *Chicken Soup for the Soul*, and subtitled *Stories To Open The Heart And Rekindle The Spirit*. There is also a parody of these books, entitled *Chicken Poop for the Soul*, and subtitled *Stories to Harden the Heart and Dampen the Spirit*. (You should know me well enough by this stage of the book to have a good guess at which I might prefer!)

One of the latter is about a near-death experience. A man 'dies' on the operating table, and sees it happen from above the scene. As the doctors shout 'We're losing him!' he finds himself in a long, narrow tunnel. 'But in the distance, far away, I saw a beautiful white light. I started moving toward it. I could feel its warmth. I felt so safe, so beautiful.' He sees a person dressed in white who he takes to be his mother. But it isn't. It's his ex-wife. '"And just where do you think you're going?" she demanded in that incredibly shrill voice of hers that had made my stomach churn for so many years.' She gives him an earful, and then he comes across someone he mistakes for his father, but who turns out to be his former boss – slave-driver might be better – who comes up to him and says, 'I've just got a little problem here and you're just the person who can solve it.' He gets away from him, but bumps straight into his eighth-grade math teacher, 'the meanest man I'd ever known', who sets him some homework. And that's what gets him to run away from the light, back to the body on the operating table![10] Our relatedness to others will need to be healed as well as transformed, or eternity may feel like quite a long time!

People sometimes suggest that the longing for an afterlife is simply a by-product of our survival instinct. We are evolutionarily wired to seek our own survival and that of our offspring. That inbuilt programming is not stopped even by the knowledge of our own mortality. It simply gets channelled into a belief that we *shall* survive. But such a theory, I suggest, mistakes the nature of our longing. For what we desire is not survival *per se*: it is a renewal of relationship. *They Stand Together* contains nearly three hundred letters that C. S. Lewis wrote to Arthur Greeves over the fifty years of their friendship. In the last of these letters, Lewis writes this:

My dear Arthur

Last July I had a 'coma' of about 24 hours and was believed to be dying. When I recovered consciousness my mind was disordered for many days and I had all sorts of delusions. Very quaint ones some of them, but none painful or terrifying. I have had to resign my Chair and Fellowship at Cambridge and now live here as an invalid; not allowed upstairs. But quite comfortable and cheerful.

The only snag is that it looks as if you and I shall never meet again in this life. This often saddens me v. much.

He goes on to say that, 'Tho' I am by no means unhappy I can't help feeling that it was rather a pity I did revive in July.' He seems to have no fear of dying. His only horror is the cessation of relationship, and he ends, 'I am glad you are fairly well and have a housekeeper. But oh Arthur, never to see you again! ...'[11]

We have evolved to be more than merely evolutionary by-products. For we do not desire relationships in order to help us survive: we desire survival in order to continue relationship.[e] And it is one of the deepest human longings which will thus be fulfilled in the final victory of God. At the renewal of all things, our relatedness will be renewed – old relationships will restart, new conversations will take place, new joy will be taken in old friends, new jokes will be laughed at, new intimacy enjoyed.

Thirdly, our relatedness to nature will be renewed. Not only shall we live in harmony with a now-harmonious creation, as we saw earlier, but our rôle vis-à-vis the created order will be re-established too. We were given the job of ruling and caring for creation (Genesis

[e] You do occasionally meet people who claim that they do not wish there to be an 'afterlife'. I can only explain this in four ways. a) they may have been put off the idea by brutal or boring 'Christian' expositions of the afterlife. b) they may be keen to avoid the corollary belief in judgment. c) they may never have enjoyed a loving relationship. d) they may have enjoyed loving relationships but been deeply hurt by them and determined never to take that risk again. I find it hard to imagine that anyone could have loved and been loved (in family, friendly or romantic relationships) and not wish for that relationship to be renewed – especially if there is to be healing as well as renewal.

1:26), and in the new creation we shall exercise that responsibility appropriately at last. Paul writes:

> For if, by the trespass of the one man, death reigned through that one man, how much more will those who receive God's abundant provision of grace and of the gift of righteousness reign in life through the one man, Jesus Christ.

Romans 5:17

As N. T. Wright comments, 'it is not, as we might have expected, "death" or "sin" on the one hand, and "God" on the other. It is the reign of death, far outweighed by the reign of – believers! Those who were pronounced dead under the haughty and usurping kingdom of death are themselves to be the rulers in God's new world.'[12] That rôle of being God's vice-regents over creation will indeed be re-established, but this time it will be exercised without the exploitation and destruction that currently characterise much of our interaction with the created order. This time, it will be God's liberating rule that we mediate to His world. And the curse that we brought upon the ground (Genesis 3:17f) will have turned to blessing and abundance (Revelation 22:1–5). And we 'will reign for ever and ever.'

d) It will renew our cultures

> You are worthy to take the scroll
>> and to open its seals,
> because you were slain,
>> and with your blood you purchased for God
>> members of every tribe and language and people and nation.
> You have made them to be a kingdom and priests to serve our God,
>> and they will reign on the earth.

Revelation 5:9–10

While it is gloriously true that, when it comes to entry qualifications for the Kingdom, or status within it, 'there is no Greek or Jew, circumcised or uncircumcised, barbarian, Scythian, slave or free' (Colossians 3:11), our backgrounds will not count for nothing. Our cultures will not be lost into an amorphous cultural uniformity. Our languages will not have to be abandoned in favour of an eschatological Esperanto! While jingoism and nationalism and warfare and exclusivism will indeed be left behind, the same will not be true of the art and the thought-forms and the music and the customs and the dance and the distinctive ways of being and thinking that are encapsulated in the different national and cultural traditions. Members of every tribe and language and people and nation will be gathered into one kingdom, but that will not iron out their individuality or the unique cultures they represent. On the contrary, they will bring these things – purged and transformed – into the new creation.

> I did not see a temple in the city, because the Lord God Almighty and the Lamb are its temple. The city does not need the sun or the moon to shine on it, for the glory of God gives it light, and the Lamb is its lamp. The nations will walk by its light, and the kings of the earth will bring their splendour into it. On no day will its gates ever be shut, for there will be no night there. The glory and honour of the nations will be brought into it.
>
> **Revelation 21:22–26**

God does not wipe the slate clean and start again. He rescues everything that is rescuable. The shame of the nations will be left behind, but their glory and honour will be taken up. Vietnamese water puppetry, and Eskimo throat-singing, and Japanese Noh theatre, and Cossack dancing, and Alpine yodelling, and West African foot dancing, and Chinese silk making, and Indonesian cork carving, and Celtic ceilidhs, and English bell-ringing, and French cuisine (now exclusively vegetarian, of course, but just as rich and tasty!) – a whole kaleidoscopic explosion of art and culture offered to the glory of God and to the enrichment of the new life of the Kingdom.

e) It will renew my 'me-ness'

Again, all that is selfish and self-centred will have to be left behind, and all that has been crushed or atrophied will have to be healed, but all that is truly me will be taken up and welcomed in. 'Today you will be with me in paradise', said Jesus to the penitent thief (Luke 23:43). You – the utterly unique person God made you to be, the person made in the image of God yet different from any other and therefore reflecting an angle on God that no one else does. *You* – the utterly loved and cherished child of God. *You* – the deep and complex bundle of thoughts, hopes, longings, affections and memories that make up you. *You* will be with Him in paradise – with those memories healed where necessary and integrated, with those thoughts purified, and those hopes and longings and affections appropriately directed.

Peter Cook once mentioned to an old school friend that he was seeing a psychiatrist, and, when asked why, replied, 'I have been talking in other people's voices for so long that, when I don't, I have a terrible sense of emptiness. I don't know who I am.'[13] And that is but an extreme case of what we all know to be true also of us. We don't fully know who we are. But then we shall. At the end of (this phase of) our journey, we shall know ourselves for the first time. We shall know who we are, we shall be who we are, we shall revel in who we are, and others will rejoice in who we are.

Is all this just wishful thinking? Have religious people dreamt up these more or less sophisticated future scenarios simply because they want to believe them? In response, we need to note that Christian hope for the future is not grounded in our own need. Christians do not believe in this future hope because we desperately want it to be true, though that is in itself a curious fact. Why would we want to believe in it unless we were made for it? If we were purely finite creatures, thrown up by the evolutionary process to strut and fret our time in pursuit of the spreading of our genes, why would we hope for anything more? C. S. Lewis said that he was once impressed by Matthew Arnold's line, 'Nor does the being hungry prove that we have bread.'[14] In other words, just because we feel the need for something doesn't mean that we'll get it. No, replied Lewis, being hungry doesn't mean that we have bread. But it does mean that we are made for food – why else would we feel hungry?

Is there any other need that we feel within ourselves which is in principle unfulfillable? We feel the need for air, and that is no guarantee that we will not suffocate, but it does mean that there is such a thing as air, and that we are made for it. We feel a craving for sex, and that doesn't mean that we shall ever get any, but it does mean that there is such a thing as sex, and that we are designed to engage in it. Similarly, if we feel the need for a renewal of life and relationship the other side of death, that may suggest that there is such a thing and that we were made for it. If the need for hope beyond death is mere wishful thinking, then it is the only need we know that must by its very nature frustrate us – which seems improbable. So the very fact that human beings have always evidenced such a hope tells you quite a lot about who we are and what we are for.

But Christian hope is not grounded primarily in our own sense of need. It is grounded in the action and nature of God. As Henri Nouwen wrote:

> If the God who revealed life to us, and whose only desire is to bring us to life, loved us so much that he wanted to experience with us the total absurdity of death, then – yes, then there must be hope; then there must be something more than death; then there must be a promise that is not fulfilled in our short existence in this world; then leaving behind the ones you love, the flowers and the trees, the mountains and the oceans, the beauty of art and music, and all the exuberant gifts of life cannot be just the destruction and cruel end of all things; then indeed we have to wait for the third day.[15]

It is in the death of Christ for us that our hope is grounded. And, as the final phrase hints, in the resurrection of Christ also. Our third day depends upon His. Our hope is grounded not on our desires, but on facts of history, and the ultimate fact of God. And of course the claim of the sceptic can be turned on its head. It is just as possible that the sceptic disbelieves in the Christian hope because she *doesn't* want to believe it, as it is that the Christian believes it because he *does*. The sceptic may be using her scepticism as a protection against the demands that such a hope would make upon her. And it is to those demands that we now turn.

9. THE FINAL VICTORY OF GOD SHOULD PROMPT US TO HOLINESS

Holiness is nearly always the context of future hope talk in the New Testament. The quotation from Romans 13 with which we began goes on to draw an ethical conclusion:

> Our salvation is nearer now than when we first believed. The night is nearly over; the day is almost here. So let us put aside the deeds of darkness and put on the armour of light ...
>
> **Romans 13:11c–12**

As does 1 John 3:2–3:

> Dear friends, now we are children of God, and what we will be has not yet been made known. But we know that when he appears, we shall be like him, for we shall see him as he is. All who have this hope in them purify themselves, just as he is pure.

The logic is that we need to be made into the sort of people who can be part of God's restored and renewed creation without ruining it, without reintroducing hatred and disharmony into it. As usual, we are not reliant entirely upon our own efforts, or we would never be able to fit into the new creation without spoiling it. God will transform us and bring His work of sanctification in us to completion

(1 Corinthians 15:50f). But if that is where we are headed, then that is how we must try and live now.

When I was at school, we had carpentry lessons, and, every term, we had to make a stool. I was one of four brothers who all went to the same school, so my parents' house was littered with these stools! Now, I have to confess that I tended to mess around a little in carpentry lessons, not being a particularly practical type, and, by the end of term, I would normally only have half a leg of the stool made. But Mr Silk, the carpentry master, would generously add three and a half legs and a top to my stool, and finish it off so that I had a nice finished product to take home to my delighted parents! If we had made no effort at all, then he wouldn't have made a stool from scratch for us, but if we had showed vaguely willing, then he would do the rest.

And it's a bit like that with sanctification. If, by our life, we show that holiness is the direction in which we are headed, the goal for which we are aiming, then God will finish the process off for us – even if we have messed around a little – and we shall be changed in the twinkling of an eye, and become the sort of people who will not distort the new creation when we become part of it. But if we do not wish to go in that direction, and make no effort to move in that direction, then God will not force us – and neither will He allow us to ruin His new creation by being a part of it.

Christian ethics is ultimately about living now, as far as is possible, the sort of life we shall be able to live when all things – ourselves included – have been renewed. We are to be pictures of, and pointers to, the beauty, harmony, goodness and purity of the new world God is committed to bringing in.

*   *   *

Whenever I speak on this subject in public, people always ask me what is to stop the whole thing from going wrong again, so perhaps it would be helpful just to address that question in conclusion. If God doesn't take away our freedom, if He doesn't rewire us, then how do we know that we won't fall again? How do we know that the new creation will prove any less vulnerable to rebellion than the old?

The answer seems to me to be that it is possible to be free, and yet to have become the sort of person who won't sin. Take Mother Teresa as an example. When she was seventy, say, she was perfectly free to go out and mug some eighty-year-old man in the street – there was no metaphysical constraint stopping her. But because of her lifetime of predominantly right moral choices, and because of her faith and her life of prayer and Bible study, and her daily celebration of the Eucharist, she had become the sort of person who wouldn't.

So if it is possible to be free and yet be the sort of person who doesn't sin, why doesn't God make us that way in the first place? Why doesn't he make us like Mother Teresa from the very beginning? Because it took time – and Mother Teresa's cooperation – to get her to that point. It was because of her lifetime of predominantly right moral choices and religious practice that she became the sort of person who wouldn't be tempted to go out and mug someone. And you can't be created with a lifetime's right moral choices and voluntarily entered-into religious practice behind you. You cannot be created with a moral history.

"I bought my moral history off the internet"

You have to make your own moral decisions. You have to forge – in dialogue with God – your own character. You cannot be created with those decisions already made – or it will have been God who made them, not you, and you will not be free.

So what is logically possible at the end of the process is different from what is logically possible at the beginning. We can be free and yet be the sort of people who won't choose wrongly *at the end of the process*, but we can't be like that in the beginning. We cannot be created like that. So God creates us with the capacity to choose the sort of people we become. That's the only way we can be free.

But if we choose rightly, if we choose to live our life in partnership with Him, if we offer ourselves to Him and ask Him to shape us and purify us and change us and sanctify us – then we will increasingly become the sort of people who, though free to do bad things, will not do them. We shall only get so far in that process, of course – as did Mother Teresa. She was not perfect by the time she died. She would still have ruined the new creation if she had been placed within it. But that is where the final transformation comes in. If we have said with our lips and our lives that we want to be the sort of people that God made us to be, that we want to be like Him and to be with Him in His new creation for ever, then He will complete the process of sanctification within us. He will finally and forever root out every wrong motive and selfish desire. And we shall be fitted for the new world as residents – and not the ruination – of a restored creation.

FURTHER RESOURCES FOR READING, PRAYER AND ACTION

David Lawrence, *Heaven … It's Not the End of the World* (Scripture Union, 1995).

C. S. Lewis, *The Great Divorce* (Geoffrey Bles: The Centenary Press, 1945).

N. T. Wright, *New Heavens, New Earth: The Biblical Picture of Christian Hope* (Grove Books, 1999).

Thomas O'Gorman (comp.), *An Advent Sourcebook* (Liturgy Training Publications, 1990).

Stephen H. Travis, *I Believe in the Second Coming of Jesus* (Hodder & Stoughton, 1982).

10 THE CHURCH

What life have you if you have not life together?
There is no life that is not in community,
And no community not lived in praise of GOD.
Even the anchorite who meditates alone,
For whom the days and nights repeat the praise of GOD,
Prays for the Church, the Body of Christ incarnate.
And now you live dispersed on ribbon roads,
And no man knows or cares who is his neighbour
Unless his neighbour makes too much disturbance,
But all dash to and fro in motor cars,
Familiar with the roads and settled nowhere.
Nor does the family even move about together,
But every son would have his motor cycle,
And daughters ride away on casual pillions.

T. S. Eliot's Choruses from *The Rock* were written in 1934, but, apart from the casual pillions, could have been written today. Community, of which he laments the loss, is even more eroded today. Individualism, which he sees as leading to dispersal, isolation and rootlessness in the first half of the twentieth century, is even more pronounced at the beginning of the twenty-first. The family, which did not move about together then, frequently does not stay together now. So many more people find themselves needing to live alone that, in Britain, four and a half million new homes will be required over the next ten years – and that with a static or slightly declining population. Our individualism is now having a direct impact on our environment and making modern Britain a less green and pleasant land.

That is part of the context for the modern church. How is it responding? In different places and in various ways, local churches continue to be a focal point for the life of their community. Many home groups and fellowship groups enable people to get to know and support one another. Many churches offer a degree of community and of intimacy that mark them out as an oasis in a relational desert.

In other ways, however, churches sometimes appear simply to have bought into the individualism and fragmentation of society. Let's look at three disturbing trends.

THE TENDENCY TO DIVORCE BEING A CHRISTIAN FROM BEING A MEMBER OF THE CHURCH

You sometimes hear evangelists saying, 'I am not recruiting for the Church: I'm recruiting for Jesus Christ'. And we know what they mean. Indeed, there is some truth to that distinction, 'For we do not preach ourselves, but Jesus Christ as Lord' (2 Corinthians 4:5). After all, it is not the Church that died for us. It was not the Church that was raised to life for us. It is not the Church that is the subject of any of the saving acts recounted in the Gospel. And it is certainly the case that the nature of the sinless Christ constitutes a far more credible and attractive call than the frequently corrupt and sometimes cruel nature of the Church.

However, it is simply not possible to divide being a Christian and belonging to the Church for at least five reasons. First, one of the things that Christ came to do was to build His Church (Matthew 16:18). You cannot therefore tell the story of Jesus without also telling the story of His Church. You cannot separate Christ from the Church without doing damage to Christ as well as, obviously, to His Church. That is how bound He is to it in purpose and love.

Secondly, we are invited to become incorporated into Christ, to become part of Christ, to be located 'in Christ'. So Christ is the sort of being that we can be included within. There is a corporate as well as a personal dimension to belonging to Christ. It is, as we saw in Chapter 8, by being in Him that we participate in the divine life, but by being in Him we also belong thereby to everyone else who is 'in Him', and participate in *their* life. Were this not the case, were Christ not a corporate being we can be included within, if the phrase 'in Christ' were cut out of the New Testament, there would be no gospel. The death and Resurrection and Ascension of Jesus would not be good news. They would set an example we could not hope to emulate instead of being events into which we may enter. Only if we died with Him, and were raised with Him and ascended in Him are these events good news for us. If he merely goes ahead and urges us to follow, we are no better off for these events having taken place. Only if we are incorporated *into* Him and thereby enter *into* these events do they avail for us. So to make too sharp a distinction between Christ and the Church is to saw off the branch we are sitting on, to cut ourselves off from the gospel, and ultimately to cut ourselves off from salvation. We can only be in Him *together*.

Thirdly, Paul tells us that Christ is the Head of the Church (Ephesians 5:23). And to be part of Christ is therefore to be part of the Body. There is nowhere else in this metaphor for us to be. There is no other place to be grafted onto. If we were grafted individually onto the Head, Christ would look like Medusa, the mythical creature with snakes for hair – only weirder! It would be as anomalous theologically as it would anatomically!

There is nowhere for us to be part of Christ other than as part of His body, which is the Church.

Fourthly, the author of the letter to the Hebrews talks of coming to the Church and coming to God as parallel ways of saying the same thing:

> But you have come to Mount Zion, to the heavenly Jerusalem, the city of the living God. You have come to thousands upon thousands of angels in joyful assembly, to the church of the firstborn, whose names are written in heaven. You have come to God, the judge of all people, to the spirits of the righteous made perfect, to Jesus the mediator of a new covenant, and to the sprinkled blood that speaks a better word than the blood of Abel.
>
> **Hebrews 12:22–24**

To come to the Church of the firstborn is synonymous and simultaneous with coming to God and coming to Jesus. (It is also synonymous and simultaneous with coming to Mount Zion, to thousands upon thousands of angels in joyful assembly, and to the spirits of righteous people made perfect – the Church is a bigger, more multi-dimensional and more glorious thing than we are usually aware of.) In fact, there is no more difference between coming to the Church and coming to God than there is between coming to God and coming to Jesus. If you cannot divide the Father from the Son, then neither can you divide the Head from the Body. Coming to Mount Zion, coming to the heavenly Jerusalem, coming to the city of the living God, coming to thousands upon thousands of angels, coming to God, coming to the spirits of the righteous, coming to Jesus and coming to the Cross are all different ways of speaking of the same reality. You cannot truly do any of these without doing them all.

And fifthly, Jesus Himself is unembarrassed about belonging to His family. 'Both the one who makes people holy and those who are made holy are of the same family. So Jesus is not ashamed to call them brothers and sisters' (Hebrews 2:11). Nor must we be.

It is easy to be. There are such pillocks and prats in the Church (!) that it is easy to be ashamed of one's brothers and sisters. But Jesus isn't. And so somehow we have to let the pillocktude bounce off us, and rejoice in the fact that they are being taken up into this process of salvation and transformation and glorification, as we are, and that a) they need us to be their companions and helpers in that process, b) we need them to be our companions and helpers in that process, c) we may not be entirely free from a degree of pillocktude ourselves, seen from a different perspective than our own, and d) they're not pillocks anyway – they are people made in the image of God, and people for whom Christ died. Indeed, e) seeing others as pillocks and prats is part of what we need to be saved from. The whole point about family members – as opposed to friends – is that you cannot choose them. And their very difference from you and your type, the very fact that they are not people with whom you would normally or happily associate, is what is going to stretch you as a human being.

It is, perhaps, not just individual Christians of whom we tend to be ashamed, but whole Christian traditions. There are whole styles of churchmanship with which we are embarrassed to be associated, and therefore from which we tend to distance ourselves with a certain disdain. Again, we need to remember that Jesus is unembarrassed to be so associated. Those who confess the risen Jesus as Lord are our brothers and sisters whether we like them or not, and whether we like their churchmanship or not. And even if we disagree with the way in which they lead their Christian life, we are not at liberty to ignore the family ties that bind us to them and them to us. As Screwtape, an old and experienced devil, says to Wormwood, his young nephew who has just set out on the business of tempting:

> The real fun is working up hatred between those who say "mass" and those who say "holy communion" when neither party could possibly state the difference between, say, Hooker's doctrine and Thomas Aquinas', in any form which would hold water for five

minutes. And all the purely indifferent things – candles and clothes and what not – are an admirable ground for our activities. We have quite removed from men's minds what that pestilent fellow Paul used to teach about food and other unessentials – namely, that the human without scruples should always give in to the human with scruples. You would think they could not fail to see the application. You would expect to find the "low" churchman genuflecting and crossing himself lest the weak conscience of his "high" brother should be moved to irreverence, and the "high" one refraining from these exercises lest he should betray his "low" brother into idolatry. And so it would have been but for our ceaseless labour.[1]

It is a package deal. You cannot have Jesus as your Brother and His Father as your Father unless you are prepared to have all other Christians – of all types and stripes – as your brothers and sisters.

During the apartheid era in South Africa, the story used to be told of Desmond Tutu and President Botha going out on a boat together across the lake. The wind gets up and blows Botha's hat off onto the water. Botha tries to retrieve it with a fishing rod, but is unsuccessful, so in the end Tutu gets out of the boat, walks across the water, picks up the hat, walks back to the boat and gives Botha his hat back. And the headline in the newspapers the next day is 'Black Bishop can't swim!' One of the things that most impressed me about Bishop Tutu was that, despite the fact that he and Botha were so at odds politically and ideologically, he nevertheless accepted him as a brother. 'If he says he is a Christian, then he is my brother', said Tutu. He was not ashamed to acknowledge him as his brother.

Joining the Church is not an event substantially separate from or subsequent to becoming a Christian. Of course, being a member of the Church doesn't make you a Christian, but being a Christian does make you a member of the Church, and does make every other Christian your brother or sister.

THE TENDENCY TO BE UNCOMMITTED TO A PARTICULAR CHURCH

Not for nothing is the story told of a man who is rescued after a year or so alone on a desert island. His rescuers notice that he has built three houses on the island, and ask him about them. 'Well, the one on the left is my home – that's where I live. The one in the middle is my church. And the one on the right is the church I used to go to!' We are somewhat promiscuous church-goers. We tend to shop around when we move to a new area in order to find a church we like, but even once we've got involved we still have a roving eye for somewhere 'better'.

An American pastor recently said, 'I'm constantly aware that my congregation is just two bad services away from going somewhere else.' And this tendency simply mirrors many of the social and intellectual currents of today's society, which, I suggest, we should be challenging, not copying. We should be offering the world an alternative to these trends, not a further example of them.

The first of these trends is social mobility. It used not to be uncommon for someone to stay with the same employer for pretty well their whole working life. Now, we seldom stay in the same job for more than a few years. We seldom stay in the same area for more than a few years. And, most sadly of all, we often don't stay in the same relationship for life, either. This tendency to move around, this restlessness, this characteristic of being 'settled nowhere', as T. S. Eliot put it, we simply import into our church life. To a certain extent, we cannot avoid being affected by this trend – but it's also fair to say that we sometimes connive with it when we don't need to.

The second trend is that of individualism, which we have already noted.[a] 'I' am the basic unit, the unit that has a vote – and exercises that vote with its feet. The basic unit is not the community, to which I therefore have certain responsibilities. The basic unit is me, and I have certain needs that I require to be met.

---

[a] 'And no man knows or cares who is his neighbour.'

The third trend is that of commitment phobia. Our generation has experienced the break-up of so many 'committed' relationships, and has suffered so much pain in consequence, that we are hesitant to enter into such relationships ourselves in order to avoid the hypocrisy of making promises that, statistically, we stand a good chance of not keeping. And this impacts the extent to which we are prepared to commit ourselves to an organisation as well as to an individual.

The fourth trend that affects – and *in*fects – us is the pursuit of fashion and novelty. Of course, the desire for all things new is not new, as Paul discovered: 'All the Athenians and the foreigners who lived there spent their time doing nothing but talking about and listening to the latest ideas' (Acts 17:21). We are not immune from this tendency, only we dress it up in spiritual language to disguise its worldly nature. We justify going off to the new church down the road by saying, 'That seems to be where God is currently at work, and I want to be at the cutting edge of what He is doing' – which, being translated, means, 'It's a bit new and a bit funky and I'm off!'

Fifthly, we follow the world in the paucity and poverty of its relationships. We cry out for community, but we fail to involve ourselves in our church in a way that would make community possible for ourselves or anyone else. And that failure has, I shall suggest, deeply damaging consequences for other members of our (would-be) fellowship and for us ourselves.

Sixthly, we follow the world in its attitude of taking rather than giving. We tend to ask whether we are getting what we want from this church, whether it is meeting *my* needs – and not whether we are giving it what it needs. Thus we forget the teaching of Jesus, that 'it is more blessed to give than to receive' (Acts 20:35).

And lastly, we are being shaped by the phenomenon of consumerism. We are used to having lots of products to choose from. And we try one brand one week and another the next – partly out of curiosity, partly because we like variety, and partly because we like to be in control. The consumer is king. And, of course, wanting to be in control is the very attitude that being part of the body of Christ is attempting to cure. For, when applied to anything other than the products we buy, it – and indeed most of these trends one way or another – amounts to little more than selfishness. Certainly, these trends give Screwtape and his demonic colleagues plenty of scope:

My dear Wormwood,

You mentioned casually in your last letter that the patient has continued to attend one church, and one only, since he was converted, and that he is not wholly pleased with it. May I ask what you are about? Why have I no report on the causes of his fidelity to the parish church? Do you realise that unless it is due to indifference it is a very bad thing? Surely you know that if a man can't be cured of churchgoing, the next best thing is to send him all over the neighbourhood looking for the church that "suits" him until he becomes a taster or connoisseur of churches.[2]

Wormwood seems to have learnt his lesson well.

THE TENDENCY TO BE UNCOMMITTED TO THE WIDER CHURCH

If we manage to resist the temptation to be uncommitted to our local church, we still have to face the temptation to leave it there and have as little as possible to do with the wider Church. It is notorious that if a church has a joint service with another local church, that is the day that we'll lie in or mow the lawn or go out for the day. Attendances for joint services are never the average attendance of the one church plus the average attendance of the other. Why? Because we don't see the need for anything other than the particular church we go to. We do our own thing in our own church and we are slightly suspicious of the structures of any wider organisation. The very word 'structure' has a somewhat forbidding and oppressive tone. We resent the amount of money we have to pay to keep those structures in place. And if we do meet up in groupings larger than the local church, it tends to be in *ad hoc* meetings of the ecclesiastically like-minded, with people who have the same basic approach that we do.

And thereby we impoverish ourselves and refuse the gifts of God. I want to suggest three in particular. First, we thereby miss out on the gift of accountability, and leave ourselves open to the abuse of leadership by a strong personality. The more churches do their own thing and cut themselves off from the wider structures of the Church, the more they become vulnerable to the maverick leader with a magnetic personality. Structures may seem slow and ponderous and finicky and bureaucratic, and we may just want to 'get on with it', but what we 'get on with' can quickly go very seriously wrong where there are no effective checks and balances. We miss out on God's gift of accountability.

Secondly, we miss out on the gift of support. The structures are there to hold us, to support us, to help and encourage us to be a faithful witness where God has placed us. And in difficult times, we draw on such networks and support structures to which we have contributed when things have gone well. In a well-functioning body, when there is a cut in the skin, corpuscles from all over the bloodstream will descend on the puncture and protect it from infection. In the body of Christ, when it is functioning properly, one part of the body will support another when it is in difficulty. Without channels of communication, without structure, the body cannot function as a body.

Thirdly, we miss out on the gift of enrichment. Different styles of churchmanship reflect different aspects of the nature of God. Some styles capture well the greatness, the grandeur, the majesty and the eternity of God. Others capture instead His nearness and approachability and warmth and acceptance. Each style has its own strengths and limitations, opportunities and dangers. To cut ourselves off from the wider Church is thus to lock ourselves in to our own limitations. It is to restrict ourselves to the categories with which we are already familiar. And it is to refuse to share our strengths with those who could benefit from them.

In Chapter 8, I suggested that the very difficulty of the doctrine of the Trinity was a sign that there might be something there that would stretch our categories and break new ground in our understanding, and not simply fit neatly and undemandingly and uninterestingly into what we already (thought we) knew. I think that the same is true of engagement with churches which do things differently and have different priorities. It is more difficult than dealing with those who do things much the same way. It can be bewildering or even distasteful. But the opportunities for learning and growing and having our understanding and our experience of God enormously enlarged are correspondingly greater. To cut ourselves off from any meaningful engagement with the wider Church is thus to impoverish and to stultify ourselves and others – and to acquiesce in division where we are called to be its antidote.

The Church in the apostolic age was by no means free from division, but the apostles took care to keep the scattered Christian communities in structured and creative contact with one another. In 1 Corinthians 16:19, Paul says, in passing, 'The churches in the province of Asia send you greetings', and thereby lets slip that there is a whole network of inter-relationships (including letters and visits and mutual hospitality and apostolic oversight) which bound the different congregations together. The churches of Asia – of which, admittedly, there would not have been very many – were sufficiently in touch with one another to be able to speak with a common voice. They knew and they cared what was going on with their brothers and sisters in Corinth. And when one congregation was in need, the others rallied round. Paul's collections for the famine-ridden churches of Judea (Acts 11:29-30) and for the impoverished church in Jerusalem (Romans 15:25–33, 1 Corinthians 16:1–4, 2 Corinthians 8-9) was one way in which he attempted to bind the Church together across geographical, racial and even theological boundaries. What might our church do to foster the same sort of links – and thus to give practical expression to the unity we have in Christ?

But what exactly is it that we belong to by virtue of our faith in Jesus? And what is it that we should be committed to, both locally and more widely? What is the Church? What are her characteristics? What may we say about her?

1. THE CHURCH IS A RESPONSE TO THE GOSPEL

As John Webster has written,

> ... the church is what it is because of the gospel. Priority has to be accorded to the good news, so that we begin our talk about the church indirectly, by talking of the gospel which calls it into being and which remains its essential theme and source of vitality.[3]

That is why I have put my discussion of the Church at the end of this book, rather than including it in its proper place in the historical sequence. I have included it here because the Church is a response to the gospel. We do not know what the Church is until we have attended to the whole sweep of God's dealings with His world and His purposes for it. We cannot properly be the Church without drawing on all that God has revealed of Himself and His acts. Now, in the light of our (hopefully) deeper understanding of who God is and what He has done, what are we called to be and to do? This chapter on the Church hopes to explore the space which God has created for us within His purposes, within His presence and within His very self, by the saving acts which we have been examining in the preceding chapters.

> At its most basic level, therefore, the church is to be defined as assembly around the gospel. 'Church' is the event of gathering around the magnetic centre of the good news of Jesus Christ.[b] Its dynamic is derived not primarily from human projects, decisions or undertakings, but from the presence of the breathtakingly new and different reality which is brought about by Jesus himself, the good news of God. The church exists because of a decision which has already taken place and which the good news declares – the divine decision to reconcile and glorify all things in Christ. ... *If the Church is what it is because of the gospel, it will be most basically characterised by astonishment at the good news of Jesus.*[4]

That is what is to characterise us as a community – astonishment that God has done what He has done, that He is doing what He is doing, and that He will do what He has said He will do. Astonishment – and gratitude. As Rowan Williams put it, '... the notion of gratitude is a fundamental thing that the Church is missing. It isn't something you'd instantly regard as the most characteristic thing about the Church: the sense that something has been given, which we're struggling to articulate and respond to.'[5] How do we make the Church a place of wonder and gratitude? By attending afresh – and prayerfully – to the revealed accounts of all that God is and has

---

[b] Hence the danger of 'magnetic' personalities in positions of authority in the Church. Our job is to draw people to Christ, not to ourselves; to make disciples of Jesus, not to create a following for ourselves. I'm not saying that people with magnetic personalities should not be in positions of leadership within the Church – we need their gifts – but just that they will need to be careful not to become the magnetic centre themselves.

said and has done. In Karl Barth's powerful analogy, '[T]he activity of the community is related to the Gospel only in so far as it is no more than a crater formed by the explosion of a shell.'[6] We need to feel the force of that explosion afresh.

2. THE CHURCH IS PART OF THE GOSPEL

The Church is not the *subject* of the gospel – Jesus Christ is the subject of the gospel. As we noted earlier, the Church did not die for us. But the Church is the fruit, the extension and the continuing locus of His ministry amongst us by His Spirit. It is part of the provision God has made for us in His Son. It is the God-given place where we benefit from all that He won for us in His Incarnation, Cross, Resurrection and Ascension. As Lesslie Newbigin put it,

> One of the most helpful ways to comprehend what Christ did for us on the cross lies in the knowledge and understanding that he has created a place where sinful men and women, despite their sins, may be accepted by God and enabled to live and rejoice in his presence. It is, if you like, the continuation of the ministry of Jesus who received sinners and ate and drank with them. The church is the place where this still happens.[7]

It is the place where all the extraordinary privileges of being God's children become ours *together*. I want to look at nine of these privileges in particular.

a) In the Church we are given a place to belong

All communities tell stories about themselves, and what is going on when we retell these stories is that we rehearse the history of the community, and we thereby locate ourselves within that history and within the ongoing life of the community. It's a way of saying, 'I belong to this community – this is part of who I am. Our stories interweave.' I have already suggested that to have meaning you need a bigger story to be part of and a wider community to belong to. In the history of the purposes of God from Creation to New Creation, God has given us a story to be part of and to contribute to. And in the Church, He has given us a wider community to belong to and to contribute to. The Church is therefore part of what we need to have meaning. It is the community of this story.

And as we retell the story, we reinforce our belonging to this story and to this community. 'A wandering Aramean was my father; and he went down into Egypt and sojourned there, few in number ...' (Deuteronomy 26:5 RSV), repeated the Jewish worshipper, year by year. 'The Lord Jesus, on the night he was betrayed, took bread ...' (1 Corinthians 11:23), we repeat week by week in the communion service. Retelling the story of the community together binds us together, and helps us to know that this is our story, this is our community. We belong.

God thus respects who we are in His dealings with us. He respects how He made us when He redeems us. He made us as social beings, in the image of the Trinity, and therefore made for relationship: He redeems us as social beings, into a community where we may relate to Him and to one another. Our salvation therefore does not make us into something we were not before: it enables us to be the relational people we were created to be. We are saved in line with our own nature. Finding a place where we can relate and belong – both vertically (with God) and horizontally (with one another) – is thus to begin to be fully ourselves.

b) In the Church we are given a healing community

A worshipping community is going to be one which helps heal us of our self-centred assumption that the universe revolves around us, thus effecting a sort of therapeutic Copernican revolution! A loving community is going, by its very nature, to help heal people of their sense of being unlovable. A community that tries to welcome people across the usual divides that fragment our human society is going to help heal those who have been on the wrong side of those divides, those who have picked up a sense of being excluded, be it from their families, their playgrounds or their place of work.

And it is also going to help heal us of our blinkers and prejudices and of our own tendency to exclude others.

Our churches will also attempt to be healing communities in the sense of being places where people care enough to want to know the needs of others, and people trust one another enough to risk sharing them, and then those needs are brought respectfully before God in prayer.

> Are any among you sick? They should call for the elders of the church and have them pray over them, anointing them with oil in the name of the Lord. The prayer of faith will save the sick, and the Lord will raise them up; and anyone who has committed sins will be forgiven. Therefore confess your sins to one another, and pray for one another, so that you may be healed. The prayer of the righteous is powerful and effective.
>
> **James 5:14–16** NRSV

This passage, of course, raises the difficult question of (apparently) unanswered prayer, of why some people are healed and others are not. Prayer is not our subject here, so here is not the place to go into this issue (as writers say when they can't think of a decent answer!). Suffice it to say that a) the Kingdom has come, and therefore God is at work amongst us to heal and to restore and to renew and to raise up. But b) the Kingdom is not yet here in its fullness, so not everyone is healed and not every prayer is answered in the way we would like. a) The same Spirit who anointed Jesus for His ministry is present amongst His people today, and therefore His ministry may take similar forms to those it took in the ministry of Jesus. But b) the Spirit has not yet flooded creation with the presence and glory of God, so we should not expect everything to reflect His will and His purpose. a) The 'already' encourages us to pray for healing. b) The 'not yet' forbids us to presume upon it.

Not everything we ask to be put right will be put right until the putting right of all things. Only at the New Genesis will all be healed. Only when there is no gap between the will of God and the way things are will there be no tension between what we pray for and what happens. As in all matters, we are called not so much to be 'successful' as to be faithful. The Christian community will attempt to be faithful in its prayer for those in need. It will attempt to be a healing community by its very nature, by the way we treat one another, and by the way we pray for one another. In all these ways, we are to mediate to one another the healing of God.

Now, I apologise for banging on about this, but do you see how destructive it is if people sit loose to the church to which they 'belong'? If you are a Christian and you don't make a point of being there when you can, or you waltz off the moment something more ecclesiastically entertaining comes on offer somewhere else, then what you are (implicitly) saying to your fellow Christians is, 'I'm not really committed to you. I'm not necessarily going to be there for you. My commitment to you is only while it suits me, and therefore it is really not far short of self-interest and exploitation.' (In that way, it shares a number of characteristics with serial monogamy.) And it thus acts to reinforce the hurt, and the rejection, and the sense that we are not committed to, and that we are not worth being with, which the Church is intended to help heal, not to exacerbate. Such a lack of commitment stops the Church from being the healing community that it is intended to be, and can gloriously be, imperfect as we are, and unrestored as the world is. Don't misunderstand me. I am not saying that we have to stay in the same congregation for life. I am saying that we need to be a little less flighty.

c) In the Church we are given all things

> All things are yours, whether Paul or Apollos or Cephas or the world or life or death or the present or the future – all are yours, and you are of Christ, and Christ is of God.
>
> **1 Corinthians 3:21–3**

Why, asks Paul, are you indulging in personality cults when the very people you are lining up behind – Paul himself, Apollos and Peter – are themselves your servants? Why are you hero-worshipping them when you yourselves are, under God, the rulers of the universe? It's not the sophisticated pagan philosophers who possess all things, as they claimed[c] – it's *you*! You're a bunch of nobodies in the world's eyes (1 Corinthians 1:26f), but it is you who own all things.

The person who has the most visionary and wonderful sense of this extraordinary truth, in the whole history of Christian theology, must surely be the great seventeenth-century writer, Thomas Traherne. He was, in my view, the greatest writer of prose that the English language has ever known. Someone – probably his publisher! – once asked C. S. Lewis why he didn't write an angelic equivalent of *The Screwtape Letters,* and he replied that if he could write like Traherne, he would – but he couldn't. Page after page flows gloriously on this theme: the following excerpts will give you a taster.

> That all the world is yours, your very senses and the inclinations of your mind declare. ... So that in the midst of such rich demonstrations, you may infinitely delight in God as your Father, Friend and Benefactor; in yourself as His heir, child and Bride; in the whole world as the gift and token of His love. ...
>
> You will never enjoy the world aright, till you see how a sand exhibiteth the wisdom and power of God: and prize in every thing the service which they do you, by manifesting His glory and goodness to your soul, far more than the visible beauty on their surface ... Wine by its moisture quencheth my thirst, whether I consider it or no. But to see it flowing from His love who gave it unto man, quencheth the thirst even of the holy angels.
>
> You will never enjoy the world aright, till the sea itself floweth in your veins, till you are clothed with the heavens, and crowned with the stars, and perceive yourself to be the sole heir of the

---

[c] Seneca said, 'all things belong to the wise man' (*De Beneficiis* 7.3.2–7.4.3). See the other examples in Richard Hays' *First Corinthians* (John Knox Press, Louisville, Kentucky, 1997), pp. 60–61.

whole world – and more than so, because men are in it who are every one sole heirs, as well as you. Till you can sing and rejoice and delight in God, as misers do in gold, and kings in sceptres, you never enjoy the world.

He remembers what it was like to be a child, and urges us to recapture a childish sense of wonder, and of everything existing for us:

The corn was orient and immortal wheat, which never should be reaped nor was ever sown. I thought that it had stood from everlasting to everlasting. The dust and stones of the street were as precious as gold. ... The green trees when I saw them first ... transported and ravished me! ... O what venerable and reverend creatures did the aged seem! Immortal cherubims! And young men glittering and sparkling angels, and maids strange seraphic pieces of life and beauty! ... The streets were mine, the temple was mine, the people were mine, their clothes and gold and silver was mine, as much as their sparkling eyes, fair skin and ruddy faces. The skies were mine, and so were the sun and moon and stars, and all the world was mine, and I the only spectator and enjoyer of it.[8]

That is what it is to be a member of the Church. All things are there for you – not to exploit, but to enjoy, and, one day, to inherit and lovingly to rule.

d) In the Church we are given God

The Chief Rabbi pays a visit to the Vatican. He is taken into the Sistine Chapel, shown all the art treasures and the archives, and finally he is invited into the Pope's private office for tea. He looks around the impressive office, admires the paintings on the wall, and notices a gold telephone on the Pope's desk. 'What's that?' he asks. 'Oh, that's my hotline to the Almighty,' replies the Pope. 'You can use it if you like.' So the Chief Rabbi dials up, has a quick chat, asks a few relevant questions about his work at the moment, and, after a couple of minutes, hangs up. 'That'll be ten thousand euros,' says the Pope. The Chief Rabbi is a little put out by this, but says nothing and pays up.

A couple of years later, the Pope pays a return visit to Jerusalem, prays at the Wailing Wall, goes to see the Dome of the Rock, and finally ends up at the Chief Rabbi's private office for tea. He looks around the impressive office, admires the design work on the walls, and notices a gold telephone on the Chief Rabbi's desk. 'What's that?' he asks. 'Oh, that's my hotline to the Almighty,' replies the Chief Rabbi. 'You can use it if you like.' So the Pope calls up the Almighty, asks one or two questions about a speech he has to give shortly, asks for a couple of illustrations and a good joke for the occasion. He chuckles at God's offering, and, after a couple of minutes, signs off and hangs up. And the Chief Rabbi says, 'That'll be two shekels, please.' 'Two shekels? How come it's so cheap?' 'Well, it's a local call from here!'

And that was how the Jewish people saw Jerusalem in Old Testament days. It would have been a local call from Jerusalem because that was where God lived. He dwelt amongst His people in the temple. That was His address. If you wanted to meet with Him, that is where you went. If you wanted to be forgiven, that is where you had to go. If you wanted a specific prayer answered, it was in the temple that you would pray it.[d] In a very literal, spatial, geographical sort of way, the temple was the earthly home of God.

So when Paul says to the Corinthian church – of all people – 'Don't you know that you yourselves are God's temple and that God's Spirit lives in you?' (1 Corinthians 3:16), he is saying, 'You are now where God lives, and where He can be met with, and where forgiveness can be found.' If you want to meet with God, it is to the Christian community that you must go.

Of course, you can meet with God anywhere. It's like a doctor's

---

[d] See Solomon's prayer at the dedication of the temple (in 2 Chronicles 6:14f), and what happened on that occasion (in 2 Chronicles 7:1f).

surgery. You may meet your doctor at a party, in the supermarket, at the gym, but the surgery is where she has agreed to make herself available. The surgery is where you know she may be found, and where you may seek treatment from her. And it's the same with God. You can meet God anywhere. You can meet Him in the garden, you can meet Him in the wilderness, you can meet Him through your own individual prayer. But the Church is where He has agreed to make Himself available. The Church is where He has covenanted to be present: 'where two or three are gathered together in my name, there am I in the midst of them' (Matthew 18:20 AV). The Church is given the promise and the privilege of the presence of God.

e) In the Church we are given harmony

> Make every effort to keep the unity of the Spirit through the bond of peace. There is one body and one Spirit – just as you were called to one hope when you were called – one Lord, one faith, one baptism; one God and Father of all, who is over all and through all and in all.
>
> **Ephesians 4:3–6**

Notice that we are called upon to 'keep' the unity of the Spirit, to 'maintain' the unity of the Spirit – not to create it. Unity is a gift. The Cross, as we saw, not only broke down the barriers between God and us, but also between Jew and Gentile, male and female, slave and free, and all the other barriers that tear apart the human fabric.

Notice too that maintaining the unity of the Spirit takes effort. And without that constant effort, in terms of prayer and listening and understanding and forgiving, we shall fragment. And so it has proved. The Cross has broken down all the barriers and we have re-erected them. Fallen men and women are great wall-builders. The Great Wall of China, Hadrian's Wall, the Berlin Wall, the peace line, the line across Cyprus. During the height of the troubles in Northern Ireland, there was a protestant estate that built a brick wall overnight to stop Catholics from the next-door estate from taking a short cut through to the school, so they had to walk miles around it to get their children to school. The authorities came in and knocked the wall down, and next morning it was back up again. Robert Frost, in his great poem, 'Mending Wall', tells of how every spring, he and his neighbour meet to rebuild the wall between their two properties, and to repair the damage that the winter has done to it. 'Good fences make good neighbors', says his neighbour. But the poet senses, not only that it is unnecessary unless you have cows to enclose, but also that there is a certain violence implicit in the act of division: 'I see him there, Bringing a stone grasped firmly by the top. In each hand, like an old-stone savage armed.'[e, 9]

The Cross is the great act of wall-demolition. The Church is to be the community that lives in defiance of the walls that divide our world, not the community that erects more and more of its own. If I were an atheist attempting to demonstrate the falsity of the Christian faith, I would not take my stand on the problem of evil. I have spent years of my life studying the problem of evil and know that the atheist case is not strong. Nor would I focus on the historical basis of the Christian faith – it is too firmly grounded. Certainly not the resurrection of Jesus – the evidence points the other way. (When I went through my year of depression and doubt, I found that I could not get around the evidence for the resurrection.)

No, I would concentrate my fire on the disunity of the Church. Here is far more fruitful territory. The Cross is supposed to have broken these barriers down. The Church is meant to be the new society living across the divides that riddle the rest of humanity. But the Church is as riddled with division as the rest of the world. It is, to my mind, the one nearly unanswerable argument against the truth of the gospel.

---

[e] Fences and walls aren't bad in themselves, of course. 'Just as homeowners set physical property lines around their land, we need to set mental, physical, emotional, and spiritual boundaries for our lives to help us distinguish what is our responsibility and what isn't.' For an excellent exploration of what is a healthy boundary which enables us to be ourselves, and what is a divisive boundary that isolates us from others, see *Boundaries* by Henry Cloud and John Townsend (Zondervan, Grand Rapids, Michigan, 1992 – the quotation above is from p. 25).

We need to make every effort, not just to maintain the unity of the Spirit, but to recover it and to live it. We need to weaken the atheist's case by doing all we can to chip away at those walls. We need to help the world to believe, by living out the unity that proclaims, 'There is one God'. We need to help the world to believe, by living out the unity that reflects the unity of the Father and the Son (John 17:21). It is an evangelistic imperative, as well as a matter of integrity. Our unity has been achieved by the Cross. It is a gift. We need to accept it and acknowledge it and, repentantly, begin to live it. When the world sees us doing that, it will not only be helped to believe: it will also be helped to peace.

f) In the Church we are given a task

The Church has been given a multi-faceted task. But it begins with hearing the gospel. John Webster again:

> The church is not called first of all to live and proclaim the gospel, but to hear the gospel. Of course, if the church really is to be a hearing church it must also live and proclaim the gospel – otherwise it will fall into a hopeless self-deception about its own hearing (James 1:22, 25). But only because it has heard, and continues to hear, the gospel is the church called to testify to what it hears in life and proclamation and, however indispensable the work and speech of the church may be, they are what they are only because they emerge from the unending attention to the good news.[10]

That's where we begin. Our first task as a Christian community is to hear the gospel, to attend to the Scriptures. That is why the reading of Scripture is utterly essential to everything we do when we meet together. Otherwise, we do not know what God is like. We do not know what His will is. We do not know how to reflect Him. We do not know how to serve Him. We do not know how to worship Him. We do not know what we are doing when we take the sacraments if we have not listened to, and attended to and heard the gospel.

But, secondly, we are called not just to hear it but to celebrate it. To quote John Webster once more: '"Church" is not a struggle to make something happen, but a lived attempt to make sense of, celebrate and bear witness to what has already been established by God's grace.'[11] Often, particularly, I suspect, for its full-time workers, Church does feel like a struggle to make things happen, a frenetic striving to get things done. To remember that Church is not primarily something we have to do, but the celebration of what God has already done is immensely liberating. An attentive hearing of the gospel leads to a natural celebration of it in praise and in sacrament.

Thirdly, we need to embody the gospel. If the gospel is about forgiveness, we need to be a forgiving community. If the gospel is about reconciliation, we need to be a reconciled community. If the gospel is about the love of God, we need to be a loving community. If the gospel is about a God who took the very nature of a servant, we need to be a community where service is not found demeaning but fulfilling. If the gospel is about the veil that separates us from God being torn from top to bottom, then we need to be a community that takes full advantage of that rip – we need, in other words, to be a prayerful community, a community that basks in the presence of God. If the gospel is about a crucified Messiah, we need to be a community which abjures authoritarian leadership and determines that it will not be so among us. If the gospel is about the one God, and our one Lord, then we shall attempt with all that we are and all that we have to be but one community, one body, one Church.

And lastly, we are called to proclaim the gospel. No one else is going to. So if we don't, how will they hear? (That is Paul's point in Romans 10:14–15.) We proclaim the gospel by balanced human example, by gentle evangelistic offer and by clear prophetic challenge. By balanced human example, because if the world sees single-issue fanatics, it will not be drawn. But if it sees men and women living out their humanity in more dimensions and greater depth than they know in their own humanity, they may be prepared to listen to our words. By gentle evangelistic offer, because if the world hears us shouting or crying out, or raising our voices stridently in the streets, it will instinctively know that we are not genuine servants of the Servant (Isaiah 42:2–3). But if we are gentle with bruised reeds and smouldering wicks then they may feel safe enough to be healed and reignited. By clear prophetic challenge, because if the world sees us locked up in our religious box, it will leave us there. But if it hears us speak out for sanity in the public arena, it will know itself to be confronted by a God who claims every area of life for His liberating rule. It will know that we are talking about God, and it will know that we are making a claim about truth. Only if Jesus is seen to be humanely relevant to every area of human life will people be prepared perhaps to acknowledge Him as Lord of all.

g) In the Church we are given the blessing of judgment

There is – of course, and gloriously – a sense in which the Church does not come into judgment. 'Truly, truly I say to you, he who hears my word and believes him who sent me, has eternal life; he does not come into judgment, but has passed from death to life' (John 5:24 RSV). Because we are in the Son, we inherit His sinlessness, we inherit His being-the-other-side-of-death-and-judgment-ness, we inherit His resurrectedness, His having-passed-from-death-to-life-ness! (And this is still true of us, despite the fact that we still sin, we still face the prospect of death and the Resurrection is still future for us.)

Yet it is also true that 'we will all stand before God's judgment seat. ... we will all give an account of ourselves to God' (Romans 14:10, 12). And that was written by Paul, from whom we learn about justification by faith, so he clearly did not see the two as being incompatible. We are justified by faith. If we have faith in Jesus then we belong to Him, we belong to His people, we belong to His new creation. If we have faith in Jesus then we hear *in advance* our acquittal and our acceptance at the final assize. Yet, says Paul, we will all stand before God's judgment. How can that be? How can we reconcile these two truths?

Paul gives an idea of how he would respond to that question in 1 Corinthians 3:10–15:

> By the grace God has given me, I laid a foundation as an expert builder, and someone else is building on it. But each one should build with care. For no-one can lay any foundation other than the one already laid, which is Jesus Christ. If anyone builds on this foundation using gold, silver, costly stones, wood, hay or straw, that person's work will be shown for what it is, because the Day will bring it to light. It will be revealed with fire, and the fire will test the quality of everyone's work. If the building survives, the builder will receive a reward. If it is burned up, the builder will suffer loss; the builder, however, will be saved, but only as one escaping through the flames.

Everyone, Christian and non-Christian alike, will come before the judgment seat of God, as is only right. No life should go unchallenged. No evil act should be overlooked. The universe would not be moral if some people were not confronted with what they had done. There would be no justice if some foul deeds were simply not followed up. And there will be justice. The universe will be moral. Every moral agent will be held to account. But the Cross has made an eternal difference. The Cross still avails. Those who have placed themselves under its protection will be ultimately secure. Those who cling to it will find that it acts as a lightning conductor for God's anger at evil. Christ *has* taken their sin and their guilt on Himself. So they will be held to account, but they won't be condemned. Their work will be tested by the fire of God's judgment, but they won't be burnt up by it themselves. Their work and their reward will be in the balance, but their salvation will not. How they have lived *will* make a difference, as justice demands; but it will not eternally undermine who they are, as the Cross ensures. Thanks to the Cross, we can and we shall be disentangled from our deeds.

But there is more to be said. As Peter puts it, 'It is time for judgment to begin with the family of God' (1 Peter 4:17). Judgment is not confined to 'the Day'. It begins now. The family of God is allowed to see the exam papers in advance! The life of Jesus, as we have it in the Gospels, judges us by the contrast between the beauty of His life and the shoddiness of our own. The Scriptures challenge us about our lifestyles, our attitudes and our motives. Day by day, through Bible reading, through prayer, through the work of the Spirit within us, through what St. Ignatius called 'the examen of conscience'[12], through confession, through the advice and challenge of others; week by week, through confession and absolution, through the liturgy of the Church, through the public reading and exposition of Scripture, through the sacraments, through the testimony and example of others, we are confronted by God *in advance of the final judgment*, so that we have time for amendment of life now. As John Webster says,

> The gospel acts as the ultimate critical point of reference for the church's life and proclamation. Here at one and the same time the church is exposed to judgement and blessed beyond measure.[13]

This judgment-in-advance is an immeasurable blessing because it is a chisel in the hands of a Master Sculptor, chipping away at all the bits of us that prevent us from being the work of art He sees we have it in us to be. It is a blessing because it enables us to become more like Him, more loving, more pure, more dependable, more consistent and transparent and solid and good. It is a blessing because it means that when the Final Judgment comes, not only will our ultimate survival not be at stake, but we shall find that judgment goes with the grain of who we have started to become. Submit yourself to the judgment of God now, and you will find that the final judgment is not a head-on collision, but a fearful and forceful pushing in the direction we are already going. However awesome and dreadful it must inevitably be, the final judgment of God will finally fulfil us, in the sense that it will finally make us the people we have set ourselves to become.

h) In the Church we are given the privilege of persecution

The New Testament is quite clear that Christians should expect persecution. Jesus, in the parable of the Sower, says 'When trouble or persecution comes ...' (Mark 4:17) – not 'if'. He promises persecutions as one of the 'rewards' of following Him (Mark 10:30). (He was never a natural in the advertising world!) He warned His disciples that 'If they persecuted me, they will persecute you also' (John 15:20). And Paul made sure that the early Christians were under no illusions about the road ahead: 'In fact, when we were with you, we kept telling you that we would be persecuted. And it turned out that way, as you well know' (1 Thessalonians 3:4). It is not hard to see why this would be the case. If we are charting our course against the flow of a fallen world, persecution is bound to be a possibility. T. S. Eliot saw the point clearly:

> Do you think that the Faith has conquered the World
> And that lions no longer need keepers?
> Do you need to be told that whatever has been, can still be?
> Do you need to be told that even such modest attainments
> As you can boast in the way of polite society
> Will hardly survive the Faith to which they owe their
> significance?...
> Why should men love the Church? Why should they love her laws?
> She tells them of Life and Death, and of all that they would forget.
> She is tender where they would be hard, and hard where they like
> to be soft.
> She tells them of Evil and Sin, and other unpleasant facts. ...
> The blood of the martyrs [was] not shed once for all ...[14]

So we are to expect persecution – but to see it as a *privilege*? Well, we are not to seek it, and we must be careful that what we are suffering is genuinely for the sake of the gospel, and not simply the consequence of our own insensitivity or pig-headedness! But persecution, when it is persecution, can be regarded as a privilege in a number of ways.

First, it puts us in good company, as Jesus remarked: '... in the same way they persecuted the prophets who were before you' (Matthew 5:12). Secondly, not only are we not abandoned in our persecutions (2 Corinthians 4:9), and not only can they not separate us from the love of Christ (Romans 8:35), but Christ Himself so identifies Himself with us that our sufferings are His sufferings, and when they persecute us, they persecute Him (Acts 9:4). Thirdly, they are an affirmation that we are 'counted worthy of suffering disgrace for the Name' (Acts 5:41). They are an affirmation that we are worth bothering to oppose. They are an affirmation that there must be some degree of substance to our witness, and some degree of reality to our faith. Fourthly, they will not go unrewarded. 'Rejoice and be glad, for great is your reward in heaven' (Matthew 5:12).

Persecution is an instance of that clear prophetic challenge of which I wrote earlier, because it lays bare the true nature of those wielding power. It erodes the authority of the régime that imposes it, and hastens its collapse. And it is a strong testimony to the reality of a higher Power, that the régime finds belief in that Power such a threat. It is a privilege to confront distorted power with the Power that is its Source and its Judge.[f]

i) In the Church we are given our destiny

The community that prays, 'Your Kingdom come', will finally see that prayer answered. And it will have a place and a rôle in that renewed, healed, transfigured creation, as it enters into the joy of its Master. It will have world enough and time to explore that restored creation, to plumb the unknown depths of fellow creatures, and to quarry the unfathomable and unutterable riches of the eternal Creator.

---

[f] Karl Barth used to say that any totalitarian régime has, by its very nature, to be anti-Semitic, because the Jewish people are, by their history and worship, evidence of a higher Power – and no totalitarian régime can tolerate such a reminder. The same is true of the Church, when it is being true to itself.

j) In the Church we are given the Eucharist

So many of the points I have been trying to make in this chapter are summed up in the Eucharist, Communion, Lord's Supper, Mass – call it what you will. In this simple act by which we are to remember our Lord, the whole nature of the Church as I have attempted to expound it receives its God-given expression. Here we are affirmed as social beings – it is, after all, communion, not union. Here we reinforce our sense of belonging both to God and to one another. Here we not only remember and recount the story of our community, but we actually enter into that story, enter into the death of Christ, participate in the body and blood of Christ (1 Corinthians 10:16). Here we kneel before God, which helps heal us of our pride; we kneel together, which helps heal us of our sense of isolation; and we are accepted, which helps heal us of our fear of rejection. Here we are given bread and wine as a token of all things. We are given Christ Himself; we have God's presence in our midst. We give expression to our harmony as we kneel at the same table. We hear and celebrate the gospel and we are strengthened to live it and to share it. We expose ourselves as individuals and as a community to God's loving examination, and seek His forgiveness and correction. We remember how they persecuted our Lord, and ask for strength to follow faithfully in His footsteps. And we anticipate the great messianic banquet which we shall enjoy with all God's people in company with Abraham, Isaac and Jacob in the Kingdom of Heaven.

Not only does the Eucharist sum up all that I have been trying to say in this chapter: it also sums up all that I have been trying to say in this book. Creation is good. Our physicality is good. It does not have to be left behind. God has not abandoned His physical world. He is active within it. He wants to redeem it, not to remove us from it. He entered into the dimensions of our time and space, and took flesh. He lived a whole human life, in all its dimensions. He died a whole human death, and thereby broke open our mortality. When He was raised, He was raised physically. When He ascended, He left no part of His humanity behind. There are now cells and molecules and sheer matter not just in the presence but in the very being of God. It matters to Him how we live in the body. He calls us to present our bodies as a living sacrifice, and to care for the physical needs of others – to feed them, to clothe them, to pray for their healing at every level and in every dimension. And when He finally remakes His world, it will happen in time and space, and it will heal and transfigure time and space. We shall not be whisked away to some spiritual existence, but we shall have our physicality renewed in the context of a renewed creation.

It should therefore not surprise us that He uses physical things, ordinary things, everyday things like bread and wine to serve His purpose and to mediate His presence. So exalted is matter – because He made it and became it and raised it – that it may stand in for Him. It may carry Him and embody Him and bring us into His life and make it part of us.

But actually we are given more than that. In the bread and wine, we see a little bit of matter, a tiny bit of God's good creation being made even now the vehicle of His grace, His love, His presence, His glory and Himself – a glimpse of that day when every particle shines with the presence of God, and the earth is filled with the glory of God as the waters cover the sea.

FURTHER RESOURCES FOR READING, PRAYER AND ACTION

David Watson, *I Believe in the Church* (Hodder & Stoughton, 1989).

Miroslav Volf, *Trinity and Community: An Ecumenical Ecclesiology* (Eerdmans, Grand Rapids, 1997).

Richard Wurmbrand, *Tortured for Christ* (Hodder & Stoughton, London, 1967). One example of the thousands of twentieth-century Christians who experienced the 'privilege of persecution'.

EPILOGUE

Having experienced a prolonged period of doubt myself, I am concerned to address, before concluding, the situation of those who find themselves unable to believe some or much of what they have read here. If that is you, I don't want you to feel excluded or ignored or unacknowledged by the experience of reading this book. I want you to know that I don't consider your reaction unusual, unreasonable or unhopeful.

Maybe you find bits of what you have read profoundly attractive, bits profoundly repugnant, and some bits just far removed from your actual experience. Maybe you long to believe, but find yourself no nearer to doing so at the end of this book than you were at the outset. Let me very briefly make five points. First, do realise, as I do, that I may have got it wrong. I may have misunderstood and distorted the true nature of the Christian faith at all sorts of points. Even where I have got it right, I may have expressed it in a way that is distorted by my own failings and limitations. And therefore you may well be right to have the reaction you do.

Secondly, might I recommend that you turn your reaction into some sort of prayer. Even if it is an agnostic prayer that begins by giving voice to uncertainty as to whether there is anyone there to pray to. Ask God, if God there be, to show you what is right, to help you sort out the wheat from the chaff in what I have written, and in your own thoughts.

Thirdly, if you want to believe, then the place to be is in the believing community. Don't wait to believe before you belong. Belonging may help you to believe. Find a church that seems to you to have a degree of honesty and integrity about it, and where you don't feel too uncomfortable. Don't say anything you don't mean, or do anything you are not comfortable with doing. But join in with what you can.

And get involved in some way that will not compromise you, ever if it's only the tea rota. Faith can be contagious.

Fourthly, commit yourself, by some means, to the pursuit of justice. Write letters for Amnesty International or get involved in Christian Aid's campaign for Fair Trade, buy fairly traded products yourself, help out in a homeless project – do anything to align yourself with the fight against oppression. For that way, you will find that you are lining up alongside the God of justice.

> If you do away with the yoke of oppression,
> with the pointing finger and malicious talk,
> and if you spend yourselves on behalf of the hungry
> and satisfy the needs of the oppressed,
> then your light will rise in the darkness,
> and your night will become like the noonday.
> The Lord will guide you always … .
>
> **Isaiah 58:9–11**

There are few better ways of getting to know someone than by working together on some project you are both passionate about. The same is true with getting to know God.

And lastly, I hesitate to hand out a reading list, but might I just recommend a book called *Free to Believe*, by Michael Paul Gallagher, in which he outlines 'Ten Steps to Faith'? It is gentle and wise and may help. (It's published by Darton, Longman and Todd, 1987.) May God reward you for your commitment to truth and meet you in your search.

NOTES

Chapter One

1. William Lane Craig & Quentin Smith, *Theism, Atheism and Big Bang Cosmology* (Clarendon Press, 1995), p. 135.

2. Robert Farrar Capon, *The Third Peacock* (Harper & Row, 1986), p. 9. He does admit this is a 'crass analogy'!

3. Richard Dawkins, *River out of Eden* (Phoenix, 1996), p. 155.

4. Ballad III: Of The Creation, from *The Poems of St John of the Cross*, translated by John Frederick Nims (University of Chicago Press, Chicago and London, 1979). I have made one small alteration to the translation, changing 'I have from my luckiest star' to 'I have from the person you are'.

5. From his poem, *Providence.*

6. From *Jubilate Agno* in *The Collected Poems of Christopher Smart*, Vol 1, edited by Norman Callan (Routledge & Kegan Paul Ltd., London, 1949), pp. 249–347, especially pp. 311, 313, 269, 302. I have quoted these excerpts in the order in which Benjamin Britten set them, not in the order in which Smart wrote them.

7. THE SCREWTAPE LETTERS by C. S. Lewis copyright © C. S. Lewis Pte. Ltd. 1942. Extract reprinted by permission.

8. PERELANDRA by C. S. Lewis copyright © C. S. Lewis Pte. Ltd. 1944. Extract reprinted by permission.

9. Extract from A BRIEF HISTORY OF TIME by Stephen Hawking published by Bantam Press. Used by permission of The Random House Group Limited.

10. *Revelations of Divine Love made to an uneducated person in AD 1373*, trans. Clifton Wolters (Penguin, 1966), p. 68. Used by kind permission of J. C. Wolters.

11. Alvin Plantinga and Michael Tooley, *Knowledge of God* (Blackwell Publishing, 2008), p. 5.

12. Corrie ten Boom, *The Hiding Place* (Hodder & Stoughton, 1971), p. 197.

13. Adaptation mine.

14. *The Irish Press*, 4 June 1976. There is, however, great dispute over what he said, and, indeed, whether he made the speech at all. It is often alleged that the bit cited here was in fact written by Ted Perry for a film made in the 1970s by the Southern Baptist Convention.

15. Thomas Traherne, *Centuries* (Mowbray, 1985), p. 91.

16. David Atkinson, *The Message of Job* (IVP, 1991), pp. 146–47.

17. Sister Mary Magdalen, *Jesus – Man of Prayer* (Hodder & Stoughton, 1987), pp. 23–24.

18. Tom Torrance, *The Christian Frame of Mind* (Helmers & Howard, 1989), p. 61.

19. Extract from THE BEST A MAN CAN GET by John O'Farrell published by Black Swan. Used by permission of The Random House Group Limited.

20. Colin Gunton, *The Triune Creator* (Edinburgh University Press, 1998), p. 12.

21. John Stott, in his foreword to Peter Harris, *Under the Bright Wings* (Regent College Publishing, 2000), pp. ix–x.

Chapter Two

1. David Nobbs, *The Legacy of Reginald Perrin* (London, Methuen, 1995), p. 1.

2. Extract from DEAD FAMOUS by Ben Elton published by Black Swan. Used by permission of the Random House Group Limited.

3. My entry on 'The Fall' in Paul Barry Clarke & Andrew Linzey (eds), *Dictionary of Ethics, Theology and Society* (Routledge, 1996), p. 368.

4. See his commentary on Romans in the *New Interpreter's Bible*, Volume X (Abingdon Press, 2002), p. 578.

5. Don Carson, (trans.), *Commentary on the Gospel According to John* (IVP, 1991), p. 415.

6. Dylan Thomas, 'Do not go gentle into that good night' from *Collected Poems 1934–1952* (Dent, 1952).

7. Derek Kidner, commenting on Ecclesiastes 7:29 in *The Message of Ecclesiastes* (IVP, 1984), first published under a different title in 1976, p. 73.

8. A GRIEF OBSERVED by C. S. Lewis copyright © C. S. Lewis Pte. Ltd. 1961. Extract reprinted by permission.

9. Shakespeare, *King Lear*, IV.i.36.

10. *The Fairly Incomplete and Rather Badly Illustrated Monty Python Song Book* (Methuen Publishing Ltd, 1994). Extract reproduced by kind permission.

11. Jack Clemo, quoted in Martin Wroe ed. *God: What the Critics Say* (Hodder & Stoughton, 1992), p. 41.

12. Semi-quoted from my article, 'Are Animals Fallen?' in *Animals on the Agenda*, edited by Andrew Linzey and Dorothy Yamamoto (SCM, London, 1998), p. 148, but with grammar corrections put in and political correctness taken out!

13. Tom Torrance, *Divine and Contingent Order* (OUP, 1988), p. 139.

14. Paul Fiddes, *The Creative Suffering of God* (Clarendon Press, 1990), p. 223.

15. N. P. Williams, *The Ideas of the Fall and of Original Sin* (Longmans, Green & Co. 1927), pp. 522–23, italics mine.

16. John Milton, *Paradise Lost*, Book 1, Line 3.

Chapter Three

1. Helen Fielding, *Bridget Jones's Diary* (Macmillan, London, UK, 1996), pp. 57–58. Extract reprinted by permission.

2. Shakespeare, *Macbeth*, V.v.26–28.

3. Richard Dawkins, *River out of Eden* (Phoenix, 1996), p. 155.

4. Extract from 'Story Time' by Joyce Grenfell in *George – Don't Do That…* (1977) (Futura, London, 1991), pp. 51–53. Text copyright © Joyce Grenfell 1977.

5. THE MAGICIAN'S NEPHEW by C. S. Lewis, copyright © C. S. Lewis Pte. Ltd. 1955. Extract reprinted by permission.

6. From the hand-out to his Wilde lectures in Oxford, 1988 quoted by kind permission. These were developed into a trilogy of books, *Warrant: The Current Debate* (OUP, Oxford, 1993), *Warrant & Proper Function* (OUP, Oxford, 1993) and *Warranted Christian Belief* (OUP, Oxford, 2000). Plantinga's discussion of Job comes in *Warranted Christian Belief*, pp. 494–98.

7. H. H. Rowley, *The Book of Job*, The New Century Bible Commentary (Marshall, Morgan & Scott, 1976, first published 1970), p. 19.

8. *The Complete Saki* (Penguin, 1982), pp. 374–75.

9. Shakespeare, *Julius Caesar*, III.ii.81–82.

10. THE MAGICIAN'S NEPHEW by C. S. Lewis, copyright © C. S. Lewis Pte. Ltd. 1955. Extract reprinted by permission.

11. Euripides, *Hippolytus*, translated by Philip Vellacott (Penguin, 1977, first published 1953), p. 127.

12. Bennett et al, *The Complete Beyond the Fringe* (Methuen, 1987), p. 104.

13. Peter de Vries, *Let me count the ways* (Gollancz, 1965), p. 307.

14. Ronald Rolheiser, *Forgotten Among The Lilies* (Spire, 1990), pp. 128–29.

Chapter Four

1. *An Almighty Passion – Meeting God in Ordinary Life* (Triangle, SPCK, 2002), pp. 57–59. Reprinted by kind permission of SPCK.

2. From The Roman Martyrology for Christmas Eve, quoted in G. Preston, *Hallowing the Time*, (Darton, Longman & Todd, 1980), pp. 48–50.

3. 'The uncontrollable mystery on the bestial floor' (*Evangel*, Spring 1985) pp. 10–13 (henceforth Webster 1985).

4. POEMS by C. S. Lewis © C. S. Lewis Pte. Ltd. 1964. Extract reprinted by permission.

5. (Webster, 1985), p. 10.

6. A composite translation. The phrase 'who rests on the breast of the Father' comes from Heinz W. Cassirer's *God's New Covenant – a New Testament Translation* (Eerdman's, 1989). 'Himself God' is based on a suggestion in Don Carson's Commentary.

7. (Webster, 1985), p. 11.

8. "M B" signifying Markus Bockmuehl, *The Epistle to the Philippians* (Black's New Testament Commentaries, Fourth Edition, London, 1997).

9. From the lectures he gave on Thirty-Nine Articles, which were later written up into *On the Thirty-Nine Articles: A Conversation with Tudor Christianity* (published for Latimer House, Oxford by The Paternoster Press, Exeter, 1986). The particular passage quoted here did not make its way into the published version, and is included by kind permission.

10. *Oratio Catechetica* 24.

11. (Webster, 1985), p. 11.

12. M B, p. 110.

13. (Webster, 1985), p.11.

14. Ruth Burrows, *Before the Living God* (1975) (Sheed & Ward, 1979), pp. 6–7, my italics.

15. From the Leonine Sacramentary, anthologised in Mary Ann Simcoe (ed.), *A Christmas Sourcebook* (Liturgy Training Publications, 1984).

16. John Osborne, *Look Back in Anger* (1957) (Faber & Faber, 1996), p. 100.

17. Rosemary Haughton, *The Catholic Thing* (Templegate Publishers, 1979), p. 230.

18. John Davies, *Be Born in Us Today – The Message of the Incarnation* (Canterbury Press, 1999), p. 89.

19. John Davies, *The Crisis of the Cross* (Canterbury Press, 1997), p. xvii, my italics.

20. John Davies, *Be Born in Us Today – The Message of the Incarnation* (Canterbury Press, 1999), p. 67.

21. *Priene Inscriptions*, edited by F. Hiller von Gärtringen, 105, 40; cited in Tom Wright's book *What St. Paul Really Said*, (Lion, 1997), p. 43.

Chapter Five

1. Douglas Adams, *The Hitchhiker's Guide to the Galaxy* (Pan, 1992, first published 1979).

2. Tom Smail, *Windows on the Cross* (Darton, Longman and Todd, 1995), p. 18.

3. *I Believe*, Volume 1 of the Collected Sermons of Alexander Schmemann, trans. John A. Jillions (St. Vladimir's Seminary Press, 1991), p. 80.

4. Lesslie Newbigin, *Discovering Truth in a Changing World* (Alpha International, 2003), p. 66.

5. From the Introduction to Confession in Morning and Evening Prayer, in the Church of England's *Book of Common Prayer*, 1662.

6. M. Scott Peck, *What Return Can I Make?* (Arrow Books, 1990), pp. 65–66. Reprinted by kind permission of the Blake Friedmann Literary, TV and Film Agency.

7. Corrie ten Boom, *The Hiding Place* (Hodder & Stoughton, 1971), p. 197.

8. John Stott, *The Cross of Christ* (IVP, 1986), p. 214. Extract used by kind permission.

9. Karl Barth, *Church Dogmatics* IV.1, *The Doctrine of Reconciliation*, translated by Revd G. W. Bromiley (T&T Clark, Edinburgh, 1988 (1956)), p. 159.

10. From a sermon in Worcester College Chapel, Oxford, on 29 April 1990, quoted here by kind permission. The Gospel reading for the day was the John 10 passage about the Good Shepherd, giving up His life for the sheep. His book, *Good Life: Reflections on what we value today* (SPCK, 1997) is full of similarly stimulating insights.

11. According to the evangelists, he taught them about His death both before (Mark 8:31f, 9:31f, 10:32–45, Luke 9:31 etc) and after (Luke 24:25f, Acts 1:1f) it happened.

12. Tom Wright, *Luke for Everyone* (SPCK, London, 2001), pp. 279–80.

13. *The Pilgrim's Progress* (1678) (Signet Classics, New York, 1964), pp. 41–42. For a moving modern version of this exchange, see Walter Wangerin's short story, 'Ragman' in *Ragman and Other Cries of Faith* (1984) (Hodder & Stoughton, 1993).

14. Graham Harrison (trans.), *Does Jesus Know Us? Do We Know Him?* (Ignatius Press, 1983), p. 30.

15. *Does Jesus Know Us? Do We Know Him?*, p. 38.

16. John G. Cumming (trans.) *The Way of the Cross*, (St. Paul Publications, 1990), pp. 32–34.

17. "NIW" signifying Tom Wright, *Paul for Everyone – Ephesians, Philippians, Colossians, Philemon* (SPCK, London, 2002).

18. NIW, p. 27.

19. I have not been able to trace this exact quotation. Bits very like it can be found in a chapter on 'The Cosmic Significance of the Cross' in *The Meaning of the Cross* (A. R. Mowbray & Co, 1959). See especially p. 67.

20. O. C. Quick, *The Gospel of the New World: A Study in the Christian Doctrine of the Atonement* (Nisbet & Co., 1944).

21. Extract from A BRIEF HISTORY OF TIME by Stephen Hawking published by Bantam Press. Used by permission of The Random House Group Ltd.

22. See Dietrich Bonhoeffer, *Letters and Papers from Prison* (SCM 1967), p. 197.

23. Edward Shillito, *Jesus of the Scars, and Other Poems* (Hodder & Stoughton, London, 1919), p. 11.

24. Jürgen Moltmann, *The Crucified God* (1973) (SCM Press, London, 1974), p.40.

25. Martin Luther, *Commentary on the Epistle to the Galatians* (1535) (James Clarke, 1953), p. 272.

26. Taken from *Christ on Trial* – Reprint by Rowan Williams. Copyright © 2002 by Zondervan 2000 by Rowan Williams. Used by permission of the Zondervan Corporation.

27. Rev Alexander Roberts & James Donaldson (eds) Fragment Llll, Volume 1, *Ante-Nicene Fathers* (T & T Clark, Edinburgh, reprinted 1996), p. 577.

28. Douglas Farrow, *Ascension and Ecclesia* (T & T Clark, Edinburgh, 1999), p. 54.

29. Sergei Hackel, *Pearl of Great Price: The Life of Mother Maria Skobtsova 1891–1945*, Second Edition (Darton, Longman and Todd, London, 1982), p. 120.

30. Quoted by Rowan Williams, *Christ on Trial*, pp. 41–42.

31. Taken from *Christ on Trial* – Reprint by Rowan Williams. Copyright © 2002 by Zondervan 2000 by Rowan Williams. Used by permission of the Zondervan Corporation.

32. P. T. Forsyth, *Positive Preaching and the Modern Mind* (The Pickwick Press, Pittsburgh, Pennsylvania, 1981), p. 344.

33. From Thomas Cranmer's Communion Service in the 1662 *Book of Common Prayer*.

34. P. T. Forsyth, *Positive Preaching and the Modern Mind*, p. 344.

Chapter Six

1. Hans Urs von Balthasar, *Mysterium Paschale*, (Aidan Nichols O. P. trans.) (T & T Clark, Edinburgh, 1990), p. 161.

2. Cited in Alexander Schmemann's *The Celebration of Faith: I Believe* (St Vladimir's Seminary Press, 1991) p. 88.

3. From *Moralia* 29 (PL 76, 489) Corpus Christianorum, Series Latina, Vol. 143b, p. 1449.

4. From his hymn, 'Lord, it belongs not to my care'.

5. Ruth Burrows, *Before the Living God*, (1975) (Sheed & Ward 1979), pp. 6–7.

6. John Saward, *The Mysteries of March: Hans Urs von Balthasar on the Incarnation and Easter* (Collins Religious Publishing, London, 1990), p. 133.

7. 'Seven Stanzas at Easter' from TELEPHONE POLES AND OTHER POEMS by John Updike (Deutsch, 1963) copyright © John Updike, 1963.

8. THE GREAT DIVORCE by C. S. Lewis © C. S. Lewis Pte. Ltd. 1964. Extract reprinted by permission.

9. Cited in Nicholas Wolterstorff's *Lament for a Son* (Eerdmans, 1987, Hodder and Stoughton, London, 1989), p. 106.

10. Nicholas Wolterstorff, *Lament for a Son*, pp. 31, 34–5.

11. Jean Vanier, *Jesus, The Gift of Love* (Hodder and Stoughton, London, 1988), p. 135.

12. Reproduced from *First Corinthians* (from the Interpretation: A Bible Commentary for Teaching and Preaching series) by Richard Hays. © 1997 John Knox Press. Used by permission of Westminster John Knox Press.

13. N. T. Wright, *The Crown and the Fire* (SPCK, London, 1992), pp. 103–104.

14. N. T. Wright, *The Letter to the Romans*, in Volume X of *The New Interpreter's Bible* (Abingdon Press, 2002), p. 418.

15. T. F. Torrance, *Space, Time and Resurrection* (1976) (T & T Clark, Edinburgh, 1998), p. 53.

16. From the tapes of his lectures, written up into *On the Thirty-Nine Articles* (published for Latimer House, Oxford by The Paternoster Press, Exeter, 1986) quoted by kind permission.

17. A. M. Ramsey, *The Resurrection of Christ* (1945) (Bles, 1946), p. 19.

18. T. F. Torrance, *Space, Time and Resurrection* (T & T Clark, Edinburgh, 1998), pp. 51–52.

19. From *The Complete Beyond the Fringe* by Alan Bennett, Peter Cook, Jonathan Miller and Dudley Moore (Methuan, London, 1987, first published 1963), pp. 112–13.

20. Gordon Fee, *Paul, the Spirit and the People of God* copyright © 1993 by Hendrickson Publishers, Inc., Peabody, Massachusetts. Used by permission. All rights reserved. I'm not sure I would agree with his use of the word 'earthly' here. I don't think first century Jews had any conception of the new age taking place anywhere other than on earth – albeit a transformed earth.

21. Gordon Fee, *Paul, the Spirit and the People of God*, p. 51. Again, I have a slight quibble with his use of the word 'world'. It is not so much this world that is on the way out – it is, after all, going to be remade and renewed. It is this age that is on the way out. But, again, his overall point is well made.

22. Eric Mascall, *Christian Theology and Natural Science* (Longmans, Green & Co., Ltd., 1956) (Ronald Press Company, New York), p. 17.

23. N. T. Wright, *The Resurrection of the Son of God* (SPCK, London, 2003), pp. 729–30.

24. N. T. Wright, *The Resurrection of the Son of God*, p. 729.

25. From the first of his unpublished Bishop's Lectures in the Winchester Diocese, 1997. (Please don't write and ask N. T. Wright for copies of his Winchester lectures or you'll get me into trouble. It's really all there in *The Resurrection of the Son of God*, especially p. 138.)

26. From *Contra Arianos* 1.61, cited by Oliver O'Donovan in his *On the Thirty-Nine Articles*, p. 36, to which I am indebted throughout this section.

27. N. T. Wright, *The Resurrection of the Son of God*, p. 655.

28. Oliver O'Donovan, *On the Thirty-Nine Articles*, p. 36.

29. MIRACLES by C. S. Lewis copyright © C. S. Lewis Pte. Ltd. 1947, 1960.

30. From the hymn, 'The head that once was crowned with thorns', by T. Kelly.

31. From the hymn, 'See the Conqueror mounts in triumph', by Bishop Christopher Wordsworth.

32. John Davies, *The Crisis of the Cross* (Canterbury Press, Norwich, 1997), p. 91.

33. From E. Milner White (ed.), *After the Third Collect* (A. R. Mowbray & Co., 1952), p. 88, my italics. This thanksgiving is based on two phrases from Sermon IV of Lancelot Andrewes' Sermons of the Nativity, published as volume 1 of his *Ninety-Six Sermons* (John Henry Parker, Oxford, 1890), p. 52. The sermon was preached before King James on Christmas Day 1609. The two phrases are in quotation marks, suggesting he is quoting someone else: I do not know whom.

Chapter Seven

1. Tom Smail, *The Giving Gift: The Holy Spirit in Person* (Hodder & Stoughton, 1988), p. 34.

2. Gordon Fee, *Paul, the Spirit and the People of God* (Hodder & Stoughton, 1996), pp. 26–27.

3. Tom Smail, *The Giving Gift*, p. 35.

4. Tom Smail, 'The Holy Spirit in the Holy Trinity', in Christopher R. Seitz (ed.), *Nicene Christianity: The Future for a New Ecumenism* (Brazos Press, Baker Book House Company, Grand Rapids, & Paternoster Press, Carlisle, 2001), p. 150.

5. St Basil the Great, *On the Holy Spirit*, Trans. David Anderson (St Vladimir's Seminary Press, 1980).

6. Tom Smail, 'The Holy Spirit in the Holy Trinity', p. 152.

7. Tom Wright, from the libretto of his *Easter Oratorio*, set to music by Paul Spicer, my italics. For a theological reflection on his collaboration with Paul Spicer on this work, see his 'Resurrection: From Theology to Music and Back Again', in Jeremy Begbie (ed.), *Sounding the Depths: Theology Through the Arts* (SCM Press, London, 2002), pp. 193–202.

8. Gerard Manley Hopkins, *Poems and Prose*, (Penguin Books, 1985), p. 27, my italics.

9. Tom Smail, *The Giving Gift*, p. 104.

10. Oliver O'Donovan, *On the Thirty-Nine Articles* (The Paternoster Press, 1986), pp. 43–44.

11. Tom Smail, 'The Holy Spirit in the Holy Trinity', pp. 150–151.

12. Oliver O'Donovan, *On the Thirty-Nine Articles*, p. 44. See also Heinz W.

Cassirer's translation of the New Testament, *God's New Covenant* (Eerdmans, Grand Rapids, 1989) which renders *paraklétos* in John 16:7 as 'the one who is to stand by your side'. Likewise, Tom Smail says that *paraklétos* means 'the one who is sent to stand with us, so that we can make a right answer and bear a right witness to Christ and his Father' (*The Giving Gift*, p. 61).

13. Derek Prince, *Foundation Series* (Sovereign World, Chichester, 1986), p. 319.

14. Hans Urs von Balthasar, *Prayer* (1955), translated by Graham Harrison (Ignatius Press, San Francisco, 1986), p. 79.

15. Tom Smail, *The Giving Gift*, p. 26.

16. Tom Smail, *The Giving Gift*, pp. 67, 73.

17. Jane Williams, *Trinity and Unity*, a booklet in the Affirming Catholicism series (Dartman, Longman & Todd, 1995), p. 6. The sentence quoted is part of her description of the Western tradition, which she sees as being dangerously limited. However, she seems from the context to be speaking with approval at this point.

18. Leonardo Boff, *Holy Trinity, Perfect Community* (1988). Trans. Philip Berryman, (Orbis Books, New York, 2000), pp.69–70.

19. Rowan Williams, from a sermon on Ephesians 4 at Holy Trinity Brompton, London, on Sunday 6 July, 2003.

20. Roy Clements, *The Church that Turned the World Upside Down* (Crossway Books, 1992), pp. 21–22.

21. Roy Clements, *The Church that Turned the World Upside Down*, p. 22.

22. Roy Clements, *The Church that Turned the World Upside Down*, p. 26. See von Balthasar's similar statements in Prayer, pp. 74–75: 'the Spirit does not splinter into multiplicity but gathers all multiplicity into one. This is his very nature as Spirit … To human reason, the mysteries of the Spirit are full of marvels and paradoxes in which unity does not destroy distinctions … In fact, the Spirit takes these distinctions as the given as He sets about His work of unification – a far more daring undertaking than anything that Monists, Idealists and Pantheists ever dreamed of.' For they aim at unity but dissolve the diversity.

23. J. I. Packer, *Keep in Step with the Spirit* (IVP, 1984), p. 66.

24. Thomas F. Torrance, *The Christian Doctrine of God, One Being, Three Persons* (T & T Clark, 1996), p. 63.

25. Oliver O'Donovan, *On the Thirty-Nine Articles*, p. 45.

26. Oliver O'Donovan, *On the Thirty-Nine Articles*, p. 45.

27. Oliver O'Donovan, *On the Thirty-Nine Articles*, p. 43.

28. George Caird, from his hymn, 'Not far beyond the sea' in *Hymns Ancient and Modern* (Canterbury Press, 1922).

29. Bianco da Siena, 'Come down, O Love Divine', translated by R. F. Littledale

in *Hymns Ancient and Modern* (Canterbury Press, 1922).

30. Tom Wright, *For All God's Worth* (Triangle, SPCK, London, 1997), p. 1. Actually, he wrote of putting the sea into a bottle and of the hurricane becoming flesh, but a hurricane in a bottle seems a better picture of the Spirit within us!

31. Hans Urs von Balthasar, *Prayer*, p. 75.

32. Thomas F. Torrance, *The Christian Doctrine of God*, p. 153.

33. Lesslie Newbigin, *Living Hope in a Changing World* (Alpha International, 2003), p. 19.

34. John V. Taylor, *The Go-Between God: The Holy Spirit and the Christian Mission* (SCM Press, London, 1972), p. 234.

35. Tom Wright, *A Moment of Quiet* (Lion Publishing, 1997), my italics.

36. Metropolitan Anthony Bloom, *Living Prayer* (Darton, Longman & Todd, London, 1966), p. 103. But he adds two important qualifiers. First, he reminds us that 'on certain occasions we may be aware of God's presence, more often dimly so, but there are times when we can place ourselves before him only by an act of faith, without being aware of his presence at all. It is not the degree of our awareness that is relevant …' (p. 95). And secondly, he insists that silence is not a substitute for speech: 'We must keep complete silence when we can, but never allow it to degenerate into simple contentment. To prevent this the great writers of Orthodoxy warn us never to abandon completely the normal forms of prayer …' (p. 110).

37. Tom Wright, from a series of meditations he gave in the Chapel at Worcester College, bits of which were published as *A Moment of Prayer*, *A Moment of Quiet*, *A Moment of Celebration*, and *A Moment of Peace* (Lion Publishing, Oxford, 1997). The bits I have quoted here were not included in the published edition, and are reprinted here by kind permission.

38. POEMS by C. S. Lewis copyright © C. S. Lewis Pte. Ltd. 1964. Extract reprinted by permission. He does not mean, I am sure, that we make no contribution of our own. He is simply enjoying standing the usual sceptical argument on its head!

39. Jane Williams, *Trinity and Unity*, p. 19.

Chapter Eight

1. Alan Bennett's *Forty Years On and Other Plays* (1969) (Faber & Faber, 1985), p. 77.

2. Lesslie Newbigin, *Living Hope in a Changing World* (Alpha International, 2003), p. 12.

3. The full text of the Athanasian Creed may be found in the Church of England's *Book of Common Prayer*.

4. N. T. Wright, *Jesus and the Victory of God* (SPCK, London, 1996), p. 653.

5. Brian Hebblethwaite, 'Recent British Theology' in Peter Toon and James D.

Spiceland (eds.) *One God in Trinity*, (Samuel Bagster, 1980), p. 169.

6. Jane Williams, *Trinity and Unity*, a booklet in the Affirming Catholicism series (Darton, Longman and Todd, 1995), p.7.

7. *Trinity and Unity*, p.6.

8. Peter Adam, *Living the Trinity* (Grove Books, 1982), p. 20.

9. H. A. Williams, *The True Wilderness* (Constable and Co., 1965), p. 124.

10. *The True Wilderness*, p. 127.

11. *The True Wilderness*, pp. 125–126.

12. Anthony Bloom, *Living Prayer* (1966) (Darton, Longman and Todd, 1973), pp. 105–106.

13. *The True Wilderness*, p. 127.

14. Walter Wink, *Engaging the Powers: Discernment and Resistance in a World of Domination* (Fortress Press, Minneapolis, 1992), p. 15.

15. *Engaging the Powers*, p. 18.

16. Lesslie Newbigin *Living Hope in a Changing World* (Alpha International, London, 2003), p.17. I am indebted to him for this whole section.

17. Leonardo Boff, *Holy Trinity, Perfect Community* Trans. Phillip Berryman (1988) (Orbis Books, 2000), pp. 13–14.

Chapter Nine

1. James Finn Garner, *Politically Correct: The Ultimate Storybook* (1994) (Smithmark, New York, 1998), pp. 71–73.

2. Alan Bennett et al. *The Complete Beyond the Fringe* (Methuen, London, 1987), p. 97.

3. From Bishop W.W. How's hymn, 'For all the saints'.

4. From 'For all the saints'.

5. Leonid Borodin, *Year of Miracle and Grief*, Trans. Jennifer Bradshaw (Quartet Books, London, 1984), pp. 95–96, my italics.

6. T. F. Torrance, *Divine and Contingent Order* (OUP, Oxford, 1981), p. 134.

7. C. S. Lewis, 'The Weight of Glory', a sermon reprinted in *Weight of Glory* (Harper, San Francisco, 2001), and in Lesley Walmsley (ed.) (HarperCollins, London, 2000), pp. 96–106.

8. *Alternative Service Book* 1980 (Hodder & Stoughton, 1980), p. 159.

9. From Private Eye's *Colemanballs books*, Vols. 5, 1 & 5 respectively (Private Eye Productions, London, 1982 & 1990 chronologically).

10. David Fisher, *Chicken Poop for the Soul* (Pocket Books, New York, 1997), pp. 24–26.

11. THEY STAND TOGETHER by C. S. Lewis copyright © C. S. Lewis Pte. Ltd. 1979.

12. N. T. Wright, in the commentary on Romans in the *New Interpreter's Bible*, Volume X (Abingdon Press, Nashville, 2002), p. 528.

13. William Cook (ed.), *Tragically I Was an Only Twin: The Complete Peter Cook* (Arrow Books, London, 2003), p. xxx.

14. From a letter published in Sheldon Vanauken, *A Severe Mercy* (Hodder & Stoughton, 1977), p. 93.

15. From his *A Letter of Consolation*, cited in Nicholas Wolterstorff's *Lament for a Son* (1987) (Spire, Hodder and Stoughton, London, 1989), p. 87.

Chapter Ten

1. THE SCREWTAPE LETTERS by C. S. Lewis copyright © C. S. Lewis Pte. Ltd. 1942.

2. THE SCREWTAPE LETTERS by C. S. Lewis copyright © C. S. Lewis Pte. Ltd. 1942.

3. John Webster, 'What is the Gospel?' in Timothy Bradshaw (ed.), *Grace and Truth in the Secular Age* (Eerdmans, 1998), p. 114.

4. 'What is the Gospel?', pp.114–115 (my italics).

5. From an interview with *Church Times*, December 6, 2002.

6. Karl Barth, *The Epistle to the Romans* (O.U.P., 1933), p.36.

7. Lesslie Newbigin, *Discovering Truth in a Changing World*, (Alpha International, 2003), p.81.

8. Thomas Traherne, *Centuries*, 1, 16, 27, 29, & lll, 3 (Mowbray, 1985). (I have modernised the spelling and punctuation.) Might I recommend the wonderful setting of some of Traherne's poetry and prose in Gerald Finzi's *Dies Natalis*?

9. From his *Selected Poems*, edited by Ian Hamilton (Penguin Books, Harmondsworth, Middlesex, 1973), pp. 43–44.

10. From 'What is the Gospel?', p. 109.

11. From 'What is the Gospel?', p. 114.

12. See *The Spiritual Exercises of Saint Ignatius* [32]f.

13. From 'What is the Gospel?', p. 114.

14. T. S. Eliot, Choruses from *The Rock*, Section Vl.

Every effort has been made to contact the copyright holders for permissions. The publishers are willing to correct any errors brought to their attention in a later edition.

STUDY GUIDE

What I most enjoy about speaking and lecturing is the 'Question and Answer' time afterwards. After all, I already know what I think (mostly!) – the interesting bit for me is hearing other people's reactions, comments, thoughts, views and questions. I wish I could sit down with readers of this book (in a café, of course!) and hear what you all have to say. Unfortunately, I would probably die of tannin poisoning if I did.

The next best (or probably better) thing is to get together and talk about the book with others. It can be enormously stimulating and helpful to talk through some of the issues raised, in the context of a small group. Other people will have different reactions and different questions. Other people will (hopefully) have liked different bits and (realistically) have disliked other bits. Talking it through with others will therefore make you think more deeply and widely about what you have read and the thoughts it provoked. Engaging with what others think – especially if they think differently from you – will 'limit your limitations'.

To that end, I have composed some questions, which I hope will inspire discussion and help you to go deeper into the nature, mind and purposes of God. This doesn't *have* to be done while eating flapjacks, but it does help.

CHAPTER ONE: CREATION

When theists call the universe 'creation', they are claiming that the cosmos does not exist randomly or necessarily, but by the deliberate will and purpose of an intelligent Person. The following questions are designed to help you unpack the significance of that claim.

1. At the beginning of Chapter 1, it is stated: 'there are basically only two possible sets of views about the universe in which we live'. Do you

agree with this statement? What are your reasons for this?

2. How should someone who believes that there is a Person behind the universe live in an impersonal world in which we are seemingly just another statistic?

3. Where do you think you personally fit into God's purposes for creation and for humankind?

4. How can we help others to believe in their own value? How can we help ourselves to believe in our own value?

5. What is there to be said for seeing the cosmos as an emanation from God – and what against?

6. What would be the implications of there being more than one source for our universe?

7. How do you fit into a bigger story, and how do you fit into a wider community?

8. Why does the doctrine of Creation mean that science is necessary and possible?

9. Corrie ten Boom wrote: 'There is no pit so deep that God is not deeper.' Yet her sister, and millions of others, died in the pit of the concentration camps. In what sense is Creation open to God, and in what sense is it not?

10. How can we open ourselves to the multi-dimensionality of creation?

11. How good do you believe creation to be? (You may like to consult your diary and your bank statements to find out what you actually believe!)

12. What are the implications of creation belonging to God?

13. Creation deserves a response from you: What one change will you make to your thinking or your behaviour?

CHAPTER TWO: THE FALL

If the universe is the deliberate creation of a good and loving Person, you would expect it to be a lot less violent and tragic and frustrating than it is – unless something has gone seriously wrong with it, so that t is no longer the way it was intended to be. This chapter argues that things *have* gone seriously wrong with it, and that it has got cut off from the person and purposefulness of God. It also argues for a particular way of understanding how that happened, which will not persuade everyone. The following questions are intended to explore this dark area more deeply.

1. Do you believe that suffering has a purpose in God's plan?

2. Does God always get His way?

3. Is suffering natural?

4. What would you say to the priest in Camus' *The Plague*?

5. What does the scene at Lazarus' graveside (John 11) tell us about our world?

6. What is hopeful about the doctrine of the Fall?

7. Has God ever felt to you like the Cosmic Sadist? What, if anything, brought you back from seeing Him that way?

8. Do you agree that the goodness of God depends on seeing the world as fallen?

9. Do you think that Jesus is at peace with nature?

10. Do you agree that we need to see nature as fallen? If so, how plausible do you find it to attribute that fallenness to the fall of the angels? Are there any other candidates?

11. If the Fall of the angels hypothesis is accepted, are human beings victims or culprits?

12. What do you think are the implications for pastoral care?

CHAPTER THREE: PROVIDENCE

Christians do not think of God as being like a Watchmaker, creating His cosmic watch, winding it up, and then leaving it to its own devices. They see Him as being committed to His world and active within it. But how? And what is He up to? What can we point to as being 'God at work', and what must we *not* see as in any way His activity?

1. Are you more inclined to see your life as determined or as random?

2. To what extent is life determined, and to what extent is it random?

3. How does providence differ from fate and chance?

4. Do you find the flexibility of God's purposes worrying or reassuring?

5. Why is it so common for people to see their own nation or race as having a special and exalted role in the purposes of God?

6. *A question for private reflection:* 'The only limitation that providence knows is the limitation we place upon His working by refusing that relationship and resisting that restorative impulse.' In what ways do you do that?

7. How do you cope when you have no idea how to understand what is going on in your life?

8. How do we 'put moral distance between God and evil' in our thinking, speaking and pastoral care?

9. Do you find the idea of God suffering from evil worrying or reassuring?

10. How useful is the Christological 'litmus paper of Providence'?

11. How do we 'take responsibility for our own actions and our own lives under God'?

12. Try and articulate 'a theology of brokenness'.

CHAPTER FOUR: INCARNATION

In the last chapter, we saw how God does not leave His creation to its own devices, but is committed to it and active within it. Just how committed and just how active and just how 'within it', we explore in this chapter as we look at the Incarnation, when God enters into creation, and works within it *as part of it*. What can we learn from what that looked like? The questions below are attempting to be a sort of prism to refract the multifarious significance of the Incarnation.

1. God 'didn't stop Adam and Eve. He didn't stop Israel. He didn't stop the prodigal son. He didn't stop the Roman executioners. He doesn't stop us, when we strike out on our own.' Should He?

2. What difference does it make to see the Incarnation as the centre-point of history?

3 What inhuman gods might we protest against today?

4. What inhuman pictures of humanity might we protest against today?

5. Why do human beings need dignity?

6. How does God sharing our life transform its bitterness?

7. 'What is not assumed is not healed.' Why not?

8. 'A church that lets go of the divinity of Jesus has no gospel.' Why not?

9. Do you fear that becoming more godly will mean having to leave bits of your humanity behind?

10. *A question for private reflection:* 'I am a human being: I consider nothing human to be irrelevant to me.' How all-embracing are your interests and concerns?

11. God 'enables everything to be fully itself'. How can we help others to see God not as threat, but as liberation?

12. 'No part of human life is outside God's domain.' What does this mean for you?

13. What would you have said to the couple who were told that it was unspiritual to take out an insurance policy, and whose house burnt down?

14. If we had the Incarnation as the model for our pastoral care, how might we do things differently?

15. 'If Jesus is Lord, then Caesar isn't.' How can we live that out, while being good citizens?

CHAPTER FIVE: ATONEMENT

Edward Shillito wrote '... not a god has wounds, but Thou alone.' There is something deeply counter-intuitive and disturbing about the death of Jesus. Yet Christians have seen it as so integral to their view of life that they have made it their central symbol. These questions try to wrestle with the simultaneously exalting and shattering nature of the Cross.

1. 'What is wrong?' is one of the basic world-view questions. What do your friends and colleagues think is wrong with the world? And what do they think is needed in order to put it right?

2. Lesslie Newbigin said: 'The Cross cannot be used as a banner for one part of humanity against another.' In what ways do we do that?

3. How do we access the love we see on the Cross?

4. In what ways do people, relationships and conflicts look different through the lens of the Cross?

5. In what sense are we no longer the people who did the shoddy things we did? And in what sense are we still the people who did them?

6. How racially, socially, educationally and theologically homogeneous are our churches? And how much do they reflect the barrier-breaking, division-defying, unifying nature of the Cross?

7. What is the 'Gospel of the New World'?

8. 'But to our wounds only God's wounds can speak.' Is that your experience? How does the Cross speak to your wounds?

9. If Christ is the One 'who sailed [in the ark] along with Noah, and who guided Abraham; who was bound along with Isaac, and was a Wanderer with Jacob', what does that mean for you?

10. How can we side with both the sinful and the sinned-against?

11. 'A world-view that is based upon a crucified Messiah ... cannot logically impose itself by force.' What kinds of force do Christians still use to impose their own agenda?

12. Repentance, faith, Baptism, Eucharist – are there other ways of appropriating the death of Christ?

CHAPTER SIX: RESURRECTION AND ASCENSION

So far, this book has argued that God intended the world to be in harmony with Him and with itself, that suffering and pain and predation and death have no place in His purposes, that He is working against them, and is committed to ridding creation of them. The Resurrection shows us the first green shoots of this good riddance.

And the Ascension speaks of the eternal *and internal* commitment of God to the world He created. These questions explore that healing commitment, and the ways in which it inspires us to join in the riddance.

1. How could we commemorate Holy Saturday?

2. In what ways is ours 'a culture that evades telling the truth about death'? In what ways could the church be a truth-telling culture?

3. How do we strike a balance between death as enemy and death as defeated?

4. What does the Resurrection tell us about the Cross?

5. What does the Resurrection tell us about ourselves?

6. 'We are given, in the Resurrection of Jesus, a vision of what creation will look like when it is finally healed, a vision of what we will look like when we are fully ourselves, and a knowledge of what will *last*.' What *will* creation look like? What *will* we look like? What *will* last?

7. What are the implications of seeing physicality as God-given?

8. What would you say to someone who claimed that Christian faith is just 'pie in the sky when you die'?

9. What lasting contribution would you like to make to the new creation?

10. Why do you think that the Ascension has not caught the popular imagination the way Christmas and Easter have done? What could we do to make more of it?

11. 'The governance of the universe is in the utterly safe, scarred hands of Jesus: He alone will use power exclusively in the service of love.' How do we use such power as we have? How should we?

12. *A question for private reflection:* Since the Ascension, 'any insult to the humanity of any person, any treating of a human being as expendable rubbish, is strictly a blasphemy; it is an insult to the nature which God has eternally taken upon himself.' In what ways do you live out of joint with the Ascension?

CHAPTER SEVEN: SPIRIT

By itself, the Ascension might encourage us to think of God as having left us. It was, on the contrary, to enable His wider and more permeated presence. This chapter explores that Presence in the person of the Spirit. And these questions try to make His work more recognisable without making it less mysterious and wild.

1. Why do you think people tend to have more of a problem with the Spirit than with the Father or Son?

2. What difference does it make if the Holy Spirit is a personal being?

3. What would be lost if the divinity of the Spirit were denied?

4. *A question for private reflection and prayer:* If the Spirit is the one who gives life, over what lifeless regions of your being and your world do you wish to pray for Him to brood?

5. If the Spirit is at work to bridge the gap between creation and recreation, where is that gap most sharply felt in your neighbourhood?

6. What can we learn from 'the *fellowship* of the Holy Spirit'?

7. If the Spirit applies 'a filial lovedness to our deepest and neediest places', how do we open ourselves to that assurance?

8. Why do you think there is so little sign of renewed creativity in the Church?

9. 'When God freezes the water … every flake is different. When we human beings freeze water, we make ice cubes!' How can we celebrate and encourage individuality and diversity?

10. 'God's plans and purposes cannot just be read off from looking at history.' Why not?

11. What can make our talk about God scientific?

12. How can we help the Spirit help us to pray?

13. What does the Spirit tell us of the future?

CHAPTER EIGHT: TRINITY

The doctrine of the Trinity is not a puzzle made up to confuse us. This chapter tries to show that it arose out of the experience of the early

Christians, and the questions that that experience forced upon them. It tries to show that the experience of Jesus and the Spirit impelled them to a new, fresh and deeply fertile understanding of God. These questions are intended to take you deeper into that fertility.

1. Why do you think people find the doctrine of the Trinity so difficult?

2. Why is it important that there is a receiving as well as a giving of love within the Godhead?

3. If human beings are made in the image of God, and God is a relationship of love, what does that tell us about what it is to be human?

4. What does it mean to 'participate in the divine nature' (2 Peter 1:4)?

5. In what ways do we manifest a craving for intimacy, and in what ways a fear of it?

6. Why do we fear that we will lose ourselves in relationships?

7. See if you can retell the story of the salt doll from a Trinitarian perspective.

8. How could we be more mutually affirming of one another, within appropriate boundaries?

9. Can you think of other examples of how the doctrine of the Trinity might reorder our value system both personally and politically?

10. Why do people tend to think of leadership in terms of status and importance? And what can we do to change that way of thinking?

11. What would a liberating hierarchy look like?

12. What are the implications of seeing peace (not violence) as basic?

13. Which person of the Trinity do I most naturally relate and pray to? Which person of the Trinity does my church most naturally relate to and pray to? How can both become more Trinitarian?

CHAPTER NINE: THE FINAL VICTORY OF GOD

Throughout this book, and throughout these questions, we have been emphasising the commitment of God to His world – to its healing, its flourishing and its fulfilment. And to ours. This chapter looks ahead to the destiny of creation in the purposes of God, and to how the world looks now in the light of that destiny. These questions attempt to unpack hope and let it do its work within us.

1. What different eschatologies are on offer?

2. How does a Christian eschatology view history and time?

3. Do we think in terms of God ultimately taking us away from this world, or returning to it to heal it?

4. How much Gnosticism have you come across in the Church?

5. How clearly do we draw the line between the good and the bad?

6. Why does there need to be an ultimate separation between good and evil?

7. How far is judgment good news and how far is it bad news?

8. *A question for private reflection:* 'The amount that we long for the appearing of Christ is probably the amount we oppose evil.' How much is that?

9. How can we point to the gathering up of all things in Christ?

10. How does the future putting right of all things help us to forgive?

11. If the goodness of God cannot be read off creation or history, on what do we ground it?

12. If the final victory of God is going to renew our otherness, our embodiedness, our relatedness, our cultures and our true selves, what does that tell us about our present life and task?

13. Why do you think that the New Testament normally speaks of future hope in the context of a call to holiness?

CHAPTER TEN: THE CHURCH

Relationship is surely the most important thing in our experience. God (says the doctrine of the Trinity) is Relationship. God saves us into relationship. These questions seek to think through the privileges and responsibilities of belonging to the Church.

1. Why does T. S. Eliot write that 'There is no life that is not in community'?

2. How much do you experience the Church as an oasis of community in a relational desert, and how much do you find that it has bought

into the individualism of the rest of society?

3. What do you think lies behind that individualism?

4. 'You cannot have Jesus as your Brother and His Father as your Father unless you are prepared to have all other Christians as your brothers and sisters.' What are the joys of that?

5. What are the benefits of structure?

6. If the Church is 'the space which God has created for us within His purposes, within His presence and within His very self', then how do we inhabit that space?

7. 'To have meaning you need a bigger story to be part of and a wider community to belong to. … And in the Church, He has given us a wider community to belong to and contribute to.' What makes the Church a community, given that many of its members live centuries – millennia, even – apart?

8. *A question for private reflection*: How can I make my church a more healing community?

9. What dangers are there in the view that, in the Church, we are given all things?

10. How do we maintain the unity of the Spirit?

11. '"Church" is not a struggle to make something happen': so why does it often feel as if it is?

12. How do we show that Jesus is 'humanely relevant to every area of human life'?

13. What does the Eucharist tell us about the world and its destiny? In what ways does the Eucharist sum up the whole message of this book?

INDEX

415

SPTC BOOKS

Holy Trinity Brompton launched St Paul's Theological Centre in 2005, following the growth of Alpha worldwide and the establishment of HTB as a major resourcing centre for other churches in the United Kingdom. SPTC continues to play a key role in the ministry of Alpha International and as developer of theological resources. In addition, in 2007 it became part of St Mellitus College, the newest theological college of the Church of England. St Mellitus is a pioneer in 'church-based' training, preparing students for ordination through a mixture of classroom learning and on-the-job church ministry. Working through Alpha International and St Mellitus, SPTC has sponsored a number of significant theological conferences, produced the popular GodPod podcast, and begun to plant branches around the world.

The central vision of SPTC is to help 'bring theology back to the heart of the church'. Rather than doing theology in a university or seminary setting, SPTC links its theology and its training as closely as possible to the life of the local church. The Centre is developing a rich seam of theological reflection on church life, following themes that arise from Christian ministry in churches like HTB and those who use the Alpha Course around the world. SPTC Books is an imprint of Alpha International, designed to help develop this theological work. It seeks to publish work linked in one way or another to the wider Alpha network, exploring theology in a way that is truly ecumenical. We will bring together the best of all kinds of theology from all parts of the church – all who are held together by a common belief in the God revealed in Jesus Christ and in the expectation of the presence and power of the Holy Spirit as the one who makes true worshipful theology possible.